MW00993799

The Grace of Christ

The Grace of Christ

Third Edition

Eric Roessing

FOREWORD BY
Jeff Roessing

WIPF & STOCK · Eugene, Oregon

THE GRACE OF CHRIST, THIRD EDITION

Copyright © 2023 Eric Roessing. All rights reserved. Except for brief quotations in critical publications or reviews, no part of this book may be reproduced in any manner without prior written permission from the publisher. Write: Permissions, Wipf and Stock Publishers, 199 W. 8th Ave., Suite 3, Eugene, OR 97401.

Wipf & Stock
An Imprint of Wipf and Stock Publishers
199 W. 8th Ave., Suite 3
Eugene, OR 97401

www.wipfandstock.com

PAPERBACK ISBN: 978-1-6667-6031-6
HARDCOVER ISBN: 978-1-6667-6032-3
EBOOK ISBN: 978-1-6667-6033-0

09/22/23

In all Scripture quotations used in this book, words in italics indicate emphasis by the author, and all words added in brackets within Scripture quotations are explanations by the author.

All Scripture quotations, including those marked "AT," unless they are marked as another translation, are the author's translation; the primary reference for the author's translations (from the Greek) and for the Greek words used in this book was *The Interlinear Greek-English New Testament: The Nestle Greek Text with a Literal Translation* by Reverend Dr. Alfred Marshall, © Literal English translation, Samuel Bagster and Sons Ltd., 1958; © Editorial Interlineation, Samuel Bagster and Sons Ltd., 1958. Used by permission of Zondervan. www.zondervan.com.

Scripture quotations marked "ATP" are the author's translative paraphrase.

Scripture quotations marked "AV" are from the Authorized Version. Those marked "AV/AT" are from the Authorized Version but altered by the author.

Scripture quotations marked "EHV" are from The Holy Bible, Evangelical Heritage Version®, EHV®, © 2019 Wartburg Project, Inc. All rights reserved.

Scripture quotations marked "ESV" are from The Holy Bible, English Standard Version. Copyright © 2001 by Crossway Bibles, a publishing division of Good News Publishers. Used by permission. All rights reserved.

Scripture quotations marked "ILT" are taken from *The Interlinear Literal Translation of the Greek New Testament* by George Ricker Berry. All rights reserved. 18th printing, Jan. 1976. Used by permission of Zondervan. www.zondervan.com. This was a secondary reference for some of the author's translations.

Scripture quotations marked "NASB" are from the New American Standard Bible®. Copyright © 1960, 1962, 1963, 1968, 1971, 1972, 1973, 1975, 1977, 1995 by the Lockman Foundation (www.Lockman.org). Used by permission.

Scripture quotations marked NKJV are taken from the New King James Version. Copyright © 1982 by Thomas Nelson, Inc. Used by permission. All rights reserved.

Scripture quotations marked "NRSV" are from the New Revised Standard Version Bible, copyright 1989, by the Division of Christian Education of the National Council of the Churches of Christ in the U.S.A. Used by permission. All rights reserved.

Scripture quotations marked "RGT" are from the Revised Geneva Translation, © copyright 2019–23 by Five Talents Audio. All rights reserved.

Scripture quotations marked "RSV" are from the Revised Standard Version of the Bible, copyright © 1946, 1952, 1971 by the Division of Christian Education of the National Council of the Churches of Christ in the USA. Used by permission. All rights reserved.

Scripture quotations marked "SAAS" are taken from the St. Athanasius Academy Septuagint,™ copyright © 2008 by St. Athanasius Academy of Orthodox Theology. Used by permission. All rights reserved; emphasis mine.

Scripture quotations marked "WEB" are from the World English Bible. Those marked "WEB/AT" are from the WEB but altered by the author.

Quotations from *Heavenly Worship* by Fr. J. Richard Ballew. Copyright 1990 by Ancient Faith Publishing, Second Edition 1995.

Quote from *St. Augustine: Against the Academics (Contra Academicos)*, translated by John J. O'Meara. Ramsey: Paulist Press, Copyright ©1951 by Paulist Press, Inc., New York/Mahwah, NJ. Reprinted by permission of Paulist Press, Inc. www.paulistpress.com.

Luther's Works. Vol. 21 Copyright © 1956, 1984 Concordia Publishing House. Used with permission. wwwcph.org cph.org.

Luther's Works. Vol. 25 Copyright © 1972 Concordia Publishing House. Used with permission. wwwcph.org

Luther's Works. Vol. 26 Copyright © 1963, 1991 Concordia Publishing House. Used with permission. wwwcph.org

Luther's Works. Vol. 27 Copyright © 1964, 1992 Concordia Publishing House. Used with permission. wwwcph.org

Pilgrim Theology by Michael Horton © 2011 by Michael Horton. Used by permission of Zondervan. www.zondervan.com.

Romans: Assurance by D. Martyn Lloyd-Jones. © Copyright 1971 by D. M. Lloyd-Jones. Used by permission of Zondervan. www.zondervan.com.

Romans: The New Man by D. Martyn Lloyd-Jones. © Copyright 1972 by D. M. Lloyd-Jones. Used by permission of Zondervan. www.zondervan.com.

Romans: The Final Perseverance of the Saints by D. Martyn Lloyd-Jones. © Copyright 1975 by D. M. Lloyd-Jones. Used by permission of Zondervan. www.zondervan.com.

From Sabbath to Lord's Day edited by D. A. Carson © Copyright 1982 by the Zondervan Corporation. Used by permission of Zondervan. www.zondervan.com.

With thankfulness to God for Christ and their one Spirit

And for Paul the apostle, and my wife Jane, without whose sacrifices this book would never have come to fruition, and for our two sons, with their families, and for all in the body of Christ throughout history whom God has used in my life.

Contents

Foreword

THE YEAR 2003 MARKED numerous changes for the Roessing household. I married my wife, Melissa; two grandparents passed away; and my dad, Eric Roessing, was diagnosed with Asperger's Syndrome. One of the grandparents who passed was my dad's mother, and upon her passing my parents received an inheritance.

Up until this point in our family life, our journey was marked by a lot of transitions. But my dad and mom worked, and for most of those years they worked full time. We made our moves from rural Minnesota, where my brother and I were born, to Chicago and back to Michigan. The biggest change occurred when my dad left his job in Grand Rapids, Michigan, as a journeyman platemaker in the graphic arts trade and moved us to Chicago so that he could attend Lutheran School of Theology at Chicago. The intent was to eventually move back to Grand Rapids for Dad to be a teaching pastor at the Lutheran church we were attending. But by the time of Dad's internship in the suburbs of Illinois, he knew that, though he was gifted in theology and did well in seminary, he was not gifted or called to be a pastor. So that opportunity fell through and, after he received his Master of Arts in theology, his dream for full-time ministry fell into disillusionment, and he returned to the graphic arts trade.

Throughout this family story there was a subtext that played its part in shaping the opportunities and lack thereof for participation in the life of the church. It also likely contributed to a lack of quality employment and our family's financial struggles that persisted until I left the house in 2003 and my parents received the inheritance. This was my dad's Asperger's, or what is now referred to as autism spectrum disorder (ASD). Although he was undiagnosed at the time, it was always clear to those who lived with him and knew him that he was markedly different. He possessed and still possesses a lot of energy and excitement, which usually made him initially endearing to people but generally led to a degree of social isolation. While he would be considered "high functioning," this has not entirely relieved him from navigating the complexities of human relationships with the added handicap of ASD. He does not lack a sense of humor, but at the same time he has some difficulty knowing if people around him are employing it. And the hallmark of ASD, having an all-absorbing interest, is what amounts to the largest obstacle in cultivating deeper friendships. For Dad, theology, particularly the gospel of the crucified and risen Christ, is a circle whose center is everywhere and its circumference nowhere. He would be happy to literally talk about nothing else. For myself, speaking as a professing Christian, there is something very beautiful and refreshing about this. I feel uniquely blessed to have grown up in a house where Jesus was invited into every conversation. Yet, for those of us who might be labeled neurotypical, being in constant company with such a person feels restrictive. In relationships most of us have desires to explore the diverse geographies of our hearts, making such a singular focus feel like we cannot be wholly ourselves in that person's company. After his diagnosis in 2003, our family gained a better vocabulary and window into what we had been experiencing for decades. I think the diagnosis also ushered in a healthier set of expectations. My hope in this foreword is to help the reader approach his writing with a different set of expectations.

I want the reader to be aware of the very real influence that autism has exerted over this book. At first glance, it might be easy to point out deficiencies. The writing style is itself atypical—choppy, wooden, technical, somewhat redundant. It can feel like you are lost in the trees and missing the forest. There is little offered in the way of context. As a result, I understand that for many it may prove too tenuous to wade through. But for those willing to approach it with patience and able to *take the time* to enter its logic, and for those who deeply desire to understand more of the depth of God's grace in Christ, I sincerely believe it will prove uniquely rewarding.

Dad has often said that he studied this topic obsessively because he had to. He said he needed this radical understanding of grace in order to stay in the faith, to stay sane—which serves as a great reminder that, although he is neuroatypical, it would be a theological mistake to reduce him or his theology or writing to his ASD. He, like all people with disabilities, is fully human, and his struggles, though always experienced with ASD present, are human struggles. Mapped onto a Roman Catholic upbringing, the late 1960s counterculture, and a conversion to faith in the early 1970s, his journey is authentic. He initially heard and believed the gospel in a Pentecostal church at the age of twenty. Then he attended a Bible church before moving to Detroit and participating in a house church on Saturdays and a Lutheran church on Sundays. He attended a Bible school but credits the library there as a crucial piece of his journey, as that is where he discovered Luther and his theology of grace. It took hold. He was primarily drawn to Reformation circles and writings, with the greatest of respect reserved for Martin Luther, Anders Nygren, Gerhard Forde, and D. M. Lloyd-Jones. Yet he would help to lead a Bible study using Bob George's *Classic Christianity* and within the same week would affirm forms of biblical criticism from scholars in the Evangelical Lutheran Church in America (ELCA) and other mainline denominations. He had become enamored with the insights of conservative Presbyterian/Reformed theologians such as Charles Hodge. However much the presence of ASD has contributed to his ability for sustained focus on this single subject matter, I am certain that his underlying hunger for Jesus is the work of the Spirit.

Almost two years ago, a friend of ours shared a project undertaken by the University of Aberdeen called the Centre for Autism and Theology. I was so encouraged to hear for the first time in my adult life a vision of inclusion and a recognition of the gifts that autistic people can bring to the church—particularly churches with the openness to learn to identify and receive these gifts. Instead of seeing ASD as a deficit, it affirms "that autistic people are to be considered a gift and a gain to the diverse Christian community." Not just a gift, but a *gain*. Admittedly, there have been many times in my life when I have been keenly aware of my dad's ASD as a deficit. And early on in my life I believe I judged him harshly as someone who talked about Jesus all the time but did not reflect that same Jesus so well. As an adult with a much broader view of reality, I now look back on my childhood and my dad and see that my perspective was very sheltered. Yes, he has shortcomings, and yes, my mother was and is a saint to love him with all his idiosyncrasies. But now I can clearly see that he has largely practiced what he preached. He has depended deeply on the grace of God. Though his rhetoric can come across as arrogant, he has consistently pleaded for God's mercy. He has had the humility to ask his family for forgiveness time and again. The older I get, the more I see how rare that is. So, on a personal note, I want to say, Dad, you—ASD included—have been a priceless gift to me. Thank you. And I believe with all my heart that you are a gain for the body of Christ as well.

This book is a part of that gain for the church. As I already mentioned, its writing style is unique. Years ago, it dawned on me that my dad's writing style—or better put, his very mode of thinking—has been so formed by the Pauline texts that he has absorbed not only Paul's theology but also his writing style and syntax. He has pored over Martin Luther's writings with a similar intensity. I have no doubt that being neuroatypical has allowed him to do this in ways the rest of us just cannot, which is a gift. The gain in this gift is that I believe he truly is a better interpreter of Paul's meaning and theology. He would argue that, as a Christian, he has the "mind of Christ" like all Christians do, which is the basis for understanding Paul. But I would add that his unique gifting allows him to have the "mind of Paul" very nearly by virtue of obsessive immersion. The benefit for the church, then, is that reading this book is like getting to read a new writing, posthumously offered by the apostle Paul (although my dad would take issue with that statement). If you can imagine Paul having written a full-length book instead of a letter to the Romans, what you would get, I believe, would look a lot like this book, *The Grace of Christ, Third Edition.*

While in most modern scholarship theologians expend considerable energy comparing the hermeneutics of fellow academics, my dad, likely because of his autism, is less concerned with substantiating his claims in this manner and more concerned with a careful exegesis wherein Paul's writing is interpreted by Paul's own texts found in his other letters in the New Testament. So, while this book could almost be categorized as a commentary on Romans, it may be more accurate to label it as a summary of Paul's overall theology, written with Paul's own syntax.

And therein also lies the challenge. Contemporary writing typically reflects contemporary writing styles and norms. But I encourage the reader to remember: This is not your typical text produced by a neurotypical author. If we are to receive this text as the gain it is, we are required to meet it halfway, to engage in some of the social translation that my dad was unable to do. So, in advance, on his behalf and mine, I say thank you for your patience and grace.

With all sincerity, our prayer is that the grace written about in these pages will move you to a deeper love for the God who first loved us, no matter where you are on the spectrum.

Jeff Roessing
MDiv, Western Theological Seminary
December 2021

Preface

THE THINKING OF PEOPLE in our day has become increasingly subjective, not desiring objective reality, with people defining their own "reality." But God and his Christ, who is the truth, does not change at the whims, beliefs, or desires of humans. The gospel is a message of objective truth in which God, in his Son, became human without ceasing to be God, and *died* for the salvation from sin and death of all who trust in him. Christ-believers do not live by feelings; they live by faith in Christ, in contrast to the subjectivism that is such a part of the American culture, and which is not in line with the apostolic gospel of God (Rom 1:1). According to the gospel, we summarize what the life of a Christ-believer is, as follows:

> The life of the person in Christ is to be one of *trust* in Christ for righteousness (being justified before God) and, through that faith, *obedience* to Christ as Lord.

Such trust and obedience are possible because Christ-believers have died with Christ to the lordship of the sin and the law and are now alive to God in Christ Jesus—owned by *him* as Lord. It is that simple—what Paul calls "the simplicity that is in Christ" in 2 Cor 11:3.

In this book, I have attempted to convey this simplicity, even while expounding what Paul paradoxically calls "the deep things of God." Both in God's gospel and in this book, the truth—that Christ's death justifies sinners, and the gospel's corollary, faith in Christ who freed believers from the lordship of sin and the law to live to God in the Spirit—are given their rightful place, that of first importance.[1] Because Christ-believers

---

1. 1 Cor 15:1–5; see Rom 5:8–9; 6:7 (author's literal translation; hereafter "lit.").

have been freed from the wrath, the sin, the law, the death, and Satan's kingdom by being joined to Christ, they are obligated to live according to the Spirit of God, putting to death the autonomous deeds of the flesh. The church is to be continually renewed according to the word of God, and this book is to that end. The gospel of God is to be preached to humans from among all the nations: both to the wise and the unwise (Rom 1:13–14), meaning both to the intellectual and the nonintellectual. For, regardless how great one's intellect may be, "the things freely given us of God" in Paul's gospel can only be known and understood by the Spirit of God, through comparing Paul's Spirit-taught words with his Spirit-taught words. In the following text, the words "we also speak" (in context—see 1 Cor 1:17, 23; 2:1–4) refers to Paul himself.

> But we have received, not the spirit of the world, but the Spirit which is from God, that we might know *the things freely given to us by God*—which things *we*[2] also speak, not in words taught from human [of the flesh] wisdom, but in *those [words] taught of the Holy Spirit*, communicating spiritual things [the things freely given us by God] by spiritual words [words taught of the Spirit]. (1 Cor 2:12–13 AT)

This means that we are to interpret Paul's words, not considering human wisdom, or philosophy, or even theologians who came after him, but essentially through Paul's own words. This book attempts to do this, going to great lengths to make the things of God's grace to be understood and grasped by those who desire to know the things freely given us by God. And the Scriptures from which we primarily deduce this grace are apostolic in origin.[3] The gospel centers, not in the unity of Jews and gentiles in Christ, or in our union with Christ, real as those things are, but in God's saving *righteousness*, which makes humans right with God.

> For I am not ashamed of *the gospel*, for it is the power of God for salvation to everyone who believes . . . for in it *the righteousness from God* is revealed—from faith to faith, as it is written, "The righteous one out of faith shall live." (Romans 1:16–17)

Throughout this book, our union with Christ is effectively explained and emphasized. And we are convinced that the Reformation's "Christ alone," "grace alone," and "faith alone" are in line with the apostolic gospel of God (Rom 1:1). But the Reformation, through its respective confessions, prematurely ceased the process of "being reformed according to the word

2. This is proved from scripture in chapter 1.
3. This is proved from scripture in chapter 1.

of God"—as if we have in those confessions the complete and error-free understanding of the gospel and the faith—all because the leaders were anxious to replace the errors of Rome with statements of truth for their churches. Right as that may have seemed and still seems to many (there are many true and good things in those confessions), it remains true that the tendency of those confessions on the "confessional churches" has been to bind (and blind) them to things that are not necessarily in line with the apostolic gospel. For centuries before the Reformation, the church subtracted from the gospel and added human teachings and traditions to the gospel that have obscured the spiritual freedom of "Christ alone" and its corollary, "faith (in Christ) alone," through which we bear fruit to God. Some of these traditions remain and have detracted from the gospel of God and thus from our freedom in Christ to live for God.

Christ-believers need to know who they are in Christ, and this book is to that end. Learning, knowing, and believing the things set forth in this book has helped me to stand.[4] And my hope is that others will also be helped and edified by the truth of the gospel set forth in these pages. If a Christ-indwelt person ever finds himself or herself reading Paul's letter to the Romans, then we believe that such a person can learn from this book. Some of the book's insights were "birthed" through much suffering.

> Chapter 1 is a foundational introduction to this book's subject: God's grace in Christ.
>
> Chapters 2 and 3 provide a gospel-background for the rest of the book.
>
> Chapters 4 through 12 deal with chapters 1 through 11 in Paul's letter to the Romans, focusing especially on texts that we believe have not been sufficiently understood or taught, while highlighting God's grace in Christ in its depth, meaning, and application, including the apostle's revelation of both sin and the law in the light of Christ crucified and risen.
>
> Chapters 13 through 20 (and the appendixes) continue to explain God's gospel according to basic themes, including freedom in Christ, the new creation, the Spirit's baptism and leading, and others, all from Paul's "revelation of Jesus Christ" (Gal 1:11–12).

Eric (Rick) Roessing
MA, Lutheran School of Theology at Chicago
1 Cor 1:27   March, 2023

---

4. Eph 6:13.

Abbreviations

AC	Augsburg Confession, in *The Book of Concord: The Confessions of the Evangelical Lutheran Church*
A&C	*Affirmation & Critique*
Ap	Apology of the Augsburg Confession, in *The Book of Concord: The Confessions of the Evangelical Lutheran Church*
BAG	W. Bauer, W. F. Arndt, and F. W. Gingrich, *Greek-English Lexicon of the New Testament and Other Early Christian Literature*
BC-T	*The Book of Concord: The Confessions of the Evangelical Lutheran Church*, edited by Tappert
CBQ	*Catholic Biblical Quarterly*
CCC	Catechism of the Catholic Church
CD	*Christian Dogmatics*
COT	*Commentary on the Old Testament in Ten Volumes*
CPJ	*Confessional Presbyterian Journal*
DB	*Dictionary of the Bible*
ECRC	*Ecumenical Creeds and Reformed Confessions*
FC	Formula of Concord in *The Book of Concord: The Confessions of the Evangelical Lutheran Church*
IB	*The Interpreter's Bible in Twelve Volumes*

IBC	*The International Bible Commentary*
ICC	International Critical Commentary
ICR	*Calvin: Institutes of the Christian Religion*
LC	Large Catechism, in *The Book of Concord: The Confessions of the Evangelical Lutheran Church*
LCC	Library of Christian Classics
LW	*Luther's Works*
MJTM	*McMaster Journal of Theology and Ministry*
MR	*Modern Reformation*
NA26	Novum Testamentum Graece
NIB	*The New Interpreter's Bible*
NPNF	*Nicene and Post-Nicene Fathers of the Christian Church*
PR	*Princeton Review*
RTR	*Reformed Theological Review*
SB	*The Standard Bearer*
SBJT	*Southern Baptist Journal of Theology*
SDB	*Smith's Dictionary of the Bible*
SML	*The Complete Sermons of Martin Luther*
SD	Solid Declaration, in *The Book of Concord: The Confessions of the Evangelical Lutheran Church*
TDNT	*Theological Dictionary of the New Testament*
WA	*D. Martin Luthers Werke*
W&W	*Word and World*
WBC	Word Biblical Commentary
WCF	Westminster Confession of Faith
WNWD	*Webster's New World Dictionary of the American Language*

ONE

God's Word of the Cross

THEOLOGIAN THOMAS F. TORRANCE, after first setting forth the theology of the church fathers (leaders who came *after* the apostles, such as Clement, Ignatius, and Polycarp), finally comes to this conclusion:

> Grace, by its very nature in the thought of the New Testament, must be the absolutely predominant factor in faith, else it is not grace. In the Apostolic Fathers, grace did not have that radical character . . . what took absolute precedence was God's call to a new life in obedience to revealed truth. Grace, as far as it was grasped, was subsidiary to that. And so religion was thought of primarily in terms of *man's acts* towards God, *in the striving towards justification*, much less in terms of God's acts for man which put him in the right with God.[1]

The Apostolic Gospel

Once Paul the apostle died, the apostolic gospel, for the most part, died with him. Church leaders did not understand his gospel and preferred focusing on other writings (like the synoptic gospels) and then writing their own literature. And in the following centuries, new leaders, in the face of heresies of all kinds, had to deal with the issues of the person of Christ and of the one triune God, and so the apostolic gospel became even more obscured. Sadly, "bishops" tended to vie for power in their various cities. The apostolic gospel, with the truth of justification in Christ's death alone,

1. Torrance, *Doctrine of Grace*, 133, emphasis mine.

1

received through faith alone, faded even further into the background. So, the apostolic gospel—with its "Christ alone" and imputed righteousness through "faith alone"—remained obscure until the Magisterial Reformation, when it was to a great extent, in many aspects, recovered by the sovereign power of God in human vessels such as Martin Luther and others. However, the far-reaching depth of some of Roman Catholicism's errors and influence remain in the Protestant churches.[2] And we realize this the more we understand Paul's gospel of God, in which God's saving righteousness, which justifies the ungodly, accomplished through Christ's death alone and received through faith in Christ alone, is God's power for *salvation from sin and death*. Other doctrinal truths, as good and important as they are, are not imbued with God's power for salvation. This is a dynamic power that provides all we need because it imputes God's righteousness, which is the basis of his resurrection life—the Holy Spirit—in us. Our goal is to aid the church in a journey of a continuing reformation and renewal of the mind in learning how to be theologians of the cross.

So, we begin with the foundation of the gospel, which is *Christ* (1 Cor 3:11), for Paul said that the gospel he preached was "not from man nor through man" (Gal 1:1). According to Gal 1:1, "It is the God who raised Jesus from the dead who also called Paul to be an apostle." And "since Paul has been called by the risen Lord, *the power of God*, who raises from the dead, stands behind his apostleship."[3] Paul says that his gospel is *not according to man*, for he neither received it from man, nor was he *taught* it by mere man, but Paul received his gospel and was *taught* it through a revelation of *Jesus Christ*, who is fully God and yet fully man (Gal 1:11–12). In the following text, the "we" in the phrase "we also speak" (see 1 Cor 1:17, 23; 2:1–4) refers to Paul himself.

> But we have received, not the spirit of the world, but the Spirit
> which is from God, that we might know the things freely given
> to us by God—which things *we*[4] also *speak*, not in words taught

2. The world lives in extreme spiritual darkness, and, in one sense, the church has been utterly affected by this darkness due to its flesh and the principalities and powers working against God and his church.

3. Ebeling, *Truth of the Gospel*, 16–17. It is the power and *the authority* of God which stand behind Paul's apostleship; see Acts 26:18, Greek.

4. By "we" Paul means himself. He does this elsewhere: "For *we* wanted to come to you—*I, Paul*, more than once—yet Satan thwarted *us*" (1 Thess 2:18 NASB; compare also 3:1); and in 1 Cor 1 and 2, where he uses the expressions "me" (1:17), "I" (2:1–3), and "my" (2:4), and first-person plurals like "we" (referring to himself in 1 Cor 1:23; 2:6, 7, 12, 13, 16), and "us" (for himself in 2:10), all interchangeably. Thus, when Paul refers to words *taught* of the Spirit (1 Cor 2:13), he means words *taught* by Christ (Gal 1:11–12; see Rom 8:9–10).

from human (fleshly) wisdom, but in *those words taught of the Holy Spirit*, communicating spiritual things ["the things freely given us by God"] by spiritual words [words taught of the Spirit of Christ]. (1 Cor 2:12–13)

This is exactly what Paul is saying when he says he received his gospel and was *taught* it through a revelation of Jesus Christ (Gal 1:12), who gave him this apostolic gospel.[5] And so we begin with the *grace* of God, for he calls his gospel "the grace of Christ" in Gal 1:6.

> Although *grace* was in God's mind and purpose from before the creation of the world,[6] grace occurred only *after* sin entered the world. We are justified without a cause in us by God's grace, through the ransom paid in Christ Jesus, which came through the eternal Son of God having come of David's lineage according to the flesh—in his obedience to God unto death, and through his resurrection from the dead, to save humans from Sin and Death, through faith in Christ, which, along with his Spirit, God gives to his elect—which will result in immortality—a body unable to die, fully alive and fully controlled by the Holy Spirit of God, when the creation itself also will be delivered from the bondage of decay into the freedom of the glory of the children of God, in the new heavens and the new earth.[7]

Christ Crucified Is God's Saving Righteousness

> For I am not ashamed of *the gospel of Christ*, for it is the power of *God* for *salvation* to everyone believing; for the Jew first, and for the Greek as well. For in it [the gospel] the *righteousness*

5. Paul, in his undisputed letters, gives full weight to his *apostolic authority* (Rom 1:1–4; 11:13; 1 Cor 3:10; 4:9–17; 9:1–6; 12:28; 14:37; 15:1–11; 2 Cor 3:1-6 and see 4:1-6, 12:12; 1 Thess 4:2–8; and especially Gal 1:1–2:9; and see "taught" in 1 Cor 2:12 and Gal 1:12). "And *God* has appointed these in the church: *first* apostles, secondarily, prophets, third, teachers" (1 Cor 12:28). And, from Pentecost onward (Acts through Revelation) the phrase "the word of God" (or "word of the Lord" or "the word") always refers to *Christ* or *the gospel* that proclaims him, which is thus "the canon within the canon" of Scripture. Thus, we deduce that Paul's gospel (Rom 2:16) with its apostolic authority means that the writings of prophets and other NT authors, though inspired, are under the authority of the *apostolic* gospel and Scriptures and are to be interpreted in light of the apostolic writings; see also chs. 17 and 20. Apostles were those to whom the risen Christ appeared and those called (chosen) to be apostles by Christ (1 Cor 9:1; Rom 1:1).

6. Rom 16:25; 1 Cor 2:7–8; (2 Tim 1:9; Eph 1:3–14).

7. Rom 1:3–4; 3:24; 5:9, 19; 1 Cor 15; Rom 8:21; 2 Peter 3:13.

3

from God is revealed from faith to faith; as it is written, *"The Righteous One [Christ, and all in him], out of [his obedience of] faith, will live [have life eternal]."* (Rom 1:16–17)

Those who are justified out of Christ's faith (as source), who thereby have faith (through union with him) will have life eternal. Notice how the central point of the gospel of Christ is that in it a *"righteousness from God"* is revealed. This is called "the gift of righteousness" in 5:17, and it is the righteousness to which Paul refers when he says, "Therefore having been *justified* by faith, we have peace with God through our Lord Jesus Christ" (5:1 NKJV). Therefore, God through his apostle is saying that justification is not simply one doctrine among many doctrines of equal importance. Rather, he is saying that what is first of all, first in importance, is that Christ died for our sins (1 Cor 15:3–4), that we are justified by Christ's blood (Rom 5:9), for this is the basis of eternal life and of our entire life in Christ—now and forever! So, in Rom 1:16–17, Paul proclaims that the heart of "the gospel of God" (1:1) is the righteousness from God as *the gift of righteousness* (Rom 5:17) that justifies sinners (5:8–9). Although many interpreters have gravitated toward and prioritized other truths found in Paul's theology, such as our union with Christ or the unity of Jews and gentiles as the people of God, by studying Paul's texts for decades I am convinced, along with Luther,[8] Nygren,[9] Westerholm,[10] and many others, that it is *the saving, justifying righteousness of God in Christ*, through which we *are*

---

8. See, for example, *LW* 26:4–10, and Althaus, *Theology*, 224–32.

9. See Nygren, *Commentary on Romans*, especially 65–92.

10. See Westerholm, *Perspectives Old and New*, xvii–97, 352–407, where he contrasts the "Lutheran Paul," that is, the basic view of Paul's gospel in terms of the centrality of *justification*, held by Augustine, Luther, Calvin, and Wesley, with that of the NPP scholars, (beginning with E. P. Sanders), who all argue against this view. It is noteworthy that (secularist) E. P. Sanders, in a lecture, said, "I have no advice to anyone as to how to live or what to believe" (Sanders, "Is Paul's Legacy?," 53:59–54:02). Can anyone imagine Paul the apostle making such a statement? He goes on to say, "My only advice is to face the facts of social change head on, and to work in order to adapt Scripture to each new age, consciously and intelligently, rather than on the basis of personal whim and gut reaction" (Sanders, "Is Paul's Legacy?," 54:02–54:21). According to Sanders, Scripture needs to be adapted by humans to each new (secular) age. But God through Paul says that the secular age (in *whatever* phase), needs to adapt to the gospel of God (see 1 Cor 1:17–2:16; 3:18–21). The roots of the NPP error (reading the NT in the light of the OT) were at work decades before Sanders's book; but there were also early, prior warnings against this error: see Nygren, *Significance of the Bible*, 12–29, and *Commentary on Romans*, 119–22. Such warnings were not heeded, and now there are innumerable books looking to writings by others before Paul lived to discover what he means by "the law," while he himself *defines* it in Rom 2:17–23 as the Ten Commandments by naming three of them and calling them "the law."

counted (considered) by God as righteous persons in Christ, that stands at the heart and center of Paul's gospel of God (Rom 1:1, 16–17). The offense of justification (the cross, Gal 5:11) to human pride—that no one can justify himself by works—is the reason that justification continues to be subverted and demoted in the church, across all its denominations, for justification in Christ without our works goes against all human wisdom and righteousness of the flesh—all that man is apart from Christ. For the flesh cannot believe the truth of justification; yet there is no excuse for such unbelief. But *this* justification is not that of most of Protestantism, for it is the one of which the real Paul says, "The one who has died [with Christ] has been justified from the Sin" (Rom 6:7). For justification from (the condemnation of) the sin[11] is freedom from *the sin as lord* of us who now walk in newness of Christ's life (6:6, 4); for such are enslaved to God—no longer to sin (6:22). And, being indwelt by Christ's Spirit, putting to death the deeds of the body by means of *the Spirit* is the other side of "no condemnation" (8:1), for *the Spirit* has replaced sin in the inner man (Rom 8:1–15; Eph 3:16). For without mortification, there is no life (8:12–13).

Christ Crucified Is the Wisdom of God

> For Jews ask for signs, and Greeks seek wisdom, but we proclaim *Christ having been crucified*; to Jews an offense, and to gentiles [the nations] foolishness, but to those who are the called ones, both to Jews and to Greeks, *Christ: the power of God and wisdom of God.* (1 Cor 1:23–24)

Thus, when Paul refers to "the wisdom of God" (v. 24), he means *Christ crucified* (v. 23). That is, *the proclamation* of the gospel (1 Cor 1:21). Paul goes on in 1 Corinthians to explain "the wisdom of God," what he elsewhere calls "my gospel":

> But we speak the *wisdom of God* [Christ crucified, 1:24] in a mystery [which was kept secret until now], *the having been hidden wisdom*, which [*crucifixion of Christ*] God foreordained before the ages began [Acts 2:23] for *our* glory [after the ages], which none of the rulers of this age has known. For had they known it, they would not have crucified the Lord of glory. (1 Cor 2:7–8)

The gospel that Paul calls "my gospel" (Rom 2:6) and "the wisdom of God" is that God foreordained, before the ages began, that *Christ would be crucified*

11. of Adam (Rom 5:12–21).

5

for us during the ages, for our glorification after the ages, in the eternal age to come.[12] This gospel is what Paul, in Rom 16, refers to when he says:

> Now to him who can establish you according to *my gospel*, even *the preaching of Jesus Christ according to the revelation of the mystery* [the *secret* formerly hidden, but now revealed]— which has been kept *secret* through long ages past, but now is *manifested*, and through prophetic writings . . . is made known for the obedience of faith to all the nations, to the only wise God, through Jesus Christ, to whom be the glory forever! Amen. (Rom 16:25–26)

Romans 16:25–26 verifies 1 Cor 2:7–8—that no human ever heard this gospel, nor did it enter the heart of any human . . . *until* God revealed it and taught it to Paul (1 Cor 1:17–23; 2:6–7) by Christ's Spirit (2:9–10; Gal 1:11–12). And Paul says in Rom 16 that there is no other way to be established (made stable in one's faith, Rom 1:11; Col 2:6) than by the gospel of God's grace (Rom 1:1; Gal 1:6).

My personal confession of faith is as follows. God, in Christ, has died for me and has thereby justified me—totally apart from my doing the works of the law. And this gospel reveals that sin is in its essence unbelief (not trusting) in Christ (John 16:9). But Christ also died for my unbelief, or I would never be saved. By God's grace I am a justified saint, and I rejoice in knowing this God through Christ and in the certainty of eternal life in the glory of God. Although I am both sinner and saint, I am not a sinner and a justified saint in the same sense, for I am essentially a justified saint. The body is spiritually dead and condemned to death because of Adam's sin, which resulted in my (spiritual unto bodily) death. Yet the Spirit of God and of Christ is eternal life (in my inner man) because of justification (Rom 8:10). Paul wrote, "Our word to you was not Yes and No" (2 Cor 1:18). This text can be applied to justification: God's word in Christ was not "Yes, you are justified," and "No, you are *not* justified, because you are still a sinner— one of those who are still condemned." Rather, God's word in Christ is as follows: "Yes, you *are* justified, for you are not in the flesh, but in the Spirit" (Rom 8:1, 9). To be "in the flesh" is to be under the law with its condemnation. To be in the Spirit is to be under grace with its justification. "For all the promises of God, including justification, are *Yes* in Christ" (2 Cor 1:19–20). Therefore, even though, in one sense, Christ-believers are simultaneously in the flesh and in the Spirit, nevertheless, the ultimate truth about believers is that we are *not* in the flesh but in the Spirit (Rom 8:9). So, Jono Linebaugh was right when he wrote:

12. See also Rom 8:29–34.

GOD'S WORD OF THE CROSS

"Sinner" is an identity word and is misapplied if it is used to name the Christian's identity—their person. Before God, identity is not a both/and (sinner and righteous); it is an either/or (sinner *or* righteous) . . . Paul does something unprecedented (in comparison with early Jewish literature) in that he designates all people outside Christ with the identity "sinner" (Rom. 5:8, for example). But even more novel and scandalous is his corresponding claim that it is precisely "sinners" who are identified as "righteous" *in Christ* (Rom 3:23–24) . . . If we do not speak in terms of two total states (100% righteous in Christ and 100% sinful in ourselves) corresponding to the coexistence of two times (the old age and the new creation) then the undeniable reality of ongoing sin leads to the qualification of our identity in Christ: the existence of some sin must mean that one is not totally righteous.[13]

If you are in Christ, know that God has chosen to know you only as his justified and adopted son. A son is also a new creation in Christ. If you are in Christ—in "this grace in which we stand"(the grace of "having been justified," Rom 5:1, 2)—you never become unjustified, even if you sin (4:1–8; 8:1). But the very faith that justifies includes mortification by the Spirit of faith (Rom 8; 2 Cor 4:13). Referring to Martin Luther's famous Latin phrase *simul justus et peccator* (*simultaneously righteous and sinner*), Linebaugh writes:

To say *simul justus et peccator* is therefore not to say that "sinner" is our identity; it is to say that while we remain sinful in ourselves, we are in Christ, totally righteous.[14]

The "Both/And" of Being In Christ

We *are* in Christ, for we are joined only to the risen Christ! And "there is then *now no condemnation for those in Christ Jesus*" (Rom 8:1 NKJV). Paul says to the saints at Corinth, "Or do you not know that the unrighteous [i.e., those who practice lawlessness] shall not inherit the kingdom of God; but you were . . . justified in the name of the Lord Jesus Christ" (1 Cor 6:9–11 NASB). Paul says we *were* "the unrighteous" (1 Cor 6:9). But now, in Christ's name and in God's Spirit, you were washed (regenerated), sanctified (made holy) and justified (made right with God)—when you

13. Linebaugh, *Liberate*.
14. Linebaugh, *Liberate*.

believed in Christ (1 Cor 6:11 ATP; see Rom 5:1). It is from this identity—as those who were regenerated (made new; heart cleansed), sanctified, and justified in the Spirit (1 Cor 6:11) that the believer is to live. On one hand, if we are still alive in this body, we are still, in one sense, *in the flesh, which Paul calls* "the flesh of sin" (Rom 8:3). "If I am to live in the flesh, that means fruitful labor for me" (Phil 1:22 ESV). "But to remain in the flesh is more necessary on your account" (Phil 1:24 ESV). Insofar as Paul is still "in the flesh," in *that* sense he can say:

> But if through my lie the truth of God abounded to his glory, why am I still being judged as a *sinner*? (Rom 3:7 NASB)

> But if, while we seek to be justified in Christ, we ourselves have also been found *sinners*, is Christ then a minister of sin? May it never be! (Gal 2:17 NASB)

But on the other hand, Paul says, "While we *were still sinners*, Christ died for us [justified us]. How much more, having now been justified in his blood [no longer unjustified sinners], shall we be saved from wrath through him?" (Rom 5:9) Our death and resurrection with Christ enable Paul to say, "When we *were* in the flesh . . . but *now* we have been released from the law, having *died*," and "*you* are not [any longer] in the flesh, but [you are] in the Spirit" (Rom 8:9). Now Christ-believers are saints, literally, holy ones. So, the truth is as follows: Christian existence in this present age is a *both/and* existence. We are in two ages—this age and the age to come. If we are in Christ, we are already saved in spirit but not yet saved in body. But the ultimate truth (the "and" of the both/and) is that we are essentially *in Christ*—we are already "justified . . . in the Spirit of our God" (1 Cor 6:11 NASB); yet we wait for the hope of righteousness, when we will be *visibly* and *bodily* justified and made righteous before all creation—when the exalted Lord comes and we are glorified with him who has been glorified since his resurrection. So, here is a description of Paul's *both/and* for those who are "in Christ."

> The *penultimate truth* is that we are both *in the flesh* and *in the Spirit*. To be in the flesh (in Adam) is to be a sinner in this present evil age. To be in the Spirit (in Christ) is to be a justified saint, one who belongs to the age to come.

> And the *ultimate truth* is that, in spirit (the inner man), we are *not* in the flesh (this age), but we are *in the Spirit (the age to come)=justified holy ones*, for the Holy Spirit alone indwells our inner man, our human spirit (Rom 8:16; Eph 3:16). Therefore,

our *true being* (ὄντες) is not according to the flesh but *according to the Spirit of Christ and of God* (Rom 8:5, 9).

So, the penultimate truth is not the eternal, ultimate reality about us, for life "in the flesh" is temporal, but our essential *being* is "according to the Spirit of God" (Rom 8:5) who is eternal life (Rom 8:10; see 6:23). We are, in spirit, already citizens of heaven (Phil 3:20), because we are essentially not in the flesh but in the Spirit (Rom 8:9); we are in the kingdom/reign of God which is "in the Holy Spirit" (14:17) of Christ (8:9), in which he presently reigns (Col 1:13; 1 Cor 15:25), which is not of this world (John 18:36). Thus, we are to seek first God's reign, setting our spiritual eyes and hearts on the things which are not seen and are eternal (2 Cor 4:17–18; Col 3:1–4). We look for Christ's coming, when we will be glorified in the redemption of our body. In other words, in spirit we are justified saints, though still in a body that is spiritually dead because of sin (Rom 8:10) and thus is a mortal body. But we shall put on a body of immortality, incorruption, and glory, when not only our inner man is alive with God's life but our body also will be alive with God's life and fully dominated by his Spirit. The law's verdict is so terrifying that only those who really believe the truth of the gospel can even begin to believe and face up to the truth about themselves in the flesh—that in the flesh dwells nothing good (before God, Rom 7:18). The gospel of God makes sense in the light of the truth that the holy law, which is called "the ministry of condemnation" (Rom 7:12; 2 Cor 3:9) condemns all who are "in the flesh." This is true whether people feel condemned or not. And the only deliverance from this condemnation is in Jesus the Messiah. It follows then, that apart from Christ, all humans are continually under condemnation, but all who are in Christ are continually under justification—under grace (Rom 5:15; 6:14). And blessed is the believer who beholds the glory of God's grace in Christ and trusts in Christ alone, knowing that there is only death outside of (faith in) Christ.

This book is about the grace of Christ, which is the gospel (Gal 1:6). The death of Christ justifies sinners who, in themselves, do not believe that they are sinners. Their essential sin is unbelief in Christ, the other side of which is self-justification. This is revealed by the word of the cross, in which justification in Christ is of first importance. In light of Paul's gospel, we find that there is both truth and error in the so-called "New Perspective on Paul." It is true that, according to Phil 3:

> Paul can say that he had been "flawless" as to the righteousness required by the law (v. 6). His encounter with Jesus Christ—at Damascus, according to Acts 9:1–9—has not changed this fact. It was not to him a restoration of a plagued conscience; when

9

he says that he forgets what is behind him (Phil 3:13), he does not think about his shortcomings in his obedience to the law, but about his glorious achievements as a righteous Jew, achievements which he nevertheless now has learned to consider as 'refuse' in the light of his faith in Jesus as the Messiah.[15]

Paul had what Stendahl calls "a rather robust conscience."[16] Paul can say:

> And to me it is a very small thing that I should be judged by you, or by man's day [of judgment]. But I do not judge myself. For I am conscious of nothing against myself; but not by this have I been justified, but [rather] the one judging me is the Lord. (1 Cor 4:3–4)

Thus, Stendahl traces what he (famously) called "the Introspective Conscience of the West"[17] back to Augustine, of whom he says, "His *Confessiones* are the first great document in the history of the introspective conscience. The Augustinian line leads into the Middle Ages and its reaches its climax in the penitential struggle of an Augustinian monk, Martin Luther, and in his interpretation of Paul."[18] If I may add my personal experience at this point, I would say that, as one who was taught in a Roman Catholic parochial school in the 1950s and early sixties, the whole emphasis was on keeping the Ten Commandments and focusing on the *sins against* those commandments, and thus on *not committing* those sins. This developed in me a conscience tuned to the letter of the law.[19] Thus, at the risk of oversimplification, I conclude the following: the unbelieving rejection (including the non-proclamation) of *the gospel of God's justification of the ungodly in Christ, apart from works of the law,* in the church that followed Paul's departure[20] issued in an increased and pervasive unbelief toward that gospel,

15. Stendahl, *Paul among Jews*, 80.

16. Stendahl, *Paul among Jews*, 80.

17. Stendahl, *Paul among Jews*, 78. Of course, we do not agree with Stendahl on other issues, e.g., his understanding of Rom 7, and he denies the centrality of justification in Paul's gospel of God (p. 27), contra Paul in Rom 1:16–17.

18. Stendahl, *Paul among Jews*, 85.

19. I was only "flesh," but also on the ASD spectrum, so it was a double whammy for me.

20. "It has always been a puzzling fact that Paul meant so relatively little for the thinking of the Church during the first 350 years of its history" (Stendahl, *Paul among Jews*, 83). "Seldom, if ever, do we find anyone who had grasped Paul's doctrine of justification" (Stendahl, *Paul among Jews*, 16). The reality of the Accuser accusing in Rev 12:9–11 could not have been written before *the death of Christ* that justifies his elect (see Rom 8:33–34), but the Accuser does not justify the prominence of unbelief (the

through which the church reaped the introspective conscience, worsening each century until we encounter Martin Luther, whose disturbed conscience found its relief through faith in Jesus the Christ. But this reality of Luther's experience (and where his theology *does* align with the gospel) does not annul the reality of the introspective conscience of the West[21] (compared to Judaism and Paul), which, through Christ in Luther (and teaching him), paradoxically *did* give further understanding of the gospel and the gospel's answer to the *sinful, human condition* in its depth.[22]

The Theology (Word of God) of the Cross

For example, Paul Althaus explains Luther's theology of the cross: "In summary, Luther's *theology of the cross* means that the cross conceals God and thus marks the end of all speculation about God on the part of self-confident reason."[23] "All speculation" here means all thinking about God with "the mind of the flesh" (Rom 8:6). On Luther's theology of the cross, Randall Zachman wrote:

> Luther contrasted the theology of the cross with the theology of glory (*theologia gloriae*). Whereas the theology of the cross comes to the knowledge of God through the indirect and hidden way of the cross, the theology of glory attempts to know God directly through what is apparent in the world . . . The theology of glory finds a direct continuity between what it sees and feels and what it believes about God, whereas the theology of the cross finds a contradiction between what it sees and feels and what it believes.[24]

Later, concerning this world's theology, with its glory, he writes:

> Thus, the conscience arrives at the following portrait of God: "God is a righteous Judge who is pleased with works of the law

---

neglect of teaching justification in Christ alone) in the church for centuries.

21. One example of this is Western "Christianity's" emphasis on "inner peace" over Paul's *having "peace with God"* (Rom 5:1), which remains in Christ whether one feels that peace or not.

22. See, e.g., Bultmann, *Theology of the New Testament*, 267.

23. Althaus, *Theology of Martin Luther*, 28, emphasis mine. Fleshly reason knows *nothing* of God's love and grace in Christ's cross.

24. Zachman, *Assurance of Faith*, 19. It is best to understand "the cross" here to mean Christ's death for justification (Rom 5:8, 9).

and who hates sin. Those who do good works have a gracious God; those who sin have an angry and wrathful God."[25]

The religion of conscience, therefore, is fundamentally a theology of glory. The attitude of God toward us may be known directly through the judgment of the conscience: if the conscience condemns, so does God; if the conscience acquits, so does God. In this way the conscience comes to know "the invisible things of God"—that is, God's will toward us—"in works as perceived by man."[26]

By the phrase "in works as perceived by *man*" Luther means by the perception of our *flesh*, which is blinded by sin and unbelief. But then the flesh, and not God's word, determines if *God* is *for* us or *against* us! Zachman continues:

The conscience portrays God and God's will to itself, and thus is certain that it already knows who God is and how God is to be worshiped; it portrays to itself a God who is pleased by works of the law. When the Word tells the conscience that God wishes to be worshiped by faith alone and not by works, reason and conscience reject the Word as an outright lie and falsehood.[27]

The natural person and the conscience have no knowledge of the theological or proper use of the law, for by nature all think that the law is given to us so that we might stand justified before God on the basis of works.[28]

The whole of the religion of conscience stands under the wrath of God. Indeed, the more pious the person tries to become, the more wrath the person finds on him/herself.[29]

In line with this gospel, Gerhard Forde wrote:

The law must not be admitted into unholy alliance with the conscience. It must not be confused with gospel. To do so is absolutely fatal. Between the work of the law and the promise

---

25. Zachman, *Assurance of Faith*, 33. The quote is from *LW* 26:396.

26. Zachman, *Assurance of Faith*, 36. The work of the law is written in the hearts of the nations, their conscience . . . bearing witness (with the law) . . . their thoughts the meanwhile accusing or excusing them (Rom 2:14–15).

27. Zachman, *Assurance of Faith*, 38.

28. Zachman, *Assurance of Faith*, 42. Zachman's reference to Luther is from *Complete Sermons*, 2:67–68.

29. Zachman, *Assurance of Faith*, 44.

of the gospel stand the cross and the resurrection, as the absolute dividing line.[30]

Therefore, all preaching and teaching on what humans are to *do* as being of
primary importance is done in ignorance of the gospel's use of law—that
humans are under sin and thus condemned and, therefore, they cannot justify themselves (Rom 3:9–20). Preaching the gospel is of first importance
(1 Cor 15:1–4). What the natural mind does not know, and what the gospel
reveals, is that the mind of the flesh, so far from *loving* God as the law commands, *hates* God (Rom 8:7–8), because humans are born spiritually dead
(Rom 8:10; Col 2:13). There is no such thing as an age, such as infancy, when
humans are not condemned to death in Adam. But God's grace in Christ is
greater than Adam's sin, indwelling sin, and all our sins, for we are justified
by the blood of God (Acts 20:28). Many Christ-believers have been spiritually "burned" by not hearing this theology of the cross, even if they cannot
articulate the fact that the preacher is not clearly distinguishing between the
law, which only works wrath (Rom 4:15), and the gospel, which justifies sinners (Rom 5:8–9). For the law, when properly preached, is shown to be the
ministry of condemnation. So, those in Christ are to live by faith in Christ
alone.[31] *Unbelief in Christ* is the great enemy; it is the essence and root of
disobedience toward God; it is self-justification, by which one seeks to justify
one's self before God. But God can "establish" believers—make them stable
in Christ through the gospel (Rom 16:25).

The gospel is the good news that when we were utterly helpless to save
ourselves from wrath, sin, and death, God came in history in Jesus and died
for sinners and rose again to a new life, that of the age to come. This is
how God makes right with himself all who believe in Jesus Christ for the
purpose of eternal life with God his Father.

> But to him that does *not* work [for right standing with God], but
> believes on the *One justifying* the *ungodly*, his faith is counted
> [by God] for righteousness. (Rom 4:5)

To believe in Christ is to have Christ as one's righteousness, to continue
to flee from our righteousness, which is of the flesh. For Christ is the end
of the law for righteousness to everyone believing (Rom 10:4). For God
continually justifies those who in themselves are the ungodly, who by his
gift of faith trust in him (Rom 4:5; Phil 1:29). The church has rarely taught
God's justification of the ungodly in Christ as a matter of "first importance"

30. Forde, "Christian Life," *CD* 2:418.

31. Rom 1:5, 16, 17; Gal 2:21—3:3; 5:1–5; 2 Cor 5:7; Col 2:6. The NT letters teach
faith in Christ and, through that faith, love toward the neighbor (Gal 5:1–15).

(see 1 Cor 15:1–4; compare Rom 5:6–10). Since Christ is the righteousness of God (2 Cor 5:21; 1 Cor 1:30), the great enemy of Christ is "my righteousness" (Phil 3:9). In "the word [of God] of the cross," God in Christ remains the subject and the power of our salvation. God's saving righteousness in Christ is now revealed *apart from the law* through Christ's faith—his obedience unto death, which justified us (Rom 3:21–22; 1:5; 5:19; Phil 2:8). Through the accomplished redemption in Christ, God adopted us and gave us the Spirit of Christ, who is eternal life (Rom 1:6; Gal 4:5, 6; Rom 8:10). This life in the Spirit is the life of the new creation, for God in Christ's death has delivered us out of this present evil, unjustified age into the age to come, that of the justified new creation (Gal 1:4; 6:15) in spirit (our inner man), and we shall be also in body at the coming of the exalted Lord Jesus Christ. We are now spiritually severed from the flesh, for we are joined to Christ.[32] But at death, the Christ-believer shall be bodily severed from the flesh of sin and be with Christ (Phil 1:21–26).

The gospel not only calls for faith, but it calls forth and grants faith to God's chosen ones (Phil 1:29). Faith in Christ believes in what we do not see, feel, or experience—Christ as our righteousness, our justification before God (Rom 5:1–2; 1 Cor 1:30; 2 Cor 5:7). This faith is inseparable from being indwelt by the Spirit of Christ and being led by his Spirit (Gal 2:21–3:3; 5:18; Rom 8:1–2, 9–15). The new creation in Christ is our rule (Gal 6:15–16). So, the words "by faith in Christ" and "by the Spirit" go together in Paul's gospel; the phrases are interchangeable in Gal 5:5. By faith in Christ, we count it as true that we have died with Christ—both to the sin and the law—and are alive to God in Christ's resurrection life (Rom 6:1–11; 7:6; 8:1–10; Eph 2:1–3; Col 2:13; 3:1–4). And by this faith, we are to yield ourselves in obedience to the Lord Jesus Christ, no longer presenting our bodily members to the power of sin, but instead yielding our bodily members as weapons of righteousness (that of faith) to God (Rom 6:12–22). This faith works (serves) through love, Christ's love for us. The gospel, that Jesus the Messiah was crucified, died, and rose again and is exalted to God's right hand for us, is outside of us. The gospel is also outside us in its form, which is the word of *the gospel as it is proclaimed*. This preached word of the gospel comes into our hearts by faith (Rom 10:4–9), which God grants to his elect by hearing with faith the preached gospel (Rom 10:17; Phil 1:29). Thereby Christ has made us a new creation, and he has done this by his Spirit who indwells us: "For the one who is joined to the Lord is one spirit with him" (1 Cor 6:17). We are both justified and a new creation in Christ. The resurrection and exaltation of Christ, through

---

32. Rom 2:28, 29; 6:2–9; 7:5, 6; 8:9; 1 Cor 6:17; Col 2:11–12.

which comes the indwelling of the Spirit of Christ with his leading, has a central place in God's gospel; the Spirit is given (to lead us) on the basis of justification (Rom 8:10–15). Thus, according to Paul and John, the indwelling of Christ has not been given enough prominence in the church, including the Reformation wing of the church. One tragic result of this lack is the idea of the so-called "third use of the law." This error is the result of not understanding the apostolic doctrine of Christ's resurrection and its corollary—Christ in us, by his Spirit, who is our rule instead of the law of Moses. This truth of Christ's resurrection does not at all nullify the word (of God) of the cross,[33] because to continue "in the Spirit" (of the risen Christ) is to continue in faith in Christ, which includes faith in Christ for justification (Gal 2:20–3:3). The opposite of God's word of the cross (the theology of the cross) is the theology of glory, which is trusting in and glorying in *something other* than the crucified Christ, who has become the exalted Lord (1 Cor 1:18, 30–31; Gal 6:14). Again, to trust in Christ for justification before God is to trust in the same Christ who lives in us (Gal 6:14–16).

This entire book aims to be in line with Paul's gospel (Gal 1:11–12) as set forth especially in Gal 2:16–21 and in Romans. In Galatians he sets forth what he calls "the truth of the gospel" (2:14). And, like the later-written Rom 3:21–26, Gal 2:16–21 is the central thesis of his gospel and is the basis of the rest of the letter. In Gal 2:16 he says that we are justified by Christ's faith (his obedience unto death) and not by (our) works of law, and that this justification is ours through faith in Christ. Then, in verses 17–20 he elaborates on the truth of the gospel, and then he summarizes what he said from 2:16 through 2:20 in the climax:

> I do not reject the grace of God, for if justification comes through law, Christ died for nothing. (2:21)

Then, Paul continues with Christ's death for justification, saying:

> O foolish Galatians, who put a spell on you, before whose eyes Jesus Christ was openly set forth among you [by my preaching Christ] as having been crucified [for your justification]? (3:1)

Then he says that the Galatians received the Spirit of God by the hearing of faith (in Christ for justification, 2:16, 21). He continues:

> Having begun in the Spirit [through faith in Christ for righteousness], are you now ending in the flesh? (3:3)

---

33. Gal 2:20–3:3; see also Forde, *On Being a Theologian*, 1, footnote.

He is saying that they began their life in Christ "in the Spirit," that is, by *faith* in Christ for justification, and that they were to continue and end the same way! This equating of *the Spirit* with *faith in Christ* (Gal 2:21—3:3), as he will later, in 5:5, continues throughout Paul's entire letter. It is Paul's gospel, and there is no other (1:8–9). So later, Paul can say, "If you are led by the Spirit (through faith in Christ, 5:5) you are not under (obligation to the) law" (5:18). Therefore, we unequivocally declare that as we *trust in Christ* for justification before God (by the obedience of *faith*, which through that trust, obeys him as Lord), the Spirit of God actively leads us in every area of our lives, apart from the law.

Gerhard Forde put it this way:

> I believe it can be argued that justification by faith alone itself and the freedom it creates, drives to utter concreteness in praxis.[34]

By "praxis," of course, Forde means "practice," and we will practice what we believe: that the God who justifies us can be trusted to lead us by his Spirit—for in Gal 2:21—3:3, Paul is saying that by trusting in Christ for justification before God, the Galatians would be trusting in this same Christ who is leading them by his Spirit, they would be continuing and "ending" in the Spirit, and this would have meant that they were not trusting in their works of the law. Christ in us is based upon his work of redemption outside us (Gal 4:1–7; Rom 8:9–10). Therefore, the imputation of righteousness to us through redemption is central to the gospel. All other apostolic doctrines and blessings are, in truth, based upon this foundation of Christ crucified for justification (1 Cor 1:21–23; 3:11; 15:1–4). The flesh, with its mind of unbelief, cannot believe the gospel. The flesh seeks to justify one's self apart from God in Christ. Therefore, we must endure the fellowship of Christ's sufferings (Phil 3:10), including the offense of the cross, that God has justified us in Christ alone, apart from our works, thereby giving us the right to eternal life with the Father and his Son in the Holy Spirit. We can acknowledge the truth about our helplessness to save ourselves only to the extent that we know and believe that we are justified in Christ, where there is no condemnation. Thus, the problem in the church all along has not been a lack of clearness in terms of the perspicuity (understandable nature) of Scripture, but rather the problem has been unbelief in the gospel of God, which is the center and key to interpreting the Scriptures. In the gospel, the contrast is made between "the righteousness of the law" (seeking to be justified before God by the works of the law) and "the righteousness of faith"—trusting in the God who raised Christ from the dead. The gospel of

---

34. Forde, "Viability of Luther," 29.

God includes Paul's contrast between *the law* and *the promise* (Rom 1:1–2; 4:13–16; Gal 3:11–28). But, now that Christ has come and been raised, this contrast is the antithesis between the law and the gospel (Rom 10:4–10; Gal 3:8–14) as well. From this antithesis comes the revelation of the depth of sin as unbelief in Christ, which we will cover in chapter 6. In 2 Cor 3 and 4, two kinds of glory are contrasted: the glory of *the law*, which is temporal, and the glory of *Christ*, which is eternal. The glory of the law blinds humans so that they *cannot* behold the glory of God in Christ. But all the glory and splendor of this age and world is temporary—it is passing away (1 Cor 2), and therefore it is deceptive, for ultimately its temporal character makes it as if it were *nothing* as compared to Christ's eternal life and glory. The death of Christ demonstrates how costly it was for God to pay the price to redeem his own from God's wrath, from sin, law, death, and the devil. The gospel reveals that all sin against God deserves God's wrath, for God is a holy God. The gospel does not in the least make light of sin against God, for it does not make light of God's wrath, which Christ bore on our behalf. But our sin is not greater than God's grace, which is infinitely greater than sin and its condemnation; therefore, we are able to rejoice, even with laughter, at the reality of the total forgiveness of all our sins, being justified as those who are of the faith of Jesus. Humans in Adam are, with their wills, in bondage to sin (unbelief), which means that they do not truly seek God and that they will not and cannot receive God's grace in Christ as they are in the flesh, for the flesh's mind hates God. Thus, the gospel reveals that unbelief in Christ is the essence of sin. But Christ died even for the unbelief (sin) of those he chose and is determined to save, otherwise no one would ever be saved from sin and death.

In the gospel, the central issue is that, in Christ, God's love is a "while we were yet sinners" love (Rom 5:8), in which God continually justifies the sinner in Christ alone, apart from works of the law—that is, apart from keeping the Ten Commandments. This "apart from law" (Rom 3:21) love for us in Christ of necessity excludes the law as a rule of life. For in Christ Jesus, my "law-keeping" and "lawbreaking"[35] neither justifies me nor condemns me, for I am justified in Christ alone. Thus, the Christian's rule of life is the new creation in Christ (Gal 6:15–16). Christ crucified and risen now *lives to God* (Rom 6:10) and it is no longer I who live, (for I died), but *Christ* (who lives to God) *who lives* in me.[36] This indwelling Christ does not

---

35. Paul's shorthand for outward "law-keeping" is "circumcision" and his shorthand for outward lawbreaking is "uncircumcision" in Rom 2:17–23 and Gal 5:1–4.

36. Gal 2:19–20. The "I" who is independent from God through the law (2:19) *no longer lives* (as lord=I am no longer self-lawed, as in Rom 2:14–15), but Christ lives in me (now as reigning Lord, Rom 8:9–10; 2 Cor 3:17).

need the law of Moses in any way. The incarnate Son of God, God himself, Jesus Christ crucified and risen, is the one who makes us holy by the Holy Spirit through the gospel, for the Holy Spirit is not less holy than the law, and against the fruit of the Holy Spirit there is no law (Gal 5:22). If we are in Christ, our "law" is the Spirit of Christ (Rom 8:2). We trust in Christ, and that includes Christ as an indwelling Lord. Since Christ is the object of faith, the flesh looks for something with which to *dis*believe God's word to us, which is essentially this: Therefore, since we have been justified by faith, we have peace with God through our Lord Jesus Christ (Rom 5:1 ESV). This is what he means: We have been made right with God through having believed in Christ. Through this justification, we have peace with God— God is no longer against us, but for us—through our Lord Jesus Christ, and through nothing and no one else.

If justification in Christ is not believed, then there simply is no sanctification, which includes mortification. Only as justification is believed do sanctification and spiritual life with its growth occur. Those "who are seeking to be justified by law" (Gal 5:4b NASB) refers to those who desire be perfect in conscience by the works of the law, but the law can never do what Christ has already done. The Reformers rightly understood that justification grants the right to freedom in terms of conscience for those who believe in Christ. This is substantiated by Paul, and the authors of Hebrews and First John. In 1 Cor 4:3–5, when Paul says that he does not judge himself, we logically deduce from all his words that he is simultaneously saying, "If I was to be conscious of something against myself, I am not by this condemned," which aligns with the teaching of the authors of Hebrews (in 9:9; 10:1–2, 11, 14) and of 1 John (in 3:19–20). Thus, the war between the flesh, which hates Christ's lordship through grace, and the Spirit of God is the primary war that rages in Christ-believers. But in Christ we are no longer obligated to the flesh with its desires, but to the Spirit, with his desires.[37] At any given moment, either God's Spirit or sin's flesh has power over a human—either life or death, either God's Spirit or sin's flesh—either the power of God, which is the gospel, or the power of sin, which is the law.[38] Unbelief in the Christ of the apostolic gospel is the root source of spiritual death, with its accompanying spiritual blindness and resulting unhealthiness—both in the church and in the world. Not using the gospel's discernment, that the essence of sin is unbelief in Christ, the other side of which is self-justification, has caused many Christians to be unaware of the corruption of some unbelieving leaders who (only) appear to stand for righteousness. (We are aware of the two

37. Rom 8:9–13; Gal 5:16–17.
38. Rom 1:16–17; 1 Cor 15:56.

kingdoms: that of this world and that of God, and that in this world there needs to be "civil righteousness," which never justifies; yet the above words are still true). For faith in Christ reveals that sin is a destructive power that is simultaneously unbelief in Christ, which causes humans to be blind to sin's/unbelief's effects on every person and every human system.

TWO

The First Importance of the Death of Christ

Now I declare to you, brothers, the gospel which I preached to you, which also you received, in which you also stand, by which also you are saved, if you hold firmly the word which I preached to you, unless you believed [the word] in vain.[1] For I delivered to you as of first importance that which I also received: that Christ[2] died for our sins according to the Scriptures, that he was buried, that he was raised on the third day according to the Scriptures, and that he appeared to Cephas, then to the twelve. (1 Cor 15:1–5 NKJV)

God is not just one but one-in-three, because he is a communion of persons who share in love with one another. The circle of divine love, however, has not remained closed. God's love is, in the literal sense of the word, "ecstatic"—a love that causes God to go out of himself and to create things other than himself. By voluntary choice God created the world in "ecstatic" love, so

---

1. That is, "unless you believed only when I first preached to you, and do not continue to hold firmly the word (the gospel) by *faith*." On the other hand, those foreknown (fore-loved) by God *will persevere in faith* (Rom 8:29–30). *Both* truths, which are paradoxically in tension, are to be held and believed.

2. God, in the person of his Son, became incarnate of the virgin Mary. He is the Messiah, fully God and fully man. On the person of Christ, see *NPNF* 9:45–76, and SD 8.1–87, 592–608.

that there might be besides himself other beings to participate in the life and love that are his.[3]

This love meant that the eternal Son of God took on human flesh, even unto his death (Rom 1:1–4; [5:6; Phil 2:8]) for those whom the triune God loved from before the foundation of the world. After referring to the Son's *incarnation* (a synecdoche that includes his death), Paul follows this by referring to the Son's resurrection from the dead (Rom 1:3–4). Then he speaks of "the obedience of faith" (Rom 1:5), which is in this Son of God who rose again. Then, before Paul mentions anything about the wrath of God, he proclaims this gospel once more, wherein the righteousness that saves from sin, wrath, and death is revealed:

> For I am not ashamed of the gospel, for it is the power of God for salvation to everyone who believes in Christ: to the Jew first and to the Greek. For in it [the gospel] *the righteousness from God* is revealed—from [Christ's] faith to [our] faith, as it is written, "The Righteous One, out of faith [as source] shall live." (Rom 1:16–17)

The remainder of the letter to the Romans is a setting forth of the gospel of God, in which the death of Christ for justification is of first importance. Romans will expound on the indicatives and the imperatives of the gospel, but it is crucial to see how Christ's death for our justification lies at the heart of the indicatives, indicating our justification in him.

The Grace of God Is the Death of Christ for Justification

The word "grace" has been defined by Rome and the Orthodox as God working in a person, primarily through their sacraments, while Protestants have defined grace as God's unmerited favor, and all three would agree that grace's basis is in Christ. But for Paul the apostle, the grace of God is the *act* of a particular person. The *grace of God* is *the death of Christ* for the *justification* of sinners. Paul wrote:

> I do not set aside *the grace of God* [by seeking righteousness by law], for if *righteousness* comes by law, *Christ died* for nothing. (Gal 2:21)

"Grace" is that which justifies sinners through the death of Christ. Paul says the same thing in Romans: "being *justified* freely by His *grace* . . .

3. Ware, *Orthodox Way*, 56.

in his [Christ's] blood" (Rom 3:24, 25). And Paul also explains justification by grace (5:1) in terms of Christ's death for sinners for their justification in Rom 5:6–9. If that was not enough, in 5:15 he speaks of *the grace* of God and then "the gift by grace." This *"gift* by grace" is "the gift of righteousness,"[4] which came by Christ's obedience unto death (5:19; Phil 2:8). "The gift by the grace of one man" (Rom 5:15) means the gift of righteousness (justification) by the grace (the death) of the one man (Christ) (5:17). So, there is union and distinction between God's "love" and God's "grace" in Paul's gospel. The love (agape) of God for us (Rom 5:8) was demonstrated by Christ's death for us, which is his grace (5:1, 9). Love preceded grace. Love for us was there in God from all eternity, but it was not demonstrated until Christ died for sinners who needed grace, and that death *was* God's grace, his love demonstrated in action (5:8), called "one righteous act" (5:9, 18). The death of Christ is God's act of truly judging his people with wrath—those who were indeed guilty—in his Son's *death on their behalf*, ahead of the day of wrath.[5] The coming day of eschatological wrath is precisely what those in Christ have been saved from, because for God's elect the day of wrath has already occurred, for Christ bore God's wrath in our stead (Rom 5:6–10). Humans think themselves to be free in their false worship and independence from God, but they are not free at all. The flesh hates justification in Christ because the flesh's pride hates Christ's grace. We want to glory in and trust in ourselves instead. It is important to take note here that the old covenant scriptures *never* say that the law cannot be kept. Rather, they imply that it *can* be kept, not only in Deut 30:12–19, but also in Deut 6, which reads as follows:

> And the LORD commanded us to do all these statutes, to fear the LORD our God, for our good always, that he might preserve us alive, as it is this day. And it shall be our righteousness, if we observe to do all these commandments before the LORD our God, as he hath commanded us. (Deut 6:24–25 AV)

In its OT context, the reward for doing the law is to not be put to death but to have a long and prosperous life. But now that Christ has died and been raised again to new life, Paul proclaims that God in Jesus Christ has provided a righteousness from God that saves from the powers of sin and of death. In the light of "the new covenant . . . of the Spirit" (2 Cor 3:6) the inability of the law being fulfilled apart from Christ is revealed (Rom 2:21–29; 3:9–20; 8:7–9), for only in the Spirit of Christ is the law fulfilled (Rom 2:25–29;

---

4. Rom 5:17; i.e., justification by an imputed righteousness, 4:1–8.

5. See Bultmann, *Theology of the New Testament*, 289.

8:3–9). There is both continuity and discontinuity between the old and new covenants, and this applies to the Holy Spirit as well. Brownson says:

> Paul's letter to the Galatians also describes how the role of the law in the life of God's people has shifted since the coming of Christ and the pouring out of the Spirit. In the New Covenant, the Spirit transforms us into the image of Christ, whereas in the Old Covenant, the law could only be imposed as an external restraint.[6]

Stephen Westerholm shows that the old covenant scriptures' view of *the law* (i.e., *the covenant*, Deut 4:13; 9:11) was not as spiritual and thus not condemning all humans as Paul now declared it to be in texts such as Rom 3:9–20 and Gal 3:12–13.

> As long as one believes that . . . Jews will be "saved" provided they show a basic willingness to comply with the laws of the covenant (some Jews set the standard higher than that; but some did not) one will naturally believe them capable of showing at least the required modicum of obedience. So Paul himself presumably believed prior to his life-changing trip to Damascus. But once he was convinced that Jesus was, after all, God's Messiah, then Christ's crucifixion, far from discrediting messianic claims on his behalf, had to find a place in the divine plan for messianic redemption. It follows that *humanity's predicament must be more desperate* than Jews otherwise imagined. Human beings must *not*, after all, be capable of the modicum of obedience required by the covenant . . . Along such lines, we may well imagine Paul's thinking developed.[7]

But does this truth—that came by Jesus Christ (John 1:17) mean that old covenant saints believed that they were without sin? No. They knew they needed the forgiveness of sins. God's forgiveness of his people was the *basis* of the fear of the Lord (Ps 130:3–4). The Old Testament saints were saved by faith in *the promise* of God. The apostle says this, not only in Rom 1:1–2 and 4:1–16 but also in the truth that, if old covenant saints were justified by works, they would not have needed the death of Christ as they did, but Paul says they did need it (in Rom 3:24–26). The psalmist could say to Yahweh (his covenant God), "Enter not into judgment with your servant, for no one living is righteous before you" (Ps 143:2 ESV). But it is only in the light of the righteousness from God *now* manifested in the gospel that Paul can use this OT text in his gospel by reorienting it according to the revelation of Jesus

---

6. Brownson, *Promise of Baptism*, 116–17.

7. Westerholm, *Justification Reconsidered*, 33, emphasis mine.

Christ (Gal 1:12), saying, "Therefore *by the works of the law* no flesh shall be justified in his sight; for *by the law is the knowledge of sin*" (Rom 3:20). Paul adds "by works of the law"—because what the law could never do, Christ did: justify us and give us the Holy Spirit as life to indwell us (Rom 8:10; 5:21). And with the words, "For by law is the knowledge of sin" (3:20), he means that, through the law is the experiential knowledge of sin, as a powerful lord, leading straight to death (Rom 7:7–13).

Before Paul met Christ, he saw himself just as Zacharias saw himself, as "righteous in the sight of God, walking blamelessly in all the commandments and requirements of the Lord" (Luke 1:6 NASB). Zacharias was adopted—in the old covenant sense (Rom 9:4) and thus was one of God's own (John 1:11). But since the new covenant has come (1 Cor 11:25; 2 Cor 3:6), OT adoption no longer "cut it." Looking at himself from a law perspective, Paul said of himself, "If any other person thinks to trust in the flesh, I more . . . I was circumcised the eighth day, of Israel's stock, of the tribe of Benjamin, according to the law, a Pharisee, according to zeal: persecuting the church; according to the righteousness which is in the law, I was *blameless*" (Phil 3:4–6). The Greek word for "blameless" here is ἄμεμπτος, the same word used in Job 1:1 (LXX):

> There was a man in the land of Ausitis whose name was Job.
> That man was true, *blameless*, righteous, and God-fearing, and
> he abstained from every evil thing. (Job 1:1 SAAS)

This is how Paul (when he was Saul) saw himself—blameless according to the law's righteousness, God-fearing, and shunning evil. But when Christ revealed himself in Paul, he discovered that Christ is *wholly other* than what humans would ever think God's Messiah would be. Paul discovered that in himself, apart from Christ, he was a condemned sinner and that God's righteousness is wholly other than the righteousness of the law and of the flesh, which is owned by sin. Through God-given faith, Paul became a believer in the Messiah. Knowing Christ as the exalted Lord meant his translation from the old covenant to the new covenant in Jesus' blood and of his Spirit: the death of the old man with Christ and the resurrection of the new man with Christ. The apart-from-works[8] character of the gospel reveals that, as flesh, we can conceive of nothing other than justification before God by our works. The gospel reveals that the unbeliever thinks of himself as righteous (as not needing Christ)—that humans continually flee the one true God of the gospel—and that existence in the flesh is one of self-justification before God, which is simultaneously unbelief in

---

8. Rom 3:28—4:6.

THE FIRST IMPORTANCE OF THE DEATH OF CHRIST

Christ. Therefore, "the righteous by nature" Jew and all others also who are trusting in themselves need to be seen for who they are: sinners before the righteous God. We will look at this in the next chapter.

THREE

"The Righteous" Are Sinners

BEFORE THEY BELIEVED IN Christ, both Peter and Paul saw themselves as righteous—as "Jews by nature, and not [as] sinners of the nations" (Gal 2:15–17). That is, they had previously seen themselves as God's own people (John 1:11), Israelites who were adopted through old covenant adoption (Rom 9:14). But through the gospel of Christ, which ushered in the new testament of the Spirit (2 Cor 3:6), they came to know that they were sinners (Gal 2:17). They realized that, since Christ had come, old covenant adoption was only a shadow, for God had now done something new; so they needed to become sons of God by believing on the name of Jesus (John 1:12). Thus, old covenant adoption was only a shadow of its fulfillment in Christ.[1]

Paul's gospel reveals the truth that *both Jews and gentiles are all under (the power of) sin* (Rom 3:9). The Jews are no better off than the nations, for "all the world stands under the judgment of God" (Rom 3:19). Now Paul knew the Psalms, and in Ps 1 he had read of the contrast between *the righteous* (the Jews, who were in the covenant) and *the sinners* (the wicked, who were outside the covenant):

> How blessed is the [*righteous*] man who does not walk in the counsel of the wicked, or stand in the path of *sinners* . . .
>
> But his delight is in the law of the Lord, and in His law he meditates day and night . . .
>
> The *wicked* are not so . . . But they are like the chaff which the wind drives away. Therefore the *wicked* will not stand in the judgment,
>
> Nor *sinners* [stand] in the assembly of *the righteous*. For the Lord approves the way of *the righteous*,
>
> But the way of *the wicked* will perish. (Ps 1:1a, b, 4a NASB)

1. Gal 4:1–7; Rom 8:15–16; Heb 10:1; Col 2:16–17; John 1:11–12.

Therefore, this way of thinking was part and parcel of what Paul calls "the Jew's religion" in Gal 1:14. The mindset that aligns with Ps 1 is evident in what Paul says to Peter, both of whom were Jews according to the flesh: We (you, Peter, and I, Paul) are *Jews by nature*, and *not sinners* of the gentiles (Gal 2:15 NASB). As Jews—those in the covenant by birth and circumcision—they had seen themselves as "the righteous" and not as sinners of the nations, as we have seen in Ps 1. The law said:

> Know therefore that the LORD your God is God, the faithful God who keeps covenant and steadfast *love* with those who love him and keep his commandments, to a thousand generations. (Deut 7:9 RSV)

On this text, Nygren says:

> God's love is shown . . . to them that fear him; it is shown to the righteous, not to the sinner. It signifies at most that God is faithful to His Covenant despite man's unfaithfulness, provided that man returns to the Covenant. But it is a far cry from this Divine love which comes to call sinners, for such love has no place within a legal scheme.[2]

And to show that what Nygren said is true, in what follows we set forth the context of the text from which Nygren quoted, Deut 7:

> The LORD did not set His love on you, nor choose you, because you were more in number than any people . . . But because the LORD loves you, and because He would keep the oath which He swore to your fathers [Abraham, Isaac, and Jacob], has the LORD brought you out with a mighty hand, and redeemed you out of the house of bondage, from the hand of Pharaoh king of Egypt. (Deut 7:7a, 8 NKJV)

> Know therefore that the LORD your God, he is God, the faithful God, who keeps covenant and loving kindness (who loves) *those who love him and keep his commandments* to a thousand generations . . . Therefore, it shall come to pass, *if* you listen to these ordinances, and *keep and do them*, that the LORD your God will keep with you the covenant and *the loving kindness* which he swore to your fathers: and [because you do them] *he will love you*, and *bless you*, and multiply you. (Deut 7: 9, 12–13 WEB/AT)

---

2. Nygren, *Agape and Eros*, 71.

And what the LORD through Moses means by those words "he will love you and bless you" is summarized in 8:1, which says, "All the commandments which I command you this day you shall observe and do, that you may *live* (not be put to death), and *multiply, and go in and possess the land* which the LORD swore unto your fathers." (Deut 8:1) And then, to further show the difference between the LORD's love for Israel in the law[3] and the agape love of God in the gospel, we may summarize the entire chapter 7 of Deuteronomy, yes, even the entire Torah, as the psalmist does in the following text.

The LORD loves the righteous. (Ps 146:8c NASB)

"The righteous" are those of the psalmist's day who "love God and keep his commandments" in Deut 7:9, which are the commandments of Moses in the law. But Paul's new perspective of the law came as the by-product of what he calls "the revelation of Jesus Christ," that is, *the gospel* given to him by Christ (Gal 1:11–12). In Galatians, Paul recounts a time in Antioch in which Cephas (Peter) had been eating with believing gentiles. When certain men from James (from Jerusalem) came to Antioch, Peter withdrew from eating with the gentile Christ-believers, fearing those Jews who came from James. The result was that the rest of the Jewish Christians followed

---

3. On God's side, God keeps the (Abrahamic) covenant that he swore to the fathers (Deut 7:12; Gen 12:1–9; 13:14–16; 15:3–5; 17:6–10; Exod 2:24–25). But on OT Israel's side, Israel must love the LORD and keep his commandments (the law, Deut 4:13; 9:11), if they are to receive loving kindness from the Lord (7:9), in the form of earthly, temporal blessings. But in Christ, we now know (from Gal 3 and Rom 4) that *the promise* of the gospel (Rom 1:1–2, and thus faith in the promise) existed alongside the law, which came *later* (Gal 3:15–25). So, God's will/testament/promise to Abraham is not abolished by the law, which came into being 430 years later (Gal 3:16–18). God's promise to Abraham, that he should be the (spiritual) father of many nations, who like him believe *the promise* (Gal 3:9, 29), was *hidden* in the OT scriptures, but is now revealed in Christ (Rom 1:1, 2; 16:25–26). Some among OT Israel proved their faith (in the promise) by loving God and keeping his commandments (in the law); others did not and were put to death (Num 15:32–36). And in the church that is Christ's body, we hold fast to God's word now revealed in Christ, through faith in Christ; for we, by the Spirit, put to death the deeds of the body, in order that we might live—have eternal life (1 Cor 15: 1–4; Rom 2:5–10; 8:9, 12–13; Gal 6:7–8)—for mortification is the fruit of the obedience of faith in Christ (Rom 1:5; 8:12–13). But *that* life is not temporal life in the land of Canaan; it is eschatological, eternal life, begun in this age, to be entered bodily in the age to come, and OT believers in the promise will be there with us (Heb 11:7, 39–40). But *now, apart from law* (Moses's), *the righteousness from God has been manifested* (Rom 3:21), and with that manifestation it is *now* revealed that the Messiah died for the *ungodly* (Rom 5:6), the *sinner* (5:8)—not "the righteous." God's elect among OT Israel (those who, through election, loved the LORD) were accounted righteous before God, just as Abraham was, through *faith* in *the promise* (Rom 4:1–16; Gen 22:18; compare Gal 3:9, 16, 29; Heb 11:4–10). Just as in Paul's day, when not all natural Israel was true Israel (Rom 9:6), so it was even in Moses's day.

Peter and likewise separated from (no longer ate with) gentile believers. Paul says that this act of Peter's implied that not only Jewish believers in Christ must keep the law of Moses but also that gentiles must also keep the law to be justified before God. Paul says of Cephas:

> But when Cephas came to Antioch, I opposed him to his face, because he stood condemned. For before certain men came from James, he was eating with the Gentiles; but when they came, he drew back and separated himself, fearing the circumcision party. And the rest of the Jews acted hypocritically along with him, so that even Barnabas was led astray by their hypocrisy. But when I saw that their conduct was not in step with the truth of the gospel, I said to Cephas before them all, "If you, though a Jew ['the righteous'], live like a gentile and not like a Jew, how can you force the Gentiles to live like Jews (according to the law of Moses)?" (Gal 2:11–14 ESV)

> We [you, Peter, and I] are Jews ["the righteous," Ps 146:8] by nature and *not* sinners of the nations. And yet, knowing that a man is not justified by works of law, but through *the faith [obedience] of Christ Jesus*; even we believed into Christ Jesus, in order that we might be justified by the faith of Christ, and not by works of law, because by the works of law no flesh will be justified. But if, seeking to be *justified in Christ*, we [you, Peter, and I, Paul] were also found to be *sinners* [not righteous]—then is Christ a minister of sin? May it not be! For if what things I [by faith in Christ] destroyed [my righteousness, that of the law], these things [of the law] I build again, I constitute myself as a transgressor [of the law]. For I, through the law, died with Christ to the law [and its transgressions, and thus to being a transgressor; Rom 4:15] in order that I might live to God; for with Christ I[4] have been co-crucified [I died], and I [in the flesh, under law, the ministry of condemnation] live no longer, but Christ lives in me; and the life I now live in the flesh, I live by the faith of the Son of God, who loved me and gave himself up for me. I do not set aside the grace of God, for if righteousness comes through law, then Christ died for nothing. (Gal 2:15–21)

In 2:16, Paul says "we believed into Christ Jesus." Through faith in Christ, we come to be "in Christ." There is no other way.

---

4. Christ has replaced the "I" (in the flesh of sin, Rom 8:3 lit.) who is a law to himself—the "I" who died with Christ (Gal 2:19, 20). The nations are a *law* to themselves (Rom 2:15). But Paul says those *in Christ* are *no longer nations* (i.e., gentiles, 1 Cor 12:2 lit.).

Under the *old covenant*, all those outside of the covenant are deemed sinners, while all those inside the covenant (by circumcision) are "the righteous."[5] In the *new covenant*, brought about by the death of Christ, all—both gentiles and Jews—by nature are revealed, through his death (justification), to be *sinners* (Gal 2:15–17).

All are sinners and remain condemned-to-death sinners if they are not in Christ (Gal 2:17) the Righteous One.[6] All are under God's judgment and wrath, except those who believe and are redeemed by Christ's blood—that of the new testament. Those who believe and are redeemed are now justified saints in Christ. The new covenant/testament did not go into effect until Christ's death[7] and resurrection.[8] Thus, in Christ we are severed from the law through his death, which justifies sinners. This justification has now been manifested in the historical redemption that occurred in Christ's blood (Rom 3:24–26). So, in Gal 2:18 Paul is saying, "For if I build again those things which I [by faith] destroyed [when I believed in Christ, I destroyed my righteousness, which is of the law, in order that I may be found in Christ for righteousness], I make myself a transgressor" (NKJV)—(that is, a transgressor of *the law*, for "where there is no law, there is no transgression," Rom 4:15b NKJV). In Christ I am not a transgressor of the law, "for Christ is the end of the law for *righteousness* to everyone who believes" (Rom 10:4 NKJV). Just like everyone else who is in Christ, Paul is not a transgressor of the law any longer, because he died with Christ to the law (Gal 2:18–21). The same applies to all in Christ. This is grace. And this is why Martyn Lloyd-Jones could say:

> You are either under the dominion of sin and Satan, or else you are under the dominion of grace and of God. If you are a child of God, you remain a child of God, and when you sin, you do not cease to be a child of God. When your child deliberately does the opposite of what you have told him to do, he does not cease to be your child. He is sinning as a child; he does not

---

5. To the extent that Reformed theology teaches that their children are born into "the covenant," as being already "God's covenant children," to that extent they tend to see and treat their children as "the righteous"—analogous to OT Israel's "the righteous" in Ps 146:8 and in Pss 1, 5, 7, 11, 14, 19, 31, 35, 37, etc., and not as *the ungodly* (needing justification in Christ), which, in truth, we all are, as now revealed in the gospel (Gal 2:14–17). But Peter and Paul, who were Jews by nature and not sinners of the nations, became sinners of the gentiles through faith in Christ (Gal 2:15–17). Becoming sinners, accepting that reality for one's self, was and is a corollary of faith in Christ.

6. 1 John 2:1; Acts 3:14.

7. 1 Cor 11:25; Heb 8:8–10; 9:12–17.

8. Rom 1:1–4; 8:1–11; 2 Cor 3:6–10; 6:16; Gal 4:4–9.

become a stranger because he sinned. The same is true of us Christians when we sin against God.

We must realize . . . that every time we sin, we sin deliberately and as a child of God. We are no longer merely breaking or offending against the Law, we are now wounding *love*. That is much more grievous, but it is not a *legal* offense.[9]

Unlike the mind of the flesh, which always reasons from the law, by God's revelation in Christ, Paul reasoned *from Christ* to all things, including *the law*. The wrath (Rom 5), the sin (Rom 6), the law (Rom 7), and the death (Rom 8) reigned over us when we were in the flesh, wherein we were sinners, condemned in Adam. But Christ died and rose to new life and we with him. So, Christ's lordship delivered us from the lordship of all those other lords. Luther says:

Now that Christ reigns, there is in fact no more sin, death, or curse—this we confess every day in the Apostles' Creed when we say: "I believe in the holy church." This is plainly nothing else than if we were to say: "I believe that there is no sin and no death in the church. For believers in Christ are not sinners and are not sentenced to death but are altogether holy and righteous, lords over sin and death who live eternally."[10]

Using Paul to interpret himself, we come to understand that:

For I, through law, died with Christ to *the law* and its transgressions, and thus I died to being a transgressor [Rom 4:15]— in order that *to God* I might live. For with Christ, I have been crucified [died to the law], and *I live no longer under the law and its condemnation*, but in *Christ* [who justified me and] lives in me. (Gal 2:19–20)

The law's penalty for transgressors is death. I died with Christ, so I died to the law with Christ. So the Galatians did not remember their union with Christ, that they had died with him to the law, in order to live to God (2:19). Since the flesh can only conceive of grace as a license to sin, it thinks Paul's Christ is a minister of sin. The flesh, the human without Christ, neither believes in nor receives God's revealed truth: that Christ is a minister of God's saving righteousness (2 Cor 3:6–18; Gal 2:17, 21). The revelation of this righteousness includes the revelation of the essence of "the sin" (metaphorically personified) as a powerful master, which is simultaneously unbelief in God's word,

9. Lloyd-Jones, *Exposition of Chapter Six*, 143–44, emphasis mine.

10. *LW* 26:285.

who is Christ. This truth is revealed through the *apart-from-works* corollary in Paul's gospel of God (Rom 3:21—4:8), where "justified apart from works" is central to the gospel of grace. This truth is revealed by God's Spirit, for the Spirit of God always works in conjunction with the word of God. Since Paul knew the law, he acknowledges this reality when he says to Peter:

> We [Peter and Paul] who are Jews by nature [the righteous] and *not sinners* of the nations.(Gal 2:15)

But, in contrast to the law, the gospel says:

> But *God shows his love* toward us, in that while we were still *sinners* [not "the righteous"], Christ died on our behalf. (Rom 5:8)

So, on this side of the cross, what theologians call "the Christ event" including his resurrection and exaltation, we are to believe the truth of the gospel, which says, "Although we are sinners in ourselves, that is, in the flesh, nevertheless, we are justified in Christ, for we are not in the flesh, but in Christ" (Rom 8:1, 9–10). In the law, God said, "I will *not justify* the wicked" (Exod 23:7c AV). But now, through Christ's redemption in the good news, God says:

> And to one who does not work, but trusts him who *justifies the ungodly*, his faith is reckoned as righteousness. (Rom 4:5 RSV)

God loved his elect under the old covenant, but they were not yet revealed to be sinners in the way that they now are in the light of Christ's accomplished redemption.[11] In 1 Cor 14:21 Paul calls the book of Isaiah "the Law." Thus, he can call the entire old covenant scriptures "the Law," including the book of Joshua. It should not surprise us, then, to encounter Joshua saying, "He is a jealous God; He will not forgive your transgressions nor your sins" (Josh 24:19b); which is why Paul can say "the law works wrath" (Rom 4:15) and that it only condemns (2 Cor 3:9). But now that Christ has died and rose again to a new life, we find that a new reality has entered into this age:

> And when you were dead in your transgressions and the uncircumcision of your flesh, he made you alive together with Him, having forgiven us all our transgressions. (Col 2:13 NASB)

Therefore, the gospel of God, in Rom 1:1–7:6, does include our release from the law with Christ. For, as we have seen, the law proclaims God's love for "the righteous," but the gospel proclaims God's love for the unrighteous, thereby revealing that all—Jews and gentiles—are not righteous but are under sin

11. See the quote from Westerholm in ch. 2.

(Rom 1:16–18; 3:9–20; 5:6–10). Because sin takes occasion through the law (Rom 7:7–13), we are dead, not only to the *sin* as our former master and lord but also to *the law* as our former master and lord. To be justified in Christ *is* to have died with him and to be dead to sin and law and co-raised with him to walk in newness of life. Life in Christ Jesus, the life to which no condemnation belongs, has freed us from the law—that of sin, of death, and of condemnation. The "life" of which he speaks in Rom 8:2 is *Christ* in us (Rom 8:10). When Paul says, "I live no longer, but Christ lives in me," who is the "I" who *lives no longer*? It is the old man in Adam, obligated under law to be righteous to be justified but utterly unable to do so. *That* is the person who was condemned to death with Christ, so that there is no condemnation for us, because of our union with Christ. Thus, we should never see ourselves apart from Christ,[12] with whom we died to and are utterly dead to and free from the law, in order that we might live to God (Gal 2:19). Christ is in me, and I am in Christ. Christ outside me at God's right hand and Christ in me by his Spirit is the *same Christ*, who has become God's righteousness to me (1 Cor 1:30). The foundational blessing of being "in Christ" is justification by an imputed righteousness (God's righteousness), which simultaneously includes the non-imputation of sin, including indwelling sin. The indwelling of Christ *in* us is based upon justification by Christ's death *outside* us.[13] We are led, not by the law, but by the Spirit of Christ (Rom 8:14; Gal 5:18). Christ alone is our righteousness and sanctification (1 Cor 1:30). In its old covenant context, "the righteous" were those led by the law, for they were people without the Spirit of the risen Christ (2 Cor 3:3–10; Gal 4:1–7; 3:21–28). Note in the following that "the law" and "the word" are synonymous.

But his delight is in *the law* of the LORD; and in His law he meditates day and night. (Ps 1:2 NKJV)	My eyes are awake through the night watches, That I might meditate on Your *word*. (Ps 119:148 NKJV)
The law of his God is in his heart. None of his steps shall slide. (Ps 37:31 NKJV)	Your *word* have I hidden in my heart, that I might not sin against you. (Ps 119:11 NKJV)
Blessed are the undefiled in the way; who walk in *the law* of the LORD. (Ps 119:1 NKJV)	Your *word* is a lamp to my feet and a light to my path. (Ps 119:105 NKJV)

12. "When it comes to justification, therefore, if you divide Christ's Person from your own, you are in the Law; you remain in it and live in yourself; which means that you are dead in the sight of God and damned by the law" (*LW* 26:168).

13. Redemption by Christ's blood, through which we are justified (Rom 3:24) by imputation (4:5–8), is the basis of God giving us the Spirit (Gal 4:4–7). The Spirit is life because of justification (8:10) by his death (5:8,9).

But now that God's righteousness, apart from law, through Christ has *come* (Rom 3:21–26; Gal 3:21–26), *God's word* is no longer (the righteousness of) *the law*—"Do this and live" (Lev 18:5; Rom 10:5)—for, "the righteousness of *faith* speaks in *this* way: that if you confess with your mouth 'Jesus is Lord' and believe in your heart that God has raised Him from the dead, you will be saved" (Rom 10:9). This is the word of faith, the gospel, *the word of God*.[14] The old covenant saints were not living in the reality of an accomplished redemption based upon propitiation, for their sins were not yet taken away, so they were not yet living in the reality of God justifying the sinner through faith in a risen Christ alone, who now leads by *his Spirit*. But in the old covenant Christ had not yet died! From Gal 2:17–19 we know that, because Christ is the end for the law for righteousness for those who believe (Rom 10:4), Paul and Peter had to die with Christ to their being "Jews by nature" and "not sinners of the Gentiles" for God justifies the ungodly (Rom 4:5). They had to divorce themselves from their former (law) source of righteousness by trusting in Christ for righteousness before God. Paul identifies himself with "sinners of the Gentiles" by believing in Christ (Gal 2:17). Paul includes himself in the "us" for whom Christ died, when he says, "Christ has redeemed *us*." But why did he do so?

> In order that the blessing of Abraham [righteousness/justification, 3:6] might come upon the Gentiles in Christ Jesus, so that *we* [believing Jews and Gentiles, v. 28] might receive the promise of the Spirit through [the] faith. (Gal 3:14)

Paul gladly puts himself on the level of gentile sinners, for he seeks to be *justified* with them *in Christ*. Therefore, Käsemann is right when he says, "The break with the law has to be proclaimed wherever the justification of the *ungodly* is the premise."[15] Käsemann's statement is why the law is not the rule of life for those in Christ. For "now, apart from law" (Rom 3:21), God's righteousness justifies the *ungodly*. So, to retain the law as one's rule, one must think with an old covenant mindset, like this: "We are the righteous (Ps 146:8) and we are to remain righteous by doing the law." But then justification through faith in Christ is nullified (Rom 4:14–16), for the gospel proclaims the justification of the *ungodly*. Sin deceives and derives its power from the law (Rom 7:7-13), the very law which says "the Lord loves the righteous," because we now know the truth that there are *none* righteous, and that God loves his sinners through Christ.[16] In the

---

14. Or possibly, (of) Christ, Rom 10:17 as in NA26. On *the word/Christ/gospel*, see Phil 1:7, 12, 14, 15.

15. Käsemann, *Commentary on Romans*, 191, emphasis mine.

16. For "the law was given through Moses, but grace and truth [not deception

following sentence, my words in brackets are inserted into the sentence quoted above by Ernst Käsemann.

> *The break with the law* ["the LORD loves the righteous," Ps 146:8c NASB] *has to be proclaimed wherever the justification of the ungodly* [God showed his own love toward us, in that while were still sinners, Christ died for us, which justified us, Rom 5:8–9] *is the premise.*[17]

Therefore, since Paul the apostle does proclaim the justification of the ungodly in Christ (Rom 4:5—5:9), he *does* proclaim the break with the law—being released from the law—for those in Christ, that we might live to God.[18] The answer to the fear of antinomianism is that we are free, but through that freedom we are to obey Christ as Lord, whose *Spirit* dwells in us (Rom 8:9–13; see Rom 6). For we are "not being without the law of *God*," but (we are) "in the law *of Christ*" (ἔν νομος Χριστοῦ) by being in Christ, having Christ in us (1 Cor 9:21), for Christ is God. The new creation submits to God's righteousness, which is the power of God resulting in the indwelling (lordship of) Christ. The gospel's righteousness of God is the power of God unto salvation, which includes sanctification.

We conclude with Anders Nygren on what God used to enable Paul to understand the gospel:

> Previously he had known a way—the way of man—to God through strict observance of the Law and righteousness of life. He was pursuing that way when he set out for Damascus. But wither had that way led him? To the great sin of his life: his persecution of the church of God. Instead of leading him to God, it had led him as far away from God as possible. Evidently, then there is no way—no way of man—to God. The way of the Law leads away from God. This means a complete inversion of values as far as Pharisaic values are concerned; *human righteousness, the righteousness that is of the law, is sin in enhanced form.*[19]

> It was the way of the Law that had landed him in sin; just when he thought he was most of all doing God's will, he had been committing his most grievous sin.[20]

---

through the-law-used-by-sin, Rom 7:7–13] came by Jesus Christ" (John 1:17 AV).

17. Käsemann, *Commentary on Romans*, 191.

18. See Rom 7:1–6; 6:14, 15; 8:1–2; Gal 2:19–21; 5:1–5, 5:18; 6:15–16; and 1 Cor 9:20–21 (not AV).

19. Nygren, *Agape and Eros*, 111, emphasis mine.

20. Nygren, *Agape and Eros*, 111.

Paul's story is not that of a proud Pharisee who is transformed by his conversion into a humble penitent. It is rather the story of a sincere and ardent Pharisee who in his very pursuit of righteousness becomes "the chief of sinners," and in the very midst of his greatest sin hears the call of Him who "came not to call the righteous, but sinners" (Mark ii 17).[21]

Followers of the Way[22] do not live by the law but by faith in Christ, who died for the *un*godly (Rom 5:6).

21. Nygren, *Agape and Eros*, 113. The righteousness of the flesh, of the religious leaders of Israel (through the Romans) is what caused them to put God (the Son) incarnate, who was without sin, to death. No greater commentary and condemnation of human righteousness is possible.

22. Acts 9:2; 22:4; John 14:6.

FOUR

God's Two Revelations

(Rom 1)

Paul lays out two revelations of God, in which God is dynamically active: the revelation of God's wrath and the revelation of God's saving righteousness. For many, even talk of "the wrath of God" triggers associations and inaccurate presuppositions. Yet, the justice of God against human idolatry is real, for "is God unrighteous who inflicts wrath?" (Rom 3:5b). But the hope of the gospel lies in Christ, who saves from wrath all those found in him. The wrath of God is revealed against all ungodliness and unrighteousness of humans, who have rejected God in his prior revelation of himself in the things that are made, that is, in creation. This *prior* revelation of God's self in *creation* is not to be confused with either the revelation of God's wrath or the revelation of God's saving righteousness.

The Son of God in Power

In Romans, after Paul's introduction, he begins his letter as follows:

> The gospel of God . . . concerning his [eternal] Son, come of the seed of David according to the flesh, ***appointed*** *Son of God in power* according to the Spirit of holiness by the resurrection of the dead: *Jesus Christ our Lord*. (Rom 1:1a, 3–4)

Notice that "the Son of God in power" is "Jesus Christ our LORD" (Rom 1:4). The Greek word ὁρίζω is rightly translated as "appointed" here, and it is also translated "appointed" twice in Acts, both times in conjunction with God's Son's resurrection/exaltation.

> But God raised him on the third day and made him to appear. . .
> he is the one who has been *appointed* by God to be judge of the
> living and the dead. (Acts 10:40, 42 ESV)

> Because he has fixed a day in which he will judge the world in
> righteousness by a man whom he has *appointed*; and of this he
> has given assurance to all by raising him from the dead. (Acts
> 17:31 ESV)

Because Jesus became obedient to God the Father even to the death on the cross, "therefore God has highly exalted him and given him a name which is above every name . . . that . . . every tongue should confess that Jesus Christ is Lord to the glory of God the Father" (Phil 2:8–11 AV). And from Christ's exaltation onward, we find Jesus as appointed by God to be Lord, which includes being the judge of the world (Acts 17:31). In Rom 1, this appointment of Jesus to the position of Son of God in power is the basis upon which Paul proceeds to speak of the already-now, saving righteousness from God, which saves us from the already-now and future *wrath* of God against all unrighteousness of humans (1:16,18). So, Paul sets forth two revelations of God: (1) the dynamic coming of God's saving *righteousness* (having now entered this age), and (2) the present (1:18–32) and future (2:5–10) coming of God's *wrath* against all ungodliness and unrighteousness of humans outside of Christ. The wrath of God is a both/ and wrath; it is both a present wrath (Rom 1:18–32) and future wrath (2:5–10), the "and" being the future day of wrath (2:5). Through Paul, God says humans are guilty of not worshiping the true God and thus they are without excuse before God. After Paul says that God's saving righteousness is revealed in the gospel, for all who believe (1:17), he says:

> For the wrath of God is revealed from heaven against all *un-godliness* and *unrighteousness* of men who suppress the truth in unrighteousness. (Rom 1:18)

Keck observes that God's wrath is "against all human *asebeia* and *adikia*."

> What Paul understands by *asebeia* he will say in verse 25, where
> he uses the related verb . . . *esebasthēsan* (reverenced; NRSV:
> "worshiped") to accuse gentiles of idolatry; what he means by
> *adikia* he will spell out in verses 29–31, where "filled with every
> kind of wickedness" introduces a list of vices. . . . the former

refers to the wrong attitude toward God and the latter to wrong behavior toward other people.[1]

Therefore, Paul is saying:

> For the wrath of God is revealed from heaven against all *impiety* [ἀσέβια/asebia=no worship of God, for they *worshiped* (*esebathēsan*) the creature rather than the Creator] and unrighteousness of men, who suppress the truth in unrighteousness. (1:18)

In creation, God has revealed that God is God; so, humans *know* that God is God: "because that which is *known* about God is *known within them*, for God made it *evident* [known] *to them*" (Rom 1:19 NASB). For, ever since God created the world, his eternal power (to create), revealing that he is God, has been perceived by humans. What follows is what is *known* in and to humans, and it is why they are "without excuse."

- God, the creator of the creation, is God (1:19–20), therefore:
- God is the one to whom humans' worship, glory, and thanks are due (1:19–21, 25).
- God is our judge (1:29–31).

Humans suppress this threefold knowledge of God "in unrighteousness" (unbelief)[2] and so God's wrath is against them (Rom 1:18—2:9). For even though they *knew God* (God's eternal power and deity were understood, 1:20, 21), nevertheless they *did not worship God* but the creature instead, as the following chart reveals, along with the *fruit* of false worship.

---

1. Keck, *Romans*, 59.

2. Since righteousness is "the righteousness of faith" (Rom 4:13; 9:30; 10:6), "unrighteousness" here *includes* the unrighteousness of unfaith; thus, Paul is saying two things at the same time (on the other, see Keck, above).

ἀσεβιαν/impiety (ungodliness) the non-worship of God	ἀδικίαν/unrighteousness the fruit of the non-worship of God
they did *not glorify* **Him** *as God or give him* thanks . . .	therefore God [in wrath] . . . *gave them over in the lusts of their heart* to impurity . . . that their bodies might be dishonored. (Rom 1:21 [margin note, lit., "glorify"], 24 NASB)
For they exchanged the truth of God for the lie; they *worshiped* and served the creature *rather than the Creator* . . .	*For this reason, God* [in wrath] gave them over to *degrading passions* for their women exchanged the natural function for that which is against nature. (Rom 1:25–27 [margin note, lit., "against nature"] NASB)
And just as they did not see fit to have God in [their] knowledge . . .	God [in his wrath] *gave them over* to a *depraved mind* . . . to do those things which are not proper . . . and, though they know [within them, 1:19] the ordinance of God, that they who practice such things are worthy of death, they not only do the same, but give hearty approval to those who practice them. (Rom 1:28 [margin note, lit., "to have God in knowledge"], 32 NASB)

In the above chart, in the left column, we find that they did not worship God as God. In Rom 1:25, when Paul says, "They *worshiped and served* the creature rather than the Creator," we deduce from Phil 3:3 (where to worship God is to trust in him and not in the flesh) that Paul means they did *not trust in God* the Creator, but instead they trusted in the creature. In the right column, we find the "therefore" of God's wrath expressed in *giving* them over to the desires of their (evil) hearts of unbelief (Heb 3:12) to impurity (1:21). Their God-lessness (1:21) was that they did not see fit to retain *God* in their knowledge (Rom 1:28). As Beker says:

> The knowledge of God, then, is not the problem in God's world; the acknowledgment of God, that is, the failure of human beings

to allow God to be God, is the problem. . . . idolatry is the primary reason for the human condition "under wrath."[3]

That is, the *essence* of impiety (not worshiping God as God) was, and is, not immorality but the unrighteousness of unbelief, which means first and foremost having (trusting in) other gods instead of the one, true God. The "lusts" (1:24) and "passions" (1:26) are desires that lord it over those of the gentiles who are outside of God's lordship. Of these desires, Keck comments, "The rule of the *desires* . . . is God's basic punishment for idolatry (1:24; NRSV: "lusts").[4] The lordship (control) that these desires have over these people *is* the expression and revelation of God's *wrath* in this present age. The sinful worship of the creation issues in *a depraved mind*, which issues in actual sins (1:29–31). The law (the work of which is in the nations), through conscience, 2:14–15, makes them know that those who practice such things are worthy of death,[5] for the law is the ministry of death (2 Cor 3:7). Thus, already in the first chapter of his letter, Paul gives the result of rejecting the one true God—it is *death*, the opposite of which is *immortality*, to be found in Christ alone (1 Cor 15:50–57; 2 Tim 1:10). Referring to those to whom Paul refers in 1:19–32, Sproul explains why they have no excuse before God:

> It is not that people refuse to allow the clear revelation of God in nature into their heads; quite the contrary, the revelation does indeed get through. The basis of the indictment is that while people *know* God, they still do not honor him as God or give thanks to him (1:21a).[6] If we rightly understand the apostle to the Gentiles then we would see that there are no "innocent" people, nor have there ever been any "innocent" people in the entire history of the world, for all people have received a clear revelation of the Creator. Every one of them has suppressed this knowledge, refusing to give him thanks and choosing to worship anything but the living God.[7]

In Rom 1:25, Paul says that they changed *the truth* of God into *the lie* (τῷ ψεύδει) that God is not God. Humans have denied their creaturehood in that they choose to be their own "God" in God's place. Though Paul is not clearly referring to Adam here, the lie goes back to Adam, when Eve and then Adam believed the lie of the serpent (a creeping thing), when it said,

---

3. Beker, *Suffering and Hope*, 60.

4. Keck, *Romans*, 165.

5. Though they suppress this knowledge by sin which deceives.

6. Sproul, *Defending Your Faith*, 77.

7. Sproul, *Defending Your Faith*, 78.

"You shall not surely die."[8] They believed the lie and died, for the wages of the sin is death (6:23a).

Law and Gospel in the Light of
"the Gospel of God"[9]

Lutheran theology is correct in its distinction between *the law* and *the gospel*,[10] which Paul sets forth most clearly in Rom 10:1–10 (but also in Gal 2:16–21; 3:8–14; Phil 3:3–9). However, from Rom 1:18–32, we find that Paul's words in stating the backdrop for the gospel are not "law and gospel," but *"wrath"* and (*saving*) *"righteousness."* In the light of the gospel of God, the primary distinction is that between the *law* and the *promise*.[11] This distinction, in the light of the "but now, apart from law" revelation of God's righteousness in Rom 3:21–26, reveals the gospel's contrast between *the righteousness of the law* (human righteousness) and *the righteousness of faith*[12] (that is, justification by God, given with faith). The gospel now reveals God's saving righteousness (Rom 3:21) which includes the gospel's use of the law, revealing that all humans are under sin. Therefore, the gospel's use of the law reveals that the law and its works cannot justify (Rom 1:18—3:20). A clear example of this is what we saw in Rom 1, where Paul, in 1:29–31, names specific sins (which are against the law of Moses).[13] And in Gal 3:10, Paul, quoting Moses, says that those who would be justified by the law are under a curse, for no one keeps the law. Thus Luther, referring to both Deut 27:26 and Gal 3:10, says, "So both statements are true and both types are accursed—those who do not abide by the law, as Moses puts it, and those who rely on works of the law, as Paul puts it; for

8. The Johannine Jesus said, "You are of your father the devil and the desires of your father [the devil] you will do. He was a murderer [spiritually killing humans unto bodily death] from the beginning [of creation], and remained not in the truth, because there is no truth in him. When he speaks the lie (τὸ ψεῦδος), he speaks of his own [nature]: for he is a liar, and the father of it [the lie]" (John 8:44; see Gen 3:4 and Rom 1:25 Greek).

9. Rom 1:1.

10. See Nygren, *Commentary on Romans*, 45–46; 379–85.

11. Rom 1:1–2; 4:13–16; Gal 3:14–29.

12. Rom 10:4–10; 4:13–16.

13. "Now, when sins are unrecognized, there is no room for a remedy and no hope for a cure, because men will not submit to the touch of a healer when they imagine themselves well and in no need of a physician. Therefore, the law is necessary to make sin known so that when its gravity and magnitude are recognized, man in his pride who imagines himself well may be humbled and may sigh and gasp for the grace that is offered in Christ" (*LW* 33:262).

they each lack the Spirit."[14] Thus, in the gospel of God, "the righteousness which is of the law" is contrasted with that of God's righteousness in the gospel, which says, "God raised the Lord Jesus from the dead—believe (this) and be saved" (Rom 10:4–9). This saving righteousness was promised in the old covenant scriptures (1:1–2), but it has now come in Christ (Rom 3:21–28; 4:13–25; 15:8–12; Gal 3:21–28). In Rom 1, the distinction is between God's wrath and God's righteousness, which saves from his wrath. The wrath of God (1:18) is the revelation of his wrath against human ungodliness (idolatry) and unrighteousness. The revelation of God's saving righteousness simultaneously reveals God's wrath, namely, that all humans are already now under the eschatological wrath of God, so that the only way out from under this wrath is Christ, which (salvation) is received by trusting in him. But then it is not the law that saves, for, during the era of the old covenant, before this revelation of Christ (Rom 1:16–18; Gal 3:23), God's wrath *could* be understood as being *avoidable* through doing the law, for in Moses's law, God's wrath visits the children of those who hate God, but God's mercy is toward those who love God and keep his commandments. Thus, in Exod 20:3–6, Moses tells OT Israel that their having no idols brings God's mercy instead of his wrath; thereby they could avoid God's wrath.[15] But having no idols was their doing (keeping) the law![16] Correspondingly, in Exod 32:7–10, we find that Israel's *having*

---

14. *LW* 33:260.

15. "You shall have no other gods before Me. You shall not make for yourself any carved image, or any likeness of anything that is in heaven above, or that is in the earth beneath, or that is in the water under the earth; you shall not bow down to them nor serve them. For I, the LORD your God, am a jealous God, *visiting the iniquity of the fathers* [with wrath, see 32:10] on the children to the third and fourth generation of those who hate me, *but showing mercy* [*not wrath*] to thousands, to those who love [which includes trust] Me and keep My commandments" (Exod 20:3–6 NKJV). So, wrath could be avoided by having no other gods, by what Israel did; and this contrasts with the gospel, which says, in effect, "Because of the 'now' of Christ, it is, in one sense, too late; it is impossible to do anything to avert God's wrath."

16. "Know therefore that the LORD thy God, He is God, the faithful God, who keeps *covenant and mercy* [instead of *wrath*] for a thousand generations *with those who love him and keep His commandments*; and He repays those who hate Him to their face, to destroy them [with wrath]. He will not be slack with him who hates; He will repay him to his face. Therefore, you shall keep the commandment, the statutes, and the judgments which I command you today, to observe them" (Deut 7:9–11 NKJV). In this way, Israel would not be destroyed by God's wrath, but could benefit from God's covenant mercy and escape *wrath* (see Exod 32:10). But this was the "wrath" of this age, *not* that of *the day of wrath and revelation of the righteous judgment of God* (Rom 2:5–10), so we can understand how the Jews of Paul's day could (willingly) misunderstand God's word in Paul.

43

idols brings God's wrath against them.[17] But now, in the light of Christ, we can know, regarding OT saints (who received mercy in this life because they loved the LORD and kept his commandments), that their love for the LORD was through faith in God's promise given to Abraham (Rom 1:1–2; 4:13–16). Therefore now, through the gospel, all humans are revealed to be what they really are: worshipers of the creation rather than of the creator and thus they are under God's eschatological wrath to come. And through the gospel it is now clearer than ever that God takes the initiative in saving us. He first loved us. God's wrath is revealed as dynamically against all who remain in unrighteousness apart from Christ. Paul contrasts these two divine revelations, setting them forth in the following order:

> The revelation of God's (saving) righteousness (1:17)

> The revelation of God's wrath (1:18)

God's "*wrath*" is the word Paul uses in Romans, where the active revelation of God's righteousness (1:17, in the gospel, v. 16) delivers us from (the revelation of) God's *wrath* (1:18). The phrase "law and gospel" has this weakness: when using the phrase "the law," people can easily think that "law" means that, since the law demands righteousness from humans, therefore *we* are the ones who must be able to do it and thus can do it for justification. But the word "wrath" gives no such connotation. Thus, even though what we have said up to this point is utterly true, according to the apostle, ultimately one either preaches the law or he preaches Christ. For Paul says of the Jew that he relies upon the law (Rom 2:17 NASB), is instructed out of the law (2:18), is a teacher of the law (2:20–21) and thus Paul says to the Jew, "You who preach" the law" (2:21). The law is what Paul as a Jew, before faith in Christ, *used to* preach—but now he does no longer. He says, "If I still preach circumcision,[18] then the offence of the cross has ceased" (Gal 5:11). In that sense, one cannot preach both law and gospel—for *my* righteousness is that of the law (Phil 3:9) and not

17. "And the LORD said to Moses, 'Go, get down! For your people whom you brought out of the land of Egypt have corrupted themselves. They have turned quickly aside out of the way which I commanded them. They have made themselves a molted calf, and worshiped it, and sacrificed to it, and said, "This is your god, O Israel, that brought you out of the land of Egypt!" And the LORD said to Moses, 'I have seen this people, and indeed it is a stiff-necked people. Now therefore, let Me alone, that *My* wrath may burn hot against them and I may consume them. And I will make of you a great nation'" (Exod 32:7–10 NKJV). God would make Moses a leader of a great nation in Israel's place, but Moses pleads with God, and he withheld his wrath, not destroying them; see 32:11–14.

18. In Gal 5:1–4, "law" and "circumcision" are used interchangeably, so he means "If I still preached the law."

"the righteousness of God by faith" (3:9; Rom 10:6; 4:13). But again, what "law and gospel" in Reformation theology intends to say is that the law shuts all humans up under sin and thus under wrath and in desperate need of Christ, who frees from the wrath to come (1 Thess 1:10; Rom 2:5-10; 4:13-15; 5:9); and reading the Ten Commandments to people can only *possibly* tend toward this end (of seeing one's need for Christ) *if* it is made clear that we cannot even begin to keep the law, that we are already under God's wrath (Rom 4:15); for our hearts and minds, insofar as we are flesh, are without trust in God, for they only hate God (Rom 8:7, 8). In Gal 3:24, Paul is saying that *the law* was the Jews' (and, in one sense, gentiles') child-guardian *up to Christ* (that is the literal translation, which point is verified in Gal 4:2, where he says it was "*until* Christ"). So Paul is *not* saying that the law leads anyone to Christ, as Reformation theology has taught. But God's wrath and God's saving righteousness are preached by the apostle, unlike many preachers who have not preached on God's wrath as something to be saved from. But Paul did not please humans (Gal 1:10). The order in Rom 1 is also of significance. Paul already preached the gospel in Rom 1:1, 3-4. Then he preached the gospel again in 1:16–17, where we encounter God's saving righteousness (1:17)—all this before the wrath of God (1:18) is even mentioned. Why? Paul, with his pastoral heart, wanted the saints at Rome to hear the good news first. For, assured of their freedom from God's wrath in Christ, he knew they were enabled to hear and handle the truth concerning the wrath of God. But how many modern preachers avoid the central apostolic truth of the already-now apocalypse of God's wrath in Rom 1:18–32, and the future day of wrath, in contrast to eternal life in 2:5–10, perhaps in part due to their not having been taught the difference between the (temporal) day of wrath and *eternal* life (in Rom 2:5–10, i.e., in Paul's gospel)? The law is an objective power. The power of Sin is the law (1 Cor 15:56).[19] The law works wrath (Rom 4:15), which is an utterly destructive power. The only freedom from the law and wrath is found in Christ, through faith in him. Christ delivers us from this present evil age, which is under the law and wrath. Christ-believers can easily and unwittingly slip back into a frame of trusting in ourselves for righteousness until God brings us to see that we are truly sinners who cannot justify ourselves. When the gospel overtakes us, restoring us to faith, we willingly know ourselves to be utterly helpless to justify ourselves and not wanting to even think of undoing our sinfulness or guilt by ourselves (Gal 2:21). This is having faith in Christ: accepting that one cannot justify himself before God, and allowing God to justify him in Christ.

---

19. I capitalize "Sin" because in Paul's gospel it is more than an act; it is a power, a lord.

Summary

- There are two kinds of righteousness: the righteousness of the law (human righteousness, that of the flesh of sin/unbelief), and the righteousness of faith: God's righteousness in Christ, which is received through faith in him.

- The law works wrath and thus only condemns sinners (Rom 3:9–20; 4:15; 2 Cor 3:9). Paul contrasted two dynamic revelations of God: one of wrath against all humans outside of Christ, and one of God's righteousness, which justifies all who believe in Christ from wrath and death. The revelation of creation (Rom 1:20) only makes all humans without excuse before God, that is, it only condemns. Thus, the attempt to know God savingly through his revelation in *creation* is in the same category as is the attempt to do so through *the law*, as Luther,[20] imitating Paul (1:19–20), taught.

- *The gospel*, that "Christ died *for our sins* and was raised"—in one sense *includes the law*, in that Christ died for *our transgressions of the law* (1 Cor 15:1–4; compare Gal 2:17–19 and Col 2:13).

- We know that, through the gospel's use of the law, we (in ourselves, apart from Christ) are revealed to be condemned sinners. But now we are justified in Christ and yet sinners as in the *flesh* (which still serves the law of sin/unbelief). Therefore, all true knowledge of ourselves is through Christ, and, thus, outside of Christ there is only spiritual ignorance, darkness, and death.

---

20. Althaus, *Theology of Martin Luther*, 26–27.

— FIVE —

The True Jew

(Rom 2)

> But he is a Jew who is one *inwardly*, and circumcision [law-ful-
> filling] is that which is of *the heart*, by *the Spirit*, and not by the
> letter [outward circumcision or law-keeping]; whose praise is
> not from men [who see the outer] but from God [who sees the
> heart, where the (true) Jew's obedience resides]. (Rom 2:28–29)

PAUL BEGINS ROMANS CHAPTER 2 by saying:

> Therefore you are without excuse, O man, whoever you are
> who judge, for in whatever you judge another you condemn
> yourself; for you who judge practice the same things [that is,
> "the same things" of 1:(28–)32, which made humans worthy
> of death]. But we know that the judgment of God is accord-
> ing to truth against those who practice such things. And do
> you think this, O man, you who judge those practicing such
> things, and doing the same, that you will escape the judgment
> of God? (Rom 2:1–3 NKJV)

Paul follows these by insisting that these haters of God continue to store up
wrath and will not escape the judgment of God (see Rom 2:5 AT).

> But in accordance with your hardness and your impenitent
> heart you are storing up for yourself wrath in the day of wrath
> and revelation of the righteous judgment of God who will
> render to each one according to his deeds: to those who by
> patient continuance in doing good seek for glory, honor, and

47

immortality[1]—[God will render] eternal life; but to those who are self-seeking and do not obey the truth [the truth of the gospel, Gal 2:14], but obey unrighteousness[2]—[God will render] indignation and wrath, [resulting in] tribulation and anguish on every soul of man who does evil . . . but [render] glory [Rom 5:2], honor and peace to everyone who works what is good [through obeying the truth/the gospel], to the Jew first, and also to the Greek [gentile]. (Rom 2:5–10 NKJV)

When Paul refers to "the day of wrath and revelation of the righteous judgment of God," he is saying that the wrath *is* a revelation, the final revelation, of God's righteous judgment.

So, in Rom 2:5–10, we find the apostle's most extensive eschatological text regarding the day of the Lord, of the future and final judgment of all by God. There are only two options for human beings: God's *wrath* for some and *eternal life* for the others. The contrast in 2:5–10 is between those who, on the one hand, seek glory, honor, and immortality, to whom God will render eternal life—which is equated with incorruption and immortality—and those who, on the other hand, do not obey the truth (Gal 2:14; see Rom 10:16) and thus receive God's fierce anger and wrath. This is never called "eternal wrath" in Romans or elsewhere in Holy Scripture, just as "death" is never called "eternal death" in the Scriptures. Nor do disobeyers receive immortality, as do the elect, for "death" and "immortality" are opposites (see 1 Cor 15:42–57; 2 Tim 1:10). God through Paul says "to those who do not obey the truth, God will render wrath" (2:8) on the day of wrath (2:5). These are the "vessels of wrath fitted to destruction." They will suffer wrath's anguish and affliction according to their individual deeds (2:6) unto destruction (Phil 3:19). The judgment according to works (in Rom 2:5–10) does not contradict the truth of justification in Christ alone through faith alone. It is through the obedience of faith (obeying the truth, 2:8; 10:16) in Christ that we "by patient continuance in doing good seek for glory, honor, and immortality—eternal life" (2:7; see 8:25; Gal 5:5; 6:7–8). Justification in Christ alone means no condemnation for everyone in him; thus, before Christ's judgment seat, the believer will appear and be totally righteous, not only by God's imputation of righteousness but in a body that is fully ruled by the Holy Spirit and glorified/righteous. Our status is one of being justified in Christ (Rom 5:1); nevertheless, we will be judged according to the works we

1. The phrase "to those who by patient endurance in doing good, seek for glory, honor and immortality" is explained by Paul in Rom 8:11–14.

3. The deeds of those who "obey unrighteousness" are trespasses, which, for those who remain unreconciled to God, are imputed to them unto the day of wrath and judgment; this is deduced from Paul's words in 2 Cor 5:19–20.

have done in the body, whether they were good (of the Spirit) or bad (of the flesh), to receive rewards for what we did by grace alone, and/or suffer loss of rewards (1 Cor 3:8–15; 2 Cor 5:10; Rom 14:10–13). Our interpretation of Rom 2:7 is in total agreement with Rom 8:11–13; Gal 6:8–9; John 5:39 lit.; 1 John 2:17; and other texts. Paul says:

> For there is no partiality with God. For as many as have sinned without *law* [the nations, who never had the law as a covenant, as Israel did[3]] will also perish without *law*. As many as have sinned in the law will be judged by *the law*. (For it is not the hearers of the law who are righteous before God, but the doers of the law will be justified. For when *Gentiles* who do *not* have *the law*, do by nature the things contained in the law, these, although not having the law, are a law to themselves, who show the work of the law written in their hearts, their conscience also bearing witness [with them], and their reasonings among themselves either accusing or else excusing them), in the day when God will judge the secrets of men, by Jesus Christ according to my gospel. (Rom 2:11–16)

For Paul, the holy, righteous, and spiritual law condemns gentiles, as it condemns the Jews (Rom 3:10–19). Adam, who was created upright, had this law written on his heart, but he had not yet taken of the forbidden tree, which made him know good and evil independently of God. Cain knew that murder was wrong (sin) even before he murdered Abel. He also had "the work of the law" written on his heart, so he was without excuse in murdering his brother. Likewise, every human being, because of this work of the law, knows that what he does is worthy of death (Rom 1:32). Therefore, they are without excuse (1:20; 2:1; 3:9–19). So, Paul is applying this same work of the law to all non-Jews, to prove that they are without excuse. Murray says:

> Although the Gentiles are "without the law" and "have not the law" in the sense of specially revealed law, nevertheless they are not entirely without law; the law is made known to them and is brought to bear upon them in another way. They are "the law unto themselves" and "they show the work of the law written in their hearts" (vs. 15).[4]

Paul is not praising the nations for their conscience, for with it they are still "alienated from the life of God" (Eph 4:18). He means that the law's work in

---

3. Rom 9:4.
4. Murray, *Romans*, 1:72.

their hearts only renders them without excuse on judgment day, when they, with their secrets, are judged (2:16; compare 1:29—2:2; 3:19).

> For not the hearers of the law [those with uncircumcised hearts] are just in the sight of God, but the doers [fulfillers] of the law will be justified. (Rom 2:13 NKJV)

This is not Roman Catholicism but Paul's gospel. For the doers of the law are those who "keep the righteous requirements of the law" (2:26) by being (true) Jews (2:29) and not Jews outwardly, but (rather) in spirit, in their hearts (2:28-29). Protestant commentators who stumble at 2:13 have not grasped the weight of importance given to the Spirit of God in the gospel of God, for in Rom 2:25-29,[5] Paul refers to the Spirit's circumcision of the heart,[6] wherein the flesh of sin is removed (Rom 8:3 lit.; Col 2:12) and replaced with God's Spirit in the human spirit, the inner man (Eph 3:16). For the law of the Spirit, of eschatological life in Christ Jesus (8:2), is that of the new creation (2 Cor 5:17). Notice "law" and "Spirit" in two OT texts on the new covenant:

> But this is the covenant that I will make with the house of Israel after those days, says the LORD: I will put *my law* within them, and I will write it on their hearts; and I will be their God and they shall be my people. (Jer 31:33 NRSV; see 2 Cor 3:3)

> I will give you a new heart and put a new spirit within you; I will take the heart of stone out of your flesh and give you a heart of flesh. I will put *My Spirit* within you. (Ezek 36:26-27a)

The Jewish rabbis believed that these scriptures were referring to life in the next world.[7] This rabbinic belief shows that what these old covenant scriptures refer to is the eschatological (last age) circumcision of the heart by the Holy Spirit, which has been inaugurated even already in this present age by Christ's death, exaltation, and his sending of the Spirit at Pentecost. From Jeremiah ("law") and Ezekiel ("Spirit"), we can see that Paul draws from both prophets as he refers to "the law of the Spirit" in Rom 8:2.

The "law" which belongs to the Spirit is the one of the Messiah's indwelling Spirit, who is eternal life (Rom 8:2, 10). *This* law has set us free

---

5. Romans 2:29 is best understood by 2 Cor 3:6, which shows that in 2:29 he means the Spirit of God.

6. See also *LW* 25:19-24.

7. See Montefiore and Loewe, *Rabbinic Anthology*, 132-33; but the rabbis applied the texts to the law.

from the law of Moses and of the flesh (Rom 8:3a, 5, 6), for *that* law occasions only sin and death.[8]

Paul refers to "the new testament . . . of the Spirit" (2 Cor 3:6), which is written "in fleshly tables of the [circumcised] heart."[9] Romans chapter 2, then, is in line with Rom 8; it is the same gospel of God. The law is fulfilled in an eschatological manner, a way utterly *unlike* that which the flesh, with its mind, expected. Thus, 2:13 is a preview of what he will say in 2:25–29. Next, Paul says that the gentiles (the nations) were never under *the law* as a covenant from God, as Israel was, yet they are still without excuse. In the following section, notice how "Jew" and "the law" go together; second, note how Paul defines "the law" by the Ten Commandments, naming three of them here. Third, note how he says that, though they preach the law to others, they themselves do not keep it.

> Indeed, if you are named a *Jew*, and rest on *the law*, and glory in God, and know his will, and approve the things that are excellent, being instructed out of the law, and are confident that you yourself are a guide of the blind, a light to those who are in darkness, a corrector of the foolish, a teacher of babies, having in *the law* the form of knowledge and of the truth. You therefore who teach another, do you not teach yourself? You [Jews] who preach that *a man should not steal*, do you steal? You [Jews] who say *a man should not commit adultery*, do you commit adultery? You [Jews] who *abhor idols* [*and thus idolatry*], do you *rob* temples? You [Jews] who glory in the law [as I did, Phil 3], through your breaking the law, do you dishonor God? (Rom 2:17–23)

Three of the Ten Commandments are listed here as "the law." Therefore, included in Paul's anathema (Gal 1:8–9) are those who, contrary to his gospel (Rom 2:16–23) separate the Ten Commandments from "the law." Such teachers, who condense the law[10] to its ceremonial aspects, are not allowing the Christ to deliver us from "all the law" (Gal 5:3), the same law to which he refers in Galatians (5:14), and also here in Romans. To those Jews (2:17) "who teach others," Paul asks them if they teach themselves; for those who preach that others should keep the Ten Commandments, are they really keeping the law? Unless the *whole* law is kept, humans are transgressors of the law. This is the New Testament's interpretation of the law:

8. Rom 7:7–13; 8:2; 2 Cor 3:7–19.

9. 2 Cor 3:3 AV; Ezek 36:26; Jer 31:33; Rom 2:28–29.

10. The NPP scholars, in defining the law, have gone to Second Temple Judaism and not to Paul in Rom 2:17–23, where *the law* is summed up in three of the Ten Commandments.

> For as many as are of the works of the law are under the curse;
> for it is written, "Cursed is everyone who *does not continue in
> all things which are written in the book of the law, to do them.*"
> (Gal 3:10 NKJV)

> Which of the prophets did your fathers not persecute? And
> they killed those who announced beforehand the coming of the
> Righteous One, whom you have now betrayed and murdered,
> you who received the law as delivered by angels *and did not keep
> it.* (Acts 7:52–53 NKJV)

> For whoever shall keep the whole law, and yet *stumble in one*
> point, he is *guilty of all.* (Jas 2:10 NKJV)

> For even those who are circumcised do not themselves keep
> the law, but they desire to have you circumcised, that they may
> boast in your flesh. (Gal 6:13 ESV)

The gospel's use of the law says to those who would be justified by law that
there is no hope of doing so. We do not find this New Testament interpretation of the law in the old covenant scriptures or even in the Synoptic
Gospels (before the Spirit came at Pentecost). In Rom 7:7, Paul defines sin
as *coveting,* and in doing so he reveals the spiritual nature of the law. So,
even if the Jew or anyone keeps the law outwardly, they are nevertheless
transgressing (not fulfilling) the law, as he says in Rom 2:27–29. Regarding
the inward requirement of the law (Rom 2:25–29), Paul shows the Jews
that they are without excuse. He includes circumcision as part of the law
(see John 7:22) in what follows:

> For circumcision is indeed profitable if you *keep the law* [that is,
> the whole law, not just circumcision, and that from the heart]; but
> if you are a breaker of the law, your circumcision [law-keeping]
> has become uncircumcision [lawbreaking]. (Rom 2:25 NKJV)

For Paul, to *keep* the law is to *fulfill* the law. Notice how he uses the words
"keep" and "fulfill" interchangeably in the following texts:

> Therefore, if the uncircumcised man keeps the righteous re-
> quirements of the law, will not his uncircumcision [lawbreak-
> ing] be counted as circumcision [law-keeping]? And will not
> the physically uncircumcised, if he fulfills the law [in spirit, in
> his heart] judge you who, even with your written code and cir-
> cumcision, are a transgressor of the law? (Rom 2:26–27 NKJV)

In the flesh no one, no matter how much he outwardly keeps the law (2:28),
fulfills the law (2:27). Rather, he *transgresses* the law, precisely because he

does not keep or fulfill the law from his inmost heart (Rom 2:29), unless he is regenerate, as elect gentiles would be, and that is Paul's point. So, to the Jew, Paul is saying:

> For "the name of God is blasphemed among the Gentiles because of you," just as it is written. For circumcision indeed profits, if you are a doer of the law (fulfiller of the law, v. 27), but if you are a transgressor of the law, your circumcision (law-keeping) has become uncircumcision (lawbreaking). Therefore, if the uncircumcised man *keeps* (fulfills, v. 27) the righteous require-ments of *the law*, will not his uncircumcision (lawbreaking) be reckoned (regarded by God) as circumcision (law-keeping)? And will not the one who is by (gentile) nature *un*circumcised, if he *fulfills the law* (in spirit, 2:28–29) judge you (the natural Jew) who, through letter (of the law—outward law-keeping) and circumcision, are a transgressor of the law?[11] For he is *not* a Jew (God's elect) who is one outwardly, neither is that circumci-sion (law-keeping) which is outward in the flesh; but he is a Jew who is one *inwardly*, and circumcision is that *of the heart*, in the Spirit (in our inner man, the Spirit who removes the flesh from our hearts), not in the letter; whose praise is not from men (who see the outer, temporal things, and love them), but from God (who sees the heart). (Rom 2:24–29 ATP)[12]

So the Jew's circumcision avails nothing if he is not a fulfiller of the law. Paul was circumcised as a Pharisee, part of his outward righteousness, which was "blameless" according to the righteousness of the law (Phil 3:5–6). So, the only way in which one fulfills the righteous requirement of the law is *in the Spirit*. The opposite of "transgressing the law" is "fulfilling the law." So, to the Jew of his day, Paul is saying, "You *rely on the law* (2:17 NASB) and thus on the flesh instead of God in Christ (Phil 3:3–9)." Paul interprets the law according to Christ, the last Adam. When he later says, "The law is spiritual" (7:14), he means that it demands one's spirit, one's heart to be in the spirit of the law; so, it requires the Spirit of Christ. Only he who is circumcised in the heart by the Spirit of the Messiah fulfills the law from his inmost heart. His "law keeping" is essentially not that which is outward in the flesh, for flesh

11. I.e., you who keep the letter of the law outwardly are really a transgressor of the law, because you constantly transgress the law in that you do not trust in God but have other gods before him, for you have not the Spirit, who alone fulfills the requirement of the law, 8:4; for not having the *Spirit of Christ*, you hate God in your heart, 8:7–8.

12. Paul concludes a section of thought with a summary. For example, there are summaries at the end of Rom 5 (in 5:20-21), at the end of ch. 6 (in 6:22–23), ch. 7 (in 7:24–25) and ch. 8 (in 8:38–39). And Paul does that already here in 2:28–29, where he is referring to the (Spirit's) circumcision of the heart.

can "keep the law" while hating and not trusting God. The righteous requirement of the law is fulfilled in us who are in the Spirit and walk according to
him (8:4, 12–13). Therefore, "the doers of the law" in 2:13 can only be those
who fulfill the law inwardly through the Spirit, which is precisely what he
says in 2:27–29. And the only basis upon which anyone has the Spirit is that
of justification through redemption (Rom 3:21–25; see Gal 4:4–7). Justification, being accounted righteous by God, logically and theologically precedes
the giving of the Spirit (Rom 3:24; Gal 4:1–7).

> For he is *not* a Jew [God's elect] who is one *outwardly*, neither
> is that circumcision which is outward in the flesh; but he is
> a Jew who is one inwardly, and circumcision [law-fulfilling]
> is that which is of *the heart*, by *the Spirit*, and not by the let-
> ter [outward circumcision or law-keeping]; whose praise is
> [therefore] not from men [who see the outer] but from God
> [who sees the heart. (Rom 2:28–29)

The radical truth here is that the real Jew, God's elect, *cannot* be defined
or observed as one who keeps the law outwardly; he is *not* one who keeps
the Ten Commandments. He knows that he cannot justify himself by his
outward works of the law, nor does he attempt to do so. His "law-keeping"
is in his heart, his mind, where he only wills the good because he is a new
creation in Christ, through the Holy Spirit, the mind of Christ. He looks
at his life in the broad, overall perspective and thinks, "I do not do the
good that *I, as a believer, really want to do*."[13] So, the bottom line of God's
gospel is that God is continually justifying the ungodly who are believing
in Christ (Rom 4:5, 25).

Excursus 1: The Gospel's Use of the Law

The gospel's use of the law is to shut humans up to *Christ* for justification—
Rom 3:19–20; 2 Cor 3:9; Gal 3:22–25. The gospel's use of the law is utterly
distinct from what the law teaches in the Torah, for the OT Scriptures say
that the law *could* be kept—see Deut 6:24, 25; 30:11–20. But Reformation
(Protestant) theologians have historically read their (Pauline) understanding
(what we call *the gospel's use of the law*; as in Rom 3:19–20) back into the
OT scriptures, wrongly assuming that that is what the OT taught in its own
context. Now there *is* an overarching *promise* in Scripture (beginning at Gen
3:15); in this we agree with covenant theology (CT). However, the Scriptures
never use CT's term "the covenant of grace." Instead, they refer to "the gospel"

---

13. See my ch. 10.

that was *promised* in the Scriptures (Rom 1:1, 2). Thus, it is *the promise of the gospel* (of *grace*, Gal 1:6) that Paul refers to in Rom 1:1–2. And Ephesians refers to "the covenants of *the promise*" (Eph 2:12 AT), not "the covenants" or "the covenant of grace." There is no such thing as "the covenant of grace" in the Scriptures—only "the covenants of *the promise*" (Eph 2:12 lit.). So, "the covenant of grace" should be called *the promise of grace*.

The law is what is called "his [God's] covenant" in Deut 4:13, and the law is called "the covenant" in Deut 9:11. Also, "the law" and "the covenant" are used interchangeably in Exod 34:28; 2 Kgs 18:12; and Ps 78:10.

This fact alone should have prevented covenant theologians from using the term "the *covenant* of grace," for, in light the above texts, "the covenant of grace" means "the law of grace," hardly compatible with what Paul is talking about when he contrasts *the law* with *grace* in Rom 6:14–15, Gal 2:21, and elsewhere! Ever since the Spirit was given at Pentecost (Acts 11:15–17), "the law" is used in contrast with "grace" and with "the righteousness of faith" (see Rom 4 and 10, Galatians, and John 1:17). So, in the light of *the New Testament*, the law covenant is now old (2 Cor 3:3–11; Heb 8–10). Therefore, it is unscriptural and unwise to use the term "the *covenant* of grace." Instead, using "words taught of the Spirit" (1 Cor 2:13 AT), a better terminology for what they mean to say would be "the promise of the gospel" (Rom 1:1, 2; 4:13–16; Gal 3:15–29) was set forth in the *covenants* of the promise (Eph 2:12 lit.) This is because the apostolic gospel says that "*grace*" did not occur until and through the (historical) *redemption in Christ's blood* (see Rom 3:24–25; Gal 2:21; Eph 1:7), whereas the term "the covenant of grace" implies that grace (redemption through propitiation, Rom 3:24–26) *already existed* at and beginning with the promise in Gen 3:15, which it did *only* in the form of *promise*, for the ransom for sin had not yet been paid. Thus, in CT, the new testament in Christ's blood and Spirit is not given its radical newness in contrast to the old covenant; for the new testament went into effect by Christ's death and the sending of the Spirit (1 Cor 11:25; 2 Cor 3:6–18; Heb 9:15,16; chs. 8 and 10), which Paul calls the newness of the Spirit (Rom 7:6; see 2 Cor 3:6)—that the Spirit of Christ indwelling those in "the church of God" (1 Cor 10:32; see 12:13) replaces the law of Moses (Rom 7:4–6; 8:1–2, 14; 6:15–16), for we are "in the law of Christ" (1 Cor 9:21). We are in Christ and Christ is in us. The central imperative of the new covenant/testament is the "*one* word: You shall *love* your neighbor as yourself" (Gal 5:13–14), which replaces the "ten words," for a "change of law" has occurred (Heb 7:12; see 8:6–13). With Christ we died to the law, in order that we might live to God (Gal 2:19–20). Abraham had the gospel in the form of *a promise* preached to him by God (Gal 3:8), but the grace of the gospel came only in Christ (Rom 1:2; 3:24; John 1:17). Michael Horton wrote:

> In the covenant that God made with Abraham (Gen 12 and 15), there are two distinct kinds of promises: an everlasting promise, with universal blessings for all nations, in a single seed of Abraham (Christ), and a conditional promise of a temporal land for Abraham's physical seed (Israelites).[14]

The promise of *the gospel*, to which Paul refers in *Gal 3:8* (see 3:29; Rom 1:1–2) is the first promise that Horton lists, but it was hidden in the OT scriptures (Rom 16:25–26; 1 Cor 2). And only the NT scriptures (Rom 4; Gal 3; Heb 11) make this promise clear, i.e., that the elect were trusting in this promise, which in one sense began in Gen 3:15 and is renewed through Abraham. This (first, in Horton's words) promise is, in one sense, conditioned on one's faith in the God of the promise; yet, in the primary sense, it is an *unconditional promise*, because God gives the faith to all whom he has unconditionally chosen before the world began. So, in the fullness of time (Gal 4:4), this gospel is called *the new testament* in Christ's blood (1 Cor 11:25), and redemption by Christ's death is the basis upon which God gives the Spirit through the faith (Gal 3:13–14). The promise of redemption was gradually revealed from Gen 3:15 onward, throughout the OT Scriptures, culminating in the once for all redemption that is in Christ Jesus (Rom 3:24–25). So, gospel *grace*, although promised beforehand (Rom 1:1–2), did not occur until the historical redemption in Christ's blood (Rom 3:21–25) occurred. So, covenant theology does not make a clear distinction between *the law* given to Israel (Rom 2:14; 9:4) and *the grace* of God in Christ given to the church: "Give no offense to Jews or to Greeks or to *the church of God*" (1 Cor 10:32), for those in Christ are no longer nations (1 Cor 12:2). The church that is Christ's body (Col 1:18–20) began at Pentecost with the giving of the Spirit; thus, the new creation (2 Cor 5:17-21) did not occur prior to Pentecost, for the Spirit of the risen Christ came at Pentecost based on our adoption as (adult) sons, which is based upon the historic, once-for-all redemption in Christ's blood (Rom 3:24; Gal 4:1–7). The church of God (1 Cor 10:32) is the Israel of "the new testament . . . of the Spirit" (2 Cor 3:6). This is true because the one in Christ is the true Jew (Rom 2:28–29; Phil 3:3), who belongs to God's Israel (Gal 6:16), the elect, including the elect of God (spiritual Israel) from among natural Israel (Rom 9:6; 11:25). The grace of God includes its own imperatives (1 Cor 14:37; Rom 6:14–23; 12:1–2, etc.). So, the promise, both

---

14. Horton, *Pilgrim Theology*, 161.

before and after Christ died, has always been received by faith alone. Before Christ's death, it was a faith in the promise that looked forward to the coming Messiah. So, *the promise* is ultimately "the promise of the Spirit" (Gal 3:14; see Acts 1:4, 5), and *the Spirit is eternal life* (Rom 8:10–11; 6:23; 2 Cor 3:6). Paul says that he preaches *the gospel of God*, which was *promised* in the old covenant scriptures (Rom 1:1–2). The righteousness from God is made manifest "now" (Rom 3:21), because what the OT scriptures promised has now come through the redemption in Christ's blood (Rom 3:21, 24–25; Gal 3:13—4:4; Eph 1:7). There is one promise to Abraham and his seed (Christ and thus all in him) and one people of God, which the elect gentiles have been grafted into (Rom 11), but there is also a radical distinction between the old and new covenants (2 Cor 3:3—4:18; Gal 4:21—5:1; Heb 8–10), one being that *all* those in the new covenant have the Spirit (Heb 8:7–12; 10:15–17). Jesus appointed, that is, covenanted (διατίθεμαι) to his disciples a *kingdom, as the Father (first) covenanted a kingdom to his Son* (see Luke 22:29). This has been called *the covenant of redemption*, made in the triune God before creation, and is the basis of the kingdom-reign of Christ's love (Col 1:13) and grace (Rom 5:21) for God's elect. The promise (of the gospel) has its source in *the covenant of redemption* (Luke 22:29; Ps 89:3; Heb 5:5–10; 2:9–14 and see 10:5–7; 13:20 [lit Greek]; John 17:4, 24; Gal 3:17–20; 1 Cor 1:23–24 and see 2:7), which was the result of *the pre-creation counsel of God's will* (Eph 1:4, 11), for the covenant of redemption is the covenantal agreement between God the Father and the Son in the Holy Spirit, before the foundation of the world, in which God the Father determined and the Son agreed that Christ would be the representative head of those whom God fore-chose to be saved unto eternal glory. This grace occurs in time (in Christ's death) according to God's promise, which gives life and immortality on the condition that one *believes* in the Messiah, which (faith) God freely gives to his elect (Phil 1:29); and the condition (faith as gift) was purchased by the Son (Gal 3:13–14).[15]

15. On the covenant of redemption, see Hodge, *Systematic Theology*, 2:354–73, and Fesko, *Covenant of Redemption*, 167-96.

SIX

Justified by Christ's Faith, for Believers

(Rom 3)

There is no one who is righteous, not even one.

The law says this, in order that all the world may come under judgment to God. Therefore, by the works of the law no human being will be justified in God's sight, for through law is the experiential knowledge of sin. (Rom 3:10, 19–20)

To CLARIFY WHAT THE apostle is saying here, *The Book of Concord* says:

Therefore, Christ takes the law into his hands and explains it spiritually (Matt 5:21ff.; Rom 7:6, 14), thus he reveals his wrath from heaven over all sinners and reveals how great this wrath is. . . . For Paul testifies that although "Moses is read" the veil which he "put over his face" remains unremoved, so that they do not see the law spiritually . . . or how severely it curses and condemns us because we could not fulfill or keep it.[1]

For as Luther says . . ., "Everything that rebukes sin is and belongs to the law, the proper function of which is to condemn sin and lead to a knowledge of sin" (Rom 3:20; 7:7). . . . Since the Gospel (which alone . . . teaches and commands faith in Christ)

1. SD V. 10 (559–60).

58

is the Word of God, the Holy Spirit . . . rebukes the unbelief involved in men's failure to believe in Christ.[2]

This truth is central in Paul's gospel: The law only condemns and kills (Rom 3:19–20; 2 Cor 3:7, 9), but Christ justifies, and the result is eternal life.[3]

Excursus 2: The Faith of Jesus Christ

Christ's obedience of faith (Rom 1:5; see 5:19) unto *death* (Phil 2:8) *justifies* sinners.

Christ is received through *faith* (Rom 5:1, 17), which is the fruit of his death and a gift from God (Gal 3:13–14; and see 2 Thess 2:13; Phil 1:29).

Paul says that "the gospel of Christ . . . is the power of God for salvation for everyone believing" (Rom 1:16). Paul uses the word "believing" (present tense), because believing in Christ for justification is and remains central throughout the believer's life. It is not (as it appears in American evangelicalism) that one begins by faith in Christ and then goes on to something else. According to *the gospel of God* (1:1), obedience is "the obedience of faith" (Rom 1:5). Thus, it follows that for Christ also, his faith (toward) God is obedience. When we compare Paul's words with Paul's words, we find that Paul's thesis statement in Rom 1:17 is best interpreted and understood by what he says in 3:21–22.

> Rom 1:17b the gospel . . . in it a righteousness from God
> is revealed *from* [*Christ's*] *faith*—*to* [*our*] *faith*
> Rom 3:22 a righteousness *from* God
> through the *faith* [obedience] of Jesus Christ—*to those*
> who have *faith.*

Paul, in Rom 3:22, uses more words to define what was tersely stated in 1:17, for in 3:22 he says that the righteousness *from* God is through the faith of Christ *to* those who have faith. Aside from the Authorized Version, most Bible translations have translated Paul's words in Rom 3:21–22, Gal 2:16, 3:21–22; and Phil 3:9 as being redundant—as if the righteousness from God is through *faith* in Jesus Christ for all who *believe.* But Paul is *not* redundant; he does not waste words; he is very terse. In Rom 3:21–23 he is saying:

> But now, apart from law [apart from human righteousness]
> a righteousness from God has been manifested, being borne
> witness to by the law and the prophets; even the righteousness

2. SD V. 17, 19 (561).
3. Rom 3:21–28; 5:21; 6:23; 8:10.

from God through the faith of Jesus Christ [his obedience of faith unto death] to all and upon all who believe, for there is no difference, for all sinned and through their own fault, lack the glory of God. (Rom 3:21–23)

Note that the faith we have in Christ is not omitted, for Paul says, "To all and upon all who believe." Rather, our faith (belief) is placed last in the text, because the *righteousness* (*from God*) which justifies is through *Christ's faith*, his *obedience unto death*. For Paul, faith *is* obedience—"the obedience of faith" (Rom 1:5). Christ's faith is the faith that belongs to Christ, that Christ has in God the Father. The Greek is in the genitive case. We acknowledge that in terms of Greek grammar, the Greek could be translated either as a subjective genitive (as "faith of") or an objective genitive (as "faith in"). But the deciding factors are other Scriptures written by Paul that prove that the subjective genitive provides the correct translation, as we will show.

The faith of Christ Jesus (πίστεως Χριστοῦ Ιησοῦ in Gal 2:16; see Rom 3:22) is not the faithfulness of Christ, nor is it our faith in Christ, any more than "the faith of Abraham" (πίστεως Ἀβραάμ) in Rom 4:16 should be translated as *faith in Abraham*, or the *faithfulness of Abraham*. It should not, for it clearly means *the faith of Abraham*.[4] In both Rom 3:22 and 4:16, the Greek πιστεως means "faith of"—both texts use the Greek *genitive* case—that of possession. Thus, Rom 4:16, referring to *the faith of Abraham*, is the key text on this issue. Going by the context of Rom 4:16 (4:1–24), we know that Paul is referring to Abraham's faith in God. Likewise, in Rom 3 Paul is referring to the faith that *Jesus* had in God, even unto his death on a cross (see 3:25). And in 3:26 he says the believer is "him who is of *the faith of Jesus*" (literal translation). Yes, in his obedience of *faith*, Jesus was *faithful* to God the Father—to God's will, to the saving of God's fore-loved people. Yet that faithfulness was the fruit of Jesus' (obedience of) *faith*—his *trust* in God. Referring to πίστις/*pistis* (the root of πίστεως, the genitive) Hays says:

> The noun *pistis* offers a range of semantic possibilities for English translators. It can be rendered as "faith," "faithfulness," "fidelity," or "trust."[5]

But Paul himself lets us know which of these words we should use for πίστις (*pistis*), for Paul's definitive and normal use of πίστις (in the gospel of God, Rom 1:1) is that of "the obedience of *faith*" (1:5) in Christ and

---

4. "Therefore it [the promise, 4:14] is of faith, that it might be according to grace, so that the promise might be sure to all the seed, not only to those who are of the law, but also to those who are of *the faith of Abraham*, who is the father of us all" (Rom 4:16).

5. Hays, *NIB*, 11:240.

not (the obedience of) "faithfulness." Paul put no *trust* in the flesh (Phil 3:3) and that means he had *faith* in Christ, the righteousness (of God) bestowed on faith (3:9c). In 3:3 Paul does not say that he puts no "faithfulness" in the flesh, and he consistently uses πίστις in this way in his letters. Therefore, in the *faith of Christ* texts, Paul is saying that we are justified by Christ's faith (obedience of faith unto death), which we receive through faith in him. In these texts we find what I have for years called Paul's "formula of justification," which consists in three parts:

(a) Justification is not by works of law.

(b) Justification is by Christ's faith—*his* obedience of faith unto *death*.

(c) Justification is for all who believe (in Christ).

First (a), we learn what justification *is not* by: It is not by works of the law, not by works of humans in Adam.[6] Second (b), we learn what justification *is* by: the one righteous act of God in Christ (his death, Rom 5:18; see 2 Cor 5:19); that is, Christ's obedience, that of the one God who, remaining God, became man in Christ Jesus (Rom 1:3–4; 9:5; Gal 1:10–12). Third (c), now that Christ has died and been raised, God makes his appeal through the gospel to believe in his Son (2 Cor 5:20); that is, for the righteousness of God in Christ to be received by faith in Christ. So, "the faith of Christ" means Christ's obedience (Rom 5:19) that justifies (5:18–19), that is, Christ's obedience of faith (Rom 1:5) in God the Father unto death (Phil 2:8). But *our* faith is in (God through) Christ, who obeyed God. What follows is the apostle's formula (the ABC's) of justification:

Rom 3:20–22
(a) By works of law no flesh will be justified in God's sight
    (b) a righteousness from God through the faith
        of Jesus Christ
        (c) for all those who believe (in him).

Gal 2:16
(a) A man is not justified by works of law
    (b) but by Christ Jesus' faith

---

6. All of Paul's antitheses, his "not (this) . . . but (that)" in his letters, center on this primary one: the "not by [human] works, but by the faith [obedience] of Christ unto death [grace]" antithesis, which is central to the gospel of God (1:1). Thus, to the extent that preachers and teachers do not say that *justification is not by works of the law*, they do not imitate Paul (1 Cor 4:16), and, to that extent, preach another gospel; see Gal 1:8, 9, 11, 12 and see 2:16, 21.

(c) we believed in Christ

(b) that we might be justified by Christ's faith

(a) and not by works of law, for by works of law no flesh will be justified.

Gal 3:21–22

(a) The law is not able to impart righteousness, for the Scripture has shut up all under sin,

(b) that the promise, through Christ's faith, might be given

(c) to all who believe (in Christ).

Phil 3:9

(a) Not having my righteousness, which is of the law

(b) but having the one (righteousness) through Christ's faith

(c) *the righteousness from God*, (bestowed) upon (ones having) *faith.*

Notice that *the faith of Christ* does not at all deny the need for *faith in Christ*. Rather, as we find in the twice-repeated use of "*Christ's faith*" in Gal 2:16, Christ's *death*—his obedience of faith—is the *priority*, precisely because Christ's faith *justifies* us (Rom 5:19)! Our faith (which is God's gift) merely receives *Christ's obedience unto death for justification*. And in this formula of justification, Paul does not omit the "*not* having my righteousness" or "*not* by works of the law," for self-righteous humans always need to hear the negative side, that is, (a) as well as the positive side (b). The error with the traditional view, which has influenced most Bible translations, so they read "faith in Christ for those who believe," is not simply their un-Pauline redundancy but primarily that they omit what is central to the apostle, that humans are justified by the faith, the obedience, of Christ, unto death.

> For I, through the law, died [with Christ] to the law; [for] with Christ I have been crucified [to death]; and I [under law] live no longer, but Christ lives in me, and the life I now live in the flesh I live by *the faith of the Son of God*, who [in that faith] loved me and delivered himself up [to death] for me [Gal 2:19–20], for my justification. (2:21)

Yes, Christ was faithful to his Father's will—through his faith in God the Father. And if Christ's obedience of *faith* (Rom 1:5) led Christ to die for us (5:19; Phil 2), is not *faith* alone sufficient for us to be obedient to God without the law? Paul lives by the faith of the Son of God; he *lives* by Christ's death, which *justified* him. This is the Son who is one with God the Father

(John 10:30), who delivered his only begotten Son up to death for us (Rom 8:32). Paul's "I," who has died, is the one who is a law to himself (Rom 2:14). Before Paul was in Christ, his heart was uncircumcised (still joined to the flesh of sin; the *flesh* was not yet removed from his heart), so that he was spiritually dead to God (Col 2:13). In giving himself for Paul, Christ ultimately gave him faith in God the Father, of which Paul, in the flesh, had none. Christ's faith does dwell in me because the crucified and risen Christ dwells in me. And where Christ is, there is faith in God the Father. I am living by his life in me, which is by his death, which put the old "I" to death, which death justified me from the sin (Rom 6:7) that condemned me in Adam (Rom 5:12–21). The Son of God *lives in me*, and he does so in *faith*, Christ's faith, which (Spirit of faith, 2 Cor 4:13) he obtained for me through his death (Gal 3:13, 14). Although there is a distinction between Christ's death and his resurrection life—Christ *for* me in his death for justification, and Christ *in* me (as life) through his resurrection—yet there is only one Christ, who is the one Source out of which I continually live and "walk." So, when Paul says, "imitate me as I imitate Christ," he includes *Christ's faith, his believing in God.* Christ's death for God's elect procured all their spiritual blessings (Rom 8:32–34), including faith (Phil 1:29). I am a new creation who now trusts God again. Christ's *person* and his *work*, though distinct, cannot be separated. That is, one cannot have Christ's righteous act for justification (Rom 5:18) apart from his person, the *Christ* who is *present* in *the Spirit* as our sanctification (1 Cor 1:30; Rom 8:10). Those who are in Christ have an imputed righteousness through his death (Rom 4:5–8; 5:9), which is their justification. But they also have indwelling righteousness, the righteousness and holiness of the new man (Eph 4:24). That is, *Christ* is in them (Rom 8:10), and so they are a new creation (2 Cor 5:17), which is the rule they are to walk in and by (see Gal 6:15–16). The lack of understanding of this truth of *the faith of Christ* by many is due to the immeasurable influence of Augustine on Luther and Calvin and, in turn, to *their* powerful influence on those in Reformation traditions, even to the point of influencing Bible translators and thus Bible translations, in that they obscure and thereby destroy this central truth of Paul's gospel. But Christ-believers need to continue to be reformed according to the word of God, for Paul says we are to imitate him (1 Cor 4:16; 11:1; Phil 3:17). In sum: Faith *is* obedience to God (Rom 1:5; 10:16); therefore, the *faith of Christ* is his *obedience* to God, even unto *death* on a cross (Rom 5:19; Phil 2:5). In ourselves (in the flesh) there is always nothing but unbelief (Rom 7:18). But in Christ (in the Spirit) there is nothing but faith. Thanks be to God: Christ's faith-obedience unto death is the basis of this same Christ dwelling in me, by which I became a new creation. Without Christ, I could not believe on him (God) who raised up Jesus our Lord from the dead (Rom 4:24 AT). But, because of the faith of the Son of God (Gal 2:20), by which and by whom I am justified (2:21) and therefore have life (2:20) in his life, I *do* "believe on God who raised up Jesus our Lord from the dead" (4:24 AT). I have Christ's resurrection life in me because I am in union with Christ, and thus in union with his faith. They cannot be separated. Thus, to have the Spirit of God and of Christ (Rom 8:9) is to have the Spirit of faith (2 Cor 4:13),[7] as it is written:

> You were . . . redeemed . . . with the precious blood of Christ . . . who . . . was manifest in these last times for you, who *by him* [you] do believe in God (1 Pet 1:18–21 AV)

Paul uses the Septuagint (LXX), which, in Habakkuk, says, "But the righteous shall live by My faith" (Hab 2:4b SAAS). With all we have learned about *the faith of Christ* in Rom 3:21–22, Gal 2:16, 3:21–22, Phil 3:9 (Gal 2:20; Rom 3:26; [and Eph 3:12]), it is easy to see how Paul, knowing the LXX translation of Hab 2:4, saw it as scriptural support for what God had revealed to him regarding the faith of Christ. So, when Paul saw the words "my faith" in the LXX, he saw it as *Christ* saying, "*My* faith." Because Paul wants to use the words of the prophets to bear witness to his gospel, he is limited in terms of the amount of words here in Rom 1:17 (Rom 3:21; 2:16). That reality, plus Paul's interpretive key, which is "a righteousness from God is manifested . . . [even] a righteousness *from God through the faith [obedience] of Jesus Christ—to* those who have *faith*" (Rom 3:21–22) give us utter confidence that what Paul is saying in Rom 1 is as follows:

> For I am not ashamed of the gospel of Christ, for in it a righteousness from God is revealed, *from* [Christ's] *faith—to* [our] *faith*, as it is written:
>
> "*The Righteous One* [Christ],[8] *out of*[9] faith [Christ's obedience of faith, which justified us, who, through *union with Christ, includes the one* who now has *faith*] *will live* [in eternal life]." (Rom 1:16–17)

Since Christ's faith, his obedience unto death, results in our faith (Gal 3:13–14; see Heb 12:2), then, as we understand Paul's "from [Christ's] faith to [our] faith" in Rom 1:17, it is still true that a person is *justified by faith in Christ alone, without works.* Therefore, those who understand the

---

7. See πνεῦμα in 2 Cor 4:13 and compare πνεῦμα (same word, for the Holy Spirit) in 1 Cor 2:12.

8. See also Keck, *Romans*, 53–54, and Hays, "'Righteous One,'" 191–215.

9. The Greek εκ here means *out of* faith as source; that is, *out of* faith in *God* the Father as source for Christ and *out of* faith in *Christ* as source for Christ-believers.

Reformation's recovery of the gospel with its "faith alone" need not fear the truth of the faith of Christ.

In Rom 1:16, Paul interprets Hab 2:4 in the light of Christ, not in the light of the law.[10] Why? Because Paul, later in the letter, says:

> But now, *apart from law*, a righteousness from God has been manifested, being borne witness to by the law and the prophets; even a righteousness from God through the faith of Jesus Christ [his obedience unto death] to all and upon all who believe, for there is no difference, for all sinned and lack the glory of God, being justified freely by his grace, through the *redemption* in Christ Jesus. (Rom 3:21–24)

On *redemption*, Augustine wisely says:

> And so the devil, in that very death of the flesh [Christ's flesh], lost [his hold on] man, whom he was possessing as by an absolute right [since Adam sinned, and we with him] . . . and over whom he ruled . . . so that He [Christ], being Himself put to death, although innocent [without sin, not deserving of death], by the unjust one [the devil] acting against us [in Christ's death] as [if] it were by just right [which it was not, for Christ was not deserving of death], might by a most just right [Christ's death for us] overcome him, and so might lead captive the captivity [of us by the devil] wrought through sin, and free us from a captivity [bondage, Heb 2:14–15] that was just on account of sin, by *blotting out the handwriting* [Col 2:13–15], and *redeeming* us who were to be justified although sinners, through His own righteous blood unrighteously [by the devil] poured out.[11]

> . . . whom God set forth a propitiatory sacrifice through (Christ's) *faith*.(Rom 3:25)

---

10. The Hebrew word behind "faith" in Hab 2:4 is "faithfulness." Thus, in the Hebrew text, Hab 2:4 is saying: "The righteous man shall live by his [*emunah*] *faithfulness*" to the God of Israel and thus to Israel's torah. The AV translates *emunah* correctly as "faithfulness" in Pss 5:9; 36:5; 40:10; 88:11; 89:1, 5, 8, 33; 92:2; 119:75, 90; 143:1; Isa 11:5; 25:1; Lam 3:23; Hos 2:20. And this same Hebrew word is the root of the Hebrew word translated "faithfully" (in AV) in 2 Kgs 12:15; 2 Chr 19:9; 31:12; 34:12. In the Hebrew text, Hab 2:4 is contrasting the proud man, who is not faithful (2:5), with the one who is *faithful* to the God of the torah. This demonstrates not only that Paul used the LXX but also how Paul has Christ's authority to interpret the OT scriptures in the light of Christ; see Nygren, *Commentary on Romans*, 81–90, and *Significance of the Bible*, 26–30.

11. Augustine, *On the Trinity*, 4, 13, emphasis and words in brackets are mine. See also the end of my ch. 11; see also (similarly) Luther's view in Aulén, *Christus Victor*, 103–4.

Concerning "Christ's faith" in Rom 3:25, Robinson says:

> This interpretation is to be preferred to the usual interpretation, for it makes much better sense to say that God's righteousness has been manifested by the character of Christ's work than to say that it has been manifested by man's faith in Christ, for how can man's faith be said to have demonstrated God's righteousness?[12]

> > By his blood, for a showing forth of the [inherent] righteousness of him because of the passing by of the [elect's] sins having previously [*before Christ's death*] occurred in the forbearance [restraint] of God [his wrath], and for the showing forth of his justice in the present time [*since* Christ's death, when he still passes by the sins of his people without destroying them on the spot], that he should be [demonstrated to be] just and justifying the one who is of the faith [obedience] of Jesus. (Rom 3:25–26)

In Rom 3:26, the Greek refers to him who is "of *the faith of Jesus*." Who are such? Paul, in Gal 3, says:

> Now to Abraham and his seed were the promises made. He [God] says not "and to seeds" as of many seeds, but as of One: "And to thy Seed," which is *Christ*. (Gal 3:16)

So, just as Abraham's promised seed is *Christ* (Gal 3:16), and so "they who are *of Christ* [χριστοῦ] are Abraham's seed" (Gal 3:29), even so, "those who are *of Christ*" (Gal 3:29), are those who are "of the faith of Jesus" (ἐκ πίστεως Ἰησοῦ, Rom 3:26b AT), and heirs according to (God's) promise (to Abraham, Gal 3:29).

> Where, then, is the boasting? [Is it in the law? No, for] it was completely excluded [by Christ's death, which justifies]. Through what law? [The one] of works? No, but [it was excluded] through a law of faith ["believe in Christ and live," 10:8–9]. Therefore, we conclude that a man is justified by faith apart from works of law. Or is God the God of Jews only? Is he not the God of Gentiles also? Yes, of Gentiles also, since indeed there is one God who will justify the circumcised by faith, and the uncircumcised through faith. Do we therefore destroy the law through *the faith*? May it not be! But we uphold the law [through *the faith* (of Christ, which procures our faith), for *faith* believes that "whatever things *the law* says, it speaks that ... the entire world may be under judgment to God. Therefore,

---

12. Robinson, "Faith of Jesus Christ," 80; see also Johnson, "Romans 3:21–26," 79–80.

by works of the law, no flesh will be justified in God's sight"].
(Rom 3:27–31; compare 3:19–21)

How is the law established and upheld? The answer is "through faith." He means through faith in Christ, which includes believing the gospel's use of the law, which Paul uses in 3:10–20 to show that there is only condemnation for Jew and gentile and thus the need for Christ. The law leaves no way out from condemnation, except through faith in Christ (see 3:19–20). For Christ, by shedding his blood to death (3:25), bore the curse of the law to redeem us from its curse (3:24–25; Gal 3:13). Therefore, through faith, the law is established (ἱστάνομεν)—that is, the law stands, it is upheld (3:31). For God's just judgment fell upon Christ on our behalf, and faith in Christ receives the faith of Christ (his obedience unto death, procuring our faith, which is a gift); thus, all boasting is excluded. Also, the righteous requirement of the law is fulfilled *in us*, who by faith have received *the Spirit* that the law, being spiritual, required. The law is also established (upheld) because the law (Gen 15:6) bears witness (Rom 3:21b) to justification through faith alone, as Paul will say in Rom 4:1–8.

Justification: Forgiveness, but More Than Forgiveness

God "passed by" the sins of his people before Christ's death; God did not judge the elect for those sins when they occurred. God waited until Christ, who bore their sins unto the *death* they deserved, that God might be just and the justifier of those of the faith of Jesus. This truth, which Rom 3:24–26 proclaims, is also taught in Heb 9:15–17, which says that Jesus is the mediator of the new covenant, and thus his redemptive death was also for the transgressions done under the first (old) covenant. God's "passing by" (πρεσιν) "of sins" that were committed *prior to* Christ's death was just, because those sins were finally propitiated and thereby righteously taken away on Christ's cross (Rom 3:25; Heb 10:1–14). Hebrews teaches that, unlike the old covenant sacrifices, which could never take away sin, Christ's death takes away the sins of his people. For "without shedding of blood is no remission" (Heb 9:22 AV). This was even true under the old covenant, because "the *life* of the flesh is in the blood" (Lev 17:11a). Therefore, Christ's *death*, in which his *life* was taken away, was the propitiatory sacrifice through which God removed his just wrath from his people. God was propitiated (3:25) through God's own act (see 2 Cor 5:19): It was the blood of God himself (Acts 20:28). The Son fully shares the *one divine* nature with the

Father and the Spirit. In Christ dwells all the fullness of the Godhead bodily (Col 2:9). Therefore, not a part of God died on the cross, but *the fullness of the Godhead* died in our place. Although Paul can, using old covenant scripture, say our sins were "covered" by God in Christ (Rom 4:7), nevertheless, the difference is that, now that God set forth Christ as a propitiatory sacrifice[13] in his blood, we have received, not "the atonement" (as in AV, an old covenant term), but "the reconciliation" (5:10, 11; see 2 Cor 5:19–21, so that we are made the righteousness of God in Christ). God has not merely "passed by" our sins (Rom 3:25) as he did in the past, but God has taken our sins away in Christ, as the writer of Hebrews says. Referring to the law, the author says that it "can never, with these same sacrifices . . . make those who approach *perfect*" (from Heb 10:1), in terms of having "*no more consciousness of sins*" (10:2), which is based upon God taking away our sins (see Heb 10:1–12). Thus, sins are no longer covered in the sense of "passed by" in the old covenant manner, but they are taken away through propitiation in the new testament in Christ's blood (1 Cor 11:25). So *justification* refers to the reality of an objective change in God's relationship toward sinners, in which God as the judge acquits the person who, prior to his acquittal, was charged with the verdict "guilty," that is, condemned. This objective change, through propitiation, is from one of God's wrath and rejection of us to one of God's grace and acceptance of us, in which God is both just and the justifier of those who are of the faith of Jesus (3:26).

God reckoned Abraham's faith to him as righteousness. To use a metaphor on this matter, *before* Christ's death and exaltation, Abraham, and all God's elect, lived in "God's house"—they had righteousness imputed to them and were thereby accepted by God, but they lived in that "house-of-righteousness" on credit, for the ransom price (redemption) had not yet been paid on "God's house," for their sins were not yet taken away, as Hebrews says in chapters 8 through 10. But, the *faith of Christ having (now) come* (Gal 3:25; see 3:22), we are justified by faith through the redemption that has now occurred. This is a justification based upon propitiation (Rom 3:24–28). So, until Christ provided a once-for-all redemption in history, when the ransom price for sin occurred, there was no real justification of anyone; the justification of saints before and after Christ's death is based upon his death for them.

> But the scriptures shut up all mankind under [the power of] Sin, in order that the promise, by the [obedience of] faith of Jesus Christ [unto death, 2:16, 21] might be given to those believing [in him]. But before the faith [of Christ] came, we

13. On propitiation, see Murray, *Romans*, 1:116–20.

were guarded under [the] law, being shut up to the faith [of Christ, through which we believe in him] being about to be revealed [see Rom 3:21, 22]. So that the law has become our supervisory-guardian [up] to Christ, in order that out of *faith* [*in Christ*] *we might be justified* [now, through the historical redemption that is in Christ Jesus (Rom 3:24–25; Eph 1:7), in a way that OT saints were *not justified*, for the redemption price has now been paid in full]. But the faith [of Christ through which we believe in Christ] having [*now*] *come*, we are no longer under a supervisory-guardian. For you are all [adult] sons of God [no longer "children," but heirs, 4:1–7] through faith in Christ Jesus. (Gal 3:21–26)

So, there is both a union and a distinction between OT justification and NT justification. We were redeemed from the authority of sin and Satan. And through that redemption we were justified (Rom 3:24). The debt we owed has been paid in full, for God in Christ paid the ransom which freed us from Satan's authority. So now God's people "live in a house" (they are justified, Rom 3:24; Gal 3:23–24) through the redemption in Christ Jesus. Redemption in Christ occurred, yes, but *how* Christ justified us before God is *incomprehensible* to us, as are all God's ways (Rom 11:33), *no less than* God's becoming man in Christ. God's justice is incomprehensible to mere creatures. Then how much more so is it to sinners in the flesh of sin (Rom 8:3; see 1:21)? So, the truth that God's blood (Acts 20:28; Rom 5:9) justifies sinners does *not* coincide with *our* concept of righteousness. As Ware wrote, "All that we affirm concerning God, however correct, falls far short of the living truth. If we say that he is good or just, we must at once add that his goodness or justice are not to be measured by our human standards."[14] Luther put it like this:

For if his righteousness were such that it could be judged to be righteous by human standards, it would clearly not be divine and would in no way differ from human righteousness. But since he is the one true God, who is wholly incomprehensible and inaccessible to human reason, it is proper and indeed necessary that his righteousness also should be incomprehensible, as Paul also says where he exclaims: "O the depth of the riches of the wisdom and knowledge of God! How incomprehensible are his judgments and how unsearchable his ways!" But they would not be incomprehensible if we were in every instance to grasp how they are righteous. What is man, compared with God?[15]

14. Ware, *Orthodox Way*, 16.
15. Luther, *Basic Theological Writings*, 221.

Similarly, Forde, and then Madson, say:

> "The cross is not to be understood by *another* system; the cross
> *is* its own system." This means that even Biblical metaphors and
> images are ultimately limited because the cross is beyond our
> understanding.[16]

Nevertheless, *that* Christ was a propitiation and did justify us by his blood
has now been revealed. God has dealt with human sin, and thus he is just
and the justifier of him who is of the faith of Jesus (see 3:25–26). Death is
the wages of sin (6:23); therefore, Christ died for the ungodly (5:6). We can
leave it at that and trust God's word. I am to live out of faith in Christ for
justification as my Source (Gal 5:5 AT). But the fear of imputed righteousness leading to sinning is a misguided fear, because the Christ who justifies
is the one who also indwells us by his Holy Spirit, who leads us to mortify
the deeds of the body—see Rom 8:9–13, for we are those who died with
Christ and are alive to God in Christ Jesus (Rom 6). Therefore, when most
preachers use the word "forgiven" rather than "justified" in their preaching,
they are falling short of preaching the apostolic gospel of God. And most of
the church has not clearly understood this distinction between the old and
new covenants, based upon the redemption that has occurred in Christ.[17]

The Old Covenant	The New Covenant/Testament
Salvation is coming.	*Salvation has come:* (2 Cor 6:2; Gal 3:22–25).
"God, be *propitious* to me, the sinner." (Luke 18:13)	God . . . sent his Son to be *the propitia-tion* for our sins. (1 John 4:10b) Thus: "Father, thank you that you have been propitious to me in Christ; so that there is now no condemnation in him."

So, to continue to use the language of Luke 18:13 now is a failure to know
and believe the truth of Rom 3:25–26 and 1 John 2:2 and 4:10. Even God's
promise of the Spirit has gone into effect by Christ's death.[18] In the undisputed letters of Paul, he only uses the words "justified" and "justification,"

16. Forde, *Where God Meets Man*, 36, quoted in Madson, *Cross and the Crown*, 16.

17. See Rom 3:24–26; Gal 3:21–26; 4:1–7. Justification through redemption issues
in the weighty blessing of the indwelling of the risen Christ by his Spirit (Rom 8:3–10;
Gal 3:13, 14). The law kept in bounds Israel's and our conduct as "children" until Christ,
in order that *we* might be justified and be adult sons by faith in Christ. But the faith having now come, we are no longer under a child-guardian (Gal 3:24, 25 AT; see 3:13–14).

18. See Gal 3:15–22; compare 3:21; Heb 9:15–28; 10:11–18.

and not "forgiveness of sins," except when he quotes the OT in Rom 4:7. Right alongside the church's continued failure in refusing to use Paul's "words taught by the Spirit" (1 Cor 2:13), for example, in not using words in the δικαιοσύνη family, such as *justified, justification, righteousness*, in its preaching, teaching, hymns and songs, is the unbelief that has not usually preached nor taught the grace of Christ in justification through faith in Christ alone, without works (Rom 4:6); with grace's corresponding lordship of Christ instead of sin—that we are now enslaved, not to sin, but to God through our union with Christ in his death and resurrection. We needed to have Adam's sin and our sins to be no longer put to our account unto condemnation and to be no longer in the flesh in which sin dwells. We have a right-standing with God, and to the Christ-believer, nothing else is as sweet as this message of peace with God through Christ (Rom 5:1). The word "forgiveness" does not convey the reality that God's own justice was demonstrated (and satisfied) in Christ's death as the propitiation for our sins; however, the word "*justification*" or "*justified*" does do so (Rom 3:21–28). In Rom 3:25, Christ's death shows forth God's inherent justice.[19] In Rom 5, he says that in the gospel, God demonstrates his love toward us. "Grace" means that both God's justice (Rom 3:25–26) and his love (5:8) were demonstrated in Christ's death for our justification (Gal 2:21). Thus, the word "grace" was not used in this apostolic sense in the old covenant scriptures, before Christ died and rose again. All those who believe in the God who raised Jesus from the dead will be saved from the wrath to come. All others are storing up wrath for themselves on the day of wrath, the day of the righteous judgment of God (Rom 2:5). The just judgment of God is that which Christ bore as our substitute, as the propitiation for the sins of his elect (3:25; 8:33–34). Only Christ could and did free God's elect from the holy and righteous law's condemnation. Murray, commenting on God's righteousness which justifies, wrote:

> (i) Negatively, it is contrasted not only with human unrighteousness but with human righteousness. It is not of human origin, not of human authorship.

> (ii) Positively, it is a God-righteousness, not simply because it is *provided* by God, nor simply because it is *approved* by God, nor simply because it is bestowed by God, but *chiefly* because it is a righteousness with divine quality or property. It is not,

19. δικαιοσύνησ (the genitive) is used, which means the righteousness that *God possesses* inherently (in Rom 3:25, 26) and which he demonstrates in Christ's death. This is different from δικαιοσύνη (the Greek dative for righteousness in 3:21, 22), which is God's righteousness (as a gift) to and for those who believe in Christ.

of course, the divine attribute of justice. But it is a righteousness with divine attributes. And, because so, it measures up to
the demands of our sinful situation and to the requirements
of a full, perfect, and irrevocable justification. And not only
does it meet these demands and requirements, but since it is
divine and therefore *perfectly corresponding with the inherent
justice of God it always elicits the divine approbation* whenever
it comes into operation.[20]

The Apostolic Definition of Faith and of Sin

Paul wastes no time at the beginning of his letter to the Romans to define
obedience as "the obedience of faith." This is key to the entire letter of Romans. Because of this revelation of *faith*, Paul says, "Whatever is *not of faith
is sin*" (Rom 14:23). Does Paul elsewhere define sin as *unbelief*? Yes. God
through Paul says that the opposite of *sin* is *righteousness*:

> And having been freed from *sin*, you became slaves of *righteous-
> ness*. (Rom 6:18 NASB)

> For when you were slaves of *sin*, you were free in regard to *righ-
> teousness*. (Rom 6:20 NASB)

Therefore, the opposite of *sin* is *righteousness*. But *righteousness* is "the
righteousness of *faith*."[21] Since righteousness is *the righteousness of faith*,
therefore *sin* is *unbelief—the unrighteousness of unbelief in Christ*.

Thus, Paul's revelation of Jesus Christ (Gal 1:12) moves *from* what
righteousness is—"the righteousness of faith" in Christ (Rom 4:13; 9:30;
10:6)—*to* sin, to define what sin is, now that God's righteousness has been
manifested (Rom 3:21–22). So, whatever is not of faith in Christ is now
revealed to be sin (3:21; see 14:23). The risen Christ taught Paul to no longer
think *from the law* to define sin. Yet this is what Western Christianity has
repeatedly done, by following the logic of both Moses and medieval Roman
Catholicism rather than the revelation of God's righteousness (1:17) given
to Paul the apostle to the nations. According to Paul's gospel, just as sin
is unrighteousness, sin is disobedience (to God). Because Adam's sin was
"disobedience" (Rom 5:12, 19), the opposite of sin is *obedience*. Because
obedience is "the obedience of faith," disobedience is the disobedience of
unfaith (unbelief). Israel sought righteousness by works and not by faith:

20. Murray, *Collected Writings*, 2:213; emphasis mine.
21. Rom 4:13; 10:6; Phil 3:9.

"Because they [Israel] sought it not by faith" (Rom 9:32 AV). And then, this "not by faith" he calls Israel's *disobedience*:

> But they have not all *obeyed* the gospel. For Isaiah says, "Lord, who has *believed* our report?" (Rom 10:16 NKJV)

To *believe* (*have faith*) is to *obey* the gospel (10:16). This is the truth of the gospel! So, for Israel to be "a disobedient . . . people" (10:21) is to say that they have not (all) obeyed the gospel (10:16), which is the same as saying they have not believed the gospel. Thus, disobedience is unbelief in the gospel, unbelief in Christ. "Christ" and "faith" go together so completely that Paul uses the terms "the word of faith" (Rom 10:8) and "the word of Christ" (10:17) interchangeably for *the gospel* (10:16). Paul never uses "obey" as obeying the law. We are not justified because of our faith but because of Christ's obedience unto death (5:9, 19). Faith (a gift) receives and trusts in Christ. When Paul speaks of "the obedience of faith" (1:5) he means the obedience that consists of faith and belongs to faith. Thus, he uses "faith" and "obedience" interchangeably in Romans:

Your *faith* is spoken of throughout the whole world. (Rom 1:8 AV)	For your *obedience* is known to all. (Rom 16:19 ESV)

Also, in the chart below, we find that Israel's trespass and disobedience is "unbelief." Therefore, Adam's trespass and disobedience is unbelief (sin). Adam *did not believe* God's word, which said, "You shall surely die" if he ate of the tree of the knowledge of good and evil.[22] Paul calls Adam's *unbelief* "the *trespass*" (παράπτωμα) and "disobedience" and "the sin."

Adam's sin is called:	Israel's unbelief in Christ is called:
The trespass (Rom 5:15,17, 20)	Their trespass (Rom 11:11, 12)
One man's disobedience (Rom 5:19)	Their disobedience (Rom 11:30 lit.)
"The Sin" (Rom 5:12, 20, 21; lit. trans.)	Their unbelief (Rom 11:20, 23)

In the above column on the right, Paul equates Israel's *trespass* (παράπτωμα, Rom 11:12) with their *unbelief* toward God's word, even Christ (11:20, 23). Therefore, we rightly deduce that Adam's *trespass* (παράπτώματι and παράπτωμα, in 5:15–17, 20) was his unbelief toward God's word. For if Adam had truly *believed* God's word, he would not have eaten of the

22. Since Adam's sin (Rom 5:12) was *disobedience* (5:19); sin's opposite is obedience, the obedience of faith in Christ (1:5; 10:16).

forbidden tree (Gen 2:17; 3:4, 6), for scriptural faith trusts God himself as the Source of all good; it really and always believes that God has only what is best for those whom he addresses. And such trust can only obey God as one's Lord and God. Thus, sin is unbelief in Christ. Not only Paul but the author of John's Gospel says the same thing, in John 16:9.

Unbelief in Christ Is the Essence of Sin and the Root of All Sins

To the question, "What is always my greatest enemy?" the answer of God in the gospel is: *unbelief in Christ.* Other definitions of sin fall short of the truth and glory of God. As we have seen, Christianity has too often defined sin as transgressing the law rather than defining sin in the light of *Christ*, as in John 16:9 and Rom 10:16–17. For Christ is God's righteousness *apart from law* (1 Cor 1:30; Rom 3:21). Paul includes the other aspects of sin in his letters, but they are still to be understood in the light of Christ[23] (2 Cor 4:4–6).

In 1 Cor 15:1–4, Paul says we are to hold fast to the gospel by faith and persevere in that faith. Disobedience, either in the form of doing the works of the law for justification or in the form of doing the deeds of the flesh, is disobedience to God. There is both a union (because faith is trust in Christ for righteousness) and a distinction (because Christ is my Lord, whom I am to obey) between *faith* and *obedience.* Legalism thinks that obedience is to the law (or, to Christ *and* the law). Libertarianism ignores the truth that faith involves obedience to the Lord Jesus Christ (Rom 6:12, 16–19). But obeying

---

23. For example, in Rom 6:19. Paul calls sin "lawlessness" (as does 1 John 3:4 lit.). Now that Christ has died and been raised to life, Paul defines sin as unbelief in Christ. We deduce this truth from the gospel: If *sin* is transgressing the law of Moses, then righteousness is keeping the law of Moses (Ten Commandments) and not "the righteousness of faith" as Paul declares it to be in Rom 4:13; 9:30; 10:6–10; Phil 3:9. Calling sin "lawlessness" is true, for one who is trusting *in Christ* has no other gods (in her heart) besides the one true God. Thus, faith in Christ alone spiritually fulfills the first commandment of the law, the first table of the law, as Luther understood (and *love* fulfills the law in terms of *the neighbor*, Rom 13:10); thus, whatever is done outside of faith (walking in the Spirit) in Christ is lawlessness (Rom 8:4). And the "lawlessness" of Rom 6:19 certainly includes acts which go against the (law's) commandments that Paul quotes in 13:9. But on the other hand, merely keeping the letter of the law does *not* fulfill the law, as we saw Paul teach in Rom 2. So, the disobedience of *unbelief* in Christ *is* lawlessness; unbelief is the root and cause of whatever form such lawlessness takes. "In Orthodox teaching, sin is not so much a violation of rules—although it is that, of course. Rather, it is always the violation of a personal relationship with God—being unfaithful to him and rebelling against him, turning away from him" (Payton Jr., *Light from the Christian East*, 119).

the Lord Jesus Christ is the norm for those in Christ, precisely because they have the Spirit of Christ. Trusting in Christ for justification is the basis for obeying him as Lord. Obeying the Lord Jesus Christ through faith in him for justification strengthens us in the inner man. Unbelief (which issues in all sin) weakens us. Yes. And faith is not a work; therefore, in faith there is no boasting (Rom 4:5; 3:27). So, "the obedience of faith" (Rom 1:5) has two sides. The obedience of faith is trust in Christ as my righteousness before God, but the faith that trusts in Christ for righteousness issues in obedience to Christ as my Lord. In other words, through *faith in the gospel* (which is the power of God), *I obey my Lord, who indwells me by his Spirit.*

The life of the person "in Christ" is to be one of continual *trust in Christ* for *righteousness* before God, and through this *faith*, obedience to *Christ* as *Lord*—to the Spirit who indwells us (see Rom 4:5; 8:9–13).

So, trust in Christ for justification without faith's other side—obedience to the Lord—is disobedience, which weakens the inner man and thus one's faith. Since he is our Lord, we are obligators to his Spirit and no longer to the flesh (Rom 6:11–23; 8:9–13; Gal 5:16). And, so long as we live in the flesh, due to the flesh, *neither faith in Christ (as righteousness) nor obedience to him (as Lord) are without (the flesh of) sin being present* (Rom 7:20, 21, 25; 8:3); thus, there is no perfection in this life. This confirms that justification is by *Christ's* faith, *Christ's* obedience to God unto death. We received faith (in him) by his resurrection power wrought in us at regeneration (1 John 5:1). So, those who say that "lordship salvation" is legalism are at best babes in Christ, for "Jesus Christ is Lord" (over sin and death and all our enemies) *is* the gospel (2 Cor 4:5). Christ cannot be divided into being Savior without being Lord. To submit to him as Savior is to submit to him as Lord, for it is as Lord that he saves. The battle at every moment is between unbelief (disobedience) and faith in Christ for justification before God, through which power a person obeys (and is to obey) Christ as Lord.

SEVEN

God Justifies the Ungodly through Faith Alone

(Rom 4)

PAUL BEGINS THE CHAPTER by saying:

> What then shall we say that Abraham our father has found according to the flesh? For if Abraham was justified by works, he has something of which to boast, but not before God. For what does the Scripture say? "Abraham believed God, and it was accounted to him for righteousness." (Rom 4:1–3 NKJV)

> But to the one not working [for righteousness], but believing in the one [God] *justifying* the ungodly, his faith is counted for *righteousness*. (Rom 4:5)

The word "justifying" (δικαιοῦντα) is a present participle. Therefore, Paul is saying that we continually need God to be justifying us as the ungodly.[1] That is why "believing" is also in the present tense in Rom 4:5. There have been teachers in the church who have implied that, once we come to faith, we are no longer "the ungodly" and thus would not need God to be justifying us. But Paul disagrees. He says, "For we, by the Spirit, out of faith, eagerly await the *hope* of righteousness" (Gal 5:5). The saving *righteousness of God, apart from law* (Rom 3:21) and without works (4:6) reveals that, if we were justified by works, we would indeed have something to boast about before God. For, according to the flesh, with its hidden proud heart, we desperately desire to be righteous in ourselves, apart from God. Therefore, Christ's cross is an offense to us—to our pride (Gal 5:11). Against

---

1. We remain, in one real sense, "the ungodly." See also my ch. 10.

the prevailing view of Judaism, that Abraham was justified by his faithfulness to God and thus ultimately by his works, Paul answers: He was not. The prevailing view among the Jews of Paul's day was that Abraham's faithfulness to God was reckoned as righteousness. What follows are some examples of what the Judaism and Jews of Paul's day believed, making the gospel of God all the more difficult for Jews to accept.

> Abraham was a great father of many nations, and no one was found like him in glory, who kept the law of the Most High, and entered into covenant with Him, and established the covenant in his flesh, and *was found faithful* in testing. (Sir 44:19–20)

> This is the tenth trial which Abraham was tried, *and he was found faithful*, controlled of spirit. . . [He begged for a place for burial in the land] because he was found faithful and he was recorded as a friend of the Lord in the heavenly tablets. (Jub. 19:8–9; see 23:9–10)

> Was not Abraham *found faithful in temptation* and it was reckoned to him as righteousness? (1 Macc 2:52)[2]

Instead of texts from Moses's law (beginning in Exod 20), Paul looked further back in Genesis, where it says that "Abraham believed the LORD, and it was counted to him for righteousness" (15:6). In Romans chapter 3, Paul said:

> Even *the righteousness from God*, through faith of Jesus Christ towards all *and upon*[3] all those that believe. (Rom 3:22 ILT)

This righteousness is imputed to, that is, it is "upon" all who believe in Christ, for we have *put on Christ* who is our righteousness (Gal 3:26–27; 1 Cor 1:30).

> Now to him who works, his wages are not counted as grace (a gift), but as what is owed to him. But to the one not working [for righteousness], but believing on the God justifying the ungodly, his faith is counted for righteousness. (Rom 4:4, 5)

> Just as David also speaks of the blessing upon the man to whom God reckons righteousness apart from works: (Rom 4:6 NASB)

---

2. Gathercole, "Does Faith Mean Faithfulness?," 32.

3. Regarding "and *upon* all" in Rom 3:22c AV, the Received Text aligns with Rom 4:9, that righteousness comes *upon* the circumcised and *upon* the uncircumcised (gentile), for we have been clothed with Christ (Gal 3:26–27).

Blessed are those whose lawless deeds are forgiven, and whose
sins are covered; Blessed is the man to whom the LORD shall not
impute sin. Does this blessedness [imputed righteousness] then
come *upon* the circumcised only, or [does it come] *upon* the
uncircumcised also? For we say that faith was accounted to him
for righteousness .(Rom 4:7–9 NKJV)

Paul's answer is, Righteousness was accounted to Abraham—not while
circumcised, but while he was still *un*circumcised. This word translated
as "reckoned"—λογίζομαι—is central to the apostolic gospel. Paul uses the
word in *every* verse from Rom 4:3 through 4:11 and then again in 4:22–24.
This is because *justification* as *imputed righteousness*[4] is central to the gospel
(Rom 1:16–17). Romans chapter 4 has one theme: God justifies the ungodly
through faith in Christ alone, without works. Paul quotes from Genesis
chapters 15 and 17, referring to the same promise, the one in which God
promised to make Abraham the father of many nations, even though it was
impossible (due to his age and especially his wife's age) for Abraham to be
the father of many nations (Gen 15:5; 17:4, 5). And Abraham *believed* God's
word regarding God making Abraham the father of many nations. Justification by faith alone, without works, Paul declares and proves from OT scripture in 4:1–8, which is the basis of the entire chapter. Because of this, we can,
for the sake of space, go from 4:3 to 4:17 and the meaning flows:

Abraham *believed God*, and it was counted to him as righteousness . . . (4:3)

As it is written, "I have made you a father of many nations,"
before him whom he *believed*, even God, who makes alive the
dead, and calls those things which are not [a *father* of many
nations] as existing; who against hope [he did not hope in his
or Sarah's flesh], believed in hope [God's promise], in order
that he might become the father of many nations, according to
that which was spoken, ["Look now toward heaven, and count
the stars, if you are able to number them": And God said unto
him] "So shall thy seed be." And being *not* weak in faith, he
did not consider his own body now dead, when he was about
a hundred years old, and [he *did not consider*] the deadness of
Sarah's womb; and at the promise of God ["I have made you a
father of many nations"] he *did not doubt* through *unbelief*, but
was strengthened in *faith*, giving glory to God, and being fully
persuaded that, what God had promised, he was also able to

4. Tragically, this truth is rarely preached or taught in American churches. The
White Horse Inn (radio program) proved this in the early 2000s, when they, on various
occasions, interviewed evangelical pastors at conferences.

perform. Therefore it [faith] was credited to him for righteousness. (Rom 4:3, 13–22 AV/AT)

In verse 17, we read, "I have made you a father of many nations," before him
whom Abraham believed, even God, who makes alive the dead (Abraham
and Sarah's bodies were dead with respect to having children) and calls those
things which are not (do not exist, for he was *not* yet a father of many nations) as *being*/existing. So God called Abraham a father before he was a
father. Similarly, to "us who believe in Him who raised up Jesus our Lord
from the dead" (4:24), God says, "I have made you the righteousness of God
in Christ" (2 Cor 5:21) before we are actually and bodily righteous (Gal 5:5;
Rom 8:30). But God *calls* the things not being righteous as *being righteous*,
before we are actually righteous, that is, glorified (4:19; 8:30; see Gal 5:5).

The Parallelism: "Did Not Consider" and "Did Not Doubt"

First, Abraham did not hope in (rely upon) his or Sarah's ("dead") bodies to
fulfill God's promise (v. 18). Then, in verse 19, we discover that, even though
Abraham knew the truth about his body and Sarah's, nevertheless, he did
not take that into consideration. Abraham "***did not consider***" his own body,
which was dead in terms of having the ability to have children, and he *did not
consider* the deadness of Sarah's womb, as if it would nullify God's promise to
him. For, to the extent that he considered himself, he would not be considering God's promise. Even so we, who have sin and know it, ***do not consider*** our
sins, because God in Christ *does not consider* them at all: "*Blessed is the man
to whom the* LORD *will by no means impute sin*" (4:8; see 4:25).

But now that God's righteousness has *come* through Christ's faith-obedience (Rom 3:21–22; Gal 3:22–25), this non-imputation of sin (4:8), this
imputed righteousness (4:6), is based upon an accomplished redemption
(Rom 3:24–26; 4:25). That is why, "now" (3:21), to "believe God" (4:3) for
us who believe on the risen Christ (4:24) means that we do *not* consider our
sins, for there are none in Christ, for God sees us only in Christ as our righteousness (1 Cor 1:30; 2 Cor 5:21). But someone may say, "Was not this 'not
considering our sin' part of faith in God before Christ came?" The answer is,
No, not in the way that it is now that Christ has come (see Gal 3:22–25; Heb
10:1–4, 11–18; Rom 4:24–25). Just as Abraham could not consider his own
body and Sarah's with respect to having a child and at the same time believe
God's promise that he would be a father of many nations (for fleshly thinking
destroys faith), even so we cannot consider or think on our unrighteousness

(as if it would condemn us) or our righteousness (as if it would justify us) in regards to our standing before God—whether or not we are justified—and, at the same time, be considering and believing God's word—that we are justified in Christ alone. Our righteousness is of the flesh of sin (Phil 3:3–9; Rom 8:3); therefore it is not God's righteousness in Christ. And our righteousness is opposed to God's righteousness in Christ. All considering, all thinking on our unrighteousness as undoing our justification, or our righteousness as being needed for justification (as if Christ has not already justified us), is already of the flesh (of sin), of unbelief in Christ.

Second, just as Abraham *"did not doubt"* the promise of God which said that he would be a father of many nations, even so we, in the new testament in Christ's blood (1 Cor 11:25), *do not doubt* the truth that we are justified in Christ (4:25), even as Abraham did not doubt God's promise to him and was justified by faith in God's promise. This means that when we sin, we are to repent of it and to not ever consider it again; for God is saying in his mind, his word on the issue is, "In Christ you are justified; *I* am not considering your sin; therefore, *you* are to not to consider it either." Therefore, thinking of your sin is the disobedience of unbelief in Christ. One cannot be considering, thinking on, both. Notice the parallelism between "did not doubt" (4:19) and "did not consider" (4:20). The fact that he considered not his own body enabled Abraham to *not doubt* the promise of God. For if he kept on considering his own possibilities, in terms of having a seed, he would not have believed God's word, which God alone could perform. Likewise, for us, *not considering* our unrighteousness nor our righteousness as having anything to do with our justification before God enables us to *not doubt* that we are *justified in Christ*. This not considering, says Paul, is what faith is all about. This is central to Paul's apostolic definition of *faith in Christ*. Therefore, Paul did not say, "He *considered* his own body now dead," for Paul preaches the word of the cross (1 Cor 1:18), in which we are weak in Christ (2 Cor 13:4). Only if Abraham was *not* "weak" and "ungodly" (Rom 5:6; 4:2–5) could he actually *think* on his bodily deadness and still believe God's promise. No, the entire chapter militates against this dream, for Abraham is the father and example (4:11–12; 23–24) of all who, now in the new covenant, believe on the God who, while we were *weak and helpless* (like Abraham and Sarah were helpless to have a child of promise on their own), died for the ungodly (the weak, Rom 5:6; Acts 20:28).

Deducing from Scripture

The Westminster Confession of Faith 1.6 says:

> The whole counsel of God concerning all things *necessary* for his own glory, man's salvation, *faith, and life,* is either expressly set down in Scripture, or by good and necessary consequence may be *deduced from Scripture.*[5]

So we have been deducing from Abraham's faith in God—to our faith in Christ crucified, who justified us through his historical redemption (Rom 3:24–26). Because we are justified in Christ, we have been delivered out of this present age, the place of our righteousness and unrighteousness. Thus, we have been *freed* to *not consider* our sin or our righteousness as justifying us before God. Our righteousness is utterly opposed to God's righteousness in Christ (Phil 3:3–9). Abraham *did not consider* his own body as a possibility or hope for becoming the father of many nations, because in Abraham and Sarah, apart from God—there was no hope of having a seed. And yet God called him a father ("I have made you") when he was not yet a father. Likewise, God calls us righteous, even while we are not yet righteous (glorified): "For through the Spirit, by faith, we eagerly wait for the hope of righteousness" (Gal 5:5 ESV). Considering or thinking on that which nullifies God's word, nullifies his word in one's mind by feeding the flesh, by feeding unbelief. So, we need to bring every thought captive to the obedience of Christ (2 Cor 10:5), wherein we only consider the truth of God in his word: We are justified in Christ. This is against Satan, who transforms himself into an angel of light[6] in order to tempt us to believe that God wants us thinking on our sins. God promised Abraham that he would have a seed apart from what was possible with Abraham and Sarah. Likewise, our righteousness is apart from and has nothing to do with our justified standing before God in Christ (Rom 5:1, 8–9; 1 Cor 1:30; 2 Cor 5:21). In Rom 4:17, the apostle, referring to Abraham, says that God is he who "makes alive the dead" in Abraham and Sarah, in giving them the child of promise despite their bodily deadness. And, in God giving Christ as Abraham's seed (Gal 3:16) in fulfillment of *the promise* (3:6–14), God makes alive the (spiritually) dead in raising up Jesus our Lord from the dead (Rom 4:24) and us with him (Rom 6:4; Eph 2:5). Jesus was raised to life because of the *justification* of us in his death (4:25), of which Paul speaks in Rom 4:5–8. God is the one who "calls those things not being" (many nations *did not yet exist* at the time when God promised this to Abraham) "as being." In like manner, we deduce that, now that Christ died and rose again, God calls (he pronounces) those *not being* righteous *as being* righteous (Rom 4:1–8, 17), and it is because of justification that Christ is life in us (8:10)—God gives

---

5. *Westminster Standards*, emphasis mine.

6. And of righteousness, see 2 Cor 11:14–15.

spiritual life to the spiritually dead (4:17; Col 2:13). Just as, in creation, God said, "Let there be light" and there was light, even so, God calls the ones not being righteous as being righteous, and they *are* righteous in his sight. For God is a creative God who merely speaks and it is done: God calls those who are not yet glorified as already glorified, for to be justified is nothing less than being *considered by God* as being already glorified (8:30; Gal 5:5). Since God considers us to be righteous ones in Christ, we are to do the same. So, now that the faith has come, and we are justified by Christ's faith (Gal 3:23–25), justification in Christ reveals both our unrighteousness and our righteousness to be of the flesh of sin (8:3).

- In Abraham and Sarah, there was no hope for Abraham to be a father. Nevertheless, he *believed God's promise* that he would *be a father of many nations.*
- In us (in the flesh) there is no hope in being justified before God (3:20). Nevertheless, we *believe God's word* that we *are justified in Christ.*

Christ has now died and been raised to be our righteousness and life (4:25; 1 Cor 1:30; Col 3:4). Therefore, Romans chapter 4 is *the gospel of God*'s definition and exposition of *faith*, now that, through the faith of Christ, "the faith has come" (Gal 3:25).

Before and after the Faith of Christ Came

But before the faith [of Christ] came, we were guarded under law, being shut up to the faith being about to be revealed. So that the law has become our supervisory-guardian up to [until] Christ, in order that out of faith we might be justified; but *the faith having now come*, we are no longer under a supervisory-guardian [the law]. For you are all sons of God through faith in Christ Jesus. (Gal 3:23–26)

And, because justification through redemption (Rom 3:24) has been accomplished, Paul, by saying, "to *us* who believe in the God who raised Jesus," distinguishes *us* who are in the new testament of the Spirit (2 Cor 3:6) from Abraham. For Abraham could not "believe in him who raised up Jesus our Lord from the dead" (4:24), because when Abraham lived, God had not yet raised Jesus from the dead, even though Abraham waited for that day. So there is a union and a distinction between Abraham's faith and our faith; the union being that both are trust in the one true God. In Romans, Paul refers to the gospel of God (1:1), which God had "promised beforehand through his prophets in the Holy Scriptures" (1:2). Therefore, Abraham heard and believed the gospel (Gal 3:8) but only in the form of a promise. So, the promise and *the confirmation* of that promise (Rom 15:8) are *two different things*, though there is a real continuity between them. Paul says:

> Christ *redeemed* us from the curse of the law . . . in order that, to the nations the blessing of Abraham [imputed righteousness] might be through Christ Jesus; in order that *we* might receive [now[7]] the promise of the Spirit through the faith. (Gal 3:13–14)

> Now it was not written for Abraham's sake alone, that it [righteousness] was imputed to him, but also for *us* [in Christ] who believe in the God who raised Jesus from the dead, who was delivered up [to death] on account of our transgressions, and was raised to life on account of our justification [by his death, 5:9]. (Rom 4:23–25)

In Genesis, Abraham at times doubts and disobeys God, though the basic tenor of his life was that of faith. But in Rom 4, Paul intentionally focuses only on the *faith* of Abraham, because Paul, in 4:16–21, is using him as *the* example of what it means to *believe God*, expecting the readers to deduce *from* Abraham's faith (his not considering his and Sarah's bodily deadness, and his not doubting God's promise to him to be a father) *to our faith in Christ (not considering our sin* as if it is still imputed to us, and *not doubting our justification in Christ*). Twice Paul says that Abraham was strong in faith (4:19–20). In faith I do not consider (4:19) myself or my strength; faith only considers and relies on God. So Paul is saying, "And not being weak in faith, he did not doubt at God's promise to him, so he did not have to bring in the issue of his body or Sarah's with or without their powers, depend on, or even think on them, for he knew (and trusted) that God would keep his word." Luther said:

> Would that I could commit some token sin simply for the sake of mocking the devil, so that he might understand that I acknowledge no sin and *am conscious of no sin*.[8]

Those are words of one who is trusting in the real Christ of the gospel. Paul says, "And being not weak in faith, he *did not consider* his own body"[9]

---

7. Now that justification through redemption ("redeemed" v. 13) has occurred; see Gal 4:1–7. "To be sure, Abraham was justified not by faith in Christ but by faith in God, but . . . the fact remains that Abraham was justified *by faith.*" *IB* 12:41.

8. Luther, *Letters of Spiritual Counsel*, 28, 86, emphasis mine.

9. When God promised Abraham that he would be the father of many nations, Abraham *did not consider* his body or Sarah's body but considered only God's promise (Rom 4:17–19). We know this, because (1) Both the Majority Text and the Received

with respect to God's promise to Abraham. And we rightly deduce that this applies to us who believe in the God who raised Jesus (4:24), in that through Christ, we are spiritually freed to *not have to consider our sin*, for the accuser would destroy us thereby.

"God, Who Gives Life to the Dead" (Rom 4:17)

First the natural (1 Cor 15:46)	Afterward the spiritual (15:46)
God gave (*this-age*) natural life to Abraham's and Sarah's "dead" bodies in order to have a child (of promise, Rom 4:16–19). God imputes righteousness before the faith (of Christ; justification) came (Gal 3:23–25).	God gave (*immortal*) life to the dead *Jesus* and to those in him (Rom 4:24), for the Spirit is life because of justification (4:25; 8:10) unto immortality (8:11). God imputes righteousness to us *after* the faith (of Christ; justification) came (Gal 3:23–25).

What Luther, following Paul, understood and proclaimed is that the imputation of righteousness in Christ is utterly and exceedingly *greater* than our sins—to the nullifying of their guilt and our condemnation. For God in Christ is both just and the justifier of him who is of the faith of Jesus (Rom 3:26). Therefore, any teaching on justification in Romans chapter 4

---

include the Greek οὐ (in English, "not"); thus, Abraham did not consider his body (or Sarah's) but only God's word. (2) In 4:19 there are *far more* (I counted sixty-seven) Greek MSS that include the Greek οὐ (not) than there are (I counted eleven) that do not have οὐ, in Swanson, *New Testament Greek Manuscripts*, 60. (3) The parallelism in 4:19–20 argues for the "not," for "did not consider" (4:19) is parallel to "did not doubt" (4:20), so that, just as Abraham *did not consider* his body or Sarah's, but only God's promise, so also, he *did not doubt* God's promise to him. (4) This reality aligns with what Paul says elsewhere. Of course believers are not to consider their sins or their righteousness, for God in Christ has justified them (4:1–8) through Christ's death (3:24–26; 4:25), which aligns with Paul's gospel, that "the ones being according to the Spirit mind the things of the Spirit (Rom 8:5)—the things unseen and eternal (2 Cor 4:18), the things freely given us of God (1 Cor 2:12), such as being justified freely by grace (Rom 3:24). For if Abraham "considered his body," the corollary would be that we are to consider our sins, contra God's declaration in Rom 4:4–8, 25. Then the NA text, which omits the Greek οὐ (not), would have us *considering, thinking upon* our sins, in contrast to the faith that believes God, who imputes righteousness without works (4:6) and does *not* put sin to our account (4:8) now that Christ has died and been raised to new life (3:21; 4:25). Thus, due to the overall scriptural witness elsewhere, we are convinced that the Majority Text and the Received Text represent the original MSS, not only in Rom 4:19 but also in Mark 9:29; Luke 1:28; Rom 3:22c; 1 Cor 2:4; 6:20; 11:24; 2 Cor 11:3 (and possibly in Gal 5:19). Conversely, we believe that the NA (UBS) text includes copies of the original Greek in Rom 8:1; 1 Cor 9:20; 12:13; Gal 5:1; Mark 9:44, 46; John 5:3b, 4; and most likely in John 1:18; Rom 6:11; Phil 1:14. Therefore, translators of the Scriptures and commentators on them should also consult the Majority and the Received Texts and not ignore them; see also Sturz, *Byzantine Text-Type*.

that does not include these things falls short of the apostolic gospel by not deducing from Paul's words what he means. Paul Althaus explains faith in the word of Christ as Luther rightly understood it:

> Faith is directed toward *the word* of promise and at first has nothing except this word. The word offers a reality which is hidden and cannot be seen. This reality therefore is not the object of "experience" but something that can be grasped only through faith in *the word*.[10]

> As *the word* is nothing less than God dealing with men in order to save them, so this same saving activity of God, and nothing else, is the content and object of faith.[11]

So, when God says, "There is then now no condemnation for those who are in Christ Jesus" (Rom 8:1), we are to believe him. This is what it means to believe in Christ, who reveals that God's righteousness in Christ is opposed to all human righteousness. The importance to God of *faith* is expressed by Luther in the following words:

> So, when the soul firmly trusts God's promises, it regards him as truthful and righteous. Nothing more excellent than this can be ascribed to God. The very highest worship of God is this that we ascribe to him truthfulness, righteousness, and whatever else should be ascribed to one who is trusted.[12]

Here Luther, following Paul in Rom 1:5, equates faith with obedience:

> This obedience, however, is not rendered by works, but by faith alone. On the other hand, what greater rebellion against God, what greater wickedness, what greater contempt of God is there than not believing his promise? For what is this but to make God a liar or to doubt that he is truthful?—that is, to ascribe truthfulness to one's self and set up himself as an idol in his heart? Then of what good are works done in such wickedness, even if they were the works of angels and apostles? Therefore, God has rightly included all things, not under anger or lust, but under unbelief, so that they who imagine that they are fulfilling the law by doing the works of . . . the law (the civil and human

---

10. Althaus, *Theology of Martin Luther*, 55, 56, emphasis mine.

11. Althaus, *Theology of Martin Luther*, 50, emphasis mine. The word of God is the gospel (1 Thess 2:9, 13; 1 Cor 15:1, 2).

12. *LW* 31:350, cited in Luther, *Martin Luther's Basic Theological Writings*, 602.

virtues) might not be saved. They are included under the sin of unbelief and must either seek mercy or be justly condemned.[13]

Gerhard Forde said:

> Justification by divine imputation creating faith is a complete break with the exodus from vice to virtue because the divine imputation is fully as opposed to human righteousness as it is to unrighteousness.[14]

> In the scriptures the divine imputation (cf. Rom. 4:1–7) is the creative reality which by the very act of imputation unmasks the reality and totality of sin *at the same time*.[15]

> By declaring us righteous unilaterally, unconditionally for Christ's sake, he at the same time unmasks sin and unfaith.[16]

So, the apostolic teaching of justification through faith in Christ alone reveals that the flesh utterly desires to see himself as a righteous person, for the flesh cannot bear to know that he is not righteous before God (nor his conscience, which he thinks is God's voice). For humans in flesh think that God will accept the works of the law for justification (Rom 2:14–15) which is not true (3:20). Humans in Adam think that they already have righteousness in them; that is, they think that their wisdom and righteousness are the true wisdom. But the crucified God reveals that all human wisdom is foolishness before God and all human righteousness is unrighteousness with God.[17] Faith itself does not justify; Christ's death justifies sinners, and faith receives Christ. Faith is that trust in Christ that does not trust in the life we live in the flesh for righteousness (Phil 3:3, 9). The righteousness of faith and the righteousness of the law are as opposed to each other as are life and death; they are of two entirely different ages, and the last Adam (Christ, our righteousness) is of the age to come.

13. LW 31:350–51, cited in Luther, *Martin Luther's Basic Theological Writings*, 602, 603.

14. Forde, "Christian Life," 2:408.

15. Forde, *Justification by Faith*, 30.

16. Forde, *Justification by Faith*, 31

17. 1 Cor 1:18–29; 3:18–21; Rom 1:18—3:20. Knowing this, we can better understand why the old man who desires to be righteous before God by his works in order to be justified and live needed to be put to *death* with Christ. To be justified in Christ (Gal 2:17) is to be justified from the sin (Rom 6:7 lit.)—already delivered out of this present evil age (Gal 1:4), and thereby freed from our unrighteousness and our righteousness, both of which are of the flesh (of sin, Phil 3:3, 9; Rom 8:3), for we are no longer in the flesh, but in the Spirit (Rom 8:9).

Excursus 3: Paul and James

The author of James rightly affirms that *genuine faith produces works (of obedience to God)*—that real faith in God is not an empty faith but obeys God in what he shows us to do (in the overall pattern of our lives). In *that* sense the Epistle of James agrees with Paul and the rest of the NT scriptures. However, it seems clear that when *the author of James* (AJ) heard something of Paul's "faith alone," he heard it as an error. AJ, a Jewish Christian, was undoubtedly influenced by the Judaism of his day, including the words about Abraham from Sirach, Jubilees and 1 Maccabees, as we have seen. The "faith without works" issue that the author is combatting in Jas 2:14–26 is a caricature of Paul the apostle's doctrine of faith. For, after teaching justification through faith in Christ alone in Rom 3:21 through 5:1, the apostle proceeds to reveal that the grace which justifies freed us from the (lordship of) sin, for we died with Christ to sin in Christ's new life; and, therefore, we are to live to God, presenting our bodily members to God as weapons of righteousness; and that *the fruit of justification from sin* is *sanctification* (Rom 6:6–22). Thus, sanctification is *the fruit of righteousness* (Phil 1:11), which is the righteousness of faith (Rom 4:13); so in Paul's gospel there is no justification without sanctification (fruit to God, Rom 6:22; 7:6—8:13). So, AJ is really attacking a caricature of Paul—his gospel and doctrine—and not the real Paul, and this partly explains the confusion that has continued since the Epistle of James was accepted into the canon of Scripture. AJ does not understand the real Paul, for, even though his defenders say that AJ is referring to a justification *before men* (they point to the words "you see" in 2:24), nevertheless, the weakness is that the author *nowhere* states that he means any other justification than that which prevails before God. So, he infers that Abraham actually was justified before God when, and only when, his faith was perfected by works, when he offered up Isaac (Gen 22). But that event occurred over a decade *after* he was *already accounted righteous* through faith alone (Gen 15:6). Therefore, since the words which James uses in 2:21–26 have historically been misused by many to nullify Paul's gospel, does not AJ fall under the curse of what Paul calls "another gospel"? For Paul, by revelation of Jesus Christ (Gal 1:12), says that even if Paul should come, or an angel from heaven, or anyone else, and preach a gospel other than the one that Paul first preached to the Galatians (defined in 2:16–21), "Let him be accursed" (Gal 1:8–9). Paul's point is as follows. Since, in Paul's apostolic gospel, *faith* means that *Christ alone* (his obedience unto death alone) justifies, then to add works to faith (in Christ) is to *nullify Christ's death* (Gal 2:21). Human works cannot justify because only Christ's death has justified us. Paul died with Christ to the law, and where *law* is, there is *transgression* (Rom 4:15). Thus, Paul (and all in Christ) live under law no longer (Gal 2:20); they are "no longer transgressors" of the law (Gal 2:18–19). Thus, when AJ calls his hearers "transgressors of the law" (2:9–11) he is building again the things (of the law), which Paul (through his death with Christ) destroyed (Gal 2:18). In summary, AJ has no clue of what Paul's gospel is really teaching, as Easton said:

> But Paul's real meaning could be grasped *only* by those who could *understand his argument* as an indivisible whole, a task quite *beyond the capacities of almost everyone in the apostolic and post-apostolic ages.*[18]

18. *IB* 12:8, emphasis mine. In place of the words "his argument," read "his gospel." Earlier (on p. 8), Easton refers to 2 Pet 3:16, because the author, referring to Paul, says, "As also in all his epistles, speaking in them of these things, *in which are some things hard to understand*" (2 Pet 3:16a, b NKJV), no doubt referring to Paul's *grace of Christ*, which the "unstable twist to their own destruction" (2 Pet 3:16c NKJV). This proves the important truth of Easton's words above, as does Torrance, *Doctrine of Grace*, quoted in my ch. 1. Therefore, Christians should not *presume* that if a NT author made it into the Bible, he *must* have understood Paul's gospel of God. Such reasoning is simply false. On the authorship and theology of the Epistle of James, see *IB* 12:4–9; 41–42; Wengert, *Reading the Bible*, 1–21; *LW* 35:396–97; and Schnelle, *History*, 388. James was written by a Spirit-indwelt man; in that sense it is inspired; on "inspired," see McDonald, *Formation*, 155–160. Would that conservatives would read these pages. There are good things in James, for example: 1:5–8; 17–20; 3:1, 9, 13–18; 4:1–8; 13–17; 5:7–9. But, as with all canonical writings, they should be read in light of the apostolic gospel.

EIGHT

God's "While We Were Yet Sinners" Love

(Rom 5)

> Therefore, having been *justified* by faith, we have peace with God through our Lord Jesus Christ (Rom 5:1 NASB), through whom also we have had the access into *this grace* [of having been justified] in which we *stand*, and we rejoice in the certain hope of the glory of God. (Rom 5:2)
>
> *Justification* is the abiding *status* of which we are to constantly avail ourselves before God. That is, we have constant access in Christ to the graciously bestowed *status* of *justified* men and women.[1]

IN THE FIFTH CHAPTER of Romans, Paul's manifesto crescendos into the unparalleled power of the gospel's epicenter, where we witness a God beyond anything we, in ourselves, could never imagine—the God who loved us while we were still sinners, even unbelievers.

Being *justified* means that we have a right standing with God, that God's wrath toward us is removed. So, Paul is saying that "this grace in which we stand" is our status and standing of *having been justified* (by his blood, v. 9), which we received by faith. Regarding the word *stand* in this phrase, Lloyd-Jones says, "The word implies stability and security. It means, therefore, continuance and establishment."[2] The justifying grace

1. Silversides, "Benefits Accompanying Justification."
2. Lloyd-Jones, *Exposition of Chapter Five*, 39.

in which we stand is stable and secure—it is an established reality. This standing in the grace of having been justified is central to the apostolic gospel. Our faith is in this (grace of) Christ (Gal 1:6) in which we stand. And we glory (with a holy boasting) in the certain hope of attaining the glory of God (5:2), precisely because we are *justified* (5:2; see 8:30), for justification is in what has been called the "golden chain" of Rom 8:29–30, which ends in glorification. Paul continues:

> And not only that, we glory in our tribulations, knowing that trials work patience, and patience works the proof [of our faith], and experiential proof works the certain hope that we will be glorified; and such hope does not disappoint, because God's love [for us] has been poured out in our hearts [to assure us] through the Holy Spirit who was given to us. (Rom 5:3–5)

In this passage one can imagine Paul's interlocutor questioning (and him answering):

> But do not the trials and difficulties of the Christian life detract from its blessedness? . . . Not at all! . . . This is because trouble produces steadfastness (endurance, perseverance, or patience). This, in turn, produces a tried and mature Christian character . . . People of such spiritual stability are inevitably those of increasing hope, for spirituality and hope are intimately related.[3]

God's Love, Shown in Christ's Death, Is a "While We Were Still Sinners" Love

In Rom 5:6–10 we find that God's *agape* for us is a "while we were yet sinners" *love*. We were helpless unbelievers in God's sight, unable to do anything toward saving ourselves, for we were under sin (3:19), wrath (1:18; 3:5), and judgment (3:19). Since Paul is terse, we will paraphrase the text, adding words that he uses, to help understand him.

> For indeed when we were still weak, in due time Christ died for the ungodly. For hardly for a righteous man will one die; yet perhaps for a good man someone would even dare to die. But God proves his own love toward us, in that while we were still sinners [unbelievers, under God's wrath, God came, not in wrath, but in love so that] Christ died for us [justified us]. How much more then, having now been justified [sins no longer put

---

3. Olyott, *Gospel as It Really Is*, 42.

to our "account" and us made God's righteousness in Christ, wherein God's wrath is no longer against us] by his blood, will we be saved from wrath [in the day of wrath] through him? For if, while we were enemies [to God, in his sight] we were reconciled to God through the death of his Son, much more, being [now] reconciled [to God, made God's friends through being justified], will we certainly be saved [from wrath] in his [resurrection, eschatological] life. (Rom 5:6–10)

Paul uses "weak" (without strength) as a word for "ungodly" in 5:6. For, to the extent one is weak, he is not like God, who is strength personified. Here "weakness" echoes the sinner's lack of God's glory (3:23), so there is nothing intrinsically good about (sin as) human weakness (lack of strength) or ungodliness (lack of God-likeness).

Paul acknowledges that human love, in certain humans and at certain times, can be incredibly self-denying, even to the point of laying down one's life for someone else. Yet even such a love cannot be compared to God's agape/love in Christ, for Christ died for God's enemies—sinners who have sinned against the holy God. In 5:8, God's "while we were sinners" love is demonstrated in an act (5:18) to the ungodly (5:6) and to law-transgressors (4:5–8). Thus, God's agape shown in Christ's death is *not* in accordance with "the righteousness of the law"—it is not some kind of restitution. So we, precisely as those being "in the law" (3:19), which only condemns (2 Cor 3:9) to death (3:7), *died*[4] with Christ out of the whole legal, condemned state and world system, so that now, in Christ's resurrection life, God calls the things not being (righteous in flesh) as being (righteous in Spirit[5])—in Christ's new, resurrection life (5:18; 6:4; 7:6; 8:1–2). We were enemies to God (5:10) and therefore under the wrath of God (5:9). And this "While you were still condemned sinners, I died for you and thereby justified you" love of God for "the called"[6] never changes. Once we are justified by faith (5:1), sin is not ever put to our account again. Since, while we were still sinners, we were loved, justified, and thus freed from wrath by God in Christ, how much more (now) shall we be saved from God's wrath in the day of wrath through Christ? (Rom 5:8–9). So, the obedience of faith means that we think and live in the truth that our sin is no longer held against us or considered by God. For justification, and the trusting in God for it, fundamentally determines

4. He endured wrath unto death/destruction.

5. As being righteous, first by imputation (4:5–8; 5:1), and on that basis (8:10), his true being is (only) according to the Holy Spirit (8:5).

6. What Paul means by "the called" in Rom 1:6 is further clarified in 1 Cor 1:23–28, where he says that "the called" are those who are "chosen" by God (for salvation in 1:21, 30).

how we live. For, trusting God here means we will not do works to attempt to undo our sins—to justify ourselves before God. Not only is there no way to make amends before God, but we are not to try. We are to stand firm in this freedom (Gal 5:1–5) and not return to the spiritual bondage unto death that comes by not believing that we are justified in him (Gal 5:1–5). God's agape/love for us is not an "I'll love you when you are justified" love. Nor is it an "I will love you when you are sanctified or holy" love. Nor is it an "I will love you when you are glorified" love. God will not love us more when we are glorified than he did when that (pre-creation) love was demonstrated toward us in Christ's death—when we were ungodly, sinners, and enemies in God's sight! Such good news completely transcends the rationalism and thinking of the flesh. And the proof of that unconditional love for the elect is that God will give them his very best: They will be conformed to Christ's image in glory (8:30). When I was unable (through bondage to sin) to trust in anything but my own righteousness before God, Christ died for me to enable me to believe in him by his Spirit (Gal 3:13–14), the Spirit of faith (2 Cor 4:13). This gospel contrasts with that of much of Christianity, in which there are conditions that first must be met before justification is ours. Paul continues:

> And not only so, but we also glory in God through our Lord Jesus Christ, through whom now we have received the reconciliation. (Rom 5:10–11)

We received the reconciliation when we were justified by faith (5:1). Outside of Christ, all humans are God's enemies—they are under his constant wrath (Rom 1:18—3:20; 4:15). But in Christ, God now always thinks of us as his reconciled friends and treats us as such, even when we are disciplined by him. Like justification, reconciliation here is objective and was accomplished by God, wholly outside of us. God was in Christ *reconciling* the world to himself, *not imputing their trespasses to them* (that is how they are reconciled), and has committed to us the word of reconciliation (2 Cor 5:19), says the apostle. So, just as "justified" (5:9) means that our sins are not put to our account but instead righteousness is (Rom 4:1–8), even so, "reconciled" means that God does not count our sins against us, so that we are no longer enemies in God's mind and sight but are now *reconciled to God—friends* in God's mind and sight. Reconciliation, in one sense, is justification with the resultant friendship included, with the result being peace with God (5:1)—no longer alienation. Reconciliation through Christ's death is the basis of his resurrection, in which Christ gives us "the mind of the Spirit" (8:6), in which our minds are reconciled to God, in contrast to the mind of the flesh which is enmity against God

(Rom 8:6–9). So here, in 5:6–10, Paul deduces that, if while we were still under God's wrath, God came, not in wrath but in Christ who died for us, so that we are now justified (not condemned), then how much more will God *not* condemn us on the day of judgment but instead save us from wrath in Christ's eschatological life? (Rom 8:1). When Paul (in v. 8) says that "God demonstrates his own ἀγάπη (agape, love) toward us" what does the word *agape* mean? Anders Nygren says it well:

> God does not love that which is already in itself worthy of love,
> but on the contrary, that which in itself has not worth acquires
> worth just by becoming the object of God's love.[7]

Sin defaced God's image; it made us unworthy. But while we were still sinners (those who cannot trust God), Christ died for us, thereby reconciling us to God. Nygren explains what a "while we were yet sinners" love means, correcting a popular notion of God's love. "When Christianity speaks of God's love for sinners, this is explained as meaning that what God really loves is not so much the sinner as what can be made of the sinner."[8] He continues, "When God seeks fellowship with sinners, it is not because he really desires fellowship with them, but because that is the only chance he has of transforming them into righteous men with whom he can really desire fellowship."[9]

But such a "Christianity" is a denial of the *unconditional* character of God's love for sinners, as sinners and while sinners (unbelievers), as was demonstrated in Christ's death (Rom 5:8). As we return to Nygren (below), I suggest that when he uses the phrase "fellowship with God" it would be more in line with the gospel to think of this phrase as meaning "fellowship *through reconciliation* with God" (5:10). Referring to what he meant by Christianity's lack of the unconditional character of God's love for sinners, Nygren continues, "Love is always an end in itself, and the moment it is degraded into a means to some other end it ceases to be love . . . To live in fellowship with God certainly means for man to be recreated in the image of God; man's sanctification is the fruit of his fellowship with God. But the fellowship does not therefore cease to be an end in itself, nor does God's love cease to be spontaneous and unmotivated."[10] By "unmotivated" Nygren means what Paul says in Romans: Those who in themselves cannot trust God (8:7–8; see Heb 11:6) are "justified without a cause [in them] by

7. Nygren, *Agape and Eros*, 78.
8. Nygren, *Essence of Christianity*, 110–11.
9. Nygren, *Essence of Christianity*, 111.
10. Nygren, *Essence of Christianity*, 111–12.

God's grace through the redemption which is in Christ" (Rom 3:24 lit.). And because God loved his own unconditionally, without them fulfilling any conditions, in his death for us, how much more are we safe and secure in that love *now* through being justified in Christ? Throughout the eternal life in glory, we will always be cognizant of the truth that God's love for us was and is a "while we were yet sinners" love. The unregenerate man does not want fellowship with God; indeed, he hates God.[11] But Christ died for us while unregenerate, while we were enemies in God's sight, and the fruit of his death is eternal life in fellowship with God.

In His Life

Regarding the correct translation of the last four Greek words in 5:10 (εν τῇ ζωῇ αὐτοῦ), meaning "in the life of him," we are convinced that it should be translated as "in his life," and not "by his life."[12] This is because, though the Greek word εν can be translated as "in" or "by," the context determines which is the better translation. And in Paul's gospel as found in Paul's letters, the phrase "in Christ" means *in union with* (the having been crucified and now risen) *Christ*, that is, "in his (resurrection) life." There is further contextual support, for in the very next sentence Paul says, "But also, [we are] boasting *in* [εν] God, through whom we have now received the reconciliation." And in 5:13, he says, "For until the law, sin was *in* [εν] the world" (not "by" the world). And in the next chapter, Paul says, "So we also should walk *in* (εν) newness of life" (Rom 6:4).

Adam and Christ

Neither "the first man Adam"—nor "the last Adam"—had a human father (Luke 3:37–38; 1:26–38; 1 Cor 15:45). On the original creation of man, Ware says:

> the notion of man as created in God's image can be interpreted in a dynamic rather than a static sense. It need not mean that man was endowed from the outset with a fully realized perfection, with the highest possible holiness and knowledge, but

---

11. Rom 8:7–8. See Nygren, *Essence of Christianity*, 120–22; and *Commentary on Romans*, 339–41. Out of love for us, God will do what is best for us—he will conform us to the image of the Lord Christ (Rom 8:28–30), who is holy.

12. See Lloyd-Jones, *Exposition of Chapter Five*, 150–53, 174–75, where he enabled me to see this truth.

simply that he was given the *opportunity to grow* into full fellowship with God.[13]

God warned Adam regarding the tree of the knowledge of good and evil,
saying, "In the day you eat of it, dying [spiritually] you shall surely die"
(Gen 2:17b). And they ate, and they immediately died in their spirits,
which death eventually brought them to death—to die in their bodies,
upon which death was complete and the victor. We begin with the following summary of Rom 5:12–21:

Just as *we sinned* in Adam, and were thereby condemned to *death*
in him, even so, *we* (our old man in him, condemned to *death*) *died with
Christ* and were thereby *justified* unto *life* in him.

We acknowledge the genuine achievements of science and acknowledge that it can be difficult in light of such to accept all of Holy Scripture
on the issue of Adam. By grace, *God's Spirit* witnesses with the spirit of all
those who are in Christ, that Christ is real and that such belong to him,
even (with) those believers who doubt the existence of a historical Adam.
But by God's grace, we believe what God says through Paul on the historic-
ity and implications of Adam[14] and Christ, for this is central to the gospel
of God as set forth in Romans (and again in 1 Cor 15). Indeed, everything
Paul says from Rom 1:1 until Rom 5:21 leads up to the truth of *Adam and
Christ* in Rom 5:12–21, and all that follows (5:12–21) is based upon the
truth of Adam and Christ,[15] such as being justified from *the sin* (6:7) of

13. Ware, *Orthodox Way*, 66.

14. On Gen chs. 1–3, see *COT* 1:27–115; see also Berghoef and DeKoster, *Great
Divide*; Bavinck, *Reformed Dogmatics*, 2:563–88; Hodge, *Romans*, 142–91; Versteeg,
Adam in the New Testament; Mortenson, *Searching for Adam*; Batten, *Creation Answers*;
White, *What about Origins?*; and Varvel, *Genesis Impact*. The days in Gen 1 are defined
by each "evening and morning" (2:1–3) and are further clarified as literal days in Exod
20:8–11. The creation and the Scriptures are not equal revelations from God; they are
different kinds of revelations, creation being that (revelation) through which humans
are without excuse before God (Rom 1:18–32). The Scriptures reveal God as creator of
all things, seen and unseen, and also humans as created in his image, the entrance of sin
into the world, the setting apart of Israel through whom the Messiah would come, and
the redemption from sin and death in the Christ who died and rose to new life, with the
hope of immortality in him alone. The concept of the age of the universe being many
billions of years old is problematic, because the One who was raised from the dead will
judge the living and the dead, ushering in the *salvation* (see Rom 13:11) of the new
creation. Thus, the idea of billions of years does not really fit on *either* side of the Christ
event. Human-caused climate change is real, regardless of what one believes about the
age of the earth. But the bottom line of the gospel boils down to this reality: *The ultimate truth* is the *objective* nature of *Christ's death* and *bodily resurrection* (resulting in
the reality of Christ in those who are his, Rom 8:9–10). Thus, "If anyone . . . seems to be
wise in this age, let him become a fool that he may become wise" (1 Cor 3:18 NKJV).

15. I came to understand this through Nygren, *Commentary on Romans*, 208–9;

Adam through Christ's *one righteous act* (5:18). The truth of imputation is explicitly taught in Romans chapter 4 and implicitly here in chapter 5. In Paul's gospel, humans are either "in the flesh" (what Paul calls "in Adam" as their representative head) or they are "in Christ" as their representative head; and they are those who are "in the Spirit," for the Spirit is the Spirit of Christ (8:9, 10). Earlier, Paul said that Christ died for us. But Paul does not leave it there. Baugh, referring to Paul's words "on our behalf" (in 5:8), explains an important point:

> The point of 5:12–21 is to explain how it is that Christ *could* die on our behalf (ὑπὲρ ἡμῶν). More pointedly, how could his mediation be effective for those who have *no active involvement* at the time when the intervention is accomplished, yet the intervention forms the *sufficient ground* of the tremendous results obtained?[16]

So, Paul immediately moves to explain *how it can be* that one man's—Christ's—death *can* justify a *multitude* of sinners. Thus, one cannot rip out 5:12–21 and remain with the gospel of God (Rom 1:1). Paul begins his transition in 5:12 and then immediately inserts a parenthetical section from 5:13–17 to explain his point in 5:12. And then he finally completes his thought with 5:18–19.

It is tragic that translators of the NT from Greek do not always include the definite articles, for they are important. In Paul's case, they show that "the sin" and "the death" are destructive powers that came into the world through Adam's one sin. Commenting on Rom 5:12, theologian Charles Hodge writes:

> *Sin entered into the world.* It is hardly necessary to remark, that χοσμος does not here mean the universe. Sin existed before the fall of Adam. It can only mean the world of mankind. Sin *entered* the world; it invaded the race.[17]

> It is clear, from Gen. ii. 17, iii. 19, that had Adam never sinned, he would never have died; but it does not follow that he would never have been changed. Paul says of believers, "we shall not all die, but we shall all be changed," 1 Cor. xv. 51.[18]

---

similarly, Lloyd-Jones, *Exposition of Chapter Five*, 176–77.

16. Baugh, "New Perspective, Mediation," 158.

17. Hodge, *Romans*, 228.

18. Hodge, *Romans*, 229–30. That is important (and in line with Rom 5:12); see also *LW* 1:153–54.

His purpose is to teach the connection between Adam's sin and the death of all men: "It was *by one man* that men became sinners, and hence all men die." As all were involved in his sin, all are involved in his death.[19]

But the only possible way in which all men can be said to have sinned in Adam, is putatively. His act, for some good and proper reason, was regarded as their act . . . when Adam incurred the sentence of death for himself, he incurred it also for us.[20]

Adam is the cause of death coming on all, independently of any transgressions of their own; as Christ is the author of justification without our own works.[21]

Although, therefore, it is true that our *nature was corrupted* in Adam, and has been transmitted to us in a depraved state, yet that hereditary corruption is *not* here represented as the ground of our condemnation, any more than the holiness which believers derive from Christ is the ground of their justification.[22]

The sin of Adam, and not our personal sin, was the original ground of condemnation; as the righteousness of Christ, and not our personal righteousness, is the ground of our justification.[23]

By nature (as a natural man), I think of my relationship with God as though he deals with me as an individual. But according to Paul, Adam was the representative head of all "in Adam" (1 Cor 15:22). Because there is no unrighteousness with God (Rom 9:14), God was just in making Adam the representative head of the race, so that if he obeyed God's commandment and passed the period of probation, all his seed would have had life in him. On the other hand, if he disobeyed, all in him would (and did) incur the guilt (condemnation) of that sin, which resulted in spiritual unto bodily *death*. God was also righteous in setting forth Christ to bear the sins of those whom he represented as head (Rom 3:24–26), and having taken upon himself Adam's sin, which condemned them all—and their many sins which also condemned them (5:16) unto death, God imputes his righteousness to those in Christ (2 Cor 5:21). As background to this, the Westminster Confession of Faith says:

19. Hodge, *Romans*, 231.
20. Hodge, *Romans*, 236–37.
21. Hodge, *Romans*, 253. On 5:12–21, see also Murray, *Romans*, 1:178–210.
22. Hodge, *Romans*, 235, emphasis mine.
23. Hodge, *Romans*, 286.

> The distance between God and the creature is so great, that although reasonable creatures do owe obedience unto him as their creator, yet they could never have any fruition of him as their blessedness and reward, but by some voluntary condescension on God's part, which he hath been pleased to express by way of covenant.[24]

Humans could *never* merit life from God. Yet, while God's covenant with Adam (Hos 6:7) was not one of grace (for there was yet no sin in the world), it was a covenant that offered life over death based upon Adam's obedience to one simple commandment through trust in God's word to him. But as soon as the serpent began to speak, the woman acted independent of her head (Adam, 1 Cor 11:3), taking it upon herself to deal with the serpent's words independently of the man. Yet, because Adam was not only the woman's head but also the covenant head of humankind, Adam's sin was far *greater* than that of the woman. As soon as the serpent contradicted God's word (Gen 3:1), Adam, who was with her (3:6), should have destroyed the serpent (see Gen 1:26–28; 2:15), thereby defeating Satan by obeying his creator. Of course, he did not, but the last Adam, through his obedience, did destroy and will destroy Satan (Rom 16:20; Col 2:13–15; Heb 2:14, 15; 1 Cor 15:24). So, what the WCF means is that God could have created man, and man would have simply owed God perpetual obedience because God was his creator and Lord, and any disobedience would have meant immediate death. But instead God, in goodness, offered to man a way to life by means of covenant. Michael Brown uses John Owen's understanding to express this important truth, saying:

> For Owen, once God established this covenant through his divine condescension, Adam had a legal claim and right to its reward upon the fulfillment of its conditions. This claim was not the result of an intrinsic merit, but a covenantally determined merit.[25]

We could not agree more. With Romans chapter 3 in mind, Michael Horton wrote:

24. WCF 7.1. Although we agree with the WCF on this point, yet, with John Owen and S. Petto, we deny that the old and new covenants are "two administrations of the same covenant," for they are two distinct covenants: old and new.

The Abrahamic covenant overlapped the old and new—that would be a better way to say it (see Gal 3:19–26).

25. Brown, "John Owen on Republication," 155. This is important, for many theologians, from Barth to the present have denied this truth, because they read their understanding of (New Testament) *grace* back *into* Genesis—God with Adam, and reason from (supposed) intrinsic merit, against (the truth of) the covenant of life with Adam.

How can Gentiles be "under the law" and therefore "under sin" and its condemnation apart from some covenantal arrangement? How can they be "held accountable to God" (3:19)—indeed, "without excuse" (1:20)—*unless they were in fact bound to God in a covenant relationship?*[26]

And Shaw said:

We are, therefore, warranted to call the transaction between God and Adam a *covenant*. We may adopt, for the use of this term, the language of Scripture. In Hosea 6:7 (margin) we read, "They, like Adam, have transgressed the covenant." This necessarily implies that a covenant was made with Adam and that he violated it.[27]

And they were in such a relationship, for that is the only conclusion one can come to from what the apostle teaches in Rom 5:12–21. The only way Paul's words in 5:12–21 make sense is if God made Adam a representative head of all in him (Christ excepted) and that all remain in that covenant, which is now broken, and are therefore under *condemnation unto death*. And many scholars have pointed out that the translation of Hos 6:7 which reads, "like Adam" makes sense, because "covenant" means there was a stipulation and a corresponding curse, but the translation "like men" does not, and that the language of Gen 2 and 3 is covenantal language, including stipulations and consequences for breaking the covenant. Just as Adam did not keep the covenant (Hos 6:7), even so the last Adam *did* keep the covenant—(only) the covenant that God the Father covenanted with him before the world began[28] (Luke 22:29 lit.). Hodge rightly says:

It is almost universally conceded that this 12th verse contains the first member of a comparison which, in vs. 18, 19, is resumed and carried out. But in those verses, it is distinctly taught that "judgment came on all men on account of the offense of one man." This then is Paul's own interpretation of what he means when he said "all sinned."[29]

After Rom 5:12, Paul uses a parenthetical paragraph in 5:13–17. Then, in verse 18 he returns to his main point (through 5:21). What follows is my

26. Horton, *Pilgrim Theology*, 136–37, emphasis mine.

27. Shaw, *Exposition of the Westminster Confession*, 125. Similar to Hos 6:7 is Job 31:33.

28. "As the Father covenanted to me a kingdom, so I covenant to you a kingdom" (Luke 22:29; see Col 1:13).

29. Hodge, *Romans*, 238.

paraphrase of Paul's parentheses in 5:13–14, which is within Paul larger parentheses of 5:13–17.

> (For, until the law was given, sin was in the world, but sin is not imputed where there is no law—[for there was *no law* in covenant form, as a covenant from God was with Adam, and then later, with Israel] over those who lived from Adam to Moses, i.e., the Law of Moses, which was a covenant [Deut 4:13; 9:11; see Rom 2:12]; therefore, the sins of those who lived from Adam to Moses were not imputed to them; that is, those sins are not why they died. But nevertheless, the Death reigned from Adam until Moses, even over those who had not sinned after the [God-given-covenant-] likeness of Adam's transgression, who is a type of the one coming, who is Christ.) (5:13–14)

The apostle is not denying that death continues to reign over all humans also after the law of Moses was given, until the end of the age, because of Adam's one sin. He is saying that sin is not imputed where there is no law (5:13b), as there was with Adam, who had the law that said, "Of every tree of the garden thou may freely eat; But of the tree of the knowledge of good and evil *you shall not eat*, for in the day that you eat of it *you shall surely die*" (Gen 2:16b, 17 NKJV). Thus, where there is and was this law, sin *was imputed* to *Adam* and to *all whom he represented*—all in Adam, unto death (1 Cor 15:22). After the parentheses of 5:13–17, Paul completes what he began in 5:12. In 5:18–19 he says that, just as Adam's disobedience *condemned* all in him, even so Christ's obedience *justified* all in him. So, here is a clarifying summary of Rom 5:12–21, without the parentheses of 5:13–17:

> Wherefore, *as by one man* the Sin entered the world, and the Death entered through the Sin, because all sinned [in one man] . . . *even so, through one man,* [Christ, by his obedience unto death] Righteousness entered the world, and through righteousness, Eternal Life entered, inasmuch as all died with Christ, that is, all those receiving the grace. (5:12, 17–21; through his death, see Gal 3:13–14)

In 5:12–21, there is a consequential chain of events: the consequences of the one *sin* are *condemnation* resulting in *death*: the *sin*—the judgment concerning it was *condemnation* (the verdict was "guilty")—the penalty being *death*.

What follows is the scriptural proof:

> For the judgment came by one *trespass to condemnation* (16b)

... as through one *trespass* [the judgment came] to all men *to condemnation*. (18a)

Then, in 5:21, Paul summarizes his argument, and we will insert his previous words to clarify the consequential chain:

In order that, as the Sin ["by one trespass to *condemnation*," v. 16] reigned in the *Death*, even so might the Grace [of Christ—his death[30]] reign through *righteousness* [*justification*] unto *eternal Life*, through Jesus Christ our Lord.

Therefore, Rom 5:16–18 can be summarized as follows:

The judgment on Adam [for his sin, and those in him] issued in [the verdict of] condemnation, which resulted in the sentence of *death* [spiritual unto bodily death] to Adam and to all in him.

The judgment—God's condemnation of the one Sin in Christ's death—issued in the verdict of justification [an acquitted and a righteous status], which resulted in *eternal life* for Christ, and for all in him.

But the free gift [in Christ] is not as the offense [in Adam]; for if through the offense of one, the many died [in Adam], much more the grace of God and the gift [of righteousness, v. 17] by grace, which is by the one man, Jesus Christ, has abounded unto many. And the gift [of righteousness, v. 17] is not like that which came through the one who sinned. For on the one hand, the judgment arose from *one* offense which resulted in condemnation, but on the other hand, the free gift [of righteousness, v. 17] was from *many offenses* [not only Adam's offense, which condemned all in him, but also our offenses, which only increased our guilt, storing up more wrath], resulting in justification. (Rom 5:13–16)

Hodge says:

For if by the offense of one many die, *much more* by the righteousness of one shall many live, ver. 15 . . . the benefits of the one dispensation far exceed the evils of the other.[31]

30. In 5:15, *the trespass* of Adam is contrasted with *the grace* (obedience unto death) of Christ; compare Christ's one just act (of deliverance for the enslaved, 5:18; see 6:20–22) and "the obedience of one" (5:19); compare also Gal 2:21.

31. Hodge, *Romans*, 224, emphasis his.

That is, the benefits of Christ, justification unto *eternal life*, which is *immortality*, far outweigh the evils of condemnation unto *death* (mortality, see 5:21).

> For if by the offense of the one man, death reigned through the one [man], by much more those receiving the abundance of the grace and of the gift of righteousness will reign in life through the one, Jesus Christ. (Rom 5:17)

"Life" in 5:17 is the resurrection life in Christ Jesus, wherein there is no condemnation (Rom 8:1–2). Although, on one hand, Christ was raised to life by God because of our justification by Christ's death (Rom 4:25 lit.; 8:10; 1 Cor 15:17), on the other, Paul never says that life belongs to justification, for "justification belongs to *life*" (5:18 AT). That is, justification is found and had only in the risen *Christ*—in his eschatological, resurrection *life* (5:10). For Paul, "in Christ" or "in him" always means in union with Christ who died for us, in his resurrection life, which includes the justifying value, worth, and application of his death for the justification (Rom 5:9, 18) of God's elect (8:33–34).

> So then, as through one trespass [the judgment came] to all men [in Adam] to condemnation, even so, through *one righteous act* [the judgment came] to all men [in Christ] resulting in justification which belongs to [resurrection] Life. (Rom 5:18)

Note that the "one righteous act" is an act of justice, of deliverance, as the psalmist says, "*Deliver* me in thy *righteousness* . . . and *save* me" (Ps 71:1 AV; see Ps 31:1 and 71:15). Again, the phrase "justification of life" means the justification that belongs to Christ's life, his resurrection life. In Christ's life there is no condemnation, only justification (Rom 8:1–2). Many Bible translations muddle this verse by neglecting to use the literal translation of the Greek. It is literally "justification of life," that is, justification belonging to life (eternal). On the words "all men" in 5:18, Strimple says:

> We must therefore see that Paul's interest in this passage is not in the question of how many will be saved, nor even, at this point, to emphasize again the clear need for faith in Christ; but his interest now is to focus upon the analogy between God's modus operandi in the two covenant heads, Adam, and Christ. Just as the disobedience of the one man, Adam, resulted in condemnation and death for all those in covenantal union with him, so also the obedience of the one man, Jesus Christ, results in justification and life for all those in covenantal union with Him.[32]

32. Strimple, "Was Adam Historical?"

Paul, in 5:17, does say that it is those who *receive* the abundance of grace who will reign in life (eternal) through Jesus Christ.

> For as by one man's disobedience many were made sinners, so, by the obedience of one, shall many be made righteous ones. (5:19)

> The word translated here as "made" . . . means "to set down in the rank of," or "to place in the category of," or "to appoint to a particular class."[33]

> As on account of the disobedience of one we are treated as *sinners*, so on account of the obedience of one we are treated as *righteous*.[34]

What kind of sinners? *Condemned* sinners—see 5:16. And the apostle says that Christ's obedience was his bearing our sin unto death (5:6, 8), because he equates Christ's "one righteous act" (5:18) with "the obedience of one" (5:19). Both 5:18 and 5:19 refer to Christ's death on the cross. This does not deny that only a spotless, sinless "lamb" could justly have our sins imputed to him, to take them away. Just as we were legally constituted sinners, so we are, by the obedience of Christ, now constituted righteous, put in the class of righteous persons (5:19). So, Lloyd-Jones says:

> "Ah," says someone, "but what if you sin tomorrow?" I reply that I am still a righteous person. The fact that I may sin tomorrow does not mean that my standing before God is changed and that I go back and am "in Adam" once more, as I was before. You cannot go back and fore like that as to your position—such a suggestion is monstrous. We are either "in Adam" or "in Christ."[35]

At the same time, this does not mean that one can live according to the flesh as the main direction of his life and still "live" (see Rom 8:12–13 and Gal 6:7–8). For mortification (and repentance when needed) through faith in Christ define the life of faith in Christ.

The condemnation through one man's sin means that all humans are *condemned* in Adam alone, before, and apart from their entire life in the flesh—what they do or do not do. Conversely, believers are *justified* in Christ through his one righteous act, in which he bore the condemnation for us having sinned in Adam and all our sins—completely apart from our entire life in the flesh, what we have done or not done. In other words:

---

33. Lloyd-Jones, *Exposition of Chapter Five*, 271.

34. Hodge, *Romans*, 232, emphasis mine.

35. Lloyd-Jones, *Exposition of Chapter Five*, 277–78.

Just as we were condemned to death by one act outside ourselves, so also, we were justified to life by one act outside ourselves.

We were condemned in Adam before we committed even one sin; therefore, our own sins are not what really and first condemned us. This knowledge actually frees us all the more to no longer focus on ourselves but instead on God in Christ. The sins humans commit only add to their already existing condemnation (storing up wrath for the day of wrath, 2:5), from which Christ delivered those in him (5:16). And yet, throughout history, most preaching has said that humans are condemned by their own individual sins. God created Adam with the potential for immortality. Adam, as federal head of humanity, transgressed the God-given covenant of life. It has been called "the covenant of life" because life was what was offered to Adam if he did not disobey the terms of the covenant (Gen 2:16 17; see 3:22). But all sinned in Adam unto death (Rom 5:12–19); his one trespass made it impossible for anyone in him to attain life based on their obedience or works (5:12–21; 11:6). Humans who are in Adam remain under that covenant, that law in which *the one trespass was imputed to all in him* unto *death*. Therefore, all in Adam are under the curse of the broken covenant—the law of works (Rom 3:27; 11:6) and of death (8:2). Thus, humans are under the curse of the law (Gal 3:10), that is, under the law (Rom 6:14; 7:1), the reign of sin and of death; and the only way of deliverance is Christ himself (Rom 3:9—8:39; 1 Cor 15:22–45). If the righteousness that justifies sinners is by grace, it is *no longer* on the basis of works (Rom 11:6 NASB), which shows that it was at one time on the basis of works, i.e., with Adam before the fall. If humans in Adam (1 Cor 15:22) were not under a covenant that Paul called "the law of works" in 3:27, then how could Paul say that now, in Christ, "it is *no longer* on the basis of works"? The natural man (the flesh) believes that righteousness and life are by the law (of works) because Adam was created upright (Eccl 7:29); Adam knew no other reality than that of obtaining life by *his* obedience, as Owen taught.[36] Therefore it is true that "the things freely given us by God" in Christ had never entered into the heart of any human until God revealed them in Christ (1 Cor 1:22–24; 2:7–9, 12). All through the Romans letter, by the words "will live" and "life," Paul is referring to eternal life (see Rom 5:21 and 6:23). Thus, from Gen 3:22

---

36. "For before [sin entered the world, by which] our understandings were darkened, and our reason debased by the fall, there were no such things [as justification by grace] revealed or proposed to us; yea, the supposition of them is inconsistent with, and contradictory to, that whole state and condition [of Adam before sin entered the world] wherein we were to live to God; seeing they all [Christ and grace in him] suppose the entrance of sin . . . For it [our reason] has no faculty or power but what it has derived from that [pre-fall] state" (Owen, *Doctrine of Justification*, 53; brackets mine).

we can deduce that, had Adam eaten of the tree of life, he would not have died, which proves that his obedience—during a period of probation—had to first be completed before he would have been granted the right to take of the tree of life and live forever (3:22).[37]

> And the law came in, that the offense might abound; and where the *Sin* abounded, the Grace super-abounded, that, as the *Sin* reigned in the Death, the *Grace* [Christ's death] might also *reign* through Righteousness for the purpose of Eternal Life through Jesus Christ our Lord (Rom 5:21).

God did not say to Jesus, "Of the tree of the knowledge of good and evil, thou shall not eat of it," nor did he say to him, "You shall keep the Ten Commandments, and after that, die." "But now, apart from law, God's (saving) righteousness is manifested, even the righteousness from God through Christ's faith, for all who believe" (Rom 3:21 AT). Yes, the Messiah fulfilled the covenant of life, but it was not by his keeping Moses's law, which was appointed, commanded, and ordered by many angels in the hand of Moses the mediator, to Israel (Rom 9:4); for in contrast to *many* angels, who needed Moses as a mediator to give the law to Israel, *God is one*, needing no mediator (Gal 3:19–20), for *God* was in Christ reconciling (those from among the nations of) the world to himself, not counting their sins against them, when he was made sin on the cross, that we might be made the righteousness of God in him (2 Cor 5:19, 21). For none of the old covenant laws said, "He shall *do the law* for others, and thereby justify the wicked." Rather, in the law, God says, "I will *not* justify the wicked" (Exod 23:7c AV). But Christ's obedience unto death *does justify* the ungodly. The writer

---

37. Many theologians, including Luther, have believed this; had he obeyed, those in Adam would have lived forever. How this would have worked we do not know. Enoch was taken to God without dying; so was Elijah. But, had Adam obeyed God, all his children would have been justified unto life. Perhaps, as those children took dominion and multiplied, God could have had a time in each of their lives when they would have been taken (without dying) to be with God, as was Enoch (and as believers who are alive when Christ returns will not die but be changed); but however long Adam's justified descendants lived (in a body not yet immortal), we deduce that they would have eventually been granted glorified bodies in a glorified creation. But God ordained that Adam would sin, even though it was entirely Adam's fault, just as God ordained that Christ would die, even though it was the fault of the wicked men who did it. The covenant with Adam involved a commandment for life (Rom 7:10), and it involved an obedience of faith to keep it, not an obedience or righteousness of works derived from unbelief, as it is now, since sin entered. Adam did not obey God. But because Christ obeyed God the Father unto death on behalf of those whom he represented, the law of works (Rom 3:27), with its universal curse and condemnation, is ended for those who believe in Christ—for Christ is the end of the law for righteousness for believers (10:4).

of Hebrews revises the words of Ps 40:7 and puts them into the mouth of Christ, as the Son speaks to God his Father:

> "Behold, I have come to do *your will*, O God, as it is written of me in the scroll of the book." When he said above, "You have neither desired nor taken pleasure in sacrifices and offerings and burnt offerings and sin offerings [these are offered according to *the law*], then he added, "Behold, I have come to do *your will.*" He [Jesus] does away with the first [covenant] in order to establish the second. (Heb 10:7–9 ESV)

Note that the writer purposely did not say, "I have come to do your Law, O God." He changed the OT law text to say that Jesus came to do "God's will," which he purposely used in contrast to "the law" because the new testament in Christ's blood for sins (1 Cor 11:25; Heb 10:9–14) is the actual doing away with the first covenant, as Hebrews says.[38] If a law-righteousness is our righteousness, Jesus could have kept the law and then ascended to heaven *without dying for us*. The key text on this, Phil 2:8–9, says that Christ was obedient to *God* (not Moses' law) unto death; therefore, God highly exalted him.

The First Adam	The Last Adam
And the LORD God *commanded* the man, saying: "Of every tree of the garden you may freely eat. But of the tree of the knowledge of good and evil, you shall not eat, for in the day that you eat of it, dying, you shall surely die" (Gen 2:16–17 AV/AT).	"I lay down my life, that I might take it again. No man takes it from me, but I lay it down of myself. I have authority to lay it down, and I have authority to take it again. *This commandment* have I received from my Father" (John 10:17–18). *Christ obeyed God* (Rom 5:19; Phil 2:8–9). According to John, he obeyed God's *commandment* (10:17–18).
Adam disobeyed God by disobeying God's *commandment*. The result was *death* for all in Adam.	The Son of God obeyed God (his Father) in his incarnation unto the death of the cross (Phil 2:7b, 8) for sinners, resulting in *eternal life* for all in Christ.

> For I have come down from heaven, not to do my own will, but *the will of him* [God the Father] who sent me. And this is *the will of him* who sent me, that I should lose nothing of all [the

38. For the priesthood being changed there is also of necessity a *change* of *the law* (Heb 7:12), which change from the law (of works and of Moses) of sin and of death to the law of *God*, the law of *the Spirit*, is explained in Rom 7:1–6; 7:22—8:15 (see 8:2); 2 Cor 3:3–10 (see 5:17–21); 1 Cor 9:20–21; and Heb 8:1—10:18.

ones, the sheep] that he has given me, but raise it up on the last day. (John 6:38–39 ESV)

I lay down my life for the sheep. (John 10:15 ESV)

In agreement with the words from the Epistle to the Hebrews—"your will" (God's will)—Jesus, in John's gospel, speaks of his "doing the will of him who sent me."

> And being found in human form, he humbled himself by becoming *obedient* to the point of death, even death on a cross. Therefore *God* has highly exalted him, and bestowed on him the name that is above every name, so that at the name of Jesus every knee should bow, in heaven and on earth and under the earth, and every tongue confess that Jesus Christ is Lord, to the glory of God the Father. (Phil 2:8–11 ESV)

Clearly, the One to whom God's Son was obedient was God the Father, who therefore exalted him; Paul says he was obedient to God and not to the law, for *God is not the law.* God's only begotten Son, from eternity past, has always been obedient to his Father, and that obedience continued when he took on human flesh. The Son's willing subordination to the Father does not mean that the Son is not equal to the Father in terms of Godhood, for he is God. They are one (John 10:30). Rather, it means that there is order and headship in the triune God (John 14:28). The Son was obedient to God the Father (God is the head of Christ, 1 Cor 11:3)—even to the point of death on a cross. This is the obedience of deep, loving *trust,* through which the Son of God trusts God the Father. Not only in God's eternal "past," as the eternal Son of God, but also, since the incarnation, he always fully trusted his Father, giving him due thanks, honor, glory, and obedience. The Gospel of John's parallel to Paul's saying, "*Not* having my righteousness, which is of the law" (which means we put *no* trust in the *flesh*[39]) is where Jesus says, "Truly, truly, I say to you, the Son can do *nothing* of *himself,* except what he sees the Father do" (John 5:19). Like Paul, who imitates Christ, Jesus did not have his own, independent-from-God righteousness, which (Paul says) is of the law, for Paul's was "of *the faith* of Christ" (Phil 3:9), but the law is not of faith (Gal 3:12). Jesus could do nothing of himself. His source of life and righteousness was that of God the Father. And so, in Rom 5, Paul is saying:

> *In Adam* I sinned, so I was (and in body still am) thereby *condemned* to *death.* (5:12; see 8:10)

39. See Phil 3:3, 9.

In Christ, I died with Christ, and I am (in spirit now, and in body will be) *justified* for the purpose of *eternal life.* (Rom 5:18–21; 8:10–11, 19, 21; Gal 5:5)

The imputation of Adam's one sin unto condemnation to all in him is the basis for the (spiritual unto bodily) death for all born in Adam. In the light of Rom 5, and calling original, indwelling sin "inherent depravity," A. A. Hodge wrote:

> If the imputation of [sin with its] guilt [i.e., condemnation for Adam's sin] is the causal antecedent of inherent depravity [the loss of original righteousness=indwelling sin, which means the death of the spirit, leading to bodily death], in like manner the imputation of [God's] righteousness must be the causal antecedent of regeneration and faith.[40]

In summary, the person of the eternal Son of God, in whom all the fullness of deity (the divine nature) dwells, put on a full humanity in the incarnation; and thus, (1) he did not become some other person than the Son of God, and (2) he was not "born of ordinary generation" as all others were born in Adam, who had Adam's sin imputed unto condemnation, resulting in (spiritual unto bodily) death. Thus, Christ was qualified to take Adam's sin with its condemnation (and our sins, with their added condemnation) upon himself—with its/their corresponding judgment, the penalty, even (spiritual unto bodily) death, on our behalf, which accorded with God's inherent righteousness (δικαιοσύνησ) (Rom 3:25) and his salvific plan.

Original Sin

The phrase "original sin" is not a scriptural one. But if it is to be used, it should contain the truth of what we have said—yes, there is indwelling sin that is corruption and spiritual death, even from our conception in the womb. But death (in all aspects) is the punishment due God's verdict of "condemned" to humans in Adam, due to Adam's one sin. Some theologians have taught this, but (sadly) not the majority. The death (Rom 5:12) that passed into all humans is the spiritual death that ends in bodily death. These are not two deaths but aspects of the *one death* of the whole man. Again, Adam's disobedience God judged, and the judgment was "guilty"—one of condemnation for all in Adam. This condemnation was unto the penalty of death. The spiritual aspect of death means that the human spirit has died through Adam's one sin, so that the spirit is no longer alive to God but dead

---

40. Hodge, "Ordo Salutis," words in brackets mine.

to God; thus, the inner person is utterly lacking that which theologians have called "original righteousness"—that which Adam had before his sin, having been changed from a likeness to God (Eph 4:24) to an unlikeness to God in impurity of heart, an evil heart, full of unbelief and covetousness. Thus, the sin entered into all humans, bringing its spiritual death, lording it over all unto bodily death, that is, mortality, corruption, and destruction. God created humans in the image of God, male and female (Gen 1:27). God saw everything that he had made, and indeed it was very good (Gen 1:31a). But sin entered the world through one man (Rom 5:12). Therefore, man in Adam, and not God, is accountable for the sin with its condemnation/guilt and corruption of humans and all the suffering of creation in its post-fall state. From the time of Adam's sin, humans have been conceived in sin, which means the death of the human spirit, leading to the death of the body. But whatever name we call "original (indwelling) sin," we agree with the Book of Concord concerning its reality:

> It is also taught among us that since the fall of Adam all men who are born according to the course of nature are conceived and born in sin. That is, all men are full of evil lust and inclinations from the mothers' wombs and are unable by nature to have true fear of God and true faith in God. Moreover, this . . . hereditary sin is truly sin.[41]

> In our definition of original sin, therefore, we have correctly expressed both elements: lack of ability to trust, fear, or love God; and concupiscence, which pursues carnal ends contrary to the word of God (that is, not only the desires of the body but also the carnal wisdom and righteousness in which it trusts while it despises God).[42]

> The deficiency and concupiscence are sin as well as *penalty*; *death*, other physical ills, and *the tyranny of the devil are*, in the precise sense, *penalties*.[43]

> Christ was given to us to bear both *sin and penalty* and to destroy the rule of the devil, sin, and death; so we cannot know his blessings unless we recognize our evil.[44]

Finally, Michael Horton wisely notes:

---

41. AC 2.1–2, 29.
42. Ap II. 26, (103).
43. Ap II. 47 (106), emphasis mine.
44. Ap II. 50 (106), emphasis mine.

Repeated attempts to dismiss the doctrine of original sin as a peculiarity of Calvin or Luther, Augustine or Paul fail to take seriously the fact that the same assumptions are articulated in the Psalms (Ps 51:5, 10; 143:2), the prophets (Isa 64:6; Jer 17:9), the Gospels (Jn 1:13; 3:6; 5:42; 6:44; 8:34; 15:4–5), and the Catholic Epistles (Jas 3:2; 1 John 1:8; 5:12).[45]

Sin and death entered into the world through one man (5:12); it was then that this present evil age began (Gal 1:14). But when God raised Christ from the dead, the age to come began and invaded, "overlapping" this age, through the life-giving Spirit.[46]

---

45. Horton, *Pilgrim Theology*, 149.

46. See 1 Cor 15:20–23; Eph 1:21; 1 Cor 15:45 AT; see also Nygren, *Commentary on Romans*, 218 (compare 20–24; 48–52).

NINE

With Christ, We Died to the Sin

(Rom 6)

THIS GRACE OF CHRIST is so incomprehensible that the flesh's response to grace is, "So, since grace is greater than sin (Rom 5:20), why not sin, that grace may abound all the more?" The answer of the only wise God to that question is found in Romans chapter 6. But at the same time, every word of truth in Rom 6 is built upon the foundation of what the apostle has said and laid in Rom 5:12–21.

- We are to *know* the truth of our union with Christ in his death to Sin and his new life in us (Rom 6:2–9).

- We are to *believe* this, to *count it as true*—for, in spirit, we died and are dead to sin and are spiritually alive to God in Christ (Rom 6:11; 1 Cor 6:17), despite appearances and feelings.

- Therefore, we are to *not let the sin reign* in our mortal bodies (Rom 6:12–23).

"Sin" is a power, a mastering power which those in Christ were formerly enslaved to but have been freed from in Christ. Unbelievers do not know not who they are! For they are deceived, so that they think that they are their *own* persons, *free and independent beings*; but they are enslaved and indwelt by their master: Sin (Satan). Because much of the church has historically not understood Romans 6, most Christians have not been knowing or counting on who they are in Christ. Holiness comes only by faith in Christ, by counting as true the truth that we are now justified and thus freed from Sin's lordship and we are enslaved to God in Christ, and are to present our bodily members, not to Sin (as power), but to God through Christ. Through union with Christ our Lord, sin no longer rules as lord over us. Everything about the life in Christ hinges on our (as under law for justification) having *died* with Christ, through which we were justified from the sin (in Adam), and our having been spiritually raised with Christ in his new, age-to-come *life*. We are to understand the implications of the words "with him" (Christ) as meaning "in union with Christ."

Our old man in Adam, under sin and sin's lordship, was crucified to death with Christ, and we have been raised with him to a new life in Christ. We are new creations in him: no longer under law (condemnation in Adam) but under grace (justification in Christ).

Romans 5:12 through chapter 6 is really one piece, with unity of thought; thus, in what follows we present it as such. Also, the Greek definite article is translated (as "the") wherever it appears in the Greek text, and the words in brackets are to aid in understanding the text's meaning.

> Consequently, [just] as through one man the Sin entered the world, and through the Sin, the *Death* [entered the world]— and so the Death entered into all men, because all sinned [in one man]
>
> . . . even so, through one righteous act [of deliverance, the judgment came] to all men [in Christ] unto justification belonging to *Life* [in *Christ*]. For, as through the one man's disobedience, the many were put in the class of [condemned] sinners, even so, through the obedience of the one, the many will be put in the class of righteous [justified] ones. But the law entered, in order that the trespass [sin of Adam] might abound [unto more trespasses (of the law)]; but where the Sin abounded, the Grace [of Christ] super-abounded, in order that, as the Sin reigned in the Death, even so might the Grace reign through righteousness unto Eternal Life, through Jesus Christ our Lord.
>
> What shall we say then? Shall we continue in the Sin [of Adam] in order that the Grace [of Christ] may abound? May it not be! *We, who died to the Sin* [thereby having been justified from the Sin, v. 7], how shall we [as such people] still live in it? Do you not know that as many of us who were baptized into Christ Jesus, into the *Death* of him we were baptized? Therefore, we were entombed with Christ through the baptism into the death [of him], in order that, as Christ was raised from the dead [out of the tomb] through the glory of the Father—so also, we might walk in newness of life [the Spirit]. For if we have become united [grafted together] with Christ in the likeness of his death, so also, we shall certainly be [united with Christ in

the likeness] of his resurrection [which resurrection-likeness is now, in the inner man, 6:4, 11, but shall be in the outer man also, 6:8]. Knowing this, that the old man of us [under Sin as lord] was crucified [to death] with Christ, in order that the body of Sin might be destroyed [live no longer, for we, as joined to the flesh of Sin, *live no longer*, for Christ lives in us[1]], that we might no longer serve the Sin as its slaves. For the one who has died with Christ has been *justified* from the Sin [of and in Adam, which was imputed to us unto condemnation, resulting in *death*]. But if we *died [that death] with Christ*, we believe that we shall also live with him [6:22–23]. Knowing that Christ, having been raised from the dead, dies no more; Death [as lord] no longer lords it over him. For in that Christ died, he died unto sin once; but in that he lives, he lives to God [in resurrection, age-to-come life]. So also, you, consider yourselves also to be dead indeed to the Sin, but alive to God in Christ Jesus. Therefore [since you died to the Sin, are justified from the Sin, and the Sin no longer reigns in your inner man where the Spirit of Jesus now reigns as Lord], do not let the Sin [as power, as lord] reign [get the upper hand] in your mortal body, that you should obey the Sin in its desires [but let Christ (the power of God) reign in your mortal bodies]. Neither present your members as weapons of unrighteousness to the Sin, but present yourselves to God, as alive from the dead [in Christ], and [present] your [bodily] members as weapons of righteousness to God. For Sin shall not lord it over you, for you are not under law [the ministry of condemnation], but under grace [the ministry of justification]. What then? May we sin, because we are not under law [the power of Sin], but under grace [the power of God]? Do you not know that the one to whom you present yourselves [as slaves]—slaves of that one you *are, whomever you obey*—whether [slaves] of Sin unto Death, or [slaves] of Obedience [to God, the obedience of faith] unto Righteousness [and Life]? [We can still choose to obey Sin rather than God (Christ, the power of God[2]), but the end is death, 6:22–23; 8:13]. But thanks be to God, that, whereas you were slaves of the Sin, you obeyed out of the heart the form of teaching [of God's gospel] to which you were delivered [by God]. And having been freed from the Sin, you were enslaved to the Righteousness. I speak in human terms because of the weakness of your flesh. For just as you presented your [bodily] members as slaves to the uncleanness and to the lawlessness unto

1. Gal 2:20.
2. 1 Cor 1:24.

the lawlessness; even so now present your members as slaves to
the Righteousness [of God] unto holiness. For when you were
the slaves of Sin, you were free [in regard] to the Righteousness
[free from Christ as Lord]. What fruit then did you have at that
time in the things of which you are now ashamed? For the end
of those things is Death. But now, having been freed from the
Sin, and having been enslaved to God, you have your fruit unto
holiness, and the end is eternal Life. For the wages which the Sin
pays is Death, but the free gift of God is Eternal Life in Christ
Jesus our Lord. (Rom 5:12, 18–21; 6:1–23)

Radical Grace

The flesh (owned by unbelief toward Christ) thinks only like this: "There
is no such thing as a God who makes people right with himself apart from
their keeping of the 10 Commandments." The flesh thinks of God as the
law personified and not as Christ. But if a person believes in Jesus, that person's inner man is no longer joined to the flesh but to the Spirit of God; he
is "in the Spirit," where he is under justification by God's grace alone. With
Christ-believers, it is only the flesh-mind that thinks that "grace" means
that we will surely use grace as a license to sin. But justification by grace
through faith only exists for the one who has died to sin's lordship and is
simultaneously a new creation, in whom Christ is his Lord. And only such
an informed faith enables the one in Christ to live and walk in the obedience of faith in Christ. So, where the sin of Adam abounded, the grace of
Christ has super-abounded. So, for us who receive that grace, the sin (in
Adam) no longer reigns as our lord but the grace of Christ that justifies,
reigns and rules believers unto eternal life in Jesus Christ our Lord (Rom
5:20–21). In Romans chapter 6, Paul builds on the foundation of chapter
5, where he only introduced our union with Christ with the phrase, "we
shall be saved in his life" (5:10). Thus, we are already now in the sphere of
Christ's resurrection *life*, as Paul reiterates in Rom 6:4, 11, and 23:

> So also, we, in the newness of *life* [*eternal*] might walk. (6:4)

> Consider yourselves also to be dead indeed to the Sin, but *alive*
> to God [because you are] in Christ Jesus our Lord. (6:11)

> The free-gift of God is *eternal Life* in Christ Jesus our Lord. (6:23)

Paul will later describe these things by saying that we are *in the Spirit* who
is *life* (8:9–10). Through our union with Christ (6:5) we participated in

Christ's death, his burial, and his resurrection (6:2–11). And our resurrection to life is in two phases: the already-now (in 6:4, 10, 11, 23) and the not-yet (in 6:5, 8, 22, 23). So, when Paul begins this chapter with the question, "Shall we continue in the Sin (of Adam) in order that the Grace (of Christ) might abound?" (6:1 AP), he does not follow that by saying, "No, because there is the law, which you are still under obligation to do and obligated to keep, and that is the way to not continue in sin." Instead, God intervened with a death and resurrection.

> The old man (in Adam, under Sin and its lordship) of us died with Christ; and we were raised to new life in Christ (his resurrection life), and now we are (a new creation in him) no longer under law (condemnation in Adam) but under grace (justification in Christ). (Rom 6:6–11, 14 summarized)

The power of sin is the law.[3] And sin is a power that totally enslaves all humans in Adam, whether they know it or not. So, Paul begins:

> What then shall we say? May we continue in the Sin [of and in Adam] in order that the Grace [of and in Christ] may abound? May it not be! How shall *we—who died to the Sin*—still *live* in it?! (Rom 6:1–2)

This, *our death with Christ to the sin* (6:3–8, 10, 11), is the central point of chapter 6. In 1 Corinthians, Paul says of the believer, "For he who is joined to the Lord is one spirit with Him" (1 Cor 6:17; see Rom 7:4). Such is our union with Christ, that we are one spirit with him; there is a union of spirits, in which the distinction between us and God remains, for we do not become God. However, when Christ died, we (as those joined to the flesh owned by sin) died with Christ to the sin as lord; we have thereby been released from the lordship and authority of sin and Satan, for "God has delivered us out of the authority of the darkness [Satan's kingdom and authority] and transferred us into the kingdom of the Son of God's love"— the reign of Christ's grace (Col 1:13; see Rom 5:21). This is true of all those in Christ, regardless of how they feel.

> Or do you not know this—that as many of us as were baptized *into Christ Jesus*, were baptized into his *death*? Therefore, we were buried with Christ through the baptism (τοῦ βαπτίσματοσ), in order that as Christ was *raised from the dead* through the glory of the Father, so also, we too [who are thereby alive in our inner man[4]] might walk in the newness of life. (Rom 6:3–4)

3. 1 Cor 15:56; Rom 7:7–13.
4. Rom 8:10; see Eph 3:16.

Called (1:6) sinners who cannot trust God, the unbelievers whom God loved (1:7; 5:8) died with Christ. As such sinners, we *passed away* (2 Cor 5:17) through the baptism into his death.

Paul, starting with the first part of 6:5, says, "For if we have become *innately grown together* [*united*] *with* Christ." Regarding the word σύμφυτοι ("grown together"), Lloyd-Jones said that it "is rather the idea of grafting a shoot into a tree. 'Planted together'—in unity, identification— that is the meaning of the term."[5] And just before Paul spoke of being *united with Christ* (v. 5), he explained the *cause* of this being united with Christ—"the baptism" of 6:4. Lloyd-Jones taught:

> This is the baptism which is carried out by the Holy Spirit when he incorporates us, plants us into, engrafts us into the Lord Jesus Christ. . . . It is because we are united with Him that we derive all these benefits from Him. The same held true when we were united to Adam. It was the one sin of Adam that brought all the evil consequences upon us. And it is the action of Christ that brings all blessings upon us. As we were united to Adam, so we are now united to Christ—that is the doctrine. And we must realize that it is the Spirit who unites us to Christ. That is the baptism about which the apostle is speaking.[6]

> What kind of baptism is taught in the New Testament which definitely says that it is a baptism that incorporates us into Christ and joins us to him? The answer is surely found in 1 Corinthians 12:13: "For by (or in) one Spirit we are all baptized into one body."[7]

James D. G. Dunn refers to Paul's use of three metaphors in Rom 6:4, 5, and 6, respectively. Of the first metaphor (in 6:4), where Paul uses "baptized" ("*baptized* into Christ Jesus"), he says:

> It is drawn from baptism, but does not itself describe baptism, or contain within itself the thought of the water-rite, anymore than did the synonymous metaphors of putting on Christ (Gal 3:27) and being drenched with the Spirit (1 Cor 12:13).[8]

Regarding Paul's second metaphor, Dunn comments on the Greek word ὁμοίωμα, which is usually translated in Bibles as "*united with*" (Christ).

---

5. Lloyd-Jones, *Exposition of Chapter Six*, 36. See also my chs. 13 and 20.

6. Lloyd-Jones, *Exposition of Chapter Six*, 36,37.

7. Lloyd-Jones, *Exposition of Chapter Six*, 35.

8. Dunn, *Baptism in the Holy Spirit*, 140.

The second metaphor (v. 5) may be drawn from . . . horticulture: "planted together in the likeness of his death" (AV).

> Our union with Christ, says Paul, was like the grafting of a branch on to the main stem so that they become one . . . it was the coming together of us and the ὁμοίωμα of Christ's death, so that henceforth we were indivisibly united with it in continuing growth. . . .[9] The third metaphor is quite independent of the other two—συνεσταυρώθη. It describes the negative side of coming to participate in the new creation—the complete breaking of the ties of the old creation (Gal. 2:19; 5:24; 6:14ff.; 2 Cor 5:14f., 17). It is only this divine operation on the spiritual plane which can effect the destruction of the body of sin, and thus end man's subjection to sin as a member of Adam and of the old order. In short, each metaphor points directly to the *spiritual reality*, and not to baptism, which is itself a metaphor.[10]

What does this "union with Christ" entail? Tipton explains:

> Union with Christ is a multi-faceted reality that includes within it distinct-yet-inseparable benefits that fall out in two basic classes: forensic/imputative and renovative/transformative. Union with Christ *per se*, is neither imputation nor renewal, but includes *both* within its compass—distinctively, inseparably, simultaneously, and eschatologically.[11]

Back to Paul, this time with the entire verse (6:5).

> For if we have become innately grown together with Christ in the likeness of his death, so also, we shall certainly be [united with Christ] in the likeness of his resurrection [which likeness is now, in the inner man (6:4, 11), but shall be in the outer man also (see 6:8)]. (Rom 6:5)

We have become, in an abiding union, united with Christ in the likeness of Christ's death to sin. Sin was never Christ's lord—he knew no sin; but our sin was imputed to him unto death, and in that sense only it lorded it over him. With him we died to the entire reign of sin. Paul says, "in the likeness of his death" because we are not Christ. So, we will never again come under sin as our lord, for we died with Christ to the sin which condemned and thus mastered us in Adam. Our death with Christ is in "the *likeness* of his death," because Christ's death is the unique death to sin,

9. Dunn, *Baptism in the Holy Spirit*, 141–42.

10. Dunn, *Baptism in the Holy Spirit*, 142, emphasis mine.

11. Tipton, "Union with Christ," 48.

which became our death through our union with Christ. His death is the source of our salvation, and his death and resurrection are ours "according to the Spirit," who is life (8:3, 5, 10).

Excursus 4: The Nature of Our Union with Christ

Paul wanted to know nothing among the Corinthians except Christ and him crucified (for our salvation).[12] This reveals that *all* fleshly wisdom and thinking, with *its* ideas and concept of God's righteousness, is a lie. Christ crucified is utterly contrary to everything we, with our own wisdom, presume we know about God. Foremost, the cross of Christ is utterly contrary to our flesh-thinking about how God would, and does, justify sinners, which is apart from law (Rom 3:21[–26]). And Paul's gospel is consistent on this "apart from law" reality.

We are justified by "the faith of Christ"—his obedience to God unto death—and not by a righteousness of the law. As we have seen, Christ's obedience is never defined as obedience to the law. Paul simply says that Christ "knew no sin"—that he was obedient to his Father who, after his death, exalted him (Phil 2:8–9). In Rom 6:3–5 Paul says we were united to Christ in his death, his burial, and his resurrection; he says nothing about us being united to Christ in his life before and up to his death. For, having been united with Christ in his death means our justification (5:9, 19; 6:7 lit.), and having been united with him in his resurrection means we have eternal life (6:4–9) to which no condemnation belongs (8:1–2). If his keeping the law, the Ten Commandments, were for our justification, then Paul would have said something like, "We were united with him in his birth, his circumcision and his doing the law." But Paul did not say that, because God's righteousness is apart from law (3:21) through Christ's obedience of faith unto death (3:22). God's way of our deliverance was that our old man (condemned in Adam, under the sin and the law) was *put to death with Christ.* Only when the law's sentence and ministration of death (2 Cor 3:6–7) killed us with Christ, so that the wages of sin were paid in full (by death), could God raise us with Christ to new life. The central truth in Rom 6 is our death with Christ to sin (6:3–8, 10, 11). And this is in accord with Paul's saying that "through *one* righteous *act* (Christ's death, 5:18–19, [9]), the free gift of righteousness (5:17) came upon all men in Christ unto justification of life" (Rom 5:18), because the one having died (with Christ) has been justified from the sin (6:7). Paul does not say "through *many* righteous acts," as the legal scheme would have it. Christ, who knew no sin—no

12. 1 Cor 1:18–23.

disobedience of unfaith, no disobedience toward God—was made sin (by the imputation of our sin to Christ unto death) for us, that we might be made the righteousness of God (by imputation) in him (2 Cor 5:21 AT). The unscriptural theory that Christ kept the law for us (*and* died for us) which justified us, is an error; his death alone justified. The *final judgment of God* occurred proleptically when *Christ* bore our *judgment* on the cross unto *death*. It was the Righteous One, through his faith/obedience to God, taking on himself our deserved death and end as sinners in Adam and in Christ's resurrection making his people a *new* creation.

The author of Matthew says that Christ fulfilled all righteousness (3:15). The author of the Gospel according to Matthew uses "fulfilled" in the sense of the old covenant scriptures being *fulfilled* in Jesus (Matt 1:22; 2:15, 17, 23; 4:14; 8:17; 12:17; 13:14, 35; 21:4; 24:34; 26:54, 56; 27:9, 35). Luke's example of this is when Jesus said to the two men on the road, "'Ought not the Christ to have suffered these things, and to enter into His glory? . . . These are the words which I spoke to you . . . that all things must be fulfilled which were written in the Law of Moses, and in the prophets, and in the psalms, concerning Me. . . . Thus it is written and thus it was necessary for the Christ to suffer, and to rise from the dead the third day'" (Luke 24:26, 44, 46 NKJV). But Jesus did this through "the righteousness which is of faith,"[13] which faith was obedience to God (Rom 1:5; 5:19).

Paul and the other NT writers proclaim Christ as one *who knew no sin*, who was without sin, *without* bringing "the law" into the equation at all; see 2 Cor 5:21; 1 Pet 2:22; Heb 4:15; John 7:18, and compare 1 John 5:17. Paul thinks from *Christ* to sin, interpreting everything in the light of his "revelation of Jesus Christ" (Gal 1:12). But someone may object as follows: But Paul says, "God sent forth his Son, made of a woman, *made* under the law, to *redeem* those who were under the law, so that we might receive adoption as sons" (Gal 4:4, 5a ESV). What then, does Christ being "made under the law" mean? Luther, commenting on this text, rightly says:

> Here Paul is teaching . . . that God sent forth His Son under the Law; that is, that He made Him bear the judgment and

---

13. The writer of Hebrews, in ch. 11, repeatedly identifies "the righteousness which is of faith" with the patriarchs and other OT believers. How? By simply obeying God "by faith" in that which God led them to do, whether it was Abel offering a sacrifice, or Noah preparing an ark, or Abraham going out to a place he should afterward receive for an inheritance, or Abraham offering up Isaac, etc. None of these things, which were done through "the righteousness which is of *faith*," were keeping the law (similarly in Jas 2). God revealed his will to his Son, and he, by faith, did his Father's will (John 6:38, 39; see 10:15; Heb 10:7). Jesus never tried to keep the law; he did not focus on the law but only (in trust) on his Father, and he knew no sin.

THE GRACE OF CHRIST, Third Edition

the curse of the Law, sin, death, etc. Moses, who is an agent of
sin, wrath and death, captured, bound, condemned and killed
Christ; and Christ endured it. Christ acted toward the Law in
a passive, not in an active way.[14]

Note that the same Greek word for "made" (under the law) in Gal 4:4 is used
in connection with "redeemed" in Gal 3. So, in both 3:13 and in 4:4, "made"
and "redeemed" go together:

> Christ has *redeemed* us from the curse of the law, [by] being
> *made* a curse for us: for it is written, "Cursed is everyone who
> hangs on a tree" (Gal 3:13 AV/AT).

Thus, Christ was made under the law to redeem us, to come under the
curse of the law, yes, to *be a curse* for us—by his *death* (3:13). His life was
without sin, and the life of the flesh is in the blood, and thus the blood of
God[15] was acceptable to God, metaphorically as an *unblemished lamb* who
was sacrificed (1 Pet 1:19; John 1:29). His life was taken away—he died—on
our behalf. The wrath of God came upon Christ when he became a curse for
us and died our death in our place. I am in the having-been-crucified and
now risen Christ—he is my righteousness (1 Cor 1:30). Paul always speaks
of "the righteousness of God" and not "the righteousness of Christ." Why?
Christ is God, but he is not God the Father. The Christ who has redeemed
me and has become righteousness to me, is the same Christ who was without
sin and was obedient unto death, for if he was not always obedient to God
(without sin), he could not have borne *our sins* in our place. His obedience
was for us, but his obedience was an obedience of faith, without sin, and
not "the righteousness of the law," for "if righteousness comes by law [even
Christ's keeping the law] Christ *died* for nothing"(Gal 2:21).

His death is righteousness/justification, for the law is not of faith (Gal
3:12). Thus, in Phil 3:9, my (flesh-of-sin[16]) righteousness, which is "of the
law," is contrasted with God's righteousness, which is of "the *faith* of Christ"
(his obedience unto death), because "the faith of Christ" *is* "the righteousness
of God" which justifies sinners.

It was by means of the obedience of one (Rom 5:19), the one righteous
act of Christ (5:18), that Christ became to us righteousness from God (1
Cor 1:30). From one perspective, the righteousness of God (in Christ) is
Christ's obedience unto death, for Christ is God (Rom 9:5; John 1:1, 14).

14. *LW* 26:372.

15. Acts 20:28. He was "made under the law," which condemned him (2 Cor 3:9).
Why? On the cross he was made *sin* for us (2 Cor 5:21). He *could* do this because he, in
himself, *knew no sin* (5:21). God was in Christ, so it was God's act (Rom 5:18).

16. It is of the flesh (Phil 3:3), which is the flesh of (owned by) sin (Rom 8:3 lit.).

At the same time: that which justifies sinners is the righteousness of God. And Christ is God's righteousness, for "Christ belongs to God" (1 Cor 3:23).

There is not only union but also distinction between God the Father and the Son of God. We are in Christ, who is the righteousness of and from God. Thus, the righteousness from God revealed in the gospel is that which justified us in Christ Jesus (3:24). Paul says, "For as many of you as were baptized into Christ have put on Christ" (Gal 3:27 NKJV). Paul does not say, "For as many of you who were baptized into Christ have put on Christ's righteousness," for Christ *is* our righteousness (1 Cor 1:30). God, through Christ's death, delivered us out of this age and into the age to come, the age of the new creation, which we are in because we are in the Spirit of Christ and not any longer in the flesh (Eph 1:21; 2 Cor 5:17; Gal 6:15–16; Rom 8:9). Again, the notion that righteousness comes by Christ's keeping the law (contra Gal 2:21) comes from the flesh, for, when it comes to God, the flesh thinks only in terms of law. But justification was accomplished by Christ's death (Rom 5:9), and justification is found, and had, in his (resurrection) life (5:10, 18), that is, "in Christ." In summary:

> "Through *one* righteous *act* [of deliverance, *Christ's death*, there came] *to all men for* [the purpose of] *justification which belongs to life*" (Rom 5:18). This is eternal *life* through Christ Jesus our Lord (5:21). Our *life in Christ* is the life of the age to come. It is not the life, nor the righteousness of this age, nor of the flesh, nor of the law. Eternal life, to which no condemnation belongs, is ours (who believe) now, in the Spirit, for we have been delivered by Christ out of this present age, into God's kingdom (Rom 14:17). The new creation in Christ is the person of the age to come, of the Spirit who raised Jesus (with whom we have died to the sin and the law) from the dead to resurrection (eschatological), eternal life.[17]

It is not that the believer remains the same person (old man in Adam), remains "alive in the flesh"—what Gerhard Forde calls "a continuously existing subject"[18]—and merely has his sins forgiven, not put to his account. No! Rather, it is that *the person* (already condemned in Adam), whose righteousness (of the flesh and thus of unbelief) and unrighteousness were his, *died* with Christ, so that *the person (as) owned by Sin, was done away with; he no longer exists*; for *Christ*, who put that old man to death with himself,

---

17. Phil 3:3–9; Rom 3:21; Gal 1:4; 2 Cor 5:17; Eph 1:21 and see Rom 8:18; Rom 4:24; 8:11; 5:21; 6:9–10, 23; 1 Cor 15:21–23, 42–57. This is in accord with FC, Epitome 3. See also Bultmann, *Theology of the New Testament*, 276.

18. Forde, *Justification by Faith*, 82.

was then raised to new, age-to-come life. And thus in Christ's risen life, Christ himself is the believer's only righteousness and life. It is in that manner that sins are not imputed to the person in Christ (for even indwelling sin is only in the flesh, not in the Spirit and human spirit), so *that* is gone also—no longer exists in the new creation, in the inner man. The problem with traditional Protestant theology is that, though it teaches an imputed righteousness, it tends to leave the believer under the law because it leaves us as old men (old creations, contra Rom 6:6 and 8:5), as *essentially sinners* in Adam. There is an ignorance of the apostolic gospel which declares that, now that God's righteousness has come (Rom 3; Gal 3), *justification cannot be separated from our death and resurrection with Christ.* Protestantism has, for the most part, not been able to grasp that imputed righteousness comes through being *joined to Christ as our life*—justification that belongs to life (Rom 5:19; see 8:1–2).

As Forde says, the righteousness which is in Christ:

> "does not merely 'take sin away' and leave the moral person intact . . ." Instead: "There is a death and a resurrection involved, which proceeds according to no immanent moral scheme."[19]

What is true of Christ as our righteousness is therefore also true of Christ as our sanctification (compare 1 Cor 1:30):

> Sanctification always comes from the whole, from the penetration of the eschaton into time, and thus involves the death of the old and the rebirth of the new.[20]

> Justification and sanctification are a dynamic unity. Sanctification is what happens when the unconditional and eschatological event of justification breaks into one's life.[21]

Because of this unity between justification and sanctification, Paul can say, "If you are led by the Spirit [in whom you are justified], you are not under law" (Gal 5:18).

> Knowing this, that our old man [under Sin as lord and condemned in Adam, in whom our inner man was joined to the flesh of sin] was crucified [to death] with Christ, in order that the body of sin [the person owned by Sin] might be brought to

---

19. Forde, "Christian Life," 2:436.
20. Forde, "Christian Life," 2:436.
21. Forde, "Christian Life," 2:437.

nothing—exist no longer, that we might *no longer* serve the sin as its slaves. (Rom 6:6)[22]

Paul the Hebrew believed in holistic dualism (a *union* and yet a distinction between body and spirit). The old man is the body and, in one sense, the person owned by sin (Rom 6:6). The "death" that occurred is a real destruction—a doing away with—of the *body* of sin, the *person* owned by sin-as-lord (6:6), the flesh[23] of sin (owned by sin, Rom 8:3 lit.). But God raised up Christ and us with him into the newness of resurrection, eschatological life, (6:4). Since we died to sin (as lord), we are to not let the sin reign in our mortal body; we should not obey sin as power (6:12).

> For the one who has died [*with Christ*] has been justified from the Sin [of and in Adam, which was imputed to us unto condemnation]. (Rom 6:7)

The man who died with Christ is "the old man of us" in Adam (6:6)—who cannot trust God, the person who is "under sin" and "under law" as lords (Rom 3:9, 19; 6:14–18; 7:1, 5). So, we no longer belong to sin but to the Lord Jesus Christ, as Paul says elsewhere:

> Do you not know that your body is a temple of the Holy Spirit in you, which you have from God, and [thus] you are not your own [you are God's possession; you no longer belong to the flesh, but to God's Spirit]. For you were bought with a price [God's blood]: therefore, glorify God in your body, and in your spirit, which are God's. (1 Cor 6:19–20)

Sin dwells in me, that is, in my flesh, but sin no longer owns me. The flesh of Sin is *no longer joined to the inner man* of those in Christ, and the Spirit (Eph 3:16) alone now dwells there. The body of the one who now lives—the new creation (2 Cor 5:17)—belongs to the Lord Jesus Christ. The (unholy) spirit that now energizes (Eph 2:2) the children of disobedience no longer energizes believers in their inner man, where God's Spirit now dwells. The old man, who could not trust God, died—passed away—with Christ. Through union with Christ, we have been justified from the Sin (6:7) and thereby released from all other lords and masters that powerfully held us (as in flesh) captive: the wrath and condemnation,[24] the sin,[25] the law,[26] and the

22. "For Christ [instead of Sin] lives in us," Gal 2:20.
23. "Flesh" is used as the whole man in 1 Cor 1:29.
24. Rom 5:9–21.
25. Rom 6:1–11; 14, 17–23.
26. Rom 7:1–6.

death.[27] Thus, we have been justified and are thereby freed from the reign of sin-as-lord through condemnation in Adam and are under the reign of grace (through justification) in Christ (5:12–21). The grace of Christ both creates and demands radical lordship—that of Christ as our Lord and owner. Christ's grace creates a new creation and obliges us to live under his lordship, to live according to the Spirit of God, not to the flesh or the law. Your eyes, mouth, mind, etc., are not yours but Christ's. So, we are to live as though that is the truth, because it is the truth (6:16–22).

> Now if we died with Christ, we believe that we shall also live with him [in glory]. Knowing that Christ, having been raised from the dead, dies no longer; death no longer has lordship over him. For in that Christ died, he died unto sin once for all, but in that he lives, he lives unto God [in resurrection life]. (Rom 6:8–10)

Because Adam's sin (5:12) was his disobedience (5:19), Paul, in Rom 6:12, is saying:

> Therefore [because you died to Sin, are justified from the Sin, and the Sin no longer reigns in your inner man], do not let the Sin [as power, as disobedience, *whatever form Sin would take*] reign [get the upper hand] in your mortal body,[28] that you should obey the Sin in its desires (Rom 6:12). (But let Christ [who *is* God's power[29]] reign in your mortal bodies by obeying Christ who is in you) (Rom 6:12).

So, it really is *trust and obey*—but it is obeying the Spirit (Christ, 8:9–10), which obedience derives its power from *trust* in Christ for righteousness (justification) before God.

So, Paul is saying: Christ, who is God's power (1 Cor 1:24) is to reign in and over our mortal bodies. In other words, now—since the exaltation of Jesus to the status of Lord over the wrath, the sin, the law, and the death— because God's saving righteousness has *now* come, *apart from law*, through Christ's faith:

> *Sin is* the disobedience of *unbelief in Christ* (Rom 1:5; see 10:16).

> Therefore, *whatever is not of faith* (in Christ) *is sin* (Rom 14:23; John 16:9).

---

27. Rom 8:1–25.

28. Paul the Hebrew (Phil 3) uses "your mortal *body*" (6:12) interchangeably with "your [bodily] members" (6:13) and "*yourselves*" (6:13).

29. 1 Cor 1:24.

> So also, you (because you, as in flesh, died with Christ, therefore, by faith) consider yourselves to be dead indeed to the sin (freed from the sin's lordship and reign), but alive to God in Christ Jesus—(because you are alive spiritually in him) (Rom 6:11).

Because *God* considers us as those who are dead to sin and alive to God in Christ, *we* (by faith in the gospel) consider ourselves to be dead indeed to the sin and alive to God in Christ Jesus.

> Neither present your members as weapons of unrighteousness *to Sin* [Sin-as-power, in whatever form], but [continually] present yourselves *to God*, as those who really are [spiritually] alive with Christ, and present your members as weapons of righteousness to God. (6:13)

Since the goal and desire of *the flesh*[30] is to sever us from Christ through *unbelief*,[31] the only way that sin as power will not reign in us is to *obey Christ* through *faith* in *Christ* for justification (that is, through *God's power*, which is the gospel[32]).

We no longer are obligated to present our bodily members to sin (8:12–13), because we died to sin as our lord. Instead of presenting our bodily members (including our minds and our eyes) as weapons of unrighteousness to sin as power, as soldiers in a spiritual war, we are (by the Spirit, 6:4; 8:12–13) to present ourselves (our bodily members) as weapons of righteousness to God by faith. So, regardless of how much we know of our union with Christ, we must continually choose to fight the fight of faith, as Richard Alleine says:

> Those who have so many battles to fight and who, on their way to heaven, must dispute every step have need of great courage . . . Let a soldier be ever so well-armed without, if he does not have a *decided heart* his armor will stand him in little stead.[33]

> There is a quick passage from the eye to the heart. If the devil can but turn the eye to behold vanity, by the eye he will easily infect the heart.[34]

---

30. The flesh's desire (Gal 5:17) is that sin as power (1 Cor 15:56) and *not Christ* (God's power, 1 Cor 1:24) reign in us (Rom 6:12; see v. 11).

31. Gal 5:1–5; see Rom 1:5; 10:16.

32. Rom 1:16; see 1 Cor 1:24.

33. Alleine, *World Conquered*, 2, emphasis mine.

34. Alleine, *World Conquered*, 36.

Next, Paul says that we are to obey *obedience:* the obedience of faith in Christ. John Owen wrote, "The more men exercise their grace in . . . obedience, the more it is strengthened and increased."[35] And this obedience is the obedience of faith in Christ.

> For *Sin* [the power of which is the law], shall not lord it over you, for you are not under law [the ministry of condemnation in Adam], but under grace [the ministry of no condemnation in Christ, the power of God, 1:17; 8:1]. (Rom 6:14)

> What then? Shall we sin because we are not under law, but under grace? May it never be! Do you not know that when you present yourselves as slaves for obedience, you are the slaves of the one whom you obey, either [slaves] of sin resulting in death, or [slaves] of obedience resulting in righteousness? (Rom 6:15–16 NASB)

Paul means that at any moment, you are serving either sin or obedience. Believers can still choose to obey *sin* as power rather than *God*,[36] the Spirit of obedience; but the end is death, not life (Rom 8:13).

Note that when he says, "*slaves* of that one you *are, whomever* you obey," that "are" is in the present tense. Paul upholds the paradoxical tension, that only those who obey God through grace (by the Spirit) will live. Luther and many Puritans upheld that tension also. One is either a slave of sin or of God. Through the obedience of faith (Rom 1:5), they are to obey obedience (Rom 6:16), that is, righteousness, for we are *slaves of righteousness* (Rom 6:18), which means we are slaves of *Christ* (1 Cor 7:22; 1:30), who is obedience personified. So, he is saying that we are to obey God (Christ) rather than sin. Those in Christ are freed from sin as lord, and therefore God actually expects them to obey *him* (not the law of Moses) by the power that he provides: justification (Christ for us; us in Christ) and the Spirit (Christ in us). Only slaves of obedience have true freedom, for everything outside of the obedience of faith in Christ is bondage that immediately leads to death. Those who present their members to obey sin are slaves of sin unto death. But if we present ourselves as slaves (of obedience) to God in and through Christ, we are slaves of obedience unto righteousness, in which Christ, our righteousness, is the one who leads and empowers us to obey, moment by moment (Rom 8:10–14). The apostolic teaching that everything hinges on the obedience of *faith in Christ*

35. Owen, *Works*, 6:170.

36. Again, the antithesis to the power of sin (1 Cor 15:56) is the power of God, which is the gospel of *Christ* (Rom 1:16; 15:19), who *is* the power of God (1 Cor 1:24). Christ is *in* us by his Spirit (Rom 8:9–10).

for *justification* (throughout one's entire life) has seldom been proclaimed as the apostle taught it. It is an offense (Gal 5:11).

> But thanks be to God, that, whereas you were slaves of the Sin, but you obeyed from the heart that form of doctrine to which you were delivered [by God]. And having been freed from the Sin, you became slaves of the Righteousness. (Rom 6:17–18)

Every human has been enslaved to sin since the moment of conception (Ps 51:5), unless and until they are freed by Christ. If you are owned by sin as lord, then your will is also bound by sin; you are not free to choose God, to believe in his Son. You, with your will, hate and reject God (Rom 8:7, 8). Before the Roman saints knew Christ, they were slaves of the sin—owned by sin as a powerful lord and master. But now they are no longer slaves of the sin, the power of which is the law (1 Cor 15:56). They were delivered by God to "that form of doctrine" (the gospel, with all it teaches). They could not free themselves, but God was active, so that we obeyed the gospel from the heart (Rom 10:16; 6:17). To be enslaved no longer to sin but to righteousness is to be enslaved to God in Christ. A person is either a slave of sin unto death or a bond servant of Christ unto eternal life (Rom 1:16–17; 6:3–7, 14–23); there is no middle or neutral ground between the two opposing powers. To be Christ's slave means to be enslaved to the power of righteousness, even the righteousness of God (Rom 1:16–17; see 6:22).

> I speak in human terms because of the weakness of your flesh; for as you presented your [bodily] members as slaves to uncleanness and to wickedness unto wickedness, even so now present your members as servants to Righteousness for sanctification. For when you were the slaves of the Sin, you were free regarding the *Righteousness* [free from *Christ's* lordship]. What fruit then did you have at that time in the things of which you are now ashamed? For the end of those things is Death. But now, having been freed from the Sin, and having been enslaved to God, you have your fruit unto holiness, and the end is eternal life. (Rom 6:19–22)

The fruit of being justified and thereby freed from sin is holiness. Those who are justified through faith in Christ *will* be made holy. Transformation is not the gospel—it is the fruit of the gospel (6:22; 2 Cor 3:17, 18). We are enslaved to God, our rightful Lord. The *fruit* of this enslavement is holiness/sanctification, and the outcome is *eternal life*, knowing God the Father through Jesus Christ. By being my Creator and my Redeemer, God has every right to my obedience to him, moment by moment, and such obedience is for my good. To the extent that some preachers (and church-es) keep their distance from God and his lordship (found in Paul's letters), they reveal that they have never really seen or understood (the glory of) the grace of Christ; and they continue on "milk" instead of "meat" and have an inordinate interest in the things of the world (2 Cor 4:4, 6, 17–18; 1 Cor 3:2; 1 John 2:15). Paul ends with these words:

> For the wages which the Sin pays is Death; but the free-gift of
> God is Eternal Life in Christ Jesus our Lord. (6:23)

How did God give us the gift of eternal life? Christ *died* (body and soul) on our behalf, for *death* is the wages of sin (6:23). But traditionalists, having been influenced by Augustine[37] and his followers, with his platonic presup-position of the *indestructibility* of the soul, must *reinterpret* everything that the apostle Paul wrote about death, for to them, "death" cannot include the soul because the soul (they claim) cannot die. However, the Scriptures con-trast God, who alone is incorruptible, with man, who is corruptible (Rom 1:23). Paul, in Rom 2:5–10, regarding the day of the Lord, says that, for those who do not obey the truth of the gospel, there will be "wrath" (2:8), which will be to the degree and duration as fits each individual's deeds and will be experienced in what Jesus calls "Gehenna," which (fiery garbage dump) was a picture of a place where "he will *burn up* the chaff with unquenchable fire" (Matt 3:12 AV). The apostle does not say that this wrath is eternal, as the *life* is eternal in 2:7. The outworking of this temporal wrath, in affliction and anguish, occurs, resulting ultimately in their destruction—as Paul says, "Vessels of wrath fitted for [the purpose of] *destruction*" (Rom 9:22), just as grace reigns for God's elect for (the purpose of) *life eternal* (Rom 5:21). The *soul*, to which the mortal body will be reunited, for judgment, will bear God's wrath in Gehenna (hell), unto what both Jesus (in Matt 7:13) and Paul (in Rom 9:22 and Phil 3:19) call "destruction."

> Then comes the end, when Christ delivers the kingdom to
> God, even the Father, when he abolishes [καταργήσῃ, i.e.,
> destroys] all rule[38] and authority and power; for Christ must

37. We admit that Augustine had his good points, e.g., teaching that in Adam hu-mans are under sin's guilt from birth.

38. The word ἀρχήν (rule) here is synonymous with the "rulers" (in Greek) in Rom 8:38; Eph 6:12; Col 2:15. And "authority" (ἐξουσία) is used in Col 2:13, 16; Eph 6:12; 1 Pet 3:22. All these texts refer to Satan's principalities and powers, including the unclean spirits who will be destroyed (Mark 1:23–27). Christ will deliver the kingdom to God the Father when he *destroys*, καταργήσῃ ("does away with") them all (v. 24) as he will with human enemies (Phil 3:18–19; Luke 19:27).

reign until he has put all his enemies[39] under his feet. The last enemy that will be *destroyed* is *death* [and that for the elect only, 1 Cor 15:24–25, 28]. . . . then the Son [having completed his mission, Rom 8:29–34] also shall be subject to him [the Father] who put all things [enemies, v. 25] under him [the Son, v. 25], that God may be all in all [those who "remain forever"]. (1 Cor 15:24, 28b; 1 John 2:17)

The holy God will no longer endure sin, unbelief, and evil anywhere, in all creation, for there will only be the new creation—the new heavens and the new earth. Those who attempt to defend the traditional idea of hell (Gehenna), use Mark 9:48, where Jesus is quoting Isaiah. But in truth:

There is no doctrine of hell in the Old Testament. In Isa 66:24, at one time a much-quoted verse, the reference is not to the continuing personality (*nephesh* . . .) of the rebels, but to their *corpses*.[40]

In the real hell (Gehenna), the fire will not be quenched[41] until it has done what God ordained it to accomplish: suffering in body and soul according to God's justice, unto destruction (Rom 2:8, 9; 9:22; Matt 3:12; Phil 3:19). Says Fudge:

The figure of "unquenchable" fire appears frequently throughout scripture and signifies a fire that cannot be resisted or put out until it has done what fire is intended to do. Because this fire is "not quenched" or extinguished, it completely consumes what is put into it. . . . Because it cannot be thwarted in its intended purpose, or stopped short of accomplishing its goal, "unquenchable" fire ("irresistible fire") fully consumes (Ezek 20:47–48), reduces to nothing (Amos 5:5–6) or burns up what is put into it (Matt 3:12).[42]

---

39. "Enemies" (ἐχθροὺς) here includes Christ's human enemies (see Luke 19:27, 43; Acts 13:10; Rom 11:28; Phil 3:18–19); as well as Satan's unseen rulers and powers (non-elect, fallen angels; 1 Tim 5:21). In 15:24–28, there are only *two* groups: God (and Christ's) *enemies* (who will be destroyed) and *friends* (Rom 5:10; John 15:13–15) in whom God will be all in all (1 Cor 15:28).

40. *IBC*, 64.

41. It refers to a fire that *destroys*, like that which happened to Sodom and Gomorrah, see Jude 5–7; compare 2 Pet 2:1–6; 3:6–7; Matt 3:12; 10:28. The fire *may* be everlasting, but (in either case) it will burn up the chaff, unto their destruction (Matt 3:12; 10:28; Rom 9:22; Phil 3:19).

42. Fudge, *Fire That Consumes*, 77.

Humans were created for life and not for death. But how much more severe will be the second death, which will express God's day-of-judgment wrath, unto the death and destruction that is never undone, which is the opposite of *immortality*. This is where Augustine's teaching is revealed to be a form of unbelief in the apostolic Christ, for Christ is the "life" that is synonymous with "immortality" (incorruptibility) in the following parallelism: "our Savior Jesus Christ, who has abolished death, and brought *life* and *immortality* to light through the gospel" (2 Tim 1:10). The opposite of death is life and immortality. Christ is "the true God and eternal life" (1 John 5:20). What the unbeliever is tragically deprived of, and that forever, is eternal life with God in Christ, enjoying God's unconditional love, immortal life, fellowship, and presence, which gives all the joyous blessings of the new creation—the new heaven and the new earth. That deprivation is the ultimate meaning of "death" in Rom 6:23 and everywhere else in Paul's letters. Ignorance of this is due, to a great extent, to the powerful influence of Augustine but ultimately to ignorance of and unbelief in the God of the apostolic gospel of God, revealed in Jesus Christ. Thus, many Christ-believers are not perceiving what eternal life (immortality) really is. For, in the light of Christ, the loss of eternal life is inexpressibly tragic and an infinite loss. The loss of *Christ* (eternal life) is what makes *death* the ultimate punishment and *loss*. But the truth is that "death" in Rom 6:23 means being deprived of life, the very life of God in Christ. So, by exaggerating hell (which is really Gehenna), traditionalists unwittingly minimize the inexpressible worth of eternal life with Christ and God his Father in the age to come. Hughes rightly says:

> There is no more radical antithesis than that between life and death. Confronted with this antithesis, the position of Augustine cannot avoid involvement in the use of contradictory concepts, for the notion of death that is everlastingly endured requires the postulation that the damned be kept endlessly *alive* to endure it. Thus, Augustine was forced to argue that for those in hell, "death will not be abolished, but will be eternal," and that "the living bodies of men hereafter will be such as to endure everlasting pain and fire without ever dying . . . " and he depicted the wicked as everlastingly doomed to "drag out a miserable existence in eternal death without the power of dying." It would be hard to imagine a concept more confusing than that of death which means endlessly existing without the power of dying. This, however, is the corner into which Augustine (in company with many others) argued himself.[43]

43. Hughes, *True Image*, 403, emphasis mine.

God's warning at the beginning, regarding the forbidden tree, "In the day that you eat of it, you shall die," was addressed to man as a corporeal-spiritual creature—should he eat it, it was as such that he would die. There is no suggestion that a part of him was undying and therefore that his dying would be in part only. The immortality, accordingly, of which the Christian is assured, is not inherent in himself or in his soul but is bestowed by God and is the immortality of the whole person in the fulness of his humanity, bodily as well as spiritual. This immortality, unearned by us, has been gained for us by the incarnate Son who, by partaking of our human nature in its fullness, both bodily as well as spiritual, and by dying our death, nullified the power of the devil and removed from us the fear and the sting of death (Heb 2:14f.; 1 Cor 15:55f.).[44]

Let us look at the text in which God warned man that through disobedience he would surely die:

The LORD God commanded the man, saying, "Of every tree of the garden you may freely eat; but of the tree of the knowledge of good and evil, you shall not eat of it; for in the day that you eat of it, *dying, you shall surely die.*" (Gen 2:15–17)

And the serpent said to the woman, "You will *not* surely die" (Gen 3:4). And, ever since Adam and Eve believed *the lie,* Satan has continued to deceive humans to believe the lie: "You will *not* surely die," especially due to the deceiver's incredible influence through Plato on this world, whereby many believe in the immortality (indestructibility) of the soul.

Then the LORD God said, "Behold, the man has become like one of Us, to know good and evil. And now, lest he put out his hand and take also of the tree of life, and eat, and live forever." (Gen 3:22 NKJV)

This confirms that the fruit of this tree is necessary for immortality, and without it humans are mortal. Hence the earlier emphatic pronouncement, "in the day that you eat of it you shall die," is seen in context to mean: "On the day you eat of it, you will cut yourself off from the tree of life and therefore eventually die." So the second creation account portrays human immortality as potential rather than actual, and ends with human death as certain because of human sin.[45]

---

44. Hughes, *True Image,* 400.

45. Johnston, *Shades of Sheol,* 41.

After his disobedience, when God said, "Now, lest he put forth his hand, and take of the tree of life, and eat, and live forever . . ." God did not desire, nor did he allow man, now under sin's power, *to live forever* in that state of being "under sin" (Rom 3:9). Adam was sentenced to death (Gen 3:19) so, eventually, to dust he returned. Until then (because of his disobedience), God drove out the man and woman and placed angels at the east of the garden of Eden and the flame of a sword that turned every way (encompassing the tree of life), so that it was impossible to "eat of the tree of life and live forever," to guard the way (the access) to the tree of life. Adam's sin brought death into all humans (Rom 5:12). Since God prevented Adam who, through his sin, joined the rebellious kingdom-reign of darkness, bringing all of Adam's descendants with them, from having such a fate as living forever in the state of being a sinner, how could God allow anyone to live *forever* in a state of rebellion against God? He will not, as it has been written:

> The wages that the Sin [of and in Adam] pays is *death*, but the
> gift of God is *eternal life* in Christ Jesus our Lord. (Rom 6:23)

To the extent a person does not understand the scriptural meaning of *death*,[46] to that extent that person will not understand the scriptural meaning and surpassing worth of *eternal life*.

---

46. Thus, for a more thorough commentary on 6:23, in light of the gospel of God, see ch. 20: "Death and Eternal Life."

TEN

With Christ, We Died to the Law

(Rom 7)

In Christ, God himself has ended our bondage to the law, in which the law was functionally a god, a destructive power, lording it over us (7:1), the result being death.[1] But through our union with Christ in his death and resurrection, we have been severed and released from the law, so that we now serve God in the newness of the Spirit (in our human spirit), and not in the oldness of the letter, the law (7:1–6 summarized).

In Rom 7:7, Paul defines sin as lust, as coveting. The one whose Lord is Jesus (7:24) delights in the law of God ("Do not covet") in his *inner* man (7:22), but with his flesh, he only serves the law of sin/coveting (7:25)—for in his *flesh* nothing good (that is, of God) dwells (7:18).

EVER SINCE HUMANS SINNED in Adam, they have been under condemnation as a result of the broken covenant (Rom 5:12–19; Hos 6:7). So, Paul calls the law "the ministry of condemnation" (2 Cor 3:9), which lords this condemnation over a person as long as he lives "in the flesh" (3:19; 7:1; see 7:5). Therefore, the sobering truth is that every moment of a person's life in the flesh is continuously under condemnation—whether that person knows it or not. Because the law is spiritual (and demands the spiritual), it condemns all who are in the flesh (3:9–20; 7:1, 14).

---

1. Rom 7:5, 9–13; 2 Cor 3:7.

> Brethren, do you not know that the law *lords it over* a man
> *as long as he lives* [in the flesh, 7:5]? For the married woman
> is bound by law to her husband as long as he lives. But if the
> husband dies, she has been freed from the law of the husband.
> (Rom 7:1–2)

The law *lords it over* (κυριεύει) a man *as long as he lives* (in the flesh, 7:5).
According to the law of Moses (which Paul uses as an illustration of where
believers are in relation to *the law*), "the law of the husband" is that which
the woman is under (obligation) until the husband dies. That is, his death
legally, under the law, *ends* their marriage just as if *she* herself *had died*. In
7:1–6, Paul uses this law-analogy to say that the only way that the law will
not *lord it over* a person is if he dies with Christ so that *Jesus* becomes his
Lord instead.

> For the married woman has been bound by law to the living
> husband; but if the husband dies, she has been discharged from
> the law of the husband. Therefore, while the husband lives, she
> will be called an adulteress if she becomes married to a different
> man; but if the husband dies, she is freed from the law, so that
> she is not an adulteress, though she is married to another man.
> Therefore, my brethren, *you* also were put to *death* to the law
> through the [crucified] body of Christ, that you [like the wife,
> in that you are now free] might belong to a different husband, to
> the One having been raised from the dead. (Rom 7:2–4)

In the analogy, the law does not die. It is the husband who dies, whereby
the married woman is now *freed from the law* (of Moses, 7:1–2) and of
works (3:27, as we saw in Rom 5), which we were under in Adam. The
"married woman" stands for those who are in Christ, who were bound by
the law and now are released from it through our union with Christ in his
death ("crucified body") and resurrection, "the One having been raised
from the dead" (7:4).

> For when we were in the flesh, the passions of sins [which were]
> through the law, were energized in our bodily members result-
> ing in bearing fruit unto *death*. But now we were severed and
> released² from the law, having died [with Christ] to that [law]

2. With Christ, I died to *the law*, in order that I might live to *God*; for with Christ I
have been co-crucified, and I (as under law/condemnation) live no longer, but Christ
lives in me (Gal 2:19–20). The word καταργέω, which is translated as "released from"
in Rom 7:6 (NASB), is translated "severed from" in Gal 5:4 (NASB). Thus, we have
been *severed* from the law through our death with Christ, through which we are
released from the law, in order to live to God (Gal 2:19–20). We believe that καταργέω

in which we were utterly bound, so that we serve in newness of [the Spirit in our] spirit, and not [any longer] in oldness of the *letter* [*the law*, written . . . in stones, which *kills*, in contrast to *the Spirit* who gives *life* (2 Cor 3:6, 7)]. (Rom 7:5–6)

Paul's analogy of being now "married to Christ" (7:4) means that we have died with Christ and been utterly severed from the law by God himself through our death with Christ, that we would be joined to Christ and live to God in newness of Christ's age-to-come life, newness of the Spirit, in contrast to oldness of the letter (see 2 Cor 3:6). The new life in him is that of the new creation (the age to come) beyond the law and the righteousness of the law, for our righteousness is the righteousness of God in Christ. We could not be more (spiritually, in our inner man) severed from the flesh and the law (7:5–6) than God has made us, for God has cut us off from the flesh (Rom 2:28–29). We wait for our bodily severance from this body of the flesh and of death (7:24).

> In the new marriage, we do not go back and obey the commandments of the first husband. We are free of all requirement to do so. Indeed, it would be adulterous to do so. We are married not to the law now, but to "another"—to the living Christ who reigns within us. We do not return to living "in oldness of the letter," for "we serve in newness of the Spirit" (Rom 7:1–6). That is why we must "cast out" the old if we are to bear fruit in the new—for the external "ought to" will always render Christ of no effect (Gal 5:1–4).[3]

We now serve in newness of the Spirit in our spirit (7:6), for the one being joined to the Lord is one Spirit with him (the Lord, the Spirit, who is God) (1 Cor 6:17 AT), and the fruit of the Spirit is love, joy, etc. (Gal 5:22). The passions (desires) were *by the law*; so we had to be released from the law through our union with Christ. The ultimate problem with the law is that it is not Christ, for to look to it instead of Christ is to trust in *ourselves* for righteousness and life, which is putting us in God's place (Rom 7:7–13). Walking ("step by step") by faith in Christ is a matter of being led by the Spirit, which equates to living by Christ's justifying love for us, which Paul contrasts with living by the law in Gal 5:1–5, 13a, 18. Paul, justly released and severed from the law by his death with Christ to the law, now serves God in newness of spirit (in newness of life, 6:4), for the Spirit of *life in Christ Jesus* dwells in Paul's spirit, whereby he serves God (1:9). This

---

includes both meanings in 7:6.

3. Ord, *What Is the Mystery*, 55.

applies for all in Christ (7:22, 8:9–10; Eph 3:16). Paul serves no longer in oldness of the letter (of the law), as he did in Judaism (7:5a; Gal 1:13), for he is in the "new testament . . . of the Spirit" (2 Cor 3:6), which means he is not without the law of God, precisely because he is *in* (the law of) Christ (1 Cor 9:21) who is God. Many Christ-believers do not realize what happened to them when Christ entered into them and what that means for them. They need to know of Christ's sufficiency in them in their living for God: Christ alone (apart from the law) living in them, for "the letter which Christ writes on the heart is not written with ink on scrolls, as the Torah was, but with the Spirit of the living God—not in tables of stone [as Torah was], but in . . . the heart" (2 Cor 3:3).

So, in 7:6, the fact that by "newness of spirit" the apostle means the Holy Spirit as joined to his human spirit (Rom 8:16; 1 Cor 6:17) is revealed by this: We were "married" to another, to Christ who was raised from the dead (7:4); and, according to 2 Cor 3, "oldness of the letter" (Rom 7:6) means "the letter, written on stones" (2 Cor 3:6, the Ten Commandments), which is contrasted with "the Spirit" who gives (eternal) life in 2 Cor 3:6–10. Paul's "married to another" aligns with our being betrothed to Christ, waiting for our wedding day (2 Cor 11:2–3). We are now-already "married" in spirit and not-yet married in body to Christ (Rom 8:23). According to Paul in 7:4–6, for a person in Christ to go back to the law (for justification or sanctification, 1 Cor 1:30) is to commit spiritual adultery. The real Paul knows nothing of the law dying or being abolished as long as this age lasts (7:1[4]). Therefore, the only hope for sinners is to die to the law—to die out of being "in the flesh" (this present age) through our death with Christ, that we might live to God as new creatures in (union with) the risen Christ (Rom 6:6–11; 7:4–6; 8:1–2, 9). We who have died to the law with Christ are dead to the law—that is, to its condemnation, with its constant obligation to be justified before God by the law (Gal 5:1–5; Rom 7:1). And this includes the obligation to the law as rule of life. If you are obligated to do the law "for sanctification," as some would have it, then you are obligated to do it for justification; for a person is either obligated to the law or one is not (Rom 7:1; Gal 5:1–5), for the Christ who is our righteousness is also our sanctification (1 Cor 1:30). The truth, that the law is not of faith (Gal 3:12), also proves that the so-called "third use of the law" (the law as rule of life) cannot coincide with justification in Christ alone, with its corollary of (justification by) faith in Christ alone, for where there is the law, there is one's own righteousness (Phil 3:9)—whether for justification or sanctification. There is a dynamic, inseparable connection between our justification

---

4. See also Nygren, *Commentary on Romans*, 272.

in Christ and our death with Christ to the law. We have died and are dead to the law, which works only wrath (4:15). This means we are dead to the law as our god—which it was by lording it over us (7:1), through having Christ as our Lord, in whom we are alive to God under his grace in Christ (Rom 6:4–15). Either the law or Christ is our God—they cannot both be so at the same time. Regarding Rom 7:1–4, Leander Keck comments:

> Not to be overlooked is that the one to whom the remarried widow belongs is the resurrected Christ, not "the Jesus of history." Why? Because the primary purpose of death to the law is a wholly *new kind of life*, one that for Paul is not to be confused with adhering to Jesus as example and teacher. For Paul, Jesus of Nazareth is not a substitute for Moses (in the same game) but an alternative to Moses *in a different sport*.[5]

This is true, because "the oldness of the letter" (7:6) includes the work of the law written in the natural heart (conscience) (Rom 2:14–15). Jesus of Nazareth—Christ according to the flesh (2 Cor 5:16)—was still under the law and teaching the law for life,[6] for he had not yet accomplished redemption through his death and he had not been raised from the dead (Rom 3:24–26; 4:25; 10:4–10). Knowing "Christ according to the flesh" is knowing him under the law (as he was before he redeemed us, Gal 4:4) and/or according to our flesh, rather than as the life-giving Spirit (1 Cor 15:45) who indwells us, for "the Lord is the Spirit," the Spirit who gives life (2 Cor 3:6; Rom 8:2).[7] Regarding Paul's "no longer knowing Christ according to the flesh," Paul is referring first to himself (2 Cor 5:11–13, 19, 20) and, secondly, to all who are in Christ. He writes:

> For the love of Christ controls us, having concluded this, that One died for all, therefore all died; and He died for all [the elect, Rom 8:33; in order] that those who *live* [in his resurrection *life*] should no longer live for themselves, but for Him who died and rose again on their behalf [for *those who* now *live*, who are alive to God]. Therefore, from now on we recognize no man

5. Keck, *Romans*, 176–77, emphasis mine.

6. Mark 10:17–19; Luke 18:18–30; Matt 19:16–26; and Luke 10:25–37, where Jesus uses Lev 18:5; contrast this with Paul's apostolic use (now that Christ has died and been raised) of Lev 18:5 in Rom 10:5–9; Gal 3:11–12.

7. Christ united himself with our old humanity in Adam, died under the law's curse (death), and rose again. Therefore, since we died and rose again with Christ, we know him no longer according to the flesh, but according to the Spirit—according to an accomplished *reconciliation* (2 Cor 5:14–21). Thus, Paul calls Christ, now that he has been raised and exalted, a "life-giving Spirit" (1 Cor 15:45), saying that "the Lord is the Spirit"—the Spirit who gives life (2 Cor 3:6).

[in Christ] according to the flesh; even though we have known Christ according to the flesh, yet now [since Christ was raised, and us with him] we know him thus [according to the flesh] no longer. (2 Cor 5:14–16 NASB)

For we know Christ according to the Spirit—according to *reconciliation* (5:[16,] 19) through our death and resurrection with him—through which the old creation died to the law, condemnation, sin, and death and rose with Christ a *new creation*, freed from those ruling, destructive powers.

Therefore, if anyone is in Christ, he/she is a new creation; the old things have *passed away* [with Christ in his death]; behold, new things have come [in his resurrection life]. (2 Cor 5:17)

The new things that have come are the things of the new creation in Christ— the righteousness and the life that are *not* of this age, not of Adam as created (soulish man) nor of man in the flesh under sin, but from the last Adam, the life-giving Spirit. And Ernst Käsemann, on Rom 7:5–6, wrote:

Now the central statement is made that *only* under the dominion of *the Spirit* . . . is the dominion of *the law* broken and vanquished.[8]

Sin, by the Law, Brought Forth Death

For when we were in the flesh, the passions of Sin, which were *by the law*, worked in our bodily members, to bring forth fruit unto Death. (Rom 7:5)

This verse is so weighty that Paul, in verses 7 through 13, proceeds to explain it. These verses reveal that "the power of sin is the law" (1 Cor 15:56). Paul began by saying that "the law lords it over a person as long as he lives" (7:1), that is, lives "in the flesh" (7:5). This is central to his gospel. How did the law "bring forth fruit unto death"? The commandment was *for life* (7:10). If *man in Adam* obeyed God's commandment, he would have lived. The apostle, using the story of Adam, proceeds to tell his readers how sin as a power (1 Cor 15:56) "through the commandment" deceived Adam by exciting lust (desire).

But the law came in, in order that *the trespass* [*of Adam*—of unbelief in God's word—with its *fruit unto death* (5:21) for all in the flesh, Rom 7:5,10] might abound. (Rom 5:20a)

8. Käsemann, *Commentary on Romans*, 191, emphasis mine.

Adam had *the knowledge of God* before his lapse into sin (which, because he and all in him sinned, lost him the knowledge of God, Col 3:10). "The heathen did not think it worth the trouble to retain the knowledge of God."[9] Thus, Adam did not at all need "the knowledge of good and evil," one derived from an independent-from-God source, as the forbidden tree offered to him. Adam was not even thinking of an independent-from-God knowledge or desiring such. He did not know that he was naked—until the evil one, through the serpent, used *the commandment* with the woman in the form of a question: "Has God indeed said, 'You shall not eat of every tree of the garden?'" (Gen 3:1 NKJV), and thereby aroused unbelief (Gal 3:12) toward God and his word. For, before sin entered the world, Adam and all in him (including Paul) were alive.

> I was *alive* once [before the serpent and the fall]—apart from *the law*, but when *the commandment* came ["of the tree . . . *you shall not* eat"] sin became alive, and I *died*. (Rom 7:9)

When Adam disobeyed God, he died, and all in him also died with him (5:12). In Rom 7:7–13, Paul uses "the commandment" (referring to Adam[10]) six times, and he uses "the law" (relating to not only Adam but primarily to OT Israel) six times. Therefore, in 7:7–13, Paul uses "*the commandment*" and "*the law*" *interchangeably*; and he thereby reveals the *universal* reality of *the law and sin unto death*. Sin is personified by Paul; he says that sin (as power) uses the law to accomplish its ultimate purpose and end, which is death. So, Paul reiterates what he said in Rom 5, that not only Adam sinned unto death (5:19), but that the law entered, in order that the trespass (of Adam) might abound (5:20), in order that, as sin has reigned (as king) unto death, even so might grace reign (as lord) through justification for the purpose of eternal life through Jesus Christ our Lord (5:21 AT). Yet Paul insists that the law is not sin. For he says that sinful passions (desires, lusts) were "by the law." And to be "in the flesh" is to be bound by *the law*, and to be *released from the law* is to be *no longer "in the flesh"* (7:5–6). So, Paul, using the terms from Genesis—"commandment," "coveted/desired," "deception," and "death"[11]—through the light of *the gospel* reveals that it is *sin* which uses *the law* to bring forth *death*—severance from God, the source of life. Ultimately, it is not the fault of the law, which is righteous and good. When the law came upon the scene, sin (as power) went from being dead (nonexistent) to being alive and thus effectively powerful. Paul says, "Sin deceived me" (Adam, and

<hr>

9. Hodge, *Romans*, 64.

10. See Gen 2:16, 17; 3:11 and Rom 7:9–11.

11. See Gen 2:16; 3:4, 6, 13 respectively.

all in him; see Rom 5) and through the law (sin) "killed me." Since this *law-and-sin* synergy (in 7:7–13) was true for Adam in his innocence, it certainly remains true for us who will die because we are in Adam (1 Cor 15:22). On Paul's use of "covet" in 7:7–13, Forde wrote:

> Even if I, as a sinner, try to obey the command "Thou shalt not covet" . . . I do not escape because now I only covet . . . a certain perfection for myself . . . I covet "sainthood." So, I have not escaped at all. Sin is aroused all the more, and precisely the law, even though it is good, arouses in me "*all* manner of covetousness." Since I am a covetous person, the command "Thou shalt not covet" can at best only change the object of my covetousness. But in the end, there is little difference *coram deo* whether I covet my neighbor's wife or my own righteousness. Now then, the point is simply that the law cannot save sinners.[12]

And since *covetousness* is *idolatry* (Col 3:5:), since I covet my own righteousness, I am desiring to trust in myself as God, for only in God is there righteousness. And any other desire also makes a god (idol) out of what I covet in place of the one true God. Paul wrote:

> Is the law sin? May it not be! For I would not have come to [experientially] know *Sin* [as power] except through law, for I would not have [experientially] known *coveting* [*i.e., Sin, as a power in me*], except the law had said, "You shall not covet." But Sin, taking occasion [finding a base of operations] through the commandment [the law], worked in me [as in Adam] all manner of lust/coveting, for, apart from law, *Sin* [as powerful master] is dead. For I was once alive without the law [before law, without the commandment]; but when the commandment came, *Sin* became *alive* and *I died*. And the commandment ["You shall not eat"], which was for life, I [in Adam] found to be [a law] unto death [5:12; 7:5; 8:2]. For Sin, taking occasion through the commandment, *deceived* me, and through it [the law, the commandment] *killed* me [severed me from Life]. Was then that which is good [the law] made death to me? May it not be! But it was Sin, that it might be revealed to be Sin, by effecting death in me through [using] that which is good [the law]; in order that *Sin*, by means of the commandment [the law] might be shown to be exceedingly sinful [and thus exceedingly deceptive]. (7:7–13)

---

12. Forde, *Justification by Faith*, 32. Forde's last sentence reaffirms the apostle's important conclusion about *the law* in Rom 3:19–20; therefore, Forde's interpretation here on 7:7–13 accords with Paul's gospel (2:16) and is correct.

It is essential to realize that Paul uses "sin" and "covetousness" interchangeably in 7:7. Sin *is* covetousness—coveting life apart from God, desiring something other than God in God's rightful place. In 7:7–13, the personal "knowing" of the *sin* to which Paul is referring is not knowing what are transgressions of the law. He knew that as a Pharisee. Paul's having "known sin" is his experientially knowing the power and lordship of sin through the law; that is, that sin-through-law occasions "death in me" (7:13; see 7:9–11; 2 Cor 3:6; 1 Cor 15:56), severing him from God's life (Gal 5:1–4). Before Christ revealed himself in Paul, he thought he was blameless according to the law (Phil 3:3-9). But now he realizes that the flesh can only covet (desire) things other than God in God's place. In Adam, I desire to take God's rightful place in my life. That was Adam's sin! The law occasions every lust or desire, every desire that is of the flesh of sin (8:3) and thus not of the Spirit of God. And this includes the desire to be righteous according to the law by way of my own righteousness, apart from God's in Christ. Paul's "You shall not covet" in 7:7 is used by the apostle through the revelation of the gospel, transcending that of Moses' use of "You shall not covet" to OT Israel. Therefore, Paul concludes by saying, "I am of flesh, sold under (the power of) sin." Käsemann said:

> What sin really is, and the nature of its dominion . . . are brought to light only by the gospel. The pneumatic alone can perceive them. Paul's theology as a whole stands or falls with this statement, since the justification of the ungodly is its center. For it the moral man is the very one who is most deeply engulfed in *the power of sin* without being able to recognize it according to 9:31 or 10:3 (H. W. Schmidt).[13]

The pneumatic is one indwelt by the Spirit of Christ crucified and risen. "The power of sin" here is the power of self-justification; for the moral ("righteous") man, with conscience tuned to the law, it is impossible to let go of his righteousness before God. Thus, preachers who teach or imply that sin is essentially breaking the law (of Moses)—and not the truth that sin is essentially the disobedience of unbelief in Christ—do not preach sin in the light of the gospel of God but are instead implying that sin is, in its essence, immorality. But the morally "righteous" person who would be justified by law is utterly under sin's power, as Käsemann said.

Not only is sin defined as lust (7:7), but this lust is involuntary. That is, I, the new man, never will or wish to lust/covet; and yet my flesh continually lusts, and that is why he says "O wretched man I"!

---

13. Käsemann, *Commentary on Romans*, 200, emphasis mine.

So next, the apostle expounds on what he just said, that, although the law is good, the problem that makes the law impotent to bring forth the good (in the one whose Lord is Jesus, 7:24) is sin that indwells his flesh, the body of this *death* (7:18, 24), the very same "death" of which he has just been speaking in Rom 7:5, 9–13! He begins:

> For we know that the law is *spiritual* [and holy, v. 12], but *I* [insofar as I am still "in the flesh"] am *of flesh*, sold under the [power of] *Sin.* (7:14)

In 7:14–25, Paul explains what he means by saying, "but I am of *flesh*, sold under the Sin." Paul has already defined "sin" as "coveting" in 7:7, and he has defined "the law" as "You shall not covet." By the revelation of Jesus Christ (Gal 1:12), he reveals that sin is covetousness (which is simultaneously idolatry, Col 3:5). Therefore, the word "sin" throughout Rom 7 should be interpreted as *covetousness* (desire), whether for life/righteousness (7:10; Gal 3:21), or any desire to carry out the deeds of the flesh (Gal 5:19–21)—every desire which has "flesh" (7:14) as its source. When Paul uses the words "my mind" in 7:23 and 25, he means "the mind of *Christ*" (1 Cor 2:16), for having the mind of Christ is the same as having "the mind of the Spirit" (Rom 8:6). Because Paul is, in one sense, still in the flesh,[14] from that perspective he can say, "I am of flesh [and in that sense], having been sold under the Sin [covetousness, 7:7]" (7:14). For Paul still lives in the flesh in which nothing good (before God) dwells (7:18). But that is "no longer"[15] the Paul who is now joined to Christ; for Paul, as a new creation, has the mind of Christ, which he calls "my mind" in contrast to "my flesh" and "my members." For the new creation, all things have become new, and that surely includes the mind of the new creation,[16] as it is written:

> Whoever has been *begotten of God* does not sin, for *God's seed* remains in him and he *cannot sin*, because he has been begotten of *God*. (1 John 3:9)
> And that you put on *the new man*, which was created according to *God*, in *righteousness* and true *holiness*. (Eph 4:24)

This is the man referred to when Paul says, "So now, no longer I [the new man] work it [covetousness], but Sin dwelling in me . . . that is, in my *flesh*" (7:17–18). Even though Paul with the mind of Christ wants to do the good, that is, God's will—wants to not lust—nevertheless, with his flesh (not the

---

14. Gal 2:20; Phil 1:22, 24.
15. Rom 7:17, 20.
16. 2 Cor 5:17; Rom 7:23, 25.

Spirit, not according to the inner man, 7:22) he lusts and thus unintentionally, as Paul says in 7:15–20.[17] So, Paul is saying:

> "I am *not* in the flesh,"[18] for I (in my inner man) am *no longer in* "the Sin dwelling in me," that is, in my *flesh*.[19] Instead, I am now "in the Spirit (God) who is dwelling in me"[20]—my inner man.

I, in my inner man (7:22), am no longer joined to the flesh (of sin), and sin is no longer in me—my inner man. Sin is only in my outer man (body),[21] which is still spiritually dead because of sin (8:10). Thus, Christ alone is my life (Col 3:4). Sin[22] was my life. But now I am only united to Christ—no longer to sin in Adam. In Rom 7:14–25, just as in 8:1–10, the believer is not fleshly minded, for his mind is "the mind of the Spirit" (8:6). Therefore, Paul delights in the law of *God* the Spirit (8:2) in the inner man (7:22), which agrees with the law: "You shall not covet" (7:7). And, even though his mind *wants* God's will to be done on earth as it is in heaven, it is not done now, in his body of flesh, *as it is* done now by those who are in heaven and will be done in heaven. We wait for the redemption of our body, when *the Spirit* will then rule, not only in our spirit but also over our body (8:11, 19–25), which remains (spiritually) dead because of sin (8:10). Therefore, Paul says:

> Who will deliver me from the body of this death? Thanks be to God [who will deliver me, see 8:21–25] through Jesus Christ Our Lord. So then, with *the mind* [of Christ] I myself serve the law of *God* [which says "You shall not covet," which is written on my heart by the Spirit, and is fulfilled by the Spirit indwelling me, the law of the Spirit];[23] but [on the other hand] with *the flesh* I serve the law of *Sin*" [*covetousness*[24]]. (7:24–25)

Spiritually, but not yet bodily, the body of the flesh of sin (the flesh that is owned by sin) has been "removed" (Col 2:11–12), cut off from the inner man by Paul's spirit being joined to the Lord (alone, 1 Cor 6:17), so Paul

---

17. Thus, circumstances which would invite, provide, and encourage involuntary lust in the flesh are wisely avoided (see Rom 13:14), for they easily weaken us, making it easier to succumb to the flesh with its desires.

18. Rom 7:5–6 (8:9).

19. Rom 7:17b, 18.

20. Rom 8:11c.

21. This is not a novel view; Dr. Lloyd-Jones holds it throughout his commentary on Rom 6: *The New Man*.

22. Unbelief in Christ.

23. 2 Cor 3:3; Rom 8:3, 4; see 8:2.

24. See Rom 7:7.

says what he does in 7:14–25 about his flesh (outer man, 2 Cor 4:16). For the flesh is still indwelt by sin, the sin he refers to in 7:7–13, where the law is not the ultimate culprit. Rather, it is sin, which uses the law for its own death-inflicting end. For the flesh, with its desire for things other than Christ, has lusts that are utterly against the desires of the new man. So, sinful flesh is what makes the law ("You shall not covet") impotent (8:3) to perform the good (as it will in glory, 8:19–25), which the new mind, the mind of heaven, desires to do. Perhaps the best commentary on 7:14–25 is in Galatians, where Paul says:

> Now I say, walk by [means of] the Spirit, and the desires of the flesh you will not perform. For the flesh lusts [sets its desire] against the Spirit, and the Spirit lusts [sets its desires] against the flesh; for these oppose each other, to prevent you from doing what you [as of the flesh, or as of the Spirit] would [do]. (Gal 5:16–17)

The first truth here is that the Spirit's desires prevent the flesh's desires from being done—as they *would* be done if the Spirit were not in us. The second thing is that the flesh's desires prevent the Spirit's desires from being done as they would be done according to the mind of Christ and as they will be done in glory. In Rom 7:14–25, Paul expounds on the second truth. So, the flesh continually sets its desires against the Spirit and opposes *the Spirit*, the mind of *Christ* in me (1 Cor 2:12, 16). The Spirit in us causes our spirit to long for our body's redemption (freedom, 7:24; 8:20–25), when the Spirit will rule the body without the hindrance of the flesh of sin (Rom 8:3). The Spirit and its desires prevent the one in Christ from being totally fleshly in his desires, and the unregenerate *flesh* and *its* desires prevent you from being totally spiritual in your desires, and thus from being able to fully carry them out, as when you are glorified, for then you *will* love God with *all* your heart and your neighbor as yourself. Luther says:

> In addition, we are opposed by half of our very selves, namely, by reason and all its powers. Moreover, because the flesh cannot believe . . . that the promises of God are true, it resists the spirit. Therefore, it contends against the spirit and, as Paul says, holds the spirit captive (Rom 7:23), to keep it from believing as firmly as it wants to (Gal. 5:17).[25]

The "members" are the members of the *body*, the *flesh*. So Luther says:

25. *LW* 26:64.

> But the law of the members striving against the law of the mind, *hinders faith in us* and suffers it not to be perfect . . . Paul himself, feeling this battle of the flesh against the spirit cries out, "Oh! Wretched man that I am, who shall deliver me from this body of death?" (Rom. vii. 24).[26]

In the flesh, there is only unbelief toward Christ, but in the Spirit there is only faith toward God.

Thus, in this life, our faith is always hindered by unfaith. What follows is Rom 7:15–25 with these insights inserted into the text.

> I [with my mind, with *its* wishes] do not understand my own actions. For I do not do what I [as a new creation] want [God's will to be done, as it is done in heaven], but I [with my flesh] do the very thing I [with my mind of Christ] hate. Now if I [in my flesh] do what I [with Christ's mind] do not want, I agree that the law is good. So then it is no longer I [new creation] that do it, but sin which dwells within me. For I know that nothing good dwells within me, that is, in my flesh. I [with my new-creation mind] can will what is right, but I [with my flesh, which serves sin] cannot do it. For I do not do the good that I [with Christ's mind] want, but the evil I do not want is what I do. Now if I do what I do not want, it is no longer I [new man] that do it, but sin which dwells within me [my flesh, 7:18]. (Rom 7:15–20 RSV)

> I find then a law, that evil [*all* manner of evil *desire*, v. 8] is present with me, the one [the new creation] who wills to do good [as though I had *no flesh* at all, as I *will* in glory]. For I delight in the law of God [the Spirit, 8:2] according to the inward man, [in which I *want* to love God with all my heart, and my neighbor as myself]. But I see another law in my [bodily] members [my flesh], warring against the law of my mind [of Christ], and bringing me into captivity to the law of sin which is in my members [my flesh, so that I *cannot* do what I *wish* to do]. O wretched man that I am! Who will deliver me from this body of death? I thank God—through Jesus Christ my Lord. So then, with my mind I myself serve the law of God [*the Spirit*], but with *the flesh* [I serve] the law of Sin [the law which occasions sin, independence from God. This is the law which Paul served as a Pharisee, for all he was then was flesh; his heart was not yet circumcised by Spirit]. (Rom 7:21–25 NKJV)

26. Luther, *Galatians*, 386.

Therefore, in Rom 7:14–25, Paul is saying, "It is *no longer I* (with *Christ's mind*) who do it (lust/covet), but Sin dwelling in me" (7:17), that is, in my flesh (7:18).

Even though the new man *wants* to do the good, that is, wants to not lust, nevertheless with his flesh he lusts, which, according to Paul's "my (new) mind," is *involuntary* lust, as he repeatedly says in 7:15–25. And regarding this lust, there is no "getting out of" Rom 7 and into Rom 8 where the desire/bondage (7:24) no longer exists—see 8:21, 23. A popular view of Rom 7:14–25 (revived many decades ago by W. G. Kummel) is that which teaches that it refers to natural man or the Jew under law, but as seen from a Christian perspective. As we have shown, this view is false. For the believer is still, in one sense, in the flesh, and, in that sense, he remains "sold under sin" (7:14) for he is still corruption (8:21; 1 Cor 15:50) and thus he awaits the incorruption of the spiritual body. Only the Spirit says, "Jesus is Lord" (1 Cor 12:3) and yet "Lord" is what Paul calls him (7:24). In 7:1–18, Paul qualifies "in me" by saying "that is, in my flesh," for with his spirit, the Spirit of Christ bears witness (8:16). With his spirit, Paul serves God (1:9). The person "under law" is only flesh, for he does not have Christ's Spirit. If it was Paul speaking as before his conversion—as under law—he would not have used the present tense as he does in 7:14–25, nor would he have seen himself as not doing the good (7:19, 20; see Phil 3:6, 9). But now, being released from the law, we serve in newness of the Spirit and not in oldness of the letter.[27] That is, "With the mind I myself serve God's law *in newness of Spirit*," according to the inner man (7:22 in light of 7:6; 2 Cor 4:16; and Eph 3:16) "but with the flesh I serve the law of sin" (7:25), which is to covet/desire things other than God in his place (7:7). When Paul says, "For according to the inner man [where Christ's Spirit dwells], I delight in the law of *God*," he does not mean, "I delight in the law of Moses," which Paul would have said were he still in the flesh (see Phil 3:3–9). But now he delights in the law of God in *the inner man*, which he strongly contrasts with the sin in *his flesh* (in 7:17, 20, 23, 25). Due to the confusion which has existed for centuries on what Paul means by "the law" in these verses, we explain them here:

> 7:17—It is no longer I (according to my inward man, 7:22), but sin that dwells in me (my flesh, 7:18).

> 7:20—(Then) no longer I work it, but the sin dwelling in me (my flesh, 7:18).

27. Rom 7:6; see 2 Cor 3:6.

7:23—I see another law (of sin) in my members (my flesh, which is) against the law of my mind (the mind of Christ, 1 Cor 2:16), in my inner man (7:22), the law of God's Spirit (8:2).

7:25—With my mind (inward man, 7:22) I serve the law of God (the Spirit, 8:2), but with the flesh the law of sin (and death, 8:2).

The body, the flesh (2 Cor 4:10–11) is the outward man (4:16), with which Paul, before Christ, served the law of Moses (Phil 3:3–9)—the gospel is that radical—but the Paul whose Lord is Jesus (7:24) says, "I delight in the law of *God*," which is defined only five verses later as "the law of *the Spirit*, the one of life in Christ Jesus." And yet, for centuries, Western Christianity has been so entrenched in the law that most Christians *presuppose* that Paul means the law of Moses when Paul says, "the law of *God*" in 7:22. But when Paul uses "the law" by itself, he means the law that says, "Do this and live," the outcome of which for sinners is condemnation unto death (2 Cor 3:7, 9). From this law Christ has set us *free* through justification and the Spirit (Rom 8:1–2). Paul delights in the law of God, but the law of *God* is now the law of the *Spirit* (Rom 8:2) who gives *life* (2 Cor 3:6), the eschatological life in Christ, that of the new creation. The author of Hebrews writes that Moses and his law are of this creation[28] and therefore not of the new creation. In the new covenant, God the Spirit has written his law in and on our new hearts.[29] The new covenant concurs with the law: "You shall not covet" (7:7), but this is the living *new* testament (heart) of the Spirit in one indwelt by the Spirit.[30] It is not a law from outside, written with ink (2 Cor 3:3), nor on stone (2 Cor 3:3, 7), nor in the outer man (2 Cor 4:16), nor in the heart of the natural human (1 Cor 2:14) who has only the spirit of the world (1 Cor 2:12). It is not the heart joined to the flesh of sin (Rom 2:14; 8:3) but the heart joined to the Lord (1 Cor 6:17). Paul writes tersely; he does not waste words in writing this letter. So, he does not waste verses 14 through 25 of Rom 7 to refer to the unbeliever, for he is writing to saints (1:6, 7). Paul writes Romans chapter 7 as complementary to what he said in Rom 6. Not only does the indicative (indicating who we are in Christ) section of 7:1–6 (we died to the law) match the similar indicative section of 6:1–11 (we died to the sin), but the second part of chapter 7 is a realistic "other side" to the experiential second half of Romans chapter 6. For, though we are to present our bodily members to God, to "not let sin reign in our mortal bodies" (Rom 6), consistently, in 7:14–25, Paul does *not* refer to sin reigning in the

28. Heb 8:1, 2; 9:19–24.

29. 2 Cor 3:3; Heb 8:10; 10:16.

30. *God the Spirit* (8:2) circumcised my heart to be owned by the Spirit (2 Cor 3:3, 6, 17; 1 Cor 6:20).

life of the one whose Lord is Jesus (7:24); but he refers to the continuous reality of coveting (sin), to its presence (v. 21), for with the flesh he continually serves the (law of) sin—which he calls "the law of sin" because sin takes occasion through *the law* (7:7–13). And "sin" here is covetousness (and also unbelief, as we have seen up to this point in Romans), which opposes the Spirit, and *sometimes the flesh wins—its desires are "carried out"* (see Gal 5:16 NASB,[31] where this opposition of the flesh against the Spirit is why he gives the command "Walk in the Spirit"). In the light of Paul's gospel, *the flesh* of sin (and Satan), if it could be articulated and heard by us, would sound something like this:

> "Feed me, give me / some fuel for my lusts /
> Feed me, feed me, for *lust* I just must.

> Vice or virtue, it matters not / I want to destroy you,
> because I hate God."

But *the Spirit of God* says:

> "Walk in the Spirit / Obey not the flesh / And you *will* be delivered / From the body of this death."

So, in Rom 7:14–25 the contrast is between Paul's *wishing* with the mind of Christ in his inner man and the *doing* of Paul, with his flesh. It's between Paul's mind and Paul's flesh, between Paul as already heaven's citizen and Paul as not yet there—as flesh[32]—between the already of the new creation and the not yet of the new creation. Five times the apostle refers to this corruption in the flesh as "slavery" from which he longs to be free (in Rom 7:14, 23–25; 8:21). In the "with my mind I serve . . . God" confession of Paul (v. 25), it is often overlooked that Christ is hidden to humans, for only God can see "the inner man" who serves in 7:22. So, to the flesh, this "serving God" is nonexistent, for flesh cannot see it! The flesh desires a seen glory. It cannot understand Paul in Rom 2:28–29. So, this service and worship of the one whose heart has been circumcised by the Spirit (Phil 3:3) is what Paul means when he says, "I delight in the law of God [the Spirit, 8:2] in the inner man" (7:22). Such delight is not seen. So, when Paul says, "But now, having died to that [law] . . . so as to serve [God] in newness of spirit," the flesh *cannot see* the spirit or heart (7:6; 2:28–29), the inner man (7:22).[33]

---

31. And so this reality is also included in 7:14–25, but not in the sense in which those deeds are *practiced* as a lifestyle, as in Gal 5:19–21.

32. Phil 3:20; see 1:20–24.

33. This interpretation of 7:14-25 accords with the word of *the cross* (1 Cor 1:18), for God is hidden there also.

Therefore, as *a new creation in Christ*, my mind's intent—my *renewed will's intent*—is *not to sin* but *to serve God*.

Thus, Luther was right when he saw in verses 14–25 the truth of "at the same time righteous and a sinner"—but, in this instance, not righteous by imputation (justification), but righteous by means of "the law of God [the Spirit] in the inner man," i.e., by *regeneration*. Thus, to covet/lust/desire (sin, 7:7) "with my flesh" (7:25) is *not* what Paul means when he says that "those who *practice* such things [fornication, idolatry, etc.] shall not inherit the kingdom of God" (from Gal 5:19, 21 NASB). Instead of going directly from Rom 5:21 to Rom 8:1, Paul wrote chapter 6 as God's corrective to *libertinism*—using the grace in Christ as a license to sin. God's (the gospel's) answer to such is that we died with Christ to sin and its reign, being no longer under law (6:7, 14) but released from it (6:1–23; 7:5–6), so now we walk in newness of life (Rom 6:11). And Rom 7 is God's corrective to the errors of legalism and perfectionism, in order that the believer (7:24) would know that he cannot do the good that he would, as he will do when he is set free from "the body of this death." So, chapter 7 reveals that, because of (continual) involuntary lust, no believer can be justified by the law (see 3:20). Although sin no longer reigns in *us*, this does not negate the truth of sin still dwelling in our flesh. A believer, with his flesh, is a continually lusting sinner/unbeliever/idolater (7:25), for the flesh is not regenerated. Ever since Paul's encounter with the risen, *glorified* Christ, he saw everything in the light of this Christ. Thus, when the *new creation* comes in its fullness, we will do the things that we want to do.[34] Now, in Christ there *is* progressive sanctification (essentially unseen, Rom 2:28–29),[35] which is the fruit of justification (Rom 6:22) because of regeneration by the Spirit. But such growth takes time, and for that we must work with God, from whom comes the power to do so (Phil 2:12–13).

---

34. If you are a new creation in him, your essential nature and being is to trust in and obey God through Christ in you; and at the same time, with your flesh you serve Sin's law—unbelief, for the body is spiritually dead because of indwelling sin/unbelief (Rom 8:10). Because of the flesh, believers have a somewhat blinded view of themselves. So, the believer's flesh causes him to think "I'm really not that bad"—and that is why he is prone to doubt that Paul is speaking of himself as a believer in 7:14–25. But the flesh not only does not improve, it actually gets worse (see Eph 4:22).

35. The real Jew (2:28–29) cannot be observed as one who keeps the law outwardly, as one who keeps the Ten Commandments.

— ELEVEN —

No Condemnation
in Christ

(Rom 8)

Christ is my life, and in his risen life there is no condemnation.

IN ROM 7 PAUL expounded on the penultimate truth of the flesh's continual desires[1] which are "present" (7:21) in the flesh of the one whose Lord is Jesus (7:24). But this is not the entire truth for the person in Christ. The ultimate truth is that the saint's essential being is *according to the Spirit of God* (8:5); that is, he is essentially *no longer in the flesh* (joined to the flesh of sin) *but in the Spirit* (joined to the Lord).[2]

> *There is therefore now* [since you have been justified by Christ's blood, and it is no longer *you* who continually covet (for *you* died with Christ), but Sin which indwells your flesh] *no condemnation for those in Christ Jesus. For the law of the Spirit, the one of* [condemnation-free, resurrection] *life in Christ Jesus, has set you free from the law—*[the one of works[3] and] *of Sin and of Death.*[4] (Rom 8:1–2 ATP)

1. Rom 7:7; Gal 5:17.

2. Rom 8:9; 1 Cor 6:17.

3. See Rom 3:27 (compare 11:6); Paul's writing is terse, so he did not include this phrase here; see my ch. 8.

4. Rom 7:7–13, 24; 2 Cor 3:7; 1 Cor 15:56.

For what was impossible for the law, in that it was impotent through the flesh, God did, sending his own Son in the likeness of the flesh of Sin, and for sin, he condemned the [lord] Sin [to death] in the flesh [of his Son, having thereby destroyed Sin, in that Sin's authority to rule us has been brought to nothing], in order that the righteous requirement of the law might be fulfilled in us, who do not walk according to the flesh [man-in-Adam], but according to the Spirit [God in Christ] in order that the Spirit of Christ could indwell us [in our inner man, instead of Sin].

For the ones being according to the flesh [flesh-beings] set their minds on the things of the flesh [the things seen and temporal[5]], but the ones being according to the Spirit [Spirit-beings; their essential being is according to *God*] set their minds on the things of the Spirit [the things unseen and eternal]. For the mind of the flesh [which serves as slave the law of Sin[6]] is death, but the mind of the Spirit [which serves the "law" of the Spirit of life in Christ, 8:2] is life and peace; because the mind of the flesh is enmity towards God; for to the law of God [the Spirit, who is God] it [the mind of flesh] is not subject, neither indeed *can* it be subject [to God in Christ]. So then, the ones being in flesh cannot please God [for without faith it is impossible to please God, and in the flesh dwells no good (of God) thing, 7:18]. But you are not in the flesh [joined to the flesh], but [you are] in the Spirit [joined to the Holy Spirit], if [it be that] the Spirit of God dwells in you. But if any man does not have the Spirit of Christ, he does not belong to Christ. And if Christ is in you, the body [outer man, the flesh] is spiritually dead because of Sin, but the Spirit is life [eternal, in your inner man] because of justification [by Christ's blood, 5:9]. But if the Spirit of him [God] that raised Jesus from the dead dwells in you, he that raised Christ from the dead shall also make alive your mortal bodies by his Spirit indwelling in you [1 Cor 15:22, 42–57]. So then, brethren, we are obligators, not to the flesh [to the law/nomism, Gal 5:1–5, or to license, 5:19–21], to live according to the flesh [to obey its desires; but you are (owned-by-God) obligators to the Holy Spirit—to obey his desires]. For if you live according to the flesh, you are about to die [now, and in the age to come], but if, by the Spirit [through faith in Christ] you put to death the deeds of the body, you will live [experience his age-to-come life now and fully in the age

---

5. 2 Cor 4:17, 18.
6. Rom 7:25. *The law of sin* is the law of *coveting* (7:7) life apart from God (7–13).

to come]. For as many as are led by the Spirit of God [not the law or the flesh], these are the sons of God (Rom 8:3–14).

Christ's death and resurrection to life *changed everything*, from the old covenant to the new testament of the Spirit, from the age of death in Adam to the age of life in Christ. Besides Paul, there is in Scripture a second witness, from the author of Hebrews:

> For the priesthood being *changed*, of necessity there is also *a change of the law.* (Heb 7:12)

"The law of *the Spirit*" has replaced the law of works (in Adam) and of Moses—yes, even of the flesh, by and of which the law was impotent to save (Rom 8:3). There is thus now *no condemnation*, because a person cannot be *in* union with *Christ Jesus*, who is the last Adam, *and* be in this present evil age *in Adam*, which is under condemnation (3:9—5:21). He is either in one age or the other. The person in Christ is no longer in the flesh but in the Spirit. If you are in Christ, you belong to Christ alone (8:9). Christ gave himself for our sins, in order that he might deliver us out of this present evil age (Gal 1:4) and into the age to come, the age of the life-giving Spirit (6:15; Eph 1:21; 1 Cor 15:45).

"For the Law of the Spirit" (Romans 8:2a)

In the flesh, the law is the ruler that *lords it over* all who are "in the flesh" (7:1–5). But for those in Christ, the "law" or rule or lordship of the Spirit *is* the rule and reign of *grace* (5:21), which justifies and gives life.[7] Jesus rules his people as their Lord. His rule, his reign of grace, has set them free from the law, the one which occasions sin and death.[8] This "law" or rule of the Spirit, which is condemnation-free *life in Christ Jesus*, is the believer's only "law" before God, by which he "walks" (8:4; Gal 6:14, 15). The old covenant law has been superseded by another law, the one of the Spirit. For the rule and reign of the Spirit is eschatological (last-age) life in Christ Jesus. This is the life of "the resurrection unto life" (John 5:29), where there is no condemnation (Rom 8:1–2). This life has set you free from the rule, reign, and lordship of sin unto death. In Christ we are free from the law, which is the power of sin, which is the potent sting and cause of death, for Romans (6:14; 7:1) refers to the lordship (κυριεύο) of the sin through the law. Therefore, if you are in Christ, when the Accuser

7. Rom 3:24; 5:17, 18, 21.
8. Gen 2:17; Ezek 18:4; Rom 5:21; 6:23; 7:9–11; 2 Cor 3:7.

comes to accuse you, believe the truth: You are in Christ Jesus and thus no longer in this present age under wrath and condemnation, the sin, the law, and death,[9] for God has translated you into the kingdom of love, the Son of God's love—that is, the rule of grace (Col 1:13; Rom 5:21 and 3:24). Paul, referring to "the law" (the rule) of the Spirit of life (8:1, 2) is elaborating on what he touched on in 6:4 and especially in 7:6, where he says that though our death with Christ, we have been severed from the law, that we might serve God in newness of *the Spirit* and not in oldness of the letter, "the letter" being the letter (the law) that kills, in contrast to the Spirit, who gives life (2 Cor 3:6). And Martin Luther rightly resonates:

> Moreover, no Law should reign in the conscience except that of the Spirit of life, by which we are delivered in Christ from the Law of the letter and of death, from its works and from sins.[10]

"Great is the mystery of godliness: God was manifest in the flesh, *justified in the Spirit*, seen of angels" (1 Tim 3:16). Now, in union with Christ, we are *justified in the Spirit* also (1 Cor 6:11 NASB; see Rom 8:1, 9). Christ took our sins on himself and became sin for us (2 Cor 5:21); and Christ, having become sin, was condemned on our behalf unto death. But in his resurrection, Christ was vindicated and justified in the Spirit. Death and condemnation have no more dominion over the risen Christ nor over us who are joined to him (1 Cor 6:17). By saying that "the law of the Spirit (of life) . . . has freed you from the law" (8:2), he means what he said earlier, in Rom 3:27, where he contrasts the law of *faith* with the law of *works*. Therefore, in 8:2 he is saying that the law of faith in Christ has set you free from "the law of works" for justification, which condemned those in Adam. Paul is saying that the person "in Christ," in his *inner man*, obeys the rule of the Spirit of Christ and of God (8:9, 10), and not the law of Moses (8:2), which is the power of sin and the ministry of death. He obeys the life (John 14:6) that God has put within him (or her), which is *the Spirit*, even Christ who justified him (8:1–2, 9–10). The new man obeys no other law. The Spirit's "law" is the one of life in Christ Jesus that has freed you from the law that occasioned sin (disobedience/unbelief) and death (7:7–13, 25). This is another way of saying that the only rule (κανών, "canon") for the person in Christ is *the new creation* in Christ (Gal 6:15–16—Christ in you). The Spirit's rule of life in Christ Jesus leads us, and this is confirmed in 8:13–16, where he says we are to live according to the Spirit and not according to the flesh and that those

9. Wrath (Rom 5:9–21); Sin (6:6–14; 7:5, 7–13, 25); the law (7:1–6); Death (6:23; 5:21; 8:1–11, 21–39).

10. *LW* 26:139.

being led by the Spirit are sons of God (8:14). So, the question asked is, "How do we know we are not being led by our feelings or flesh?"

The Spirit of Christ's "law" (rule) is the one of *condemnation-free, eternal life* in *Christ Jesus* (8:1, 2), which *frees* us to *know the true God, including his Spirit's leading*—in distinction *from all other gods or lords, even the law*, and all other powers and spirits, including the flesh of sin. When you are trusting in Christ for no condemnation—Christ as your righteousness before God—be assured that the Spirit which is leading you is the Spirit of life in Christ Jesus and no other god, spirit, or power! Faith in Christ for justification grants the discernment, the distinguishing of spirits, between the one true God and *all other* gods, powers, or spirits.[11]

Paul tells the Galatians, "Since you began by faith in Christ for righteousness (which is to *begin by the Spirit*—to be led by him), you are to continue and 'end' by the Spirit also, and not end in the flesh by returning to works of the law for justification" (2:21—3:3). Thus, we are led by the Spirit of the God who justifies the ungodly (Rom 8:14; see 4:5–8) in Christ (Gal 2:17). So, Paul can say, "Walk by the Spirit" (Gal 5:16), for he knows that there is *no other God* except *this* Spirit—of *the God who justifies the ungodly in Christ without works* (Rom 4:5–8). "But if you are led by the Spirit [who is God and trustworthy], you are not under law" (Gal 5:18). Thus, disobeying the Spirit is disobeying God! It comes down to that. Therefore the primary apostolic command for those who are in Christ is this:

But I say, walk by the Spirit, and you will not carry out the desire of the flesh. (Gal 5:16 NASB)	That is, walk, moment by moment, by the strength and leading of the *Holy Spirit of God*, through *faith** in *Christ*.
	*For we, by *the Spirit*, out of *faith*, eagerly expect the hope of righteousness (Gal 5:5 AT), the hope of glory (Col 1:27).

The phrase "the law [the rule] of the Spirit, the one of life in Christ Jesus, has set you free from the law of sin and of death" (8:2; see 2 Cor 3:17) is described well in Luther's words: "Wherever the Spirit of God exists, there is freedom, as St. Paul says [2 Cor. 3:17]; there no teaching or law is needed; everything happens as it should happen. It is just like the man who has healthy, good vision; he does not need anyone to teach him how he should see. His vision is unhindered, and he has more than any teaching could help him get or give to him."[12] So, in 8:2 Paul is saying, The law—the

11. See also Käsemann, *Perspectives on Paul*, 152.

12. *LW* 39:189.

rule, the lordship, the leading—of the Spirit, the one of Christ's indwelling Spirit, who is eternal life, has set you free from *the law* of Moses (of works and of the flesh), the law of works[13] (Rom 3:27), which only occasioned sin and death (7:7–13) and condemns sinners to death (2 Cor 3:7). "The law of the Spirit" is written "with the Spirit of the living God, not on tablets of stone, but on tablets of human hearts" (2 Cor 3:3 NASB). Here, the Spirit (with *his* law/rule) is contrasted with the law of Moses, which was a recapitulation of the law of works, with its sanction: "*You shall not eat*, for in the day that you eat of it you shall surely die."[14]

The following texts show that Paul the Hebrew uses "death" and "destruction" interchangeably:

But what fruit were you getting at that time from the things of which you are now ashamed? For the **end** of those things is *death* (Rom 6:21).	For many walk, of whom I have told you often . . . that they are enemies of the cross of Christ: whose **end** is *destruction* (Phil 3:18–19a).
The wages of the Sin is *death* (6:23).	

Paul's word καταργέω (translated in italics below) means "destroyed," "brought to nothing."

> But we speak wisdom among those who are mature; yet a wisdom not of this age, nor of the rulers of this age, who are *coming to nothing*. (1 Cor 2:6)
> The last enemy that will be *destroyed* [*done away with/exist no longer*] is death [when we put on immortality]. (1 Cor 15:24, 26)

When we put on immortality, death will be *destroyed*—it will no longer exist for God's chosen ones.

Paul says that we died with Christ, in order that "the body owned by Sin might be *done away with* [as joined to the Sin, we *live no longer*, for Christ lives in us], that we might no longer serve the Sin" (Rom 6:6). And he says that "as through one man *the Sin* [ἡ ἁμαρτία] entered into the world" (5:12). We saw that in Rom 5:12–21 there is a consequential chain of events: the consequences of Adam's one *sin* were *condemnation*, which resulted in (spiritual-unto-bodily) *death*—"in the day you eat of it, dying [spiritually] you shall surely die [bodily]" (Gen 2:17b). Through the Sin,

---

13. "*Do* this and live"—be justified.

14. The Spirit's law is not the law of Moses, which includes the Sabbath commandment (Exod 20:8–11) and only condemns (2 Cor 3:9). When I go to be with Christ, I will be *bodily* severed from the flesh of sin, but already now I am *spiritually* (in my spirit) severed from "the flesh of sin" (Rom 8:3 lit.; see 2:29 [Col 2:11–12]).

the death entered into all men (Rom 5:12) in the form of indwelling sin. (Eastern Orthodox theologians understand this: indwelling sin is death.) The judgment concerning the one *sin* was *condemnation* (*guilty*), and the penalty was *death*. But this sin-condemnation-death (destruction) "chain" also applies to Christ and those in him. For here we find that the *Sin*, which *condemned* us to *death* in Adam, was *itself condemned* to *death* (*destroyed, brought to nothing*) by God *in Christ's death* (for the elect, 8:33):

> For what the law could not do . . . God [did], sending his own Son in the likeness of the flesh of Sin, and for sin, [he] condemned *the Sin* [τὴν ἁμαρτίαν] in the flesh [to *death*, that is, God thereby *destroyed* the Sin, so that its authority to rule us has been *brought to nothing*]—in order that the righteous requirement of the law might be fulfilled *in us*, who do not walk according to the flesh [of Sin], but according to *the Spirit* [of God—that is, in us who have the Spirit of Christ in us (8:9)]. (Rom 8:3a, 4)

"For the *one having died with Christ* has been justified from *the Sin*" (Rom 6:7 lit.)—imputed and thus indwelling. "The one having died with Christ" is the Christ-believer, who was, in the past, indwelt by "*the spirit* of the world" (1 Cor 2:12), *the spirit* now operating in "the sons of disobedience [but no longer in the elect]" (Eph 2:2). The world (1 Cor 2:12) consists of the sons of disobedience; you *were* such, but *as such*, you *died with Christ*, thereby having been *justified* from the sin (6:7; see 8:3, 4). I am free from the *unholy* spirit that works in unbelievers, because God's *Holy* Spirit now indwells me (Rom 8:9). Satan, the ruler of this world, has been judged on the cross (John 16:11) and this is precisely what Paul is saying in 8:3–4: "The Spirit is life (eternal) because of justification (from the Sin, 6:7; 8:10)." Thus, in Christ's resurrection life (5:18)[15] the Spirit indwells us—instead of the Sin. Therefore, Paul can say, "We have received, not *the spirit* of the world [which, with its lordship, was destroyed for and in us], but we have received *the Spirit* which is from God" (1 Cor 2:12a)[16] in sin's place. "For the one being *joined to the Lord* is one spirit [with him]" (1 Cor 6:17). Thus, Aulén, when comparing the Latin with the classic idea of the atonement (the cross), can say, "And while the Latin type of view regards the Atonement as primarily the remission of the *punishment* of sin, the classic idea

---

15. 'To all men unto the justification of life [justification which belongs to life eternal]" (5:18b AT).

16. Just as there is union and distinction between *the Spirit* of God and *Christ* (Rom 8:9–10), even so there is union and distinction between "*the spirit* of this world" (Satan) and *Sin*. Thus, the flesh of Sin (8:3) has a connection with Satan's demons, so that when one yields to *the flesh*, the door is opened to God's adversary.

directs attention not primarily to the punishment or other consequences of sin, but to the sin itself. It is the sin itself that is overcome by Christ, and annihilated; it is from the power of sin itself that man is set free."[17] Paul deals with the remission of the *punishment* (condemnation unto death) of sin in Rom 8:1–2, but he deals with the Sin itself and its replacement by the Spirit in 8:2–10, based upon 8:3–4. But has the church heard him?

In the Flesh: The *Outer Man*	In the Spirit: The *Inner Man*
We have indwelling sin (Rom 7:17–23).	We have not *sin*, for *Christ* indwells us (Rom 8:3–10).
We are in the flesh (of Sin) (Phil 1:21–24; Rom 8:3)	We are no longer *in the flesh of Sin* (Rom 7:17; 8:3), for we are in Christ (Rom 8:9–10)
and have sins (Rom 4:5–8)	and sins are not imputed to us (4:5–8).

For those in Christ, sin now only indwells the flesh, "the outer man" (2 Cor 4:16) and not the inner man as we have seen: "For I delight in the law of *God* (*the Spirit*, 8:2), according to *the inner man*" (Rom 7:22). "If then I do what I *wish* [desire, by the Spirit[18]] *not* to do [i.e., covet/desire life apart from God][19] . . . it is no longer *I* [new man] who do it, but the *sin which dwells within me* . . . that is, *in my flesh*" (Rom 7:16–18b). But *you* are *not* in the flesh, but in the Spirit (Rom 8:9). This gospel truth sheds light on why the Spirit's leading is sufficient without the law (Gal 5:18; Rom 8:11–14). So, in a paradox, in the believer there are two men: the old man and the new man; yet there is only one man.

> But if Christ is in you, on one hand, the body [outward man] is [spiritually] dead [the end of which is bodily death] because of Sin; on the other hand, the Spirit is life [eternal, in the inward man, the end being immortality (8:11; 1 Cor 15:50–56)], because of righteousness [justification]. (Rom 8:10)

So, a human person consists of both an inner man and an outer man: "Therefore, we do not lose heart. Even though our *outward man* is perishing,

---

17. Aulén, *Christus Victor*, 148n2. Notice that sin is "annihilated" (see chart, right side). It is no wonder then, with that kind of insight, he says of Luther, "In him we find sin once again treated as an objective power" (Aulén, *Christus Victor*, 148). "The life that the Christian now lives *is*, an ontologically real manner, Christ himself" (Mannermaa, Christ *Present in Faith*, 39); see Rom 8:5, 9; Gal 2:20.

18. Gal 5:17; compare Rom 7:22.

19. Rom 7:7–13.

yet the *inward man* is being renewed day by day" (2 Cor 4:16). In a mystery, there is a mutual indwelling: God's Spirit dwelling in my (human) spirit and my spirit dwelling in God's Spirit (Rom 8:9, 10). Believers are no longer in sin (in Adam), but we are now in God (1 Thess 1:1; Rom 8:1). Therefore, as a new creation, you are free from the law of sin and of death. To be in Christ is to be in the new creation, where there is neither sin nor death, for our citizenship is in heaven (Gal 1:4; Col 1:17; 2 Cor 5:17; Phil 3:20). Paul had the Shema in mind when he wrote the following:

The LORD	the grace of the *Lord* Jesus Christ
our *God*	the love of *God* the Father
the LORD is one (Deut 6:4)	the communion of *the Holy Spirit* (2 Cor 13:14; 3:17)

So, knowing that there is only *one* God, Paul is saying:

> For the rule of the *kingdom* [*reign*] *of God in the Holy Spirit* [Rom 14:17], has set you free from the *law*, with its reign of *Sin* and of *Death*. (8:2)

The point is that, in 8:2, when Paul refers to "the Spirit," he does not mean one-third of God, or someone less than God, but God in all God's fullness, for the Spirit *fully* shares the one divine nature with the Father and the Son. The flesh is impotent in that it cannot fulfill the law (8:3).

God condemned the lord sin to death, to destruction, and on that basis God's Spirit cleansed my inner man from the sin, "circumcised" my heart (Rom 2:28–29) from the flesh of sin (8:3). Concerning the gentiles, Peter said, "And God . . . bore witness to them, giving them the Holy Spirit, just as He did to us, *cleansing* their hearts by faith" (Acts 15:8, 9 NASB). *The Spirit in us* is the fulfillment of the law, what the law always required (8:3–4). In Rom 8:4, Paul is not referring to "the righteousness (δικαιοσύνην) of the law"[20] (to which he refers in Phil 3:9, and rejects), but rather to "the righteous requirement [δικαίωμα] of the law" (8:4 ESV, NASB). For "the righteousness of the law," human righteousness, is of the flesh (Phil 3:3–9). The righteous requirement of the law is "the law of the Spirit" (Rom 8:2), "written on our hearts . . . written not with ink, but by the Spirit of the living God . . . on . . . the heart" (2 Cor 3:3; see 3:15–17; 4:6; Rom 2:28–29; Heb 8:10–13).

> For the ones being [ὄντες] according to the *flesh*, mind the things of the flesh [the things seen and temporal], but the ones

20. As the AV wrongly translates the Greek in 8:4.

[being] according to *Spirit* [mind] the things of the Spirit [the things unseen and eternal]. (Rom 8:5 AT; see 2 Cor 4:18)

The mind of the flesh thinks on the things seen and temporal, including humans and their sins, instead of God in Christ.[21] The mind of the Spirit trusts in Christ and sets its affection on him. The Spirit's mind perceives those in Christ as essentially no longer in the flesh (in this present and temporal age) but in the Spirit, in the eternal age to come. Christ is the mind's Lord, focus, and object of grateful worship. Those who belong to the Spirit have their thoughts informed by the gospel, that is, on the things freely given us in Christ (1 Cor 2:12). In 2 Corinthians chapters 3 and 4, Paul contrasts the glory of *the law* with the glory of *Christ*. Then in chapter 5 he continues the contrast, climaxing with the truth that believers do not look at the things seen and temporal (including the law, with its transgressions) but at the things unseen and eternal (Christ and his glory). In Rom 8:5 he says that the true being of the person in Christ is according to God the Holy Spirit. He is no longer an unbeliever at the core of his being; he trusts God and thinks on the things of the Spirit, for he no longer belongs to the flesh. In 8:5 the apostle contrasts the ontological difference between those in Adam and those in the last Adam. Then, in 8:6, he reveals the *thinking* that is innate in each Adam's sphere of lordship and its results. In 1 Cor 1:29, "flesh" means man, the whole person, with all his powers, apart from Christ—and that whole man includes his conscience. So, Zachman says:

> As part of a person's fleshly nature, the conscience cannot be seen as a highest consciousness (apex mentis) that has direct contact with the divine . . . Although the conscience does make inferences about the attitude of God toward us, it does so on the basis of what it can see and feel . . . and not on the basis of some form of consciousness that transcends the temporal, sensible world. For Luther, the conscience is as worldly and fleshly as any other power of the soul. It has as its object human works.[22]

---

21. It is a privilege to function out of the mind of Christ (1 Cor 2:16), in whom there is neither Jew nor gentile, neither male nor female (neither conservative nor liberal, etc.), for the ultimate, eternal issue is that we belong to Christ. With Christ's mind, and that renewed (12:2), we are enabled to discern the folly of the "conservative" flesh-mind and of the "liberal" flesh-mind (8:6). Both sides of the mind of the flesh think only on the things seen and temporal, though it can be argued that, though both are *void of trust in God*, the conservative flesh-mind thinks even more of self than of others. If conservatism (or progressivism) is your god, it is certainly not the Lord Jesus Christ. All the lies that idolaters believe are rooted in *the lie* of not believing in *the truth* of the gospel (Gal 2:14).

22. Zachman, *Assurance of Faith*, 21.

The following quote by Luther, and typical of him, verifies just what Zach-man said:

> For Paul, therefore, "flesh" means the highest righteousness, wisdom, worship, religion, understanding, and will of which the world is capable.[23]

Comparing Paul's words with Paul's words, we find that the mind of the flesh is one of self-justification. The natural man (who is only flesh) knows that God is God (1:19–21, 25), which includes the truth that his sin is considered by God (1:18–32) although he suppresses this truth. By the flesh, which is owned by sin, the man of flesh rejects God. Paul sets before saints the two different minds in Rom 8:6: the mind of the flesh and the mind of the Spirit. The spiritual man *believes* that he is justified: that in Christ God does not consider his sin. God, for Christ's sake, refuses to consider his sins; therefore, we are not to consider or think on them either. If the spiritual man turns from Christ through unfaith, he is no longer walking in the Spirit; he is walking in the flesh, contrary to Paul's commands in Rom 8:12–13 and in Gal 5:16 and 25. The mind of the flesh is not just ill, it is dead to God. It is *enmity against* God, and thus it is against life. The Spirit points us to Christ for justification. No matter how sanctified a believer becomes, due to the flesh, he always needs Christ as his righteousness. The mind of the flesh is death (8:6) and ends in death; it is all about destruction, for it is a mind of unbelief; it is unable to trust God. The mind of the flesh is utterly bound by sin to hate God and not trust him, for the one "in the flesh" is enslaved to sin (7:14), so the flesh's mind is not free to trust or love God (8:7–8). Paul says:

> . . . while we look not at the things which are seen, but at the things which are not seen. For the things which are seen are temporal, but the things which are not seen are eternal. (2 Cor 4:18)

"The things which are seen and temporal" belong to what Ballew calls "a four-dimensional space-time continuum. Length, width, depth and time are four coordinates that govern . . . *this world*."[24] And this world, this *cosmos* (κοσμοσ, which had a beginning, Matt 13:35), includes the visible, "seen" (2 Cor 4:18) universe. But God "dwells in His heavenly kingdom, outside the bounds of space and time."[25] Therefore "Christ's ascent was

23. LW 26:140.

24. Ballew, *Heavenly Worship*, 1, emphasis mine.

25. Ballew, *Heavenly Worship*, 2. When Paul says, "But you are not in the flesh, but *in the Spirit*," Ephesians says that we are (blessed) "*in the heavenlies* in Christ" (1:3). Heaven is *not spatially distant*, e.g., beyond our physical universe, but is a *different dimension* than the universe; therefore "our life with Christ in the heavenly dimension is

not to a time and space heaven. Rather, he left the earthly and visible dimension of space and time and entered the invisible and eternal heavenly dimension, governed by its own laws."[26] Therefore, when Paul says, "But you are not in the flesh, but in the Spirit, if indeed the Spirit of God dwells in you," he is saying:

> But you are not in the temporal, seen kingdom of this present-age-world, for the inner man of you is no longer joined to the flesh of sin; but you are joined to the Lord, in the *unseen, heavenly, eternal kingdom of God*, for Christ alone is your life and your righteousness—they are hidden with and in Christ. For the kingdom of God is—in the Holy Spirit. (2 Cor 4:18; 1 Cor 1:30; Col 3:4; Rom 14:17; Eph 1:3)

Therefore, the mind of the flesh, set on the flesh (that is, on the law, which is seen and temporal) is death (8:6), for the things seen and temporal include *the law* (with its works, Rom 2:14–15). Thus, we are to set our mind on Christ (apart from law, Rom 3:21)—on Christ for justification before God, and not on the law—and *God will lead us* by his Spirit to do the will of God (Gal 5:18; Rom 12:1–2).[27] Therefore, we conclude that to set the mind on the law is death.

> Therefore, the mind of the flesh is enmity [hatred] towards God [thus it cannot trust God]; for to the law of God [the Spirit] it is not subject,[28] neither indeed *can* it be [subject to God in Christ, 10:3]. So then, the ones being in flesh cannot please God [for without faith it is impossible to please God, and in the flesh, there exists no trust toward God (7:18); for the flesh cannot trust God, whom it hates]. (Rom 8:7–8)

The mind of the Spirit (8:6) is the mind owned by the Spirit of Christ (8:9). In Paul's inner man he serves only this law of God the Spirit (7:6, 22; 8:2), which now fulfills the law: "You shall not covet" (7:7; 8:4). Paul is not without the law of *God*, but *in* (the law of) *Christ* who is *God* (1 Cor 9:21; see Rom 9:5; Gal 1:10; Heb 1:8; 1 John 5:20). For those who are according to the Spirit (8:5), their mind *is* indeed subject to the law of God, which is "written with the Spirit of the living God in the heart" (2 Cor 3:3). In

---

real and actual, not positional. One *can* be in the heavenly and earthly at the same time, for the heavenly circumscribes the earthly, moving invisibly . . . through it continually" (Ballew, *Heavenly Worship*, 5).

26. Ballew, *Heavenly Worship*, 3.

27. See also Nygren, *Commentary on Romans*, 419–20.

28. This is the same reality as not subjecting to God's righteousness in Christ (his Spirit, 8:9–10; see 10:3).

contrast to the old (first) creation, the new creation, with its mind of the Spirit, is reconciled to God.[29]

> But *you* are not in the flesh, but in the Spirit [in union with Christ, 8:1; 1 Cor 6:17] since the Spirit of God dwells in you. But if anyone has not the Spirit of Christ, that one does not belong to Christ. (Rom 8:9)

Flesh and blood cannot inherit the kingdom of God (1 Cor 15:50), because the existence in "flesh and blood" is an existence in the flesh of sin (8:3), which only merits God's wrath. But, Paul says, "You are in the Spirit, in whom no sin, condemnation, or death exist!" This is because the Lord Christ is your *righteousness* and your *life*. Eternal life comes to us in regeneration by the Holy Spirit, who renovates and makes alive again our formerly dead human spirits, enabling the elect to believe in Christ unto salvation. Sin is unbelief in Christ, the primary characteristic of indwelling sin. Christ died for us and justified us from the Sin and all our sins—for the purpose of giving eternal life to us in him.

> But if the Spirit of the one [God the Father] having raised Jesus from the dead dwells in you, the one [God] having raised Christ Jesus from the dead will also make alive your mortal bodies through the Spirit of him [God] indwelling in you. (Rom 8:11)

If you are in him, Christ, who is eternal life (Col 3:4; 1 John 5:20), indwells your inner man (Rom 8:9, 10; Eph 3:16), so, in spirit you cannot die (John 11:26; 1 Thess 5:10); and God will give this very life to make alive the dead (elect) at the resurrection of the dead. What follows are imperatives that are based upon the truth of who we are in Christ, which he explained in 8:1–11. Since Paul's writing style is terse, we insert words in parentheses to help us more fully understand his meaning.

> But you are not in the flesh [joined to the flesh of Sin], but in the Spirit [joined to Christ],[30] since the Spirit of God dwells in you . . . So then, brethren, we are obligors, not to the flesh, to live according to the flesh [of Sin, to obey *its* desires,[31] but we are

---

29. The mind of the flesh in Rom 8:7–8; the mind of the Spirit in Rom 8:4–6, 9; 2 Cor 5:17–19.

30. "The Spirit" and "Christ" are used interchangeably in Rom 8:9, 10; see 1 Cor 6:17.

31. This includes not being obligated to think according to the flesh; see my ch. 7. We must be attentive, for if the affections are beginning to affect the thoughts toward disobedience, they must be mortified before sin occurs. The idol-seeking flesh is far more powerful that we think it is.

obligors to the Spirit, who indwells us, to live according to the Spirit (to obey his desires and leading[32])].

> For if you live according to the flesh [not putting to death its deeds; not obeying the Spirit of God], you are about to die, [now and in the coming age]; but if, by the Spirit[33] [his rule of Christ's condemnation-free life in Christ Jesus] you put to death the deeds of the body, you will live [now, and in the age to come]. (8:9, 12–13; compare 1–2)

In other words, in Rom 8:5, 9–13, Paul is saying, "Your true being is according to (the Spirit of) God; you are no longer joined to sin, but to Christ in your inner man. But if you think and live like an unbeliever, you will die. But if you are in Christ and think and live as such, you will live: You will experience Christ's life now, and then at his coming you will put on immortality."[34] Therefore, it is true that:

> The doctrine of justification by free grace cannot be rightly preached, except the doctrine of mortification and destroying of sin be preached with it; for the same faith which lays hold on Christ for righteousness, does rest upon him also for grace and strength to subdue corruption and sin.[35]

The Spirit is life (8:10), but this life is quenched if we do not put to death the deeds of the flesh. Non-mortification is the un-filling of the Spirit (contra Eph 5:19 and Gal 5:16). A weakened state diminishes the ability to endure temptation without sinning. By the Spirit of obedience (of faith) we must choose to participate in the salvation (with its battle, Rom 6:14–23) that is in Christ Jesus (Phil 2:12–13). In Rom 8:13, when Paul says, "If you, by the Spirit, put to death the deeds of the body," by the phrase "by the Spirit" he means "by faith in Christ."

> For we, by *the Spirit*, out of *faith*, eagerly expect the hope of righteousness. (Gal 5:5)

In context, Paul is referring to faith in Christ for justification. Since sin leads to death (6:21–23), mortification is not an option (8:12–13) So, if you, by

---

32. We are to obey God the Spirit's desires, to be led by him (8:14, 15; see Gal 5:16–18.)

33. By the Spirit (out of faith in Christ, Gal 5:5) do not allow such deeds to be carried out (Gal 5:16). Along with prayer, one is filled with the Spirit (1 Cor 15:45; see Eph 3:16; 5:19) through letting God's word (the gospel) richly dwell within (him) (Col 3:16a NASB w/ margin; see Eph 5:19). *Filled* with the Spirit means *controlled* by him.

34. This accords with what Paul says in Rom 2:5–10 and Gal 5:19–21.

35. Fergusson, *Exposition of the Epistles*, 41; modern English mine.

faith in Christ for justification, put to death the deeds of the body, you will *live*. Life is a gift (6:23), but mortification is the means to that end.[36] It is the only way to have and experience life, spiritually in this age and bodily also in the one to come. The power of God is the gospel (1:16) of unconditional justification in Christ alone through faith in him alone. By that very power we are to mortify the deeds of the flesh, not yielding our bodily members (ourselves) to sin, but to God (Rom 6:7–13; 8:9–13), but this can only occur as we are strengthened by God's Spirit in the inner man (Eph 3:16), which involves spending sufficient time with the Lord in prayer[37] and its corresponding close relationship with him. That is central. Paul means we are to put to death works and deeds that have the flesh as their source. Sin as power will not reign is us as we obey the Spirit (8:12–13) through the empowerment of faith in Christ for justification. Because we are no longer joined to the flesh (of sin), we are no longer obligated to succumb to its desires; so he says, "Walk in [obedience to] the Spirit, and you will not carry out the desires of the flesh" (Gal 5:16). I know when I am walking by faith in Christ. As I do, *I* come against the desires of the flesh; *I* turn (my mind and heart) away from those desires, for God will not do it for me. Only through the renewing of my mind and prayer will I be sufficiently "strengthened by the Spirit" (Eph 3:16) to be able to mortify the deeds of the flesh. Paul says:

> God is not outwitted; for what a man sows, that will he also reap. For the one who sows to the flesh will from the flesh reap corruption [he will die], (Rom 8:13)
> but the one who sows to the Spirit shall from the Spirit reap eternal life. (Gal 6:7–8)

If we do not put to death the deeds of the body, since God is not outwitted[38] (Gal 6:7), we will reap death, which begins with and includes chastisement (Heb 12:6–11) aimed at our restoration. We are to put on the Lord Jesus Christ, and make no provision for the flesh (Rom 13:14), for the flesh is of Satan's kingdom—that of unbelief in Christ. We should not provide fuel for our flesh, which is our greatest enemy. This is not legalism but the reality of the lordship of Christ. To live according to the flesh is to live under the lordship of the law (Rom 7:1, 5, 6).

36. See Owen, *Works*, 6:6.

37. Scripture's example is (basically) first thing every morning and *Spirit*-led fasting when needed and led to do so, to curb the flesh with its desires.

38. No one ever gets away with disobedience; there is always a reaping, for God is God.

Käsemann says that, if we do not have "a doctrine of the Spirit"[39] like Paul's, then "the struggle between Spirit and flesh no longer has as its deepest issue, as in 1 Cor 15:25, the question *whether Christ reigns.*"[40] That is, if Christ is not allowed to reign over us, then the flesh, with its autonomy, does reign. And that, Paul says, is death, even now (8:13). By faith we can and do know the Spirit—the reality of being led by the Spirit, for we know Jesus, because the Holy Spirit *is* this Spirit of Christ. Now that the faith of Christ has come, whatever is not of faith is sin (Gal 3:21–28; Rom 14:23). By the Spirit, you put to death the deeds of the flesh, starting with its desires (5:16–17). Because God works in us, we work (Phil 2:12–13). But we have to work *with him*, not without him. A person cannot seek to be justified by the law or habitually sin and at the same time hold fast to the gospel. If we do not (by the Spirit's enablement) kill the deeds of the flesh (i.e., obey the Spirit), we will die; the deeds of the flesh will kill us (8:13). To practice the deeds of the flesh is not the lifestyle of a genuine believer in Christ (1 Cor 6:9–11; Gal 5:19–21), for then Christ is being rejected as Lord by those who practice such deeds. Spiritual libertarians (taking grace as license to sin) ignore the truth that faith involves obedience to the Lord Jesus, thinking, "I believe, and salvation is by grace; so, I do not need to mortify the deeds of the flesh by the Spirit." But the obedience of faith has two sides: one is trust in Christ as my righteousness before God; the other is obedience (through faith) to Christ as my Lord. Paul says that to us who are *being saved*, the gospel is God's power (1 Cor 1:18). Since it is by the Spirit that we mortify the deeds of the body, we need to be filled with the Spirit through the word and prayer. For if we are not, then we will be filled with the flesh and will have no power to control our mind, eyes, tongue, etc. In this battle, says Owen, we are to:

> cease not a day from this work; be killing sin or it will be killing you. Your being dead with Christ virtually and quickened with him, will not excuse you from this work.[41] The Spirit "works *in us* and *with us, not against us* or *without us.*"[42]

That is, because God is working salvation in us, *we* are to work it out through repeated acts of the renewed and freed will (Phil 2:12, 13).

We saw in chapter 6 how sin is a power; with that in mind:

---

39. Käsemann, *Commentary on Romans*, 226.

40. Käsemann, *Commentary on Romans*, 227, emphasis mine.

41. Owen, *Works*, 6:9.

42. Owen, *Works*, 6:20.

> Sin is always acting, always conceiving, always seducing and tempting. . . .
>
> If, then, sin will be always acting, if we be not always mortifying, we are lost creatures. . . .
>
> And it unframes our spirit, and thence it is called "The sin that so easily besets us," Heb xii 1 . . . There is not a day but sin foils or is foiled, prevails or is prevailed on; and it will be so whilst we live in this world.[43]

If you are in Christ, mortification is not an option—it is the only way to life, not only in this age in terms of experiencing the life and fruit of the Spirit and the peace of God but also in the age to come, the prize of eternal life (1 Cor 9:24–27). All warning passages in the NT scriptures are for the sake of God's elect, to bring them to glory. They are to be taken with utmost seriousness, not ignoring them by one-sided thinking that looks only at Christ's grace without its corresponding lordship. The warnings are real and are ultimately for our salvation. If we are led by the Spirit, that is, if we obey the Spirit, we are then not experientially under the law, we are living in the freedom that Christ bought for us. The church has, for the most part, not clearly taught justification through faith alone, with its corresponding doctrine of mortification as central to the life in Christ. Nor have they warned clearly enough that disobedience to God radically weakens (and, in one sense, destroys) faith. It is totally out of character for the new creation to live in the disobedience of unbelief, because we are, by God's new creation, believers in Christ, the ones who are according to the Spirit of God (8:5). It is not the law that compels the person from outside (which includes the flesh, the outer man), but it is the Spirit of Christ, God himself in us, energizing the new creation from within through faith in Christ for justification. The freedom Christ purchased for us is the freedom from death and condemnation and the fear of them, including the obligation to do the law for justification—the freedom to be led by the God who continually justifies the ungodly who trust in Christ Jesus—in whom God is working, both to will and to do of God's good pleasure (what pleases him). So, we are free from the law to serve God in Christ and to serve one another.

> For as many as are led by the Spirit of God [not the law or the flesh], these are sons of God. (Rom 8:14)

The reality that characterizes sons of God is that they are led by God's Spirit and not by the law. In the leading of the Spirit, we are passive,

---

43. Owen, *Works*, 6:11.

and God the Spirit is actively leading us, acting upon and in us to do of his good pleasure; we only need to listen and follow his leading. God in Christ redeemed, justified, and adopted his elect, and therefore he is their indwelling Lord by his Spirit (Gal 4:4–7), and therefore the Spirit of the God who justifies us in Christ is constantly leading those whom he indwells. "But if you are [passively, with God acting in you] *being led by the Spirit*, you are not under law" (Gal 5:18). If you are being led by the Spirit, you are not under obligation to do the law, the letter. You are led by Jesus, who said, "Follow me" (Mark 2:14, 23–27).

> For you have not received a spirit of slavery again unto *fear* [of condemnation and death, regardless of how you may feel with your flesh]; but you received the Spirit of adoption, whereby we cry "Abba, Father." (8:15)

So, the Spirit of adoption is a spirit of freedom (2 Cor 3:17–18). Being led by the Spirit (8:12–15) is based upon our being in the Spirit of Christ and having the mind of the Spirit. So here is what living by faith in Christ comes down to—this is Paul's command with its corresponding promise:

> Walk in obedience to the Spirit of Jesus Christ who indwells you.

> The Spirit himself witnesses with our [human] spirit, that we are children of God. And if God's children, also God's heirs— on one hand, heirs of God, on the other, joint-heirs with Christ, since we suffer with him, in order that we may also be glorified together with him. For I count it to be true [because it is true] that the sufferings of the present time are not worthy to be compared with the glory which shall be revealed in us [in the coming age]. (Rom 8:16–18)

Although (unless we are alive when the Lord comes) we will endure the outer man's death (the first death), nevertheless we live (in our spirit/inner man, joined to God's Spirit), and we will not endure the second death but will be raised incorruptible for the purpose of eternal life at "the resurrection of the dead" (1 Cor 15). We know the Lord Jesus Christ through suffering with him in this present age, in order that we might know him also in the power of his resurrection, which enables us to endure now and know him in his glory in the age to come (Rom 8:18; Phil 3:9–12). Suffering with Christ includes every kind of suffering that God ordains for each child of God uniquely. God ordained Christ's suffering and cross, and he ordains ours as well. I have been and am crucified with Christ. The purpose of suffering with Christ is that we *will* be conformed to the image of Christ, God's Son, the heavenly One.

> For the creation was subjected to futility, not willingly, but be-
> cause of him who subjected it, in hope that the creation itself
> will be set free from its bondage to corruption and obtain the
> freedom of the glory of the children of God. For we know that
> the whole creation has been groaning together in the pains of
> childbirth until now. (Rom 8:20–22 ESV)
> And not only they, but we also ourselves, who have the first-
> fruits of the Spirit, groan within ourselves, eagerly waiting for
> adoption, the redemption of our body. (Rom 8:23)

It is the creation's slavery to corruption that Paul, by saying "even we ourselves," includes all those who belong to the Lord. "Who will deliver me
from the body of this death?" (7:24). This is the body of flesh and blood,
the body of corruption: "Flesh and blood cannot inherit the kingdom of
God; nor does *corruption* inherit incorruption" (1 Cor 15:50b, c). For this
corruptible (body) must put on *incorruption*, and this mortal (body) must
put on *immortality* (1 Cor 15:53).

Charles Hodge insightfully comments on 8:20–23 as follows:

> The irrational creation was subjected to vanity, not willingly,
> but by the authority of God. It shared in the penalty of the fall:
> "Cursed is the earth for thy sake." Gen viii. 17.[44] The creature
> was subjected (ὑπετάγη, historical aorist: the fact referred to oc-
> curred at the fall, when the curse fell on the earth).[45] The subjec-
> tion was with the hope *that* the creature [the irrational creation]
> should be delivered.[46]

The "futility" of 8:20 is revealed in the light of, and in contrast to, the
eternal life that has come in Christ. For through Christ we can see that
all the glory of *this* present age is ultimately futile and empty, because
all such glory is temporal; it is a fading glory, which ends in death. This
aligns with Paul's words regarding the temporal and fading glory of the
law in 2 Corinthians chapter 3. Regarding this futility and the bondage of
corruption, even we who have the Spirit are also subjected to it. Therefore,
we look forward to the redemption of our body. In our inner man we have
the Spirit who leads us (8:14), as he will do in the age to come; but then
we will have no bodies of sinful flesh, but each will have a Spirit-ruled
(spiritual) body. Hodge says, "Salvation, in its fullness, is . . . a matter of
hope, and of course future; and if future, it follows that we must wait for it

---

44. Hodge, *Romans*, 427.

45. Hodge, *Romans*, 430.

46. Hodge, *Romans*, 431.

in patient and joyful expectation . . . the nature of the blessing waited for, enables us patiently to endure all present evils.[47]

> And in the same way the Spirit also helps us in our weakness; for we do not know how to pray as we should, but the Spirit himself intercedes for us with groaning [heard by God the Father] too deep for words ["with words which cannot be uttered" (AV) by our mouths of flesh]. (Rom 8:26 NASB)

Regarding this text, Luther said:

> But He . . . which searches the hearts, *knows* what is *the meaning of the Spirit*" &c. (Rom viii. 27). To this Searcher of the hearts, this small and feeble groaning (as it seems to us) is a loud and a mighty cry [to God the Father].[48]

God the Spirit continually does what we in our weakness cannot adequately do for ourselves: intercede to God the Father on our behalf, so that the Father hears and understands. Next, note the "golden chain" of God's sovereign purpose, consisting of five "links"—God's *foreknowledge* (his love that chose and knew his own before creation); *predestination* (of them unto glory); *calling* (unto faith), *justification*, (which results in) *glorification*.

> We know that all things work together for good for those who love God, to those who are called [by God] according to his purpose [to be conformed to the image of his Son, v. 29]. For whom God *foreknew* [fore-loved, fore-chose], [that elect people] he also *predestined* [before the ages] to be conformed to the image of his Son [the image of the heavenly One, 1 Cor 15:49, i.e., to glory], that he might be the firstborn [from the dead] among many brethren. Whom he predestined [to glory], those he also called. Whom he *called* [unto regeneration, being thereby enabled to believe], those he also *justified* [by faith granted in the calling]. Whom he justified, those he also *glorified* [glorification is as certain as if it is already done and we are there]. What then shall we say about these things? If God is for us [the called], who can be against us? He [the Father] who did not spare his own Son, but delivered him up [to death] for us all, how will he not also with him freely give us all things [including faith, Phil 1:29]? Who shall bring a charge against God's elect? [Will] God, who justifies [the elect]? Who is the one who condemns? [Shall] Christ, *who died* [for the elect], who rather is risen, who is even

47. Hodge, *Romans*, 435.
48. Luther, *Galatians*, 375.

at the right hand of God, who also makes intercession for us
[the elect]? [No way!] (Rom 8:28–34)

Because God foreknew us (fore-loved us), he sent his Son to justify us; and
through this death for our justification, God does work all things together
for good (whatever God considers to be good), which ultimately is to be
conformed to Christ's image, to be glorified with Christ, which includes
being adopted sons who are like the Son in that we, through trust, are obedient sons and participate in the love between the Father and the Son in the
Spirit. That is God's one "purpose." Regarding "the called" in 8:28, we have
already shown that in 1 Cor 1:24–28, Paul identifies "the called" as the "chosen"; they are those who are "beloved of God" (Rom 1:6–7). And the "*whom
he foreknew*" is a people: "God did not reject his *people*, whom he *foreknew*"
(Rom 11:2). So, it is not *what* God foreknew, but "whom" God foreknew,
whom God knew *intimately beforehand*; i.e., *loved before* the creation of the
universe by God. The opposite of this knowing is true of the reprobate, who
were never known by God: "And then I will declare to them 'I never knew
you; depart from me'" (Matt 7:23 ESV). "All things" in 8:28 includes all that
happens and excludes nothing. "The called" love God, who first loved them
(5:8), and they demonstrate loving God by putting to death the deeds of the
body (8:13). God chose a remnant from among the Jews and the gentiles
(9:24), and that group is who Paul is referring to in Rom 8:29: "whom he
foreknew." It is those whom God also *predestined* to be conformed to the image of his Son—predestined to be glorified, in order that the Son might be
the firstborn (from the dead) among many (resurrected) brethren (see Heb
2:10–11). "We were chosen as his inheritance, having been foreordained
according to the purpose of the One operating all things according to *the
counsel*[49] of his will" (Eph 1:11). The pre-creation purpose and will of God
to save his elect is unchangeable—so they will inherit eternal life. There is
no such thing as an election by God in which some of God's chosen will
not in the end be glorified. Whom God predestined to glory, these he also
called effectually unto regeneration; and whom he called, these God also
justified through faith, for all of "the called" will come to faith in Christ. In
8:28, Paul does not only say that all things work together for good for those
who are the called according to God's purpose. That would be showing only
one side of reality. To be called is to be chosen by God, yes. And those who
love God can only do so because God first loved them and therefore gave
them faith in Christ (Phil 1:29). So, if Paul omitted "those who love God,"
whose love is expressed by mortification (8:12–13), one could say, "I am

49. "βουλή—1. *purpose, counsel* 2. *resolution, decision* b. of the divine will . . . *the
unchangeable nature of his resolve*," BAG, 145.

chosen by God, so I can live as I wish, and all things will work together for my good." But Paul holds both truths—God's elective call and our love for God—in tension, for it is a both/and reality, the "and" falling on the side of a secured salvation in Christ, for "by God's doing you are in Christ Jesus" (1 Cor 1:30 NASB). God's guarantee of perseverance unto life in the words "those he also glorified" are words of loving comfort that motivate the new man. All the warning passages in Scripture are to the end that the elect will be saved. But the warning passages are true, as are the ones about the safety we have in Christ. So, to use Paul's analogy in 1 Cor 9:23–27, we are called to do the things God has called us to do by his Spirit, chiefly to mortify the deeds of the flesh, the body—to put to death those things which are against and not of the Spirit and faith in Christ, that we might win the race that we are to run, enduring in faith (its fruit being mortification) until the end. If anyone stops running midway, he will be disqualified and not obtain the imperishable crown (1 Cor 9:25, 27),[50] which is incorruption (1 Cor 15:50–57). Discipline is involved, both on God's side toward us (when we need it) and on our side (self-discipline) toward ourselves, including our bodies. Paul says that the foreknown of God's elect will be glorified, but the means to glorification is persevering in faith in Christ, which involves the obedience of faith in Christ through his grace. We live confidently assured of salvation through our faithful God in Christ (Rom 8:28–39; 1 Cor 1:9; Phil 1:6), simultaneously knowing that God is not mocked or outwitted, that we will reap what we sow, now and in the age to come.[51]

The effectual call of God results in regeneration, which creates a new creation, who trusts God in Christ. Regeneration precedes faith in John 11:25–26; 1 John 5:1 (lit.).[52]

And whom God justified, these God also glorified (Rom 8:30), for the foreknown were predestined for glory. "Glorified" is in the past tense, for it is as good as already done.

---

50. 1 Cor 15:1–4; Gal 5:1–5; 19–21; Col 1:22, 23; Rom 2:5–10; 8:12–13; Gal 6:7–8; and Heb 11:38–39; Rom 6:6–23; 8:9–14. On perseverance of the saints, see Hoekema, *Saved by Grace*, 234–56; and Hoeksema, *Voice of Our Fathers*, 399–488.

51. Gal 6:7, 8; Rom 8:12, 13, and so we work out (not for) our salvation with a faith-based fear of God in Christ (Phil 2:11, 12), which is not the fear of condemnation (see Rom 8:1–16), which (fear) is unbelief in Christ.

52. "Having been born again, not of corruptible seed, but of *incorruptible* [seed], through the word of God [the gospel], which [incorruptible seed] lives and remains forever" (1 Pet 1:23 WEB). And John says, "Everyone having been begotten of God does not sin, because [the *incorruptible*] *seed* of God remains in him, and he cannot sin, because of God he has been begotten" (1 John 3:9). Such a new man (Eph 4:24) cannot not have *eternal* life.

What then shall we say to these things? If God is for us, who can be against us? He who did not spare his own Son, but delivered him up [to death] for us all, how will he not also with him freely give us all things? Who shall bring a charge against God's elect? [Will] God, who justifies [God's elect]? Who is the one who condemns? [Shall] Christ, who died [for God's elect], who rather is risen, who is even at the right hand of God, who also makes intercession for us [the elect]? (8:31–34)

Excursus 5: Christ Died for the Elect

"Christ *redeemed* us from the curse of the law . . . in order that we [for whom he died] might receive the promise of the Spirit through [the] faith" (Gal 3:13, 14). And the Spirit here is the Spirit of faith (2 Cor 4:13; 2 Thess 2:13–14). He died for us that we might be given faith to trust in him and be saved. Paul's words in Rom 8:33–34 reveal that Christ died for (redeemed) the elect. Referring to Gal 3:13 and to Matthew's Gospel, where Jesus says that he came "to give His life as a ransom for many" (20:28), Mack says, "The very word 'ransom' conveys with it the idea that a price has been paid and that price has been accepted."[53] And it has been accepted by God. It is "the called" (8:28), those whom God foreknew (fore-loved) and predestined to be in glory (8:29–30), the "us" whom God is *for* (8:31), for whom God delivered up his Son to death (Rom 8:32) of whom Paul speaks in 8:33–34— that no one is now able to bring an accusation "against God's elect," because it is God who justifies (the elect). "It is Christ who died [for them], and furthermore who is risen [for them], who is even at the right hand of God, who also makes intercession for them" (8:34). God purchased the church with his own blood (Acts 20:28; compare Eph 5:25–27 and John 10:10–18). Paul begins Romans saying, "To bring about the obedience of faith among all the Gentiles . . . among whom *you* [at Rome] also . . . are *the called* of Jesus Christ; to all who are *beloved of God* in Rome, *called* as saints" (Rom 1:5–7 NASB). To those who are "the called" he (later) says, "While we were still *sinners*, Christ died for *us*" (5:8). And his death paid for all our sin, including unbelief, so that we can again trust God in Christ's resurrection life, by regeneration. If Christ died for all humans, then in the case of the lost it would be double jeopardy (the prosecution of the person twice for the same offences), for the sins of those who will be judged under the wrath of God were (supposedly) already judged in and borne by Christ, and yet they would still have to bear them with their deserved wrath on the day of the Lord. But

53. Mack, *To God be the Glory*, 9.

Paul's argument in Rom 8:32–39 is that, because Christ died and rose again for the elect, Christ died for all their sins, even their unbelief. If Christ died for the sins of every human, head for head, then he died for their unbelief toward Christ also; then *all* humans would be saved and universalism is true, for there would be nothing in the way of them being saved. But Christ died for all the sins of the elect (Rom 8:33–34); he redeemed them from the bondage of sin (Rom 3:24; 6:2–7) including their unbelief, with the curse of death, in order that they might (be enabled to) receive the promise of *the Spirit through the faith* (see Gal 3:13–14) and make each of them a new creation who do believe in Christ. But since Christ *died, for a multitude* which no man can number, *out of* every tribe and nation (Rev 5:9), then all of that multitude will be saved. He purchased them and thereby gives them his Spirit of faith, as we find in 2 Cor 4:13 and 2 Thess 2:13–14. This *must* be so because flesh, with its mind, only hates God (Rom 8:7–8). If God can elect some (many) to salvation, then he can, in Christ, die for some (many). All those whom Christ redeemed will come to faith and be saved. Paul spoke God's wisdom (Christ crucified, 1 Cor 1:23–24), which (crucifixion) God ordained *before* the ages *for our glory* (after the ages, 2:7). Humans in Adam are born spiritually dead; they cannot and would never come to faith, even if they lived in the flesh for a billion years, for "without faith it is impossible to please God" (Heb 11:6), and those who are in the flesh cannot please God (Rom 8:7); therefore, there is no faith toward God in the flesh. The natural man *cannot receive* the things of *the Spirit* of God, which includes the Spirit of *Christ* himself (1 Cor 2:14–16; see Rom 8:7–10). In the preaching of the apostles throughout the entire book of Acts, they preached Christ crucified and risen and that those who believe in him receive the forgiveness of sins and the Holy Spirit. They did not say, "Christ died for each and every one of you" or even "Christ died for you." John's Jesus said:

> I am the good shepherd. I know my own, and I am known by my own; even as the Father knows me, and I know the Father. *I lay down my life for the sheep.* I have other sheep [elect gentiles], which are not of *this* [elect from Israel, Rom 9:6] fold. I must bring them also, and they will hear my voice. They will become one flock with one shepherd. (John 10:14–16 WEB/AT)

Therefore, here is what the beloved disciple is saying:

> For God so loved the world [not only Israel, but the nations], that he gave his only begotten Son, that those *believing* in him should not perish, but have *eternal life*. (John 3:16)

But you do *not believe, because* you are not of my sheep. (John 10:26)

I lay down my life for *the sheep.* (John 10:15b AV)

God loved "the sheep" from both Israel and the nations; and this aligns with Paul in Rom 5:8–10; see 8:29–39 and 9:22–26.

[1] . . . the riches of his glory on vessels of mercy, which he prepared beforehand for glory: us, whom he also called, not from the Jews *only*, but *also from the gentiles*? (Rom 9:23–24) And the called (8:30) are the elect (8:33) whom God justifies through Christ's death. (8:33–34)	And he is the propitiation for our sins (Jewish Christians*), but *not* for ours *only*, but *also* for the sins of *the whole world*. (1 John 2:2) * John was sent to the Jews; see Gal 2:9.

Those who will be *glorified* are the ones for whom Christ died and those for whom *God (before the ages) predestined Christ to be crucified* (1 Cor 2:7). Christ tasted death for every man, but "every man" in context means *the sons* led to *glory*, that is, the children *God has given to Christ* (Heb 2:9–12). Christ's intercession for the elect is based upon his death which justified the elect,[54] without which no one would be saved (Luke 22:32). Jesus prays not for the world but for those the Father has given him (John 17:2, 9).

---

54. Whoever believes in Christ will have eternal life (John 3:16), but later Jesus says to unbelieving Jews, "But you *do not believe, because* you are not of my sheep" (John 10:26a). God's election precedes faith; the sheep believe because they were the elect from before the world began; and "the Good Shepherd gives His life [died] for the sheep" (John 10:11b). "The world" in John 3:16 means not only Jews but nations also (John 10:15, 16; Rom 9:23–24; see 1 John 2:2). John 3:18 has been taken to mean that all those who do not yet believe in Christ have already had their sins paid for, that their *condemnation* is because they *do not believe in Christ*. But in John's gospel it says that unless they believe in Christ, they will die in *their sins* (8:24). Yet, the implication in 3:18, that humans are condemned for not believing in Christ, has been used against Paul's gospel of God, to spread the idea that the *cause* of condemnation is unbelief in Christ, *as if* Christ already took away the sin of every person who has ever lived in the world. But the apostolic gospel knows no such doctrine. For in the gospel of God (Rom 1:1), man's *condemnation already exists in Adam* (Rom 5:12–21; see 1 Cor 15:21, 22), before and apart from Christ's death and resurrection and thus before and apart from one's faith or unbelief in Christ. Therefore, just as John 3:16 needs to be read in the light of John 10:26; even so, John 3:18 should be interpreted in the light of 8:24, the rest of John's Gospel, and Paul's gospel of God. Scripture does not teach universal salvation (Matt 7:13–14; John 5:29; Rom 2:5–10).

God, who did not spare his only begotten Son, but delivered him up to death for us all, loves us no less than he loves his Son (John 17:23–26). Haldane wrote:

> God justifies them. There is none that justifies besides God. None can absolve and acquit a sinner from guilt, and constitute and pronounce him righteous, but God alone. . . . It is God alone that condemns, and therefore it is God alone that justifies . . . God Himself is pleased to justify the elect, to deliver them from condemnation, and view them as possessing perfect righteousness.[55]

Christ is the propitiation for our sins. Therefore, God is faithful to be the justifier of those who are of the faith of Jesus (3:25–26; 1 Cor 1:9). On 8:34, Lloyd-Jones said of Christ:

> He cannot be the cause of our condemnation because His very death proves that He has taken our condemnation upon Himself. How can the One who has taken our condemnation upon Him be our condemnation? It is impossible.[56]

God himself provided the propitiation for our sins (3:25), so we have an objective peace *with* God through an objective justification (5:1), which is the basis for having the subjective peace *of* God, as we walk by faith in Christ for justification and not by our sight or feelings. Paul finishes this section of his letter with the following finale:

> Who shall separate us from the love of Christ? Shall tribulation, or anguish, or persecution, or famine, or nakedness, or peril, or sword? Even as it is written, "For your sake we are killed all day long. We were accounted as sheep for the slaughter." Yet in all these things we are more than conquerors through Him who loved us. For I am persuaded, that neither death, nor life, nor angels, nor principalities, nor powers, nor things present, nor things to come, nor height nor depth, nor any other created thing, shall be able to separate us from the love of God which is in Christ Jesus our Lord. (Rom 8:35–39 NASB)

When Paul says that "neither death, nor life, nor angels, nor principalities . . . will be able to *separate* us from the love of God," he is saying that these powers most certainly *would separate us from God* and his love if they *could*. But Jesus, in his death, *put off* Satan's rulers and authorities,

55. Haldane, *Epistle to the Romans*, 413, 14.
56. Lloyd-Jones, *Exposition of Chapter 8:17–39*, 416.

along with the law.[57] The forgiveness of sins (Col 2:13) *is* the "wiping out the handwriting in *ordinances [in the law] which was against us*" (2:14), *thereby putting off* (from Christ and us, in union with him) the satanic rulers and authorities (2:15)—their authority over us, through redemption—the forgiveness of sins (Col 1:14; 2:13).

> Since then, the children [whom God gave to Jesus] have shared
> in flesh and blood, he also himself similarly partook of the same,
> in order that through death he might *bring to nothing* him who
> had *the dominion*[58] [of Death] *over them*, that is, the *devil*, and
> might deliver all who, *through* fear of *death*, were all their lifetime
> subject to bondage [to Death and thus to its *fear*]. (Heb 2:14–15)

Satan's dominion through death (along with its fear) lost his and its hold on God's people through Christ's death (for death is the wages of sin). For Satan, who had the dominion of *death* over all in Adam, had no right to put Christ, the righteous one, to death; thus he lost his dominion over those for whom Christ died. The Devil (Heb 2:14–15), who possessed the power and dominion of death, through his control of Judas (John 13:37) and others,[59] was allowed by God to use it on Christ. But Satan had no clue that God would raise Christ from the dead. Christ delivered us out of the authority (ἐξουσίας) of darkness—of Satan (Col 1:14 and Acts 26:18). Nothing in all

---

57. "And you being [spiritually] dead in your trespasses and in the uncircumcision of your flesh, God made alive together with him [Christ, by] *forgiving us all our trespasses, wiping out* the handwriting in ordinances [of the law, 2 Cor 3:3] which was *against us*; and he has taken it [the accusations of our trespasses against the law, which were against us] out of the way, nailing it to the cross; [thereby] putting *off* the rulers and the authorities, he made a show of them openly, triumphing over them in it [the cross]. (Col 2:13–15)

58. The Greek word κράτος is translated as *dominion* in 1 Pet 4:11; 5:11; Jude 25; Rev 1:6. The whole world lies in the Evil One (the power of Satan, 1 John 5:19 AT/AP). Satan was a murderer from the beginning, bringing (spiritual unto bodily) *death* into the world through inciting the one man to sin (John 8:44; Rom 5:12, 18, 19). Through that death, Satan has ever since had dominion over all in Adam (Heb 2:14, 15; Rom 5:12-21). But (all) the *rulers* of this present age had absolutely no clue that Christ's death would mean the breaking of the power, bondage, and dominion of death over all those for whom Christ died (1 Cor 2:6-9; see Rom 8:33-34).

59. The rulers (ἄρχων) of this age/world, who are coming to nothing (1 Cor 2:6), are among the rulers and authorities who will come to nothing (be destroyed, [same word as in 2:6]) at "the end" (1 Cor 15:24). They crucified to death the Lord of glory (see 1 Cor 2:8 and 2:6), where Paul means that flesh and blood rulers put to death the flesh and blood Christ. Since Satan is the ἄρχων (ruler) of this world (John 16:11), then clearly this age's rulers (ἀρχόντων, 1 Cor 2:6-8) were *ruled by* Satan in Christ being put to death, for when Jesus said "the ruler of this world is coming" (John 14:30; 16:11) he meant Satan's involvement in his being crucified (13:27, in his being destroyed 10:10).

creation will be able to separate us from the love of God which is in Christ Jesus our Lord (8:35–39). To illustrate, it is as though each of God's elect, at regeneration, is placed in a passenger train and kept therein by a seal (2 Cor 1:22). They will have to suffer with Christ according to his wisdom as to what each of his children must endure regarding suffering, to be conformed to the image of God's Son. At times the train enters tunnels of inexplicable suffering. But our faithful God guarantees that they will safely arrive at their destination: the glory of eternal life—experientially knowing the Father and the Son in the fellowship of the Holy Spirit.

TWELVE

The Promise Is to God's Chosen Ones

(Rom 9–11)

It is not that the word of God has taken no effect; for they are
not all [true] Israel who are [descended] from Israel. (Rom 9:6)

Romans Chapter 9

MANY PEOPLE STILL BELIEVE that natural Israel is "God's chosen people,"
because in the old covenant Scriptures, from Exodus through Malachi,
there are times when the Lord calls Israel "my people" (e.g., Exod 9:1). But
when we come to the revelation of God's saving righteousness in the gospel
of God, based on Christ's death and resurrection, we not only find that
God's righteousness in Christ is not that of the law (3:21–26; 10:1–9), but
we simultaneously discover that God's chosen people are not the nation of
Israel, for not all who are descended from Israel according to the flesh (1
Cor 10:18) are (true) Israel (Rom 9:6). Israel is the people of the promise.
The gospel of the crucified God, the Messiah, was hidden in Israel's scriptures.[1] This hiddenness of the gospel has not been sufficiently taught in the
church, yet it is a main reason that the Messiah was not recognized to be
the Messiah, even after his death and resurrection and Pentecost. In Rom
9:6 Paul says that the word of God has not failed. This is because the gospel
that was promised by God's prophets in the Holy Scriptures has come to us
in Jesus Christ (Rom 1:1–4). So, it is not as though the word—the promise

1. See 1 Cor 1:23; compare 2:6–8; Rom 16:25; 2 Cor 3:14–16.

of God—has failed, for it has not failed. God's word has accomplished—and will accomplish—all it was meant to do, for God's chosen people will be saved.

> It is not that *the word of God* has taken no effect; for they are not all Israel who are [descended] from [natural] Israel. (Rom 9:6 AT/AV)

This is a key verse in chapter 9. What Paul calls "the word of God" here in 9:6, he also calls *the word of promise* in 9:9, which is God's promise to Abraham.

> Nor are they all children [of the promise] because they are [physically] the seed of Abraham; but [rather], "In Isaac your seed will be called."[2] That is, those who are the children of the flesh [natural Israel], these are not the children of God; but the children of the promise are counted as the [true] seed [the children of God]. For this is the word of promise: "At this time I will come and Sarah shall have a son." (Rom 9:7–9)

And the "son" here is not Ishmael, but Isaac, in whom God's promise to Abraham was fulfilled in Abraham's lifetime, though it had not yet been spiritually fulfilled, as it was in Christ, the seed (Gal 3:16) for all God's elect, all who would believe (Gal 3:29). Abraham's descendants, from Isaac to the Messiah (Matt 1:2–17), are connected to *God's promise* of the seed, which is *Christ* (Gal 3:16). Isaac was chosen by God—not only through God fulfilling his promise to Abraham in Isaac's supernatural birth, but also and primarily in terms of spiritual birth. That is, Isaac was effectively called and chosen by God (Rom 9:11) and thus was a child of God (9:8–9; Gal 4:28–29). Paul is saying that all "the children of the promise" are like Isaac was in this way: They are the called, the chosen (9:7).

Then, in like manner, Paul says that when Rebecca conceived by her husband Isaac, although she had twins, God chose not Esau but Jacob.

> And not only this, but when Rebecca also had conceived by one, even by our father Isaac (for the children [of Isaac] being not yet born, neither having done any good or evil, that the purpose of God according to *election* might stand, not of works, but of God who calls); it was said to her, "The elder [Esau] will serve the younger" [Jacob]. As it is written, "Jacob have I loved [chosen], but Esau have I hated." (Rom 9:10–13 AV/AT)

---

2. Paul uses "the called" as meaning the people chosen beforehand by God (1 Cor 1:24–27; Rom 9:24; 11:2).

Paul chooses these OT examples to prove that the promise of God was, and is, not to natural Israel but to (the true) Israel, those *from among* natural Israel (9:6). They are children of God. So, although Paul here uses Isaac and Jacob as examples of *the children of the promise* (the children of God, 9:8), nevertheless, in context (9:8, 23–24) this "not having done anything good or evil, that God's purpose according to election might stand" applies to all "the children of the promise" throughout history. And those whom Paul calls "the children of the promise" (9:8), he also calls "the vessels of mercy."

> In order to make known the riches of his glory for *the vessels of mercy* which he has prepared beforehand for glory, even us whom he has *called* [to salvation, 8:30], not from the Jews only but also from the Gentiles. (Rom 9:23–24 RSV)

Here Paul says that "the children of the promise" (9:8) are those (effectually) called by God to salvation from among the Jews and the gentiles (9:24). And that is why, from 9:25 through 9:29, Paul quotes from the OT scriptures to prove his point that God had all along planned to call the gentiles (who were not his people) "God's people," and that unless God himself had kept a remnant from among natural Israel, not one of them would have been saved (for in the flesh, there is no ability to trust God, Rom 7:18; 8:7–8). God *never promised* to save (from sin and death) all who belong to Israel according to the flesh. Here, Paul contrasts the gentiles who believed, with (the majority of) Israel, in terms of their stance toward Christ, saying:

> What shall we say then? That the Gentiles, who did not pursue righteousness, have attained to righteousness, even the righteousness of faith; but Israel, following after righteousness, has not attained to the law of righteousness. Why? Because they did not seek it by *faith*, but as it were, by the works of the law. (Rom 9:30–32b NKJV)

Paul is not saying that the gentiles, who did not follow after righteousness and who have attained to righteousness by faith, now that they have believed, follow after righteousness. No. Even now they do not follow after righteousness, for *Christ is* the end of the law for righteousness—for those who *believe*. The only righteousness that elect gentiles do follow after and know is Christ, in whom God continually justifies the ungodly who believe (4:5). Again, since Paul includes the elect gentiles in "the children of the promise" in Gal 3:14 and 4:28–29, then "the children of the promise" in Rom 9:8 includes elect gentiles as well, as he will finally say when he comes to 9:23–25.

So, what Paul says regarding "Israel" from here on, through the end of Rom 11, will not depart from this distinction between (true) Israel and

"Israel according to the flesh" (see 1 Cor 10:18). The bottom line is that salvation is not by works or anything from humans, including *their* choice of God, that they could point to and glory in, but rather it is by God's sovereign, gracious choice of them for the purpose of salvation (glory) in Christ.

> What shall we say then? Is there unrighteousness with God? Certainly not! For He says to Moses, "*I will have mercy on whom I have mercy, and I will have compassion on whomever I will have compassion.*" So then, it [mercy, saving grace] is *not* of him who *wills* [for the sinner, with his will, is enslaved to sin, Rom 6:20], nor of him who *runs* [who does *works*], but of *God* who shows mercy [upon whom God wills to show mercy]. (Rom 9:14–16 NKJV)

Paul asks the rhetorical question, "Is there unrighteousness with God?" And of course, by that he is saying that *there is no unrighteousness with God.* This is paramount. We understand and accept this truth by faith in the God revealed in the gospel and throughout the Holy Scriptures.

Next, Paul gives an example of God's sovereignty over Pharaoh of Egypt in the time of Moses and applies it to God's sovereignty in salvation:

> So then he has mercy on whomever he wills, and he hardens the heart of whomever he wills. You will say to me then, "Why does he still find fault? For who can resist his will?" But who are you, a man, to answer back to God? Will what is molded say to its molder, "Why have you made me thus?" Has the potter no right over the clay, to make out of the same lump one vessel for beauty and another for menial use? What if God, desiring to show his wrath and to make known his power, has endured with much patience the vessels of wrath made for destruction, in order to make known the riches of his glory for the vessels of mercy, which he has prepared beforehand for glory, even us whom he has called, not from the Jews only, but also from the Gentiles. (Rom 9:18–24 RSV)

The Scriptures teach that all who will be saved were chosen before the foundation of the world (Eph 1:3–6). Now if the elect were chosen (foreknown, fore-loved) by God before the world began, then the others were not chosen before the world began, and in both cases it was independent of their works, or Adam's sin, or personal sin or sins. Therefore, when Paul says, "As the potter has no right over the clay, to make out of the same lump one vessel for honorable use and another [one] for dishonorable use" (Rom 9:21 ESV), then the vessels not only for honorable use (salvation, glory) but also the vessels for dishonorable use (destruction) were both predetermined to be such before the foundation of the world. But Paul says, "Who are you, O man, to answer back to God?" (v. 20a). Again, Paul's important and final word on this is "What shall we say then? Is there unrighteousness with God? Certainly not!" (Rom 9:14). So, there is no unrighteousness with God in reprobation, which Scripture teaches in Rom 9:13, 14, 18–22; 11:7–10; 1 Pet 2:8; and Jude 4. On the level of human responsibility, the fault lies entirely with those who are lost (see Rom 9:30—10:3). And in Acts, it says that the Jews had the word preached to them, yet it was *they* who judged themselves unworthy of eternal life by rejecting the gospel (13:44–46); and yet Acts continues to say that (paradoxically) when the gentiles "glorified the word of the Lord," "as many as had been *appointed to* eternal life [by God] believed" (Acts 13:48b NASB). God's sovereign, free, electing grace appointed them to life.

So, both are true: The elect, those upon whom God, who is utterly free, has chosen to have mercy (9:15) are such "according to the purpose of God who works all things according to the counsel of his own will" (Eph 1:11b AV), that is, "according to his *good pleasure* which he has purposed in himself "(1:9 AV); "according to the *good pleasure* of his *will*, to the praise of the glory of his grace" (1:5b), "wherein he has made us accepted in the Beloved" (1:6 AV). It is according to the good pleasure of God's will that he chooses some to salvation and passes by others unto destruction (9:22). Now our righteousness, which is of the flesh of sin (Rom 8:3 lit.), judges this God to be not good. But there is no unrighteousness with God (9:14). Humans in their sin judge God in that they think they know better than God, that their wisdom is wise and God's is not. That is why this chapter is the most offensive chapter in the Scriptures to the flesh. But what has made this chapter even more offensive than it truly is, is the lie ("You shall *not* die"), which death Paul calls "destruction," is not believed to be destruction because of the extent to which Platonic philosophy affected the church fathers and then Augustine and other theologians down to this very day.[3] But "destruction" and "death" are used interchangeably throughout Scripture, beginning with the Torah, all the way to and including the Synoptic Gospels, and then in the NT letters. All of God's enemies will be done away with (destroyed, 1 Cor 15:24), in order that God might be all in all (15:25–28). From all that we know from Holy Scripture, we say this:

God is love. God is just. God is love toward his chosen ones, who are vessels of mercy, and God is just toward those he passes by, who are fitted to destruction (9:18–24), for God owes no one salvation or eternal life. There is no justice of God that is not loving, and there is no love of God

---

3. See comments on Rom 6:23 in my ch. 9 and also ch. 20.

that is not just. God has justly justified his elect in Christ's death, and, for the reprobate, God's justice is not unaffected by his love; thus, they will not receive eternal conscious suffering, but what is justly due each of them in gehenna, unto destruction (Matt 10:28; Rom 9:22).

The one God does not have two wills: one that fore-loved the elect and determined to save them alone, and another will that loves all humans with a love that genuinely and strongly desires to save all humans but is too weak and thus unable to do so. Second Peter 3:9 has been used by some to teach this "genuine desire." But those who do so ignore the words "promise" and "us" in their context:

> The Lord is not slack concerning his *promise* . . . but is longsuf-fering toward *us*, not willing that any [of us] should perish, but that all [of us] should come to repentance. (2 Pet 3:9 NKJV)

The letter is written "to those who have obtained a faith of equal standing with ours by the righteousness of our God and Savior Jesus Christ" (2 Pet 1:1). God's promise is for those who have obtained a faith, that all the elect should come to repentance. Peter preached:

> For *the promise* [of salvation] is to you and to your children, and to all who are afar off, as many as the Lord our God will *call.* (Acts 2:39)

And "call" here means "chosen," as Paul teaches in 1 Cor 1:24–29. So, Peter means "as many as the Lord our God has chosen" he will call to faith in Christ that saves. Although God demonstrates his *common* kindness to-ward all, so that the rain falls on the just and on the unjust, he loves only the elect unto salvation. Thus, 2 Pet 3 should be interpreted in the light of 1:1 and Rom 8:28–34 and chapters 9–11.

Romans Chapter 10

Paul continues, saying his heart's desire is that Israel would be saved:

> For I testify about them that they have a zeal for God, but not according to knowledge. For being ignorant of God's righteous-ness, and seeking to establish their own righteousness, they did not subject themselves to the righteousness of God. For Christ is the end of the law for righteousness to everyone who believes. (Rom 10:2–4)

The law of Moses is righteous and good; it is filled with wisdom on how to live in this world. Many Jews and others who, to this very day, follow the law's wisdom find that they live decent and often prosperous and fulfilled lives (in the realm of soul and body, not their inner being). Therefore, the only "problem" with the law is when it is used to be right with God unto eternal life by doing it. That is what God, through Paul, is saying.

Again, unlike Paul's letters, in which we find the gospel's use of the law, which shuts up all under sin, the old covenant scriptures never say that the law of Moses *cannot* be kept.[4] And, in line with the OT scriptures in their context, Michael Horton points out:

> The Mosaic Law (i.e., the Sinai covenant) was never given to save sinners from God's everlasting judgment. The promises of the Mosaic Law were limited to a single nation and to temporal blessing ("long life") in a geo-political theocracy ("in the land that I am giving you to possess"). Therefore, the Mosaic law is much more specific and limited than the promise that God made to Adam and Eve after the fall and renewed with Abraham.[5]

And that nation to whom God's angels, through Moses, gave the law was old covenant Israel (Exod 19:2–7; see 20:1–22). Moses's words to old-covenant Israel, which portrayed the *simplicity* of doing the law, that is, it is *"not too difficult* for you" (Deut 30:11 NASB), evidently inspired Paul to use that OT text in Romans but without all the "do's" of Moses' law! So, Paul now applies that OT text, not to the law, but instead to the gospel. Paul does this in the premier text that contrasts the righteousness of the law with the righteousness of faith (in Christ)—that is, which contrasts the law with the gospel. When the apostle says, "The one who does those things will *live* by them" in 10:5, by "live" he means have *eternal life,* for the word "live" means *saved* and *salvation* in 10:9–10. Also, that "live" means have *eternal life* (in 10:5) is clear from the words "eternal life" in Rom 2:7; 5:21, and 6:23. In contrast to the law, which says, "The one doing those things will live (have righteousness and life by or in them)" (Lev 18:5; Rom 10:5), Paul says:

> But what does *the righteousness of faith* say? *"The Word* is near you, in your mouth and in your heart (that is, the word of *faith* which we are preaching): That if you confess with your mouth 'Jesus is Lord' and *believe* in your heart that *God raised Jesus from the dead,* you will be saved" [justified for the purpose of eternal life]. For with the heart, one believes unto *righteousness*; and with the mouth confession is made unto *salvation.* (Rom 10:6–10)

4. See Deut 30:12–16.
5. Horton, *Pilgrim Theology,* 160.

First, notice that in the last verse, "righteousness" (justification) is synonymous with "salvation." Next, in this entire text, note the antithesis between fleshly reason and gospel revelation, that is, between human righteousness and God's saving righteousness, through the Messiah (Phil 3:9). The gospel draws a clear distinction between the law of Moses and Christ, for Christ is not the law (of Moses) and God is not the law (of Moses). Only the gospel of God reveals this. Whether or not a person is saved unto eternal life comes down to whether he remains in Adam with his own righteousness or he receives God's justification in Christ. It is the distinction between not obeying the gospel—and obeying the gospel through faith. Such faith occurs through *the gospel* in those who are (savingly) called by God. Life was promised in the law of works—the commandment was for life (7:10). But humans are under the (now broken) covenant of works (transgressed) in Adam and thus under sin (Rom 3:9) and judgment to God (Rom 3:19; 5:12–21). But now that Christ has come, we know that the flesh renders the law impotent to give us life (Rom 7:10–13; 8:3; 10:5–9; Gal 3:21); for Christ is the end of the law for righteousness for believers (10:4). Note the contrast between "man" and "God" in Paul's preaching of the gospel.

> For Moses writes about the righteousness which is of the law, that the *man* who does those things will live [have eternal life] by doing them. But the righteousness [which is] of faith says this:
>
> "Do not say [think] in your heart, 'Who will ascend into heaven?' (that is, to bring Christ down [as if the Word had not become flesh and died for us]), or, 'Who will descend into the abyss?' (that is, to bring Christ up from the dead [as if Christ has not been raised from the dead])."
>
> But what does the righteousness of *faith* say? "The word is near you, in your mouth and in your heart, (that is, the word of faith which we are preaching): That if you confess with your mouth "Jesus is Lord" and believe in your heart that *God* raised Jesus from the dead, you will be saved [justified to eternal life]." (Rom 10:5–9)

In those words, Paul spoke the antithesis between the law and the gospel for salvation. By revelation of Jesus Christ (Gal 1:12), the apostle was taught that he must include this central truth in the gospel of God (Rom 1:1), which contrasts what *man* does with *God's* raising Christ from the dead. We can accept the truth that we are sinners—those who cannot justify ourselves—when we know and believe that, while we were still such sinners, in love Christ died for us and thereby justified us before God. Thus, we are simultaneously sinners (in flesh) and yet justified (in Christ) through faith in the God who justifies the ungodly in Christ (4:5, 25). "The word" and "the word of faith" in Rom 10:8 is called "the word of God" (or "the word of Christ") in 10:17. They are all expressions for the gospel, for the terms "the word of God" and "the gospel" are used interchangeably in Paul's letters.[6] Faith comes by hearing and hearing by the word of Christ (the gospel) (10:17). In fact, Christ, through Paul, is so far from equating *the scriptures* with *the word of God* that he uses "the law" (Rom 3:10–19) and "the scripture" (Gal 3:22) interchangeably—both as having the very same function: as imprisoning, as shutting up all humans under (the power of) sin unto condemnation—in contrast to the gospel of Christ, which justifies and frees believers from sin and death, as the following chart shows.

For we previously charged both Jews and Greeks, that they are all *under sin* (Rom 3:9 NKJV). Now we know that whatever things **the law** says, it speaks . . . in order that . . . *all the world* may be brought *under the judgment of God* (Rom 3:19).	But **the scripture** shut up *all mankind under sin*, in order that the promise . . . might be given to those believing (Gal 3:22).

Below, we put both of the above columns (on the law and the scripture) on the left, in contrast to the gospel (on the right).

The scriptures and *the law* shut up all under *sin*	*Christ* justifies sinners who believe
All are *under sin* (Rom 3:9) as *OT scripture (the law)*, quoted in 3:10–18, proves, and brings the whole world under judgment to God (3:19). *The scripture* has imprisoned all *under sin* (Gal 3:22a) . . .	But now apart from law, the righteousness from God is revealed (Rom 3:21 = come, Gal 3:23–25). . . . in order that the promise (righteousness and life, Gal 3:21) by Christ's faith, might be giving to those believing (Gal 3:22b).

So, what is Christ for? "Christ is . . . for *righteousness*" (Rom 10:4). Therefore, justification is "no longer on the basis of works" (11:6b NASB) as it was in God's covenant of life with Adam. For the bottom line is that there was a historical fall into sin from which we must be redeemed in order to have eternal life. Thus, now that the faith of Christ has come (Gal 3:22–25),

6. See 1 Cor 15:1–4; Phil 1:14–18; 1 Thess 1:5 and 2:13; Rom 10:8, 17; 2 Cor 4:2–3; also, Acts 4:2–4; 8:4–5, 25; 15:7; 19:4, 5, 10; 20:24, 32.

every other way of righteousness, including the law of Moses, is *ended* for all who believe in Christ, which is precisely what Paul says in Rom 10:4. God never said to Abel, Abraham, Moses, or David, "Believe on the Lord Jesus Christ, and you shall be saved," because Jesus had not yet come, died, or risen from the dead. They were saved through faith in the promise (of the gospel, Rom 1:1–2; see 4:13–16). No one, including Peter, *believed on the Lord Jesus Christ* until God appointed Jesus to be both Lord and Christ through his exaltation to God's right hand.[7] As in the OT scriptures, so also in Gal 3:21, "righteousness" and "life" are used interchangeably, for they always go together. Paul says that unbelieving Israel did not subject themselves to God's *righteousness*, for the mind of the flesh does not subject itself to God's life, that is, God's Spirit (Rom 10:1–3; 8:6–10). In light of Paul's gospel, we paraphrase Paul in Rom 10:5–9 as follows:

> It does not matter what Moses, in his old-covenant context (in Lev 18:5), meant by the words "those statues of the law, which, if a man does, he shall *live* by (doing) them." For I know that for Moses, to "live" meant to not be put to death, but live a full, prosperous life. But now, by the authority given me by the exalted Lord Jesus Christ, I make Moses the representative of "the righteousness which is of the law."[8] I make those words of Moses mean what the mind of the flesh (Rom 8:6a) universally thinks concerning how a person is to be right with God, namely, that *righteousness* comes by *doing the works of the law*.[9] But now, by the truth of *the gospel of God* I expose the lie,[10] for the righteousness which justifies before God came by the death of Jesus Christ (Rom 3:21–26; 5:9), whom God raised from the dead (4:25), who gives eternal life in Christ alone, through faith in him alone.[11]

7. See Rom 1:4 lit.; Acts 11:17 and 2:32–36; Phil 2:8–11.

8. This insight comes from Nygren's understanding in his *Significance of the Bible*, 24–28.

9. By "the works of the law" Paul means a human's keeping of the law, summarized in the Ten Commandments (Rom 2:17–23), which, due to sinful flesh, is in reality only an *outward* keeping and is thus a lie. It is not a keeping or fulfilling of the law from the heart. For the flesh, with its mind, hates God (8:7–8; 2:29), and it is impossible to trust one whom one hates; and thus the flesh cannot please God (Rom 8:7–8; see Heb 11:6).

10. Paul speaks of sin being used by the law to deceive him (Rom 7:7–13). This is why John says that "the law was given through Moses, but grace and truth [not deception] came through Jesus Christ" (1:17), because the law speaks of "the righteous" as the ones who are loved by God (Ps 146:8), but in the gospel, we know that there are *none* who are righteous, that God loved his chosen sinners while we were still sinners (Rom 5:6–8; Gal 2:15–17).

11. So, there are only two kinds of righteousness: the righteousness of the law

Regarding this righteousness that saves, we cannot do better than to quote from Stuart Olyott, who comments on verses 9 through 17 as follows:

> *vv. 9–10* What must the inward heart believe in order to receive it? It must believe in the lordship and saviourhood of Christ, and that he is forever alive to save, God having raised Him from the dead. This belief must be a living faith, sufficiently real to lead the person concerned into open confession . . . *v. 11* Those who thus believe, as the Scriptures promise, will never be let down. Unlike the striving Jew, trying to get right with God by his own efforts, they will not be unsuccessful. No such disappointment awaits them. Those who believe are certainly saved. . . . *vv. 12–13* Salvation is thus available to all, Jew or Gentile. There is no difference in their standing before God (ch. 3) and there is no difference in the way each is saved. The righteousness which God imputes is for all without distinction. God's saving mercy is lavished upon sinners without discrimination or partiality. Whoever cries, whether he be Jew or Gentile, the Lord hears him and saves him.[12]

> It is worth noting that Paul holds to both the doctrine of election and the free offer of the gospel, and finds no embarrassment in doing so. Nor should we . . . The gospel really is for "whosoever," and its invitations exclude nobody.[13]

> *v. 15* And how can someone go and tell him, unless that person is sent to do so? To understand this final question we need to realize that the New Testament teaches that the main business of spreading the gospel is the work of men specially commissioned to do so.[14] *v. 16.* However, we must not think that everyone who hears the gospel comes to believe. If this were so, Isaiah would not have said, "Lord, who hath believed our report?" (Isa 53:1). *v. 17.* On the other hand, we must be clear that no one will believe at all, unless he *does* hear. Faith comes only by hearing the Word of God.[15] The electing God who has decreed who should

---

(human righteousness in Adam) and the righteousness of God in Christ, which Paul calls "the righteousness of faith" (4:13; 9:30; 10:6), the phrase of the apostle that Luther rightly used so often. Adam sinned, and all sinned with and in him and are thus condemned sinners sentenced to death. Therefore, only the righteousness of God in Christ avails before God for the justification of sinners, unto life eternal.

12. Olyott, *Gospel as It Really Is*, 92.

13. Olyott, *Gospel as It Really Is*, 93.

14. Olyott, *Gospel as It Really Is*, 93.

15. Olyott, *Gospel as It Really Is*, 94.

be saved has also decreed that there is no salvation without gospel preaching.[16]

In Rom 10:17, Paul refers to "the hearing of faith" which saves (Gal 3:2).

He is saying, "So then, faith comes by hearing, and hearing by the word of God" (10:17), that is, the preached gospel (Rom 10:6–10). By "the word of God" he means the gospel, "the word of faith," the word of (concerning) Christ (10:8).

Romans Chapter 11

Paul himself is proof that God has not completely rejected Israel, for Paul is an Israelite!

> I say then, has God cast away His people? Certainly not! For I also am an Israelite, of the seed of Abraham, of the tribe of Benjamin. (Rom 11:1)

Paul then clarifies: "God has not rejected his people whom he *foreknew*" (Rom 11:2a ESV), whom God intimately knew and loved beforehand. And then Paul calls God's people whom he foreknew "the remnant [chosen from among natural Israel] according to the election of grace" (11:5b). They were loved before the ages by God. Those whom God foreknew (fore-loved) are the called—the chosen for salvation.

> What then? That which Israel is seeking for, it has not obtained, *but those who were chosen* obtained it, and the rest were hardened. (Rom 11:7 NASB)

This reveals that those whom God loved beforehand (11:2) are the remnant according to the election of grace (11:6)—those who were chosen from among natural Israel, for they are not all (true) Israel who are descended from natural Israel (9:6). By Israel's transgression, their rejection of the Messiah, and their rejection by God, salvation has come to the gentiles (nations)—the world, says Paul in 11:11.

> Now if their [Israel's] transgression be riches for the world, and their failure be riches for the Gentiles, how much more will their [Israel's] *fullness* be [riches for the nations]? (Rom 11:12 NASB w/ margin)

Do we have light from any other text to enable us to know what Paul means by Israel's "fullness" here? Yes. Commenting on Rom 11:25, Olyott says:

16. Olyott, *Gospel as It Really Is*, 94.

There the word "fullness" means "the total number of the elect," and there seems to be no reason why it should not be taken in the same way here.[17]

In 11:25, "fullness" means the full number of all the elect gentiles. Thus, Israel's fullness means (the salvation of) *the full number of the elect from* among *natural Israel*, which will be riches for the world, even life from the dead[18] (11:15). The branches that were broken off from the holy root, Abraham's natural seed, are the unbelieving majority, amazing as it may seem to the flesh. The branches grafted into God's people are the gentiles who believe (11:16–19). Because of unbelief, most of natural Israel was broken off, "but you [gentiles in Christ] stand by faith" (v. 20). If the natural branches (v. 21) from among Israel do not remain in unbelief, God is able to graft them in again. God will do so, as history moves on, as they believe in the Messiah.

> Lest you be wise in your own sight, I want you to understand this mystery, brothers; a partial hardening has come upon Israel, until the fullness of the Gentiles has come in. And in this way [by means of a remnant continually being saved from among natural Israel, until Christ returns, 11:5, 1–7; so that the gentiles might be grafted in, v. 19], all Israel will be saved. (Rom 11:25–26a ESV)

"All Israel" here could mean "all of the elect from among natural Israel (9:6). Or it could mean "all the elect from the Jews and the Gentiles" (11:16–24; 9:23–24). Because of our comments on Romans chapter 9, we believe it is the latter.[19] So then, how will (true, elect) Israel be saved?

> As it is written, "The Deliverer will come out of Zion. And He will turn away ungodliness from Jacob; *For this is my covenant with them, When I take away their sins.*" (Rom 11:26 NKJV)

But when and how did God take away the sins of the remnant among Israel? In the new covenant/testament in Christ's blood (1 Cor 11:25). And of this, Hebrews says:

> *This is the covenant that I will make with them*: "After those days," says the Lord, "I will put my laws on their heart, I will also write them on their mind"; then he says, "*I will remember*

---

17. Olyott, *Gospel as It Really Is*, 99.

18. In light of 1 Thess 4:16; 1 Cor 15:36, 42, in 11:15 we believe Paul to mean that "life from the dead" means resurrection out from the dead (1 Cor 15).

19. See also White, "Israel in Romans 11."

their sins and their iniquities no more." Now where remission of
these is, there is no more offering for sin. (Heb 10:16–18 WEB)

This is the salvation of "all Israel" (11:26): being saved from sin and death
"when I take away their sins" (11:26). And Israel, in 11:25–26, is not that Israel which is according to the flesh (9:6) but according to the Spirit. Christ is
truly reigning now as Lord[20] and therefore must be received as Lord now, in
this present age, by all who would be saved. Paul summarizes it as follows:

> For just as you [Gentiles] once were disobedient to God but now
> have been shown mercy because of their [Israel's] disobedience,[21]
> so these [natural branches of Israel according to the flesh, Rom
> 11:16–21] also now have been disobedient[22] [in rejecting the
> Messiah] in order that because of the mercy shown to you
> [Gentiles] they may also now [be made jealous[23] by the Gentiles
> receiving salvation and thereby] be shown mercy [to a remnant
> of Israel, (in order) that all (elect) Israel may be saved, 11:25–26].
> For God has shut up all [Jew and Gentile] in disobedience[24] [in
> order] that He might show mercy to all [that is, "even us, whom
> he has *called, not from the Jews only, but also from the Gentiles*"
> Rom 9:24 RSV]. (Rom 11:30–32 NASB)

So, the Christ-believer cannot think like this: "*I* made the (righteous) choice
by choosing Christ, while others did not."

The *righteousness* that is *of faith* (Rom 4:13) means *not having* my righteousness but that righteousness that is of the faith of *Christ* (his obedience of
faith unto death, which redemptive death for our justification procured *the
promise of the Spirit through the faith* [Gal 3:13–14]) bestowed upon faith (Phil
3:9), which God grants (Phil 1:29).

So, there is *no boasting* (Rom 3:26-28), for even faith did not come
from any one of us (Rom 7:18; 1 Cor 2:14). Election is "the election of grace"
(11:6 AV), God's sovereign freedom to choose those whom he pleases[25] for
salvation by grace (Christ's death) alone, while he passes by others unto
destruction, not life. Paul sums up chapters 9 through 11 as follows:

---

20. Rom 1:3, 4; 1 Cor 6:14; 12:3; 15:25; Heb 2:8; Eph 1:21.

21. Rom 10:1–3; 16–21; 11:11, 12, 15.

22. Rom 10:1–3; 16–21; 11:11, 12, 15.

23. Rom 11:11, 14.

24. Rom 3:9; Gal 3:22.

25. Eph 1:5; see 1:9b.

Oh, the depth of the riches and wisdom and knowledge of God! How unsearchable are his judgments and how inscrutable his ways! (Rom 11:33 ESV)

For from him and through him and to him are all things [including the mercy of *salvation*]. To him be the glory forever. Amen. (Rom 11:36 ESV)

Excursus 6: God's Sovereign Will and God's Revealed Will

"The *secret* things (concerning God's sovereign will and plan) belong to the LORD our God, but those things which are *revealed* belong to us and our children forever" (Deut 29:29 NKJV).

On the sovereign will of God, Scripture says:

Even as God chose us in Christ before the foundation of the world, that we would be holy and unblemished before him; in love predestinating us unto adoption as sons through Jesus Christ to himself, according to the good pleasure of *his will*. (Eph 1:4–5)

We were chosen [by God] as his inheritance, having been foreordained according to the purpose of the One operating *all things* according to *the counsel* [*wise, unchangeable purpose*] of *the will of him*. (Eph 1:11)

The above use of "the will of him" refers to the sovereign, secret, immutable will of God, known to God alone, except to the extent he has revealed it in Scripture—for example, those who are foreknown (fore-loved) by God will be glorified (Rom 8:29–30). Of this will of God, the Westminster Confession of Faith says:

God, from all eternity, did, by the most wise and holy counsel *of his own will*, freely, and unchangeably *ordain whatsoever comes to pass*: yet so, as thereby neither is God the author of sin, nor is violence offered to the will of the creatures; nor is the liberty or contingency of second causes taken away, but rather established.[26]

On the other hand, the *revealed will of God* is what God would have humans do; such as:

26. WCF 3.1, emphasis mine.

Our Father . . . *Your will* be done on earth as it is in heaven. (Matt 6:10 NKJV)

Be transformed . . . that you may prove what is that good . . . *will of God.* (Rom 12:2 NKJV)

For this is *the will of God,* your sanctification. (1 Thess 4:3 NKJV)

── THIRTEEN ──

Freed for the Freedom

For *the freedom* [of justification], Christ has *freed* us [by his death, in order to be led in resurrection life by his Spirit]. —Paul[1]

Christ and the law can by no means agree and reign together in the conscience. —Martin Luther[2]

PRIOR TO THE COMING of "the faith of Christ," the law was on the side of righteousness; for the law was all that old covenant Israel, without the Spirit of the risen Christ, had. But now that "the faith of Christ" has come (Gal 3:23–25), which includes his Spirit (Gal 4:1–7), the law (with its righteousness) is on the side of "the flesh" and not on the side of the new creation.[3] J. Louis Martyn explains this well:

> (1) The Spirit and its opposite, the Flesh, are not timeless first principles, called into being by God at the beginning.

> (2) This pair of opposites owes its birth to God's *new*-creative act. It is born of the new event, God's sending both his Son and the Spirit of his Son into the present evil age (Gal 1:4; 4:4-6).

> (3) The advent of the Son and of his Spirit is thus *the* cosmic apocalyptic event. There was a "before" and there is now an "after." And it is at the point at which the "after" invades the "before" that the Spirit and the Flesh have become a dynamic pair

---

1. From Gal 5:1. Justification=freedom: 3:13–14; 4:1–7, 21–31; to be led by the Spirit (5:18) with its fruit (5:22).

2. Luther, *Galatians*, 69.

3. See Rom 7:4–6; 8:1–4; Gal 3:21–28; 5:17; 6:14–16.

of opposites. They form an apocalyptic antinomy characteristic of the dawn of God's new creation.[4]

What time is it? It is the time after the apocalypse of the faith of Christ (3:23–25), the time of things being set right by that faith, the time of the presence of the Spirit, and thus the time of the war of liberation commenced by the Spirit. In a word, it is the time of the dawn of the new creation with its new antinomies.[5]

Martyn lists two of two of these antinomies (opposites) as follows:

There is, first, the Spirit and the Flesh. Paul speaks of these two powers as one would speak of a cosmic pair of opposites (5:17) . . . The Spirit and the Flesh are an oppositional pair that cause the world to be what it *now* actually is. Second, Paul speaks several times of a new-creation antinomy made up of the death of Christ versus the Law.[6]

Here is Paul's text to which Martyn refers:

For the flesh sets its desire against the Spirit, and the Spirit [sets its desire] against the flesh; and these [two powers] oppose each other, so that you cannot do the things that you [as of Spirit, or even as of flesh] wish [to do]. (Gal 5:17)

Thus, Martyn concludes:

And since the Law (*scil.* religion) is in fact impotent to curb the Flesh, it is crucial to see that the true and potent opposite to that monster is the Spirit, rather than the Law.[7]

In the light of all of the above, the following text in Galatians becomes even more clear. Note that, because *circumcision* became part of *the law* for Israel, Paul uses "circumcision" and "the law" interchangeably, just as he does in Rom 2:25–27.

For *the freedom* [of justification in Christ, the spiritual freedom of conscience before God], Christ has *freed* us. Stand firm, therefore [in that freedom] and do not be entangled again with a yoke of [spiritual] bondage [through the law]. Behold, I, Paul, tell you that if you are *circumcised* [keep the law for justification], *Christ* will profit you *nothing*. And I testify again to every

4. Martyn, *Theological Issues*, 120–21.
5. Martyn, *Theological Issues*, 122.
6. Martyn, *Theological Issues*, 120.
7. Martyn, *Theological Issues*, 120.

man being *circumcised* [for justification] that he is a debtor to do *the whole law* [for justification]. You are severed from Christ [deprived of all effect from him], whoever of you would *be justified by law*; you fell from the grace [and its corresponding faith]. For we, by the Spirit, out of faith, eagerly expect the [certain] hope of righteousness [Gal 5:1–5], which is "the hope of glory." (Col 1:27)

If one is going to be justified by circumcision or the law, that one is obligated to *keep the whole law* to be justified by it. But in Gal 5:1–5, Paul says that in Christ you are not under obligation to keep the law. For if you are led by the Spirit, to whom you *are* obligated,[8] you are not under law (Gal 5:18). The apostolic commandments in the New Testament letters are consistent with the truth of justification in the grace of Christ.[9] The law, with its obligation to do it, is gone, for we died with Christ to the law (Rom 7:1–6). For if a person is obligated to do any part of the law, that person is obligated to do all of it (Gal 5:1–5). For spiritual freedom, Christ has freed us—by justification. So, in Gal 5:1–5, "circumcision" means "law-keeping"—the words are used interchangeably. When Paul in 5:6 says, "Neither circumcision nor uncircumcision means anything" he means that neither law-keeping nor lawbreaking means anything before God, but faith (in Christ) working (serving one another) through (Christ's) love,[10] is the norm for those in Christ.

There are those who would say, "You are not under (obligation to the) law for justification, but you are for sanctification." Such language betrays an ignorance of Paul's gospel of God: Christ has become to us not only righteousness but also sanctification. Ultimately, such "third use" teachers do not understand the centrality of justification before God with its organic connection to the Spirit. For not only justification is "in the Spirit" but sanctification is also (see 1 Cor 6:11), which is not apart from the justification's resultant lordship and leading of the Spirit of Christ. In 5:7–12 he again admonishes the Galatians not to listen to the false teachers who hindered them from obeying (through faith) the truth of the gospel. And then in 5:13 he reiterates this truth about their freedom in Christ:

8. Rom 8:9, 12, 13.

9. For example, in Eph 4:28, to the one who is presently stealing, the writer says, "Steal no longer; but rather let him work, that he may have something to give to those who have need." There is nothing of the law (Num 5:5–8) here. And the NT imperatives are based upon having been justified in Christ alone.

10. "The love of Christ [for us] controls us" (2 Cor 5:14 NASB) is what Paul means here; see Nygren, *Agape and Eros*, 116–33 and 211–19.

For you were called [by God] *for freedom,* only do not use *the
freedom* [τὴν ἐλευθερίαν, of justification] for an occasion to the
flesh, but through *the agape* [τῆς ἀγάπης] serve one another.
(Gal 5:13)

Therefore, two times—in Gal 5:1 and in 5:13—using the definite article in
Greek, Paul says that those in Christ were called by God "for *the freedom*"
of justification in Christ, for in 5:4 he reveals that he has been talking about
justification all along in this text. Then he says, "but through the *agape*" by
which he means God's love demonstrated in Christ's death for our justification ("the freedom" of 5:1), "serve one another" (in the body of Christ, 5:13,
15). Because God our Father loved and loves us unconditionally, he does
not love and free us so that we will love others. The ultimate end of justification's freedom is eternal life (Rom 5:21). God, because of his love for us,
simply wants us to be *free;* and freedom is found in God's loving acceptance
in Christ alone. Love for others is simply a fruit of this freedom of justification in Christ (Gal 5:22). God's love in Christ freed us *for* the freedom (5:13
lit.), the freedom of being justified in Christ, through which we have God
in Christ as our Lord, the only true freedom (Rom 6:7–11, 17–18, 22; 2 Cor
3:17–18). Saints are not to use this freedom as an occasion to the flesh, but
instead we are to serve one another in love (Gal 5:13). Bible translations
radically weaken Paul's words in 5:13 to "you were called *to* freedom." But
"called *for* the [purpose of] *freedom*" is the correct translation, meaning that
"the freedom" is, in one very real sense, an end in itself. Paul is saying that
this freedom *is* God's unconditional love in Christ for those whom God,
in love, chose before the foundation and creation of the universe, through
which he died for us (Rom 5:8–9). The words "the love" in the phrase "but
through the love, serve one another" (Gal 5:13) is the love of Christ (in his
death) for us, through which we are to serve, to love one another (5:13).
According to the false teachers who came to Galatia, circumcision was the
main aspect of the law that they impelled, tempting the Galatians to depart
from faith in Christ alone for justification. Thus, Paul ends this part by saying, in effect, "(But we do not trust in the flesh), for we, by the Spirit, out of
faith, eagerly expect the hope of righteousness in Christ" (5:5). Remembering that in Gal 5:1–4 and Rom 2:17–23 "circumcision" and "law" are used
interchangeably, let us now look at Gal 6:15:

For in Christ Jesus, neither is circumcision anything, nor is uncircumcision anything, but a new creation. (Gal 6:15)

Paul is saying, "For in Christ Jesus, circumcision (law-keeping) is nothing, and uncircumcision (not keeping the law) is also nothing; but a new creation in Christ is everything."

The mind and righteousness of the flesh thinks that law-keeping is everything in God's sight. Therefore, as a Christ-believer, my own righteousness is my greatest enemy, just as, throughout the world, human righteousness is what keeps people from believing in Christ—see 2 Cor 4:4 in light of 3:6–18. But we know that God's righteousness in Christ is apart from "my righteousness, which is of the law" (Phil 3:9). Thus, since a new creation in Christ is everything, then my righteousness or unrighteousness is nothing. If a human's keeping the law is anything in God's sight, then law-keeping justifies. If lawbreaking is anything before God (then we should not break, but rather keep the law), then law-keeping justifies. Therefore, neither is circumcision (doing the law) anything nor uncircumcision (not doing or keeping the law for justification) anything, but a new creation (being a new creation according to God in righteousness and holiness, Eph 4:24) is everything (6:15).

In Gal 6:15, Paul does not need to say, "But *a justified saint, who is* a new creation," because the person who is a new creation is also justified through Christ's death (6:14). Regeneration unto a new creation and justification are two distinct blessings, but they are both present realities in Christ. For in Christ Jesus, law-keeping is nothing and lawbreaking is nothing, because I am justified and a new creation in Christ. Paul does not have a different meaning of "the law" in 5:1–4 than in Phil 3:3–9 or elsewhere.

Thus, he is saying, "For in Christ Jesus neither my righteousness, which is of the law, nor my unrighteousness means anything to God, but God's righteousness in Christ, in whom I am a new creation, is everything to God; and that is all I have in Christ!"[11]

The real Jew is one inwardly, and the true circumcision (true law-fulfilling and law-keeping) is that which is hidden in the Spirit and in the heart (Rom 2:25–29), the inner man. God's righteousness is not of this age but of the last age and of the last Adam. The Accuser can say something like, "Did you keep the law in that instance?—otherwise you are not just before God." The enemy of our souls desires the answer to be, "Yes, I kept the law in that instance," which is reliance on the flesh (of sin, Rom 8:3; contra Phil 3:3) for justification and not on Christ. For the flesh desperately wants to see itself as good, that is, as a law-keeper.

---

11. See Phil 3:3–9; compare 1 Cor 6:17; Gal 2:20–21.

> For it is of the very essence of the self-consciousness and need of
> the world, that it should consider itself to be good.[12]

My flesh's desire to be righteous without God begets the thinking that considers myself as righteous only when I do the works of the law. But all such thinking is a lie, for the gospel's use of the law condemns everything that is of the flesh, including its "law-keeping" (its righteousness, which is not of faith and therefore is sin in God's sight). Therefore, in faith I must hold fast to Christ and stand firm in him and this freedom of justification in Christ. Commenting on Gal 6:15, Gerhard Forde said:

> So now God has acted finally in this very proclamation by his
> apostle to have his way with us. God has taken the whole business
> out of our hands. Neither your lawlessness nor your lawfulness,
> your immorality nor your morality, your ungodliness nor your
> holiness—none of it matters a bit now, but a new creation.[13]

If my law-keeping means *anything* to God, then I do not need Christ at all, for I am righteous before God through my law-keeping, my righteousness; but we are not justified by any "law-keeping" and we are not condemned by any lawbreaking.

> With Christ I have been put to death, and I, as joined to the flesh
> of Sin, live no longer; but Christ lives in me; for the one being
> joined to the Lord is one spirit with him. (Gal 2:20; 1 Cor 6:17
> ATP).

So now, instead of being joined to the flesh of sin/unbelief, we are joined to the Spirit of God and of faith.[14]

Again, our true being is *according to the Spirit of God* and no longer according to the flesh (Rom 8:5). Thus, in our inner man, we are those who trust God, even though according to the flesh we cannot trust God. Regardless of our feelings, we are, through faith in Christ, to obey Christ, who indwells us by his Spirit. We know that, beginning with Satan through the serpent's tempting Eve, there has been a spiritual battle. But the opposition between the Spirit and the flesh (Gal 5:17) only began with the coming of the Spirit (Gal 4:4–7).

> But before the faith [of Christ] came, we were held in custody
> under the law, being shut up to the faith being about to be

---

12. Bultmann, *This World and Beyond*, 66 and following.

13. Forde, *Captivation of the Will*, 118.

14. See πνεύμα in 2 Cor 4:13 and compare πνεύμα (same word) in 1 Cor 2:12 where it is the Spirit of God.

revealed; so that the law has become our disciplinarian [up] to Christ, in order that out of *faith* we might be justified; but the faith [of Christ, through which we have faith *in* Christ] having come, we are no longer under a disciplinarian. For you are all [adult] sons of God through faith in Christ Jesus. (Gal 3:23–26)

On the word "disciplinarian," Taylor Jr. makes the following comments:

> The disciplinarian had essentially a restraining function (so vs. 23, "we were imprisoned and guarded under the law"). In addition . . . his work was limited to the boy's legal minority (as long as the boy was under age). Usually, the slave had responsibility for the boy from around the age six or seven to the late teens. When the boy became legally an adult, the guardian's function ceased, so Paul uses the example of the disciplinarian to indicate the restraining and limited nature of the law. Note that the law is not a tutor or teacher who leads us to Christ but a disciplinarian until Christ comes.[15]

And Kingston Siggins, on this same text, says:

> Luther is perfectly explicit: when Paul calls the law a custodian until the time of faith, "he is referring to the time of fulfillment when Christ came. However, it should be applied not only to that time, but also to experience, because what happened historically at the point in time when Christ came—His abrogating the law and bringing liberty and eternal life to light—the same happens personally and spiritually to every Christian."[16]

That freedom from the law applies to Jew *and gentiles* in Christ is proven by the use of "us," "we," and "you" in Gal 3:13–14; see 4:5–7. Living according to the law rather than faith is to *not* walk in the Spirit. For the Spirit sets its desires against the flesh, both sides of the flesh: legalism—doing the works of the law for righteousness, and license—practicing the deeds of the flesh. Christ freed us for *the freedom* (Τῇ ἐλευθερίᾳ); stand firm therefore in *the freedom* (Gal 5:1), for only those who stand firm in the freedom of justification in Christ are walking by faith and led by him (5:1–18). Paul's apostolic gospel's *law/Christ* antithesis is as follows:

"In the law" (Rom 3:19 lit.) there is no justification, but only condemnation.	"In Christ" there is only justification and no condemnation whatsoever (Gal 2:17; Rom 8:1).

15. Taylor Jr., *Paul, Apostle*, 150.
16. Kingston Siggins, *Martin Luther's Doctrine*, 174.

Therefore, as we have shown, the NPP scholars obscure Paul's primary reference to the law, which he summarizes by using three of the Ten Commandments (in Rom 2:17–23) and which he calls "the ministry of condemnation" (2 Cor 3:6–9 [see Rom 3:9–19]). As Steven M. Baugh says:

> The new perspective Paul can never break out of the box of his supposed pre-Christian convictions about the nature of the law and its righteousness. Paraphrased, the reconstructed ancient *Judaism of the new perspective* acts as a *filter* through which Paul must pass. Anything he says that *does not conform* to the views of this censorship board must be scrubbed of all *offending* material.[17]

Christ Is Our Object of Faith

Sin, as power, deceives through the law (of sin[18]), the ministry of condemnation (Rom 7:7–13; 2 Cor 3:7–9), and *sin* through the law finds its own *object of unbelief* toward God, to nullify Christ as the one in whom you trust (Rom 8:3; Gal 5:1–4). But this is to call God a liar—in response to Satan's lie, which is, "Yea, has God said (of Christ), that you are now justified in him?[19] You are not!" In Gen 3:1, Satan, through the serpent, began with the words, "Has God said?" when tempting Eve, through which she began to not believe God's word, his commandment that "in the day that you eat thereof, dying, you shall surely die" (Gen 2:17). Then the murderer (John 8:44) went in for the kill. He said "You shall *not* surely die" (Gen 3:4b). This was the lie that Eve and then Adam believed. To us, the same liar, accuser, and murderer, using our flesh, says, "You sinned, therefore you are not justified," in utter defiance of God's word that says, "You were justified in the name of the Lord Jesus" (1 Cor 6:11 NKJV) and "having been justified by faith . . . through our Lord Jesus Christ'" (Rom 5:1 NASB). As with Eve, this is how the murderer operates—by *the lie*. As soon as the flesh of sin directs you to some sin that you have done, to tempt *you* to make yourself right with God, the immediate natural-man thinking is to justify yourself, to make sure that you did *not* sin, and if you did, to "make it right" for justification. But we are led by the Spirit of the God who justifies the *ungodly* (Rom 4:5; 8:14; Gal 5:5). Unbelief in God's word supposes that if you sin or have sinned, then you are condemned, contrary to God's word in Christ.

17. Baugh, 147, emphasis mine.
18. Rom 7:24–25.
19. Yes, God *has* said it, in Rom 5:1, 9; 8:1; 1 Cor 1:30; 6:11, and elsewhere.

This is the flesh's *fear* of condemnation and of death,[20] for the flesh cannot trust in Christ for justification. But to fear condemnation from God (by thinking on your righteousness or unrighteousness) is unbelief and thus death, for Christ is your righteousness and your life (1 Cor 1:30; Col 3:4; see Gal 5:1–4). It is to gratify the flesh in its desire to be righteous apart from Christ/grace/faith. This is important: The flesh[21] *looks for something* about which to not believe the gospel (to not believe that there is no condemnation in Christ)—something with which *to sever the believer from Christ, from faith in him*[22] (Gal 5:1–4)—thereby bringing death and condemnation into his conscience.[23] But you are under obligation, not to the flesh (Rom 8:12–13), says Paul. This fleshly fear of condemnation is the source of a legal fear of sinning, which is not the fear of God but of condemnation; for we have not received a spirit of fear (of death and condemnation, Rom 8:15; see 2 Cor 3:7, 9). Therefore, we can know for certain that such a fear is not from God. Christ is the object of faith, for faith trusts in Christ. Paul says, "We are the ones who . . . put no trust in [the life we now live in] the flesh," that is, "not having my righteousness" (Phil 3:3, 9). So, the flesh, in rebellion against Christ, actually looks for an object of unbelief. But God says:

> You are severed from Christ, you who are seeking to be justified
> by law (Gal 5:4), that is, your own righteousness (Phil 3:9).

20. Heb 2:14–15; see 2 Cor 3:7, 9.

21. The flesh desires to have some other god (in our hearts) to replace Christ as God (Gal 5:17 and 1 John 5:20–21).

22. For faith not to be weakened, we are, through faith (Rom 1:5), to obey obedience (Rom 6:16), i.e., righteousness, for we are slaves of *righteousness* (Rom 6:18), i.e., of *Christ* (1 Cor 7:22); for faith is a precious treasure (2 Pet 1:1).

23. With Christ, I died to the law, out of this present evil age (where my righteousness of the flesh and of the law exists, Phil 3:3, 9), and I am a new creation in him (Gal 1:4; 2:19–20; 6:14–15). Therefore, the law is to be kept out of the conscience; Christ alone is to reign there. Paul writes of the gentiles, "The work of the law written in their hearts [which (gentiles) we are not, 1 Cor 12:2 AV], their *conscience* also bearing witness [with the law]" (Rom 2:14–15 AV). So, the corollary between "*the works of the law*" and "*conscience*" is to be applied to "*the law*" as used throughout this book. Therefore, when the Accuser comes to accuse you, neither justify nor condemn yourself (for to do so is to usurp God's place as judge), because in Christ, God has already condemned (to death) the one owned by sin, with his or her sins, so that one is justified in Christ alone; see also 1 Cor 4:3–4. On law and conscience, see Forde, "Christian Life," 2:407–22; *LW* 27:10–21; Zachman, *Assurance of Faith*, 19–76; Thielicke, *Theological Ethics*, 1:313–18, 329–30; Bultmann, *Theology of the New Testament*, 1:267. There is a tension, for there are two sides as to the truth about conscience: On the one hand, we do not listen to its accusations, because God is our justifier in Christ (Rom 8:33–34); we do not judge ourselves, because God is Judge (1 Cor 4:5); on the other, we are to be fully convinced in our mind (Rom 14:5) before we act, or else we sin (14:23).

> But we, by the Spirit, wait for the hope of righteousness [glory]
> through *faith*. (Gal 5:5)

For not in this life will we see the righteousness which justifies, for righteousness is by faith and not by sight (Gal 5:5; 2 Cor 5:7). The desire of the wicked flesh is that unbelief (sin as power), and not Christ (the power of God), reign in us, control us. Since the goal and desire of the flesh of sin is to sever us from Christ through unbelief, the only way that sin (as power) will not reign in us is to trust in Christ for righteousness before God and through that faith obey Christ as Lord.

For the power of God is the gospel (Rom 1:16; 1 Cor 1:18, 24). God says that "you are under obligation, not to the flesh, to live according to the flesh" (Rom 8:12 NASB). To live according to the flesh begins with thinking according to the flesh; but we do not have to do that (Rom 8:12–13). So we are to resist the flesh and, by the Spirit (by faith in Christ), put its autonomous deeds and works to death, denying our feelings and believing God's word. Just as, when the flesh is enlivened and strengthened by a lustful look (e.g., at someone who is attractive) and seeks to gratify that desire (but the Spirit-led response is to deny feelings and, by the Spirit, put to death the deeds of the flesh), even so, when the flesh of sin comes through the law and its accusations, we are to recognize Satan and death in it; we are not to give in to those thoughts, for Satan sometimes accuses of things we have not done, but his accusations always include the lie (as if we are not in Christ, Rom 8:1). So do not defend yourself or condemn yourself as the gentiles do, for *in Christ* you are no longer a gentile (1 Cor 12:2). If we do not believe God's word in Christ, that "there is therefore now no condemnation for those who are in Christ Jesus" (8:1 RSV), such unbelief is sin, which severs us from Christ, who is life. Luther understood and proclaimed this. Commenting on Gal 5:4, he said:

> Therefore, this is the final conclusion: You must give up either Christ or the righteousness of the law. If you keep *Christ*, you are righteous in the sight of God. If you keep *the law*, Christ is of no avail; then you are obligated to do the whole law, and you have as your sentence (Deut 27:26) "Cursed be he who does not, etc."[24]

> The more someone tries to bring peace to his conscience through his own righteousness, the more disquieted he makes it. For, as Paul says, it is impossible for the conscience to find peace through the works of the law.[25]

24. *LW* 27:17. See also *LW* 27:11–21.
25. *LW* 27:13.

The "disquieted conscience" to which Luther refers *is* "the wrath/anger/displeasure of God revealed against all *unrighteousness*" (Rom 1:18), in this case the unrighteousness of *unbelief,* which is the opposite of "the righteousness of faith" (4:13; 9:30; 10:6), for such a person, even if he is in Christ, is not trusting in God through Christ. It is God, in wrath, giving a person over to a heart of unbelief, *for* his unbelief, because God's wrath is against all unbelief in Christ, as Paul (and Luther) clearly taught. Therefore, standing firm in the freedom of justification is not an option for those in Christ, for we are in a spiritual war, which is the ultimate war.

To further support the truth contained in the last paragraph, we look at how the truth that God desires our trust in him existed even in the old covenant era. Moses' law begins as follows:

> Then God spoke all these words: I am the LORD your God, who brought you out of the land of Egypt, out of the house of slavery; *you shall have no other gods besides me . . .* For I the LORD your God am a jealous God, punishing children for the iniquity of parents, to the third and fourth generation of those who reject me, but showing steadfast love to the thousandth generation of those who love me and keep my commandments. (Exod 20:1-3, 5b, 6 NRSV ["besides" is in the NRSV margin])

Luther commented on this text as follows:

> Learn from these words, then, how *angry God is* with *those who rely on anything but himself,* and again, *how kind, and gracious* he is to those who *trust and believe him alone* with their whole heart.[26]

In the new testament in Christ's blood (1 Cor 11:25), this same God, who is angry with all who rely on anything other than himself in Christ for righteousness before God, is the only true God—the God of the Christian Scriptures. But is he preached as such today?

Yet, a reading of Paul's Romans convinces us that Luther was right: Central to Paul's preaching is that it is always either wrath *or* mercy from God. Luther said:

> For what follows from the righteousness of the law is nothing else than true idolatry; and the righteousness of works is *idolatry* itself because it creates another God . . . I am an idolater when I adore myself with my own works, because I think that

---

26. LC 32, 369, emphasis mine.

God takes them into consideration. That imagination is an *idol* of my heart.[27]

Those who trust in or rely on anything other than the God of Jesus Christ who justifies sinners through faith alone are under God's wrath. This was consistently Paul the apostle's doctrine (Rom 1:18–32; 4:14–16 [see 24–25]). There is only one way out from the wrath:

> The only way is that Christ and his work simply throw out the law, expel all dependence on our own work, from the conscience. Faith means to be so grasped by Christ that the demands of reason and law are simply no longer heard.[28]

And that faith is standing firm in Christ's freedom (Gal 5:1). Therefore, any trust in one's feelings[29] as a gauge to determine if one is right with God or not is an ultimate and essential trust in one's self, in the flesh, rather than in God who raises the dead—for *God* is *wholly other* than man with his feelings. God's word (gospel) is able to distinguish between which intentions of the heart are of the flesh and which are of the Spirit through grace and reveal them to that person, that he may walk in the Spirit by faith in Christ.[30]

Paul uses the terms "the world" and "the flesh" interchangeably:

> But God chose the weak things of *the world*, and the low-born of *the world* . . . the things not being anything, in order that he might bring to nothing the things that are [something: the strong and high-born], so that [whether through the cross working in believers, or through the perishing of the lost] no *flesh* should glory in his presence. (1 Cor 1:28–29)

Therefore, "the world" in the following scriptural text means "the flesh" as well.

---

27. Althaus, *Theology*, 124, emphasis mine. The unbeliever lives in this idolatry, unawares.

28. Forde, *Preached God*, 261.

29. This includes feelings of guilt; for the heart and mind of *the flesh* (of sin/unfaith, Rom 8:3, 6) is *deceitful* above all things and desperately wicked (Jer 17:9).

30. Hebrews 4:12 says that the Lord Christ sees the thoughts and intentions of the heart; those intentions are *open before him* (*the Lord—the Word of God*) with *whom* we have to do. On "the word of God," see Heb 4:13 and Rev 19:3, which reveal that Christ is God's Word, who through the gospel reveals the thoughts of our hearts, making known to us our intentions: whether they are self-justifying (of the soul [ψυχῆς], Heb 4:12, the soulish/natural man, 1 Cor 2:14) or of the spirit, where the Spirit of God dwells.

For since, in the wisdom of God, *the world*, by [its] wisdom ("the power judging rightly,"[31] having in Adam taken from "a tree desirable to make one *wise*" [Gen 3:6] without God), did not know God, God was well-pleased through the foolishness of the proclamation [the gospel], to save those who *believe* [in Christ—who do not live by the world's wisdom, the flesh's power of judging rightly]. (1 Cor 1:21)

That is Paul's definition of how the believer lives. This is the word (of God) of the cross. Walther von Loewenich expressed Luther's way of saying this as follows:

One must be zealous for God "in pious ignorance and mental darkness," "without understanding, without feeling, without thinking."[32]

By "without thinking," Luther means (through Christ) not allowing the mind of the flesh (Rom 8:6) to rule, for we are no longer obligated to the flesh (8:12–13). Therefore, Luther says of the believer, that:

he *believes* that which he neither sees nor feels nor comprehends.[33]

Regardless of his feelings, he believes that God has justified him and continues to justify him in Christ Jesus. The opposite of the Spirit-led life is not trusting in God in Christ for justification and for one's other needs. God's wisdom (Christ crucified) looks like utter foolishness to the world with its wisdom—for God's righteousness in Christ crucified appears to be unrighteousness to the flesh. Therefore, the cross is an offense and a stumbling block to human righteousness (Gal 5:11; Rom 9:30–33). Christ reveals human righteousness to be what it is: of the flesh of sin, therefore, as feces (Rom 8:3; Phil 3:3–9).

Casting Down Reasonings

Paul in the following passage refers to the nations, which are only flesh; therefore, what he says applies to the flesh that remains with Christ-believers.

For whenever nations do by nature the things of the law, these . . . are a law to themselves [they are self-lawed], who show the

31. *WNWD*, 1678.

32. *LW* 25:404, cited in von Loewenich, *Luther's Theology*, 80. Note his "without thinking" and compare to "not thinking on" in my ch. 7 on faith in Rom 4. Thus, behind Luther's words here stands Paul—his gospel.

33. *LW* 21:304, cited in von Loewenich, *Luther's Theology*, 86, emphasis mine.

work of the law written in their hearts, their *conscience* bearing witness [with the law], and their *reasonings* accusing [condemning] or else defending [justifying] them. (Rom 2:14–15)

Their "conscience" and their "reasonings" form a parallelism; they mean the same thing. These "reasonings" are of *the flesh*, which *cannot* please God (Rom 8:7, 8), though the flesh thinks they are godly. In Rom 2:15, Paul says that these reasonings either accuse (condemn) or defend (justify) one's self. But even accusing one's self is an attempt to justify one's self. In line with the word "reasonings" in Rom 2:15 is the word "reason" as Luther usually used it, to stand for fleshly reason, "the devil's whore." Note how Luther uses "reason" when commenting on how we are to stand firm in the freedom of justification in Christ. He says of Christian freedom:

> It is easily lost. Therefore, he bids them to stand fast, lest that, through negligence or security, they fall back again from grace and faith, to law and works. Now, because reason judges that there can be no danger in preferring the righteousness of the law over the righteousness of faith, therefore with a certain indignation he weighs against the law, and with contempt he calls it a yoke, yes, a yoke of bondage.[34]

The Greek word in Rom 2:15 which we translated as "reasonings" is λογισμῶν. The only other time λογισμός is used in the NT scriptures is in 2 Cor 10, where it reads as follows:

> We war [fight] not according to the flesh [with fleshly weapons], for the weapons of our warfare are not fleshly, but mighty to God to the pulling down of [satanic] strongholds; casting down *reasonings* [λογισμούς], and every high thing [thought] raised up against the knowledge of God [in Christ], and taking captive every thought [νόημα, *noeema*] to the obedience of Christ. (2 Cor 10:3b–5)

First, note that "reasonings" here are the accusing and/or justifying thoughts which the nations have, of which Paul speaks in Rom 2:14–15. But Paul says that (in Christ) *we* are *no longer nations* (1 Cor 12:2 lit.), for we have the Spirit of God, so such thoughts are not to be entertained by us. Second, when Paul (in 2 Cor 10) says that we are "taking every *thought*[35] captive," he is referring to the "thoughts" (reasonings) to which he just

34. Luther, *Galatians*, 456; modern English mine.

35. On the issue of *thoughts*, believers are not to *think of their righteousness or unrighteousness as having anything to do with their justification* before God: see my ch. 7, which fully aligns with the above quotes by Luther.

referred in this same verse. But this time, for "thought" Paul uses the word
νόημα. Now, νόημα is used in 2 Corinthians for "thoughts" that are from
Satan, Christ's adversary. In the following texts, the "thoughts" (in italics) to which Paul refers (which he takes captive to Christ) is the English
translation of the Greek νόημα.

> We are not ignorant of Satan's *thoughts*. (2:11)

> But Israel's *thoughts* were blinded; for until this very day, at the
> reading of the old covenant, the same veil remains, it not being
> unveiled that it, the law, is done away in Christ. (3:14)

> The god of this age [Satan] has blinded the *thoughts* of the un-
> believers. (4:4)

> And I fear lest somehow, as the serpent [Satan] deceived Eve by
> his cleverness, your *thoughts* should be seduced from the sim-
> plicity that is in Christ. (11:3)

Of these texts from 2 Corinthians, the only one that does not mention
Satan is 3:14; but clearly Satan is involved in 3:14 also, because the law
condemns, and Satan is the accuser (2 Cor 3:9; Rev 12:9–10). The god of
this present age blinds the minds of the unbelieving, who blinds the hearts
of unbelieving Israel so that they do not see Christ (2 Cor 4:4–6). And the
cause of their blindness is that to Israel it is not unveiled (the truth is still
hidden from them) that the law (old covenant) is done away in Christ.
For Christ is the end of the law for righteousness for believers (Rom 10:5
AT). So, Rom 2:15 and the other above texts reveal what Paul in 2 Cor 10
is saying. It is basically this:

> For though we walk in the flesh, we do not fight according
> to the flesh [with fleshly weapons]. For the weapons of our
> warfare are not fleshly, but mighty through God to the pull-
> ing down of [satanic] strongholds [satanic thoughts]; casting
> down *reasonings* [accusing and justifying thoughts, because
> Christ is our defense, our justification], and every high
> [proud, un-humbled by the gospel] thought raised up against
> the knowledge of God [in Christ, 4:4–6], and taking captive
> every [satanic] thought to the obedience of Christ [his obedi-
> ence which justified us].[36] (2 Cor 10:3–5)

36. Rom 5:19, which we receive through the obedience of faith (Rom 1:5).

Because the nations are under the authority of Satan[37] and sin (Rom 3:9), and, in one sense, believers "walk in the flesh,"[38] these "reasonings" become Satan's thoughts against believers. As weapons, Satan uses the fleshly reasonings to attempt to get them to not trust in Christ, and he desires to create strongholds over them through unbelief in Christ for righteousness. But in Christ we are no longer nations (gentiles), no longer in this present age, for we are a new creation.[39] Thus, as these reasonings come to us through the flesh, we are to not depend on the flesh to fight them, but we are to cast the reasonings down and reject them and thereby bring every accusing or defending (self-justifying) thought captive to the obedience of Christ our righteousness (1 Cor 1:30). The gentiles, with their reasonings either accusing (condemning) or else defending (justifying) them, have only "the mind of the flesh" (Rom 8:6); and when Paul refers to "the mind of the Spirit," this Spirit is the Spirit of faith. Ever since Christ died to justify his people in and by his blood, ever since the faith (of Christ) has come (Rom 5:9; Gal 3:23–25; 8:33–34), there is a real sense in which Satan has changed his tactics,[40] so that faith in Christ means to not consider our sin or our righteousness, because in Christ, God no longer considers either. The chart below distinguishes between the mind of flesh and that of the Spirit.

The mind of the flesh (Rom 8:6) thinks either:	The mind of the Spirit (Rom 8:6) thinks:
"I am righteous in the flesh" (defending thoughts), or	"I am the Righteousness of God
"I am unrighteous in the flesh" (condemning thoughts).	in Christ" (2 Cor 5:21; see Rom 8:1, 9).
Either way, I am still in the flesh.	I am *in Christ*, no longer in the flesh.

37. Col 1:13 lit.; Acts 26:18 lit. Satan transforms himself into an angel of light (2 Cor 11:14). Just as some serpents transform their shape to *appear* to be what they are not (e.g., to have larger heads than they have), even so, Satan, who came to Eve through a serpent (11:3), transforms himself into an angel of *light*, i.e., of *righteousness* (11:15).

38. The flesh, with every means at its disposal, opposes the Spirit of God. And those powers that oppose the Spirit include the reasonings of the flesh, which are Satan's thoughts, in order to bring us back into bondage (Gal 2:4), which is death (Gal 5:1–5; see Col 3:4). To add the law to Christ is to destroy and nullify faith and the promise (Rom 4:13, 14; Gal 2:18, 19; 3:1–3; 5:1–5; Rom 10:4), the promise of the Spirit who leads (Rom 8:13–14; Gal 5:18), and is to preach another gospel (Gal 1:8–9). Continued faith in Christ is the issue.

39. 1 Cor 12:2; Gal 1:4; 3:28; 2 Cor 5:17; Eph 4:24.

40. See Rev 12:9–11.

"But you are *not* in the flesh, but *in the Spirit*, if indeed the Spirit of God dwells in you" (Rom 8:9)—and faith in Christ believes that. Since we are in Christ, through him we can think the truth in Christ, that is, in faith, for we are not under obligation to the flesh, to think or live according to it (Rom 8:9–12). God accepts us because of Christ alone.[41] Are we stronger than he (1 Cor 10:22b AV)? Are we better than he?[42] (As though we could accept ourselves on a different or better basis than that on which *God* accepts us?) God has received us by his Son's death on our behalf, through which we died and were raised anew with him. So, we are to accept ourselves on the same basis that God accepts us, which is justification by God's blood. Forde says:

> When God imputes righteousness . . . He makes it plain that we do not have righteousness and never will. By declaring us righteous . . . unconditionally for Christ's sake . . . sin is revealed and attacked at the root in its *totality:* our unfaith, rebellion, and blindness . . . God's justification, you see, is fully as opposed to human righteousness as it is to human unrighteousness. It cuts both ways, both at the ungodly and the super-godly. Only faith in the flat-out judgment of God is equipped to do battle with human sin . . . That is the only salvation from both . . . immorality and super-morality.[43]

Only faith in Christ for justification is sufficient to battle and overcome human unbelief. Just as in the (OT) law, "going to the right or to the left" of what the law commanded meant disobeying the LORD (Deut 17:19–20), even so, now in the gospel, going to the right into nomism (doing law-works for justification [Gal 5:1–5]) or to the left (practicing the deeds of the flesh [5:19–21]), are both of the disobedience of unbelief in Christ. Believers are to know and believe that they, as joined to the flesh, died with Christ, and live no longer in the flesh (under condemnation), but Christ (their righteousness) lives in them (Gal 2:19–20; Rom 8:1, 9; 1 Cor 1:30). To be justified is to be *freed for the freedom* of no condemnation in Christ, which is simultaneously the freedom to be led not the flesh, but by the Spirit of God, the fruit of which is the fruit of the Spirit (Gal 5:22). And God does truly lead. This freedom must be maintained against both sides of the flesh, which would bring us back into bondage unto death (Rom 8:12–13). So, we are not to allow Satan to create a stronghold in our flesh through unbelief in Christ. In regard to Satan trying to bring you back into bondage, into self-justification, say to him (and to yourself), "I am not going there; I am trusting in Christ,"

41. Rom 14:3 NASB; Rom 15:7 NASB.

42. See Phil 3:9; Gal 6:3.

43. Forde, *Justification by Faith*, 31.

because you are no longer in the flesh but in the Spirit.[44] You died with Christ out of the flesh and this present age, where your righteousness and unrighteousness are; and now, *all that you have* (in spirit-reality, as joined to Christ alone) is *Christ* as your righteousness, in the new creation—the age to come.[45] So, walk by faith in this reality and not by sight.

44. Rom 8:9; 7:4–6.
45. See Gal 1:4; 2:19, 20; 6:14, 15; Phil 3:3, 9; 2 Cor 5:17.

──── FOURTEEN ────

The New Creation in Christ

The new creation is our *canon*—our *rule* of life.

FOR IN CHRIST JESUS neither circumcision nor uncircumcision avails anything, but *a new creation*. And as many as walk according to *this rule* [χανών, *canon*], peace and mercy be upon them, and upon the Israel of God. (Gal 6:15–16)

The Holy Spirit[1] does not need the law.[2]

In Christ, my true being is according to the Spirit of God.[3] Therefore, I am a new creation (2 Cor 5:17). And the new creation has been created in righteousness and holiness, which differs from the natural morality of the natural man, who is of the flesh, for I am no longer a natural (soulish) man.[4]

We Believed into Christ (Gal 2:16)

The Greek word εἰς is rightly translated as "into" in the above text (Gal 2:16); and εἰς is translated as "into" (in italics) the following texts:

And when they had come *into* the house . . .(Matt 2:11 NKJV)

---

1. In Paul's words: "*If you are being led by the [Holy] Spirit, you are not under law*" (Gal 5:18). Not to all believers has God *revealed* this truth (see Phil 3:15, which applies here also). "You" in Gal 5:18 is the one joined to the *Lord*, one spirit with him.

2. The law indeed is holy (Rom 7:12).

3. We are the ones being according to the Spirit, not the flesh (Rom 8:5).

4. Eph 4:24; 1 Cor 2:14; see 2:12–16.

> Then He said to them, "Let us go *into* the next towns." (Mark 1:38 RGT)

> For this cause a man shall leave his father and his mother and the two shall be *into* one flesh. (Matt 19:5)

> For this cause a man shall leave his father and his mother and the two shall be *into* one flesh. This mystery is great and I refer to Christ and [him] *into* the church. (Eph 5:31–32)

Just as the two in marriage are made into one flesh, likewise Christ and his bride are made one spirit with him (1 Cor 6:17), for to "believe into Christ" is to believe into union with Christ. In the following texts, to believe in Christ (Gal 3:26) is also described as to "believe into Christ."

> Even we believed *into* Christ Jesus, in order that we might be justified by the faith [obedience] of Christ. (Gal 2:16)

> How will they believe *into* him whom they have not heard? (Rom 10:14b)

When the Spirit of God comes into man's spirit, an organic union is created; and the new creation has been created in righteousness and true holiness (Eph 4:24) by the Holy Spirit.

The new creation in Christ (alone) is the Christ-believer's canon—his or her rule of life (Gal 6:15–16). Paul also calls this rule "the law of the Spirit" (Rom 8:2). The crucified and now risen Christ lives to God (Rom 6:10), and so it is no longer I who live, but Christ (who lives to God) who lives in me (Gal 2:20). The new creation has been created according to God in righteousness and true holiness (Eph 4:24). Therefore, following this rule, we cannot go wrong. Many decades ago, while reading Phil 3:3–9, I realized that the phrase "the law" is used three times and the words "the flesh" are used three times. I also noticed that the "not" in "*not* in *flesh* trusting" (3:3) is parallel to "*not* having my righteousness, which is of *the law*" (3:9). Therefore, to the extent that the law is brought in to one's life, to that extent is "my righteousness," that of the law (3:9) and of *the flesh* (3:3), brought in; and the flesh is "the flesh of Sin" (Rom 8:3). Thus, to bring in the law as "a rule of life" is to bring in one's own righteousness, which is of the law (Phil 3:9) and of the flesh (3:3). So, any church that teaches their people the Ten Commandments, simultaneously implying they are to live by it, is not distinguishing between Old Testament Israel and the church which that is Christ's body, New Testament Israel,[5] in which we died to the law in order to live to God (Gal 2:19). In so doing, they destroy the gospel's distinction between the law,

5. Rom 2:28, 29; 9:6; Phil 3:3; Gal 6:16.

which condemns sinners, and the gospel, which justifies the ungodly. To the extent that this distinguishing is not taught, the hearer will (tend to) trust in his own righteousness and be inoculated to the grace of Christ, for human righteousness is the greatest enemy of the gospel.

Again, to the extent that a person looks to the law as the "rule" for righteousness or life, even for sanctification, there will be a righteousness of the flesh (Phil 3:3, 9). So, it should not surprise us that Paul says to the *unbelieving* Jew, "You who preach the law" (Rom 2:17–23). Paul no longer preached the law. He says, "If I still preached circumcision [the law, 5:1–4], why do I still suffer persecution? Then the offense of the cross has ceased" (Gal 5:11 NKJV). One cannot preach Christ and at the same time preach the law for a rule of life (Gal 2:16, 19–20), for such is another gospel, which is not really another but a false one (Gal 1:6–7). When Paul says "in the flesh," he means this present life in the flesh.

> For to me, to live is *Christ*, and to die is gain. But if I am to live on *in the flesh*, this will mean fruitful labor for me . . . But I am hard-pressed from both directions having the desire to depart and to be with Christ, for that is very much better; yet to remain *in the flesh* is more necessary for you. (Phil 1:21–22a, b, 23–24 NASB)

So when Paul says, "We are those glorying in Christ Jesus and *not in flesh* trusting" (Phil 3:3), he means we put *no trust* in the life we now live in the flesh for righteousness, as he concludes his points about how he could have boasted in the flesh by saying, "*Not* having my righteousness, which is of the law" (but having that which is Christ's faith, which is God's righteousness bestowed on faith, Phil 3:9). Paul is saying, "For me, to live [in this body] is Christ [alone, not Christ and the law, for Christ is sufficient]" (Phil 1:21). Paul does not say, "My mind and conscience are in the gospel, and my flesh is in the law," as some have taught. Why? Because Paul is essentially not in the flesh but in the Spirit (Rom 8:9). And since he died with Christ to the law, in order to live *to God*, the new creation (Christ in him) is his rule (Gal 2:19; 6:15–16). Therefore, "for me to live [in this life, this flesh] is Christ"—means "I died to the law and live (under law) no longer; but Christ instead lives in me (joined to me in my inner man); and the life I now live in the flesh, I live by the faith of the Son of God (Gal 2:19–20a) and not by the law." When Paul, concerning Christ, says that he wants "to be found in him, *not having my righteousness*, the one of law, *but [having]* the one of the faith of Christ [his obedience unto death]—*the righteousness of God* bestowed on faith in Christ" (Phil 3:8d, 9), he is not only saying that he is not trusting in the flesh (3:3), but he is also saying that in spirit-reality he does not have *his* righteousness any longer, for he is now in Christ, joined to him; so the only righteousness that he has now is "the one of the faith of Christ" (his obedience unto death)—"*the righteousness of God* by faith" (3:9).

> The gospel of Christ . . . is the power of God for *salvation* to everyone believing . . . For in it the *righteousness from God* is revealed from [Christ's] faith to [our] faith. (Rom 1:16–17)

Notice that the words "righteousness" and "salvation" here are used in synonymous parallelism (see Rom 10:10). For, to be saved there must be a righteousness which can save, deliver us from the flesh of sin (Rom 8:3) unto death (8:2, 10). And this salvation includes sanctification, for the word of the cross is the power of God to us who are "being saved" (1 Cor 1:18); so the gospel, as God's power, needs no help from the law. The flesh continually serves the law of sin (Rom 7:25). And "every lust" (Rom 7:8) includes the desire for life and righteousness apart from God, for the desires are either for doing the works of the law or doing the deeds of the flesh,[6] neither of which is the third path, which is walking by the Spirit through faith in Christ. For "the law is not of faith" (Gal 3:12a); for "if by the Spirit [not the law] you put to death the deeds of the body, you will live" (Rom 8:13). Therefore, those who hold to a so-called "third use of the law," (1) underestimate the power of sin in the flesh, for the flesh looks for something in one's life to sever one from Christ, and it does this through the law (Gal 5:1–5; Rom 7:7–13); and/or (2) underestimate the trustworthiness of Christ in them, the new creation (Gal 6:15–16; Eph 4:24). And the Christ who justified us is the same Christ that indwells us, sanctifies us, and sufficiently leads us (Gal 2:21–3:3). Because we died to the law and are joined to Christ instead, that death to the law includes the law as rule of life. For where the law is the rule of life, then the Spirit's rule is rejected and faith is nullified.[7] *Nomos* (νόμος) means "law"—thus nomism is living by the law. Thus, Gerhard Forde rightly said:

> Nomism is the refusal to allow the eschatological gospel to have its way in our lives. While some Christians will think this route preferable to antinomianism, it finally is a denial of Christ's efficacy in human life.[8]

> Precisely the *gospel* determines Paul's attitude toward the law, not the rabbis or his own "conscience" or psyche—exactly as he himself says (Phil. 3:6ff.).[9]

6. Gal 4:9, 21; see 5:17, 24.
7. Rom 8:1–2; 4:14 and 3:27.
8. Forde, *Preached God*, 24.
9. Forde, "Christian Life," 2:423n16.

Amen. The new creation is our rule because Christ is sufficient for living the life in Christ.[10] Any other rule is saying that Christ is not sufficient. If our rule is the law, we are depending on the flesh (Phil 3:3, 9). Definitive sanctification includes our being cut off from the flesh and being joined to Christ by his Spirit in the inner man. In Christ, there is not only an imputation of righteousness (justification), there is also an impartation of righteousness (sanctification) because of the indwelling life of Christ.[11] Christ is the end of the law for Christ-believers (Rom 10:4), so the law, through Christ's victory, has no legal or spiritual right to reign in my conscience. God has justified me so that I have the right to have a conscience freed and cleansed by Christ (1 Cor 4:3–5; Heb 10:1–4). The new man is alive and holy in the Holy Spirit because of justification (Rom 8:10; 2 Thess 2:13). The old man is a sinner, and the new man is a righteous person by imputation (Christ for us) and impartation (Christ in us) through faith in Christ and not by the law or love, which is the law's fulfillment. For the risen Christ, in whom there is an accomplished redemption, is our righteousness and our sanctification (1 Cor 1:30).

Paul could not be further removed from the idea of the law as the rule of life for those indwelt by Christ. We now live out of the same (new creation) *mind of Christ* that we shall have in glory. The difference is that now we still have the flesh to hinder us and not a Spirit-dominated body, a "spiritual body." The indwelling of God in us in Christ is sufficient for the Christian life—he leads us and empowers us to put to death the desires of the flesh and to love our neighbor. We are free from the law—through which sin, condemnation, and death lorded it over us—for the Spirit of the *Christ* (in whom there is no condemnation), is our *guide, canon, and law* (Rom 8:1–2). It is the Spirit of Christ alone who produces fruit as we walk in the Spirit. As Hays says:

> Galatians 5:13–26 is the most impassioned defense anywhere in Scripture of the sufficiency of the Spirit to guide the community of faith. . . . We fear that without firm guidelines we will fall into chaos. . . . Paul insists, however, that the security offered by the Law is a false security and that the gospel summons those who belong to Christ to live in freedom. . . . Paul's counsel is a daring summons, urging the church to trust that it can live without being subject to the Law of Moses as long as the Spirit guides

10. Phil 1:21; 1 Cor 1:30 and Gal 2:19–21; Rom 7:5, 6; Col 3:4.

11. Those in Christ are not under sin's lordship; their mind is subject to the law of God (the Spirit) in Christ (Rom 8:2, contra v. 7). And because the power of sin is the law (Rom 7:8–13; 1 Cor 15:56), the contrast is also between *the law* and *the Spirit* (Rom 7:6; 2 Cor 3:6), that is, between the law and Christ (Rom 10:4–10).

THE NEW CREATION IN CHRIST

and shapes the community, for the community will organically produce fruit formed by the Spirit.[12]

Hays adds that, in Gal 6:1–10, in contrast to "the elaborately detailed law of Moses as a guide to life," Paul "sketches only a few short strokes in his portrayal of a community guided by the Spirit. He could hardly have done otherwise: If it is the Spirit that provides guidance, it is impossible to be narrowly prescriptive in advance."[13] And Christ is our indwelling Lord by his Holy Spirit; Christ's resurrection life in the Spirit is our law, our rule (Rom 8:1–2).[14] To the extent that believers do not apprehend that, in Christ, God has made them a new creation—to that extent it will seem right that the law is needed as the Christian's rule of life. But the law is for sinners (1 Tim 1:9) and not for the new creation in Christ—those who are saints (1 Cor 1:2; 6:11). Christ lives to God (Rom 6:9, 10); therefore, since I (as in flesh) live no longer but Christ lives in me, Christ is living to God in and through me (Gal 2:20). When Paul says that the new creation (Christ in us, 1 Cor 6:17; Gal 2:20) is our rule of life (Gal 6:15–16), he is saying that we can trust the new creation that God has made us *in Christ*, for it has been created according to God in righteousness and in holiness of the truth (Eph 4:24). Salvation means not being under the law, that is, being delivered and severed from the law through being joined to Christ, for *Christ* has become our wisdom, righteousness, sanctification, and redemption (1 Cor 1:30). Therefore, our rule (of life) is the "law" of the Spirit and *not* the law of the flesh, of which Paul speaks in Rom 2:14–15. The accusatory/condemning function of the law shuts humans up to Christ alone for justification. Luther said:

> Moreover, *the law*, when it is in its principal use and office, can do nothing but *accuse, terrify, condemn, and kill.*[15]

In contrast, the teaching known as "the third use of the law" abounded in the Western church even after the Reformation. Why? Because the Western church's most influential teacher was (the Roman Catholic) Thomas Aquinas. Michael Brown writes:

12. Hays, *NIB* 11:329.

13. Hays, *NIB* 11:338.

14. The authority of Christ as Lord has freed us from that of the law as lord for those who have died and been raised with Christ (Rom 7:1–6). The law is not of faith, for the word of faith says, "Believe in Christ and live," but the law says, "Do this and live." Then how could the law, which is *not of faith*, be the Christian's rule of life? The word says, "Out of faith [ultimately, Christ's faith] we live" (Rom 1:17; Gal 3:11; 10:8–9); but the law says, "Do this and live" (Rom 10:5); therefore, the law is not of faith (Gal 3:12).

15. Luther, *Galatians*, 356, emphasis and modern English mine.

In the Thirteenth Century, Thomas Aquinas carefully divided the Mosaic Law into ceremonial, judicial, and moral, as seen in Q.99.3–4 of his Summa Theologiae (Westminster: Christian Classics, 1989). This tripartite division is ordinarily found in Reformed theology as well.[16]

Many Reformation leaders unwittingly followed the Roman Catholic Thomas Aquinas and thus remained with the law as rule, by believing that it *could* be divided and thereby un-scripturally dividing the law into what they called "the moral law," "the ceremonial law," and "the civil (or judicial) law." But Luther did not. Forde wrote:

> Luther categorically rejected all attempts to qualify the claim that Christ is the end of the law, the whole law. Freedom is not a defensive doctrine. It is "offensive." It is about the new crea-ture, the new creation. Both early and late Luther attacked the idea that Christ is the end of the ritual law but not the whole law. In both the early (1519) and later (1531–36) Galatians lectures he pounded away on this issue whenever he got the chance. In his argument against Erasmus he said that this *error has made it impossible to understand Paul and has obscured the knowledge of Christ.*[17]

The law *cannot* be divided into various parts—the law is one law. Paul's "words taught by the Spirit" (1 Cor 2:13) do *not ever* include the phrase "the moral law," which many churches use, even in their "statements of faith," thereby ignoring the apostle's words in Rom 2:17–23, where "the law" is defined by the Ten Commandments, and in 6:14–15; 7:1–6; 8:1–2; Gal 2:19–21; 5:1–18; 6:14–16; and 1 Cor 9:20. Such churches not only go above and beyond what is written (1 Cor 4:6) but are preaching another gospel (Gal 1:8–9). The teaching of the Roman Catholic Aquinas, that of *separating the law into three parts,* led to Philip Melanchthon, in his fight against John Agricola, to come up with his "third use of the law." Then John Calvin picked it up from Melanchthon and it has influenced those in the Reformed church and tradition up to this very day. Timothy Wengert wrote:

> From the 1534 commentary or from the 1535 (second) edition of Melanchthon's theological textbook, the *Loci Communes Theologici,* John Calvin picked up this notion of the law's third

---

16. Brown, "John Owen on Republication," 151n2. But centuries before Aquinas, Jerome taught similarly; see *LW* 33:257–61.

17. Forde, *Preached God,* 259–60, emphasis mine. This error undoubtedly seems right to the flesh.

use for his famous compendium of theology, *The Institutes of the Christian Religion.*[18]

Thus, Melanchthon (though he did help Luther become clearer on imputed righteousness) even later in his life did not understand Paul here, and thus he opposed both Paul and Luther not only against the truth of the bondage of the will, but he remained Thomistic in his view of the law. What those who follow Melanchthon (and whomever he influenced, including Calvin), do not understand is that what they call "the third use of the law" for believers is already there in the law over *all flesh* (including the flesh of Christians) because the law applies to all who live in the flesh (Rom 7:1, 5). All humans have the work of the law written in their hearts,[19] for even Christ-believers are in Adam (in flesh) according to the body, and that is why they *die* (Rom 8:10; 1 Cor 15:22; 1 Thess 4:16). In that sense all in Christ also know the law, for it is written in the flesh (Rom 2:14–15). Insofar as they are still in flesh, Christ-believers, led by the Spirit, will (in the main) obey the law (civil righteousness) in/of this world, for they are, in one real sense, still in this world. However, their true and essential citizenship is in heaven (Phil 3:21). So the ultimate authority over them is the Lord Jesus Christ.[20] Therefore, although Paul knows that the flesh is under law (Rom 3:9–20; 7:1), his point is precisely that *you* (Spirit-beings, Rom 8:5) are *not* in the flesh but in the Spirit (8:9). Thus, the Spirit, that is, God, with his leading will take care of both realms (the kingdom of this world and the kingdom of God), for the Holy Spirit leads you in your *whole life*; there is no realm in your life in which the Spirit of *God* is not to lead you. As Paul said to believers at Galatia:

> But if you are led by the Spirit (not by the flesh, which is under law), then you are not (objectively and experientially) under law (the letter, Rom 7:5–6). (Gal 5:18 ATP)

In sum, the law applies to all who live in the flesh (Rom 7:1, 5), which in one sense includes believers (Gal 2:20; Phil 1:22, 24). What we mean is that, in "the hands" of God, the law (the work of which is written on the hearts of all humans) has two uses: (1) the "civil use" that restrains evil through the work of the law in the conscience and in the state (Rom 1:32;

---

18. Wengert, *Formula for Parish Practice*, 91.

19. Rom 2:14–15. All nations, which include Christ-believers according to the flesh, have (the work of) the law written in their hearts in the flesh (the outer man).

20. Similarly, Caesar (human government) does not ultimately stand in the way of allegiance to the Lord Christ. Regarding Rom 13 and governing authorities, see the insightful and balanced view of Stott in *Romans*, 338–47.

2:14, 15; 13:1–7), and (2) the "theological use" (what I call "the gospel use"), in which the law condemns (2 Cor 3:9) and leaves all without excuse before God (Rom 3:10–20), who uses the law in this way in God's elect to "kill" them (Rom 7:7–13; 2 Cor 3:6–9) so that they reject their righteousness and cling to God's in Christ (Rom 3:19–20). Since the civil (of this world) use applies to all people living in the world, there is no scriptural "third use" just for Christ-believers, for they are still, in one sense, in the flesh. Because the believer in this age is not only new man but old man (two, yet one), he must "put off the old man" with his deeds and put on the Lord Jesus Christ (Rom 13:14), the new man (Col 3:19, 20). This why John could write, "Everyone who has been begotten of God [the new man of Eph 4:24] does not sin; because the seed [of God] remains in him; and *he cannot sin* because of *God* he has been begotten" (1 John 3:9). Because God cannot sin, the new man, the one begotten (born) of God cannot sin. No wonder the new creation (*Christ* in us) is our rule (Gal 6:15–16). But someone might quote Jesus as saying:

> Do not think that I came to destroy the Law or the Prophets. I did not come to destroy but to fulfill. For assuredly, I say to you, till heaven and earth pass away, one jot or one tittle will by no means pass from the law, until all be fulfilled. (Matt 5:17–18 NKJV)

But the word "fulfilled" in Matt 5:18 must be interpreted in light of Scripture, namely, chapter 24 of Luke, which says that all things in the Law of Moses and the Prophets and the Psalms were *fulfilled* concerning Christ, as Jesus says.

> "These are my words which I spoke to you while I was still with you, that everything written about me in the Law of Moses and the Prophets and the Psalms must be *fulfilled*." . . . and said to them, "Thus it is written, that the Christ would suffer and on the third day rise from the dead, and that repentance and forgiveness should be proclaimed in his name." (Luke 24:44, 46, 47a ESV)

What needs to be understood is that the death of Christ (including our death with him) was an eschatological event in which heaven and earth *have passed away for those in Christ*:

> But God forbid that I should glory, except in the cross of our Lord Jesus Christ, through whom the world [the cosmos, including this present age, Gal 1:4] has been put to death to me and I [have been put to death, 2:19, 20] to the world/present age. (Gal 6:14)

To have died to the world is to have died to "the elements of the world." Paul says:

> So we also, when we were children, were held in bondage *under the elements of the world*. But when the fullness of the time came, God sent forth his Son, having become of a woman, having become *under law*, in order that he might redeem the ones under law, in order that we might receive the adoption of sons. (Gal 4:3–5)

Not only here, but also in Gal 4:9, 21—by comparing v. 9 with v. 21—we see that to desire to be under "the elements of the world" is to desire to be "under the law." So, how can Paul change the then-accepted meaning of "the elements of the world" to mean, or include, *the law*? Martyn explains:

> Prior to hearing Paul's letter, the Galatians will have connected the expression *ta stoicheia tou kosmou* with the traditional earth/air and fire/water, the stars being added.[21]

> Having accented the baptismal confession of 3:28, with its reference to the dissolution in Christ of certain pairs of *opposites*, Jew/Gentile, slave/free, male/female, Paul takes for granted the widespread tradition in which pairs of opposites are themselves identified as "the elements of the cosmos." Thus, in 4:3 he uses that expression itself to refer to the pairs of opposites that are passé, noting indeed that these oppositional elements had in fact enslaved all human beings prior to Christ. By juxtaposing Gal 3:28 and 4:3 Paul instructs the Galatians as to the identity of the oppositional elements. In a word, Paul employs the ancient equation of the world's elements with archaic pairs of opposites to interpret the *religious* impact of Christ's advent.

> These are the cosmic elements that have found their termination in Christ.[22]

All those in Christ, with Paul, have died to *the world* with its Jew and gentile, law-keeping and lawbreaking, or, as Martyn says, "the Law/Not Law, 4:9–10."[23] Through our death with Christ, the world (κόσμος, *cosmos*, with the law lording it over those living in it, Rom 7:1) has been put to death to *us*, and *us* to the world (cosmos, Gal 6:14). Therefore, regarding Matt 5:17–20, as it relates to Paul's "Christ is the end of the law for righteousness for everyone who believes" (Rom 10:4), Forde says of the law:

21. Martyn, *Galatians*, 404.
22. Martyn, *Galatians*, 405–6, and n56, emphasis mine.
23. Martyn, *Galatians*, 405.

When the end and the goal are not *given*, the law becomes endless, insatiable, and threatens to devour everything and destroy everyone. It becomes the irresistible weapon in the hand of the accuser, Satan, the attorney for the prosecution.[24]

Unable to rhyme Matt. 5:17–18 with Rom. 10:4, the dogmatic tradition has experienced nothing but trouble over the law. When one does not see that "heaven and earth" *do* "pass away" in the eschatological fulfillment (in Christ) anticipated and grasped by faith, and that just such fulfillment *is* the end and the goal, Paul and Matthew are at irreconcilable odds.[25]

Something to Consider

Although Martyn and Forde are correct when interpreting Paul here (see Gal 6:14 above), there are also good and legitimate reasons to question whether Matt 5:17–19 includes the actual words of Jesus.[26] Please let me explain.

> After the destruction of Jerusalem in 70 C.E., Jewish leaders gathered in Jamnia . . . and began a reorganization of Judaism based in the synagogue instead of the temple. Competition quickly developed between the traditional Jewish leaders, primarily Pharisees, and the upstart Jewish Christians, and the battleground was the synagogue. In Matthew, the author makes a point to refer to "their synagogues" (9:35; 10:17; 12:9) in reference to the opponents of Jesus, suggesting that there was a distinction between the synagogues of the traditional Jews and synagogues of the Matthean community. Indeed, Matthew's community . . . needed to define their own religious stance and find a means to survive their having been thrust into a Gentile world. They saw Jesus as the new Moses who gave a new law . . . *Matthew presents his gospel as an apologetic, a defense of what his Jewish community believes.*[27]

---

24. Forde, "Christian Life," 2:446–47.

25. Forde, "Christian Life," 2:447.

26. On Matt 5:17–18 being an "interpretation by the evangelist," see Bornkamm et al., *Tradition and Interpretation*, 67, and 65–67; and Beare, *Gospel According to Matthew*, 138–42.

27. Crowder and Smith, "Jewish-Christian Gospel," 153, 157, emphasis mine. See also Beare, *Gospel According to Matthew*, 351–56.

Related to the issue of 5:17–18, most scholars believe that the primary source of Mark's gospel came from Peter; and in Mark's gospel, Peter confesses that Jesus is the Messiah (Mark 8:27–30). It is as short and simple as that. But the author of Matthew, who had an agenda *for* Peter over *against* Paul, adds, "You are Peter, and upon this rock I will build my Church" (and more). By accepting Matthew's account, one ultimately rejects Mark's account; for one cannot have it both ways.[28] Matthew's addition in 16:16b–19 has been used by Rome to teach an "apostolic succession" from Peter until today, giving them papal authority, in which the teaching office of the Church has the *exclusive authority* to *interpret Scripture*[29]—which is not at all true—and such authority that their priests supposedly have the authority to *forgive sins*; thus, there is no need for (faith in) Christ. We need to understand that "Mark was Peter's companion and interpreter during his mission to Rome in the seventh decade of the first century."[30] Thus, if anyone knew what Jesus said to Peter, it was Mark, whose gospel here is trustworthy.[31] For further proof of this, words about Mark from Papias, which were recorded by Eusebius in his *Ecclesiastical History*, are as follows:

> And the Elder said this also: Mark, having become the interpreter of Peter, *wrote down accurately everything that he remembered*, without however recording in order what was either said or done by Christ. For neither did he hear the Lord, nor did he follow Him; but afterwards, as I said, (attended) Peter, who adapted his instructions to the needs (of his hearers) but had no design of giving a connected account of the Lord's oracles. *So then Mark made no mistake, while he thus wrote down some things as he remembered them; for he made it his one care not to omit anything that he heard, or to set down any false statement therein.*[32]

Matthew's "dependence upon the gospel of Mark . . . makes it *very improbable* that the Gospel of Matthew could have been written by the man named

---

28. On the problem of attempting to *harmonize* the Scriptures to protect them, see Achtemeier, *Inspiration and Authority*, 54–56, 64.

29. See Madson, *Cross and the Crown*, 35, citing *Dei Verbum* 10, Vatican II.

30. Swanson, "Gospel of Matthew," 70.

31. On the authenticity of Mark's account of Peter's confession in 8:27–30, see Dunn, "Messianic Secret in Mark," 103.

32. Papias, "Fragment 2," 15. "Mark created a distinctive new narrative form as the vehicle of the Christian faith. Matthew and Luke then adapted, expanded, and reinterpreted Mark for their later situations" (Boring and Craddock, *People's New Testament*, 284; emphasis mine). Trusting in Christ and critical scholarship are utterly compatible.

Matthew in the list of disciples (Matt 10:3)."[33] And under the heading "The Preeminence of Peter in Matthew's Gospel,"[34] Swanson quotes eight other texts from Matthew (besides the "You are Peter'" text), which focus solely on Peter, making nine Peter-focused texts found in none of the other gospels.

Then, referring to what Swanson said (pp. 75–76) about Paul's inclusion of the gentiles through faith, and to Matthew's addition in 16:16b–19, Swanson asks, "What more logical procedure is there than to view this addition against the backdrop of the controversy over the admission of Gentiles into the community of faith?"[35] In light of Gal 2:11–21, what most readers of Galatians have not noticed is that, when Paul recounts his rebuke of Peter for separating from eating with the gentiles (upon the arrival of men from James), he never says that Peter responded in repentance by returning to eat with the gentiles; so it is presumptuous to presume that he did (or else Paul would likely have added it). Therefore it is not stretching the point to consider the possibility that "Matthew is a spokesman for the point of view reflected by the men from James who caused schism and controversy in the churches of Galatia. Even though Paul had been dead for a decade." Matthew "was compelled to attack his point of view . . . in the subtle way of singling out Peter as the one to whom Jesus had given special dispensation of authority even to the binding and loosing of sins (Matthew 16:19)."[36] Of the four Gospels, Matthew alone

> is replete with anti-Pauline references. How else are we to explain the charge of Jesus to his disciples, "Go nowhere among the gentiles, and enter no town of Samaritans, but go rather to the lost sheep of the house of Israel" (Matt 10:5–6)? Or the response of Jesus to the Canaanite woman, "I was sent only to the lost sheep of the house of Israel" (Matt 15:24)? . . . These are singular readings in *Matthew's* gospel. In fact, the author of *Luke represents Jesus in quite a different way*, for Jesus says in his initial proclamation of the gospel in Nazareth, "There were many widows in Israel in the days of Elijah, when the heaven was shut up three years and six months, when there came a great famine over all the land; and Elijah was sent to not of them but only to Zarephath . . . And there were many lepers in Israel in the time of the prophet Elisha; and none of them

33. Swanson, "Gospel of Matthew," 72, emphasis mine.
34. Swanson, "Gospel of Matthew," 77.
35. Swanson, "Gospel of Matthew," 77; see 75–6.
36. Swanson, "Gospel of Matthew," 78.

were cleansed, but only Naaman the Syrian" (Luke 4:25–27. Did Jesus speak with forked tongue?[37]

> The author of the gospel affirms that the law is the very center of all faith and practice, for "until heaven and earth pass away, not an iota, not a dot, will pass from the law until all is accomplished" (Matt. 5:18). The law . . . will stand as long as the constituent elements of the universe itself. Whom did the author have in mind as he continues with the following? "Whoever relaxes one of the least of these commandments and teaches men so, shall be called least in the kingdom of heaven; but he who does them and teaches them shall be called great in the kingdom of heaven" (Matt 5:19). Does not this fit the apostle Paul most appropriately in the eyes of the Jewish-Christian community? Was he not the great relaxer of the law?[38]

After quoting Matt 5:17, Swanson says, "Is this too directed against Paul's gospel . . . ? For Paul states emphatically again and again that the believer is no longer under the law (Roman 6:14), is dead to the law (7:4, 6)."[39] In Matthew:

> The teaching of Jesus is an extension of the Mosaic law, not a replacement. Jesus is the successor to Moses and his teaching is a reinterpretation and reapplication of the Mosaic law in the new age. In fact, *Jesus is superior to Moses and at the same time the great conserver of all that Moses has given* . . . The member of the new community must produce a righteousness that exceeds that which has been accomplished by the scribes and Pharisees (Matt 5:20).[40]

Referring to the author of Matthew, Swanson says:

> It is evident that it was essential for this writer and for his community to preserve those basic structures of the Mosaic religion that did not appear to be in contradiction with the new righteousness in order to assure continuity with the past and stability for the future. . . . Paul, on the other hand, with impeccable Jewish credentials had been set free from dependence upon every external support in favor of reliance upon the immediate presence and witness of the Holy Spirit of God.

---

37. Swanson, "Gospel of Matthew," 78, emphasis mine.
38. Swanson, "Gospel of Matthew," 80–81.
39. Swanson, "Gospel of Matthew," 79.
40. Swanson, "Gospel of Matthew," 81, emphasis mine.

He writes: "We are discharged from the law (the Mosaic law), dead to that which held us captive, so that we serve not under the old written code but in the new life of the Spirit (Rom 7:6). The believer is led by the Spirit (Rom 8:14)."[41]

Later, Swanson observes:

> "Go and make disciples of all nations, baptizing them . . . , *teaching them to observe all that I have commanded you*" (Matt 28:19-20). The teaching of Jesus consists of commands that are to be observed or obeyed and this is the substance of the gospel for this writer.[42]

Included in the Commission's "all I have commanded you" is Matt 5:18-19; 8:4. Compare this with all that Paul says in his letters, especially Galatians chapter 2, regarding the freedom of gentiles in Christ. According to Paul, who is not lying (Gal 1:20), Peter (Cephas), James, and John went with the gospel to the Jews (Gal 2:7-9) and *not* to the nations, contrary to Matt 28:16–20.[43] And I fully believe Mark's account of Peter's confession of Jesus as the Messiah (8:29-30) over against that of Matthew (16:16-19).

Finally, on the basis of what we have shown, we believe that there are good reasons to believe that the author of Matthew used 5:17-20 to purport his Jewish Christianity over against Paul's gospel on the issue of *the law*, for in the history of the church this text has tended many to question Paul's gospel, the result being that is it obscured and/or negated. Please note that we are being critical only of these three texts in Matthew because of *our knowledge of Paul's gospel*, which should *not* be annulled due to Matthew's words. And, regarding Rome's papacy historically deriving its authority from Peter (as if from God himself) through the use of Matt 16:16b-19—this text has been used (illegitimately) for many centuries to support their claim: "Outside the [Roman Catholic] Church, no salvation."[44] Nevertheless, having put forth these things to at least consider, we conclude that: (1) Matthew is canonical Scripture; (2) the author of Matthew was not an apostle; (3) the apostles preached one and the same Christ, crucified and risen. Therefore, there is no theological pluralism among the apostles regarding the gospel and its essence; see Gal 1:23 and 1 Cor 15:3-11.

41. Swanson, "Gospel of Matthew," 83.

42. Swanson, "Gospel of Matthew," 87-88. Due to the legalistic mind of the flesh of Christians and ignorance of Paul's law-free gospel, this truth about Matthew's commission, which Swanson reveals, has not been understood; but rather, the "Commission" is heralded as the central task of the church, especially among Baptists.

43. See Beare, *Gospel According to Matthew*, 444-45.

44. See CCC, sect. 846. See also 424, 552, on the Primacy of Peter.

Not sufficiently *knowing* God's righteousness (Rom 10:1–4) in Christ, including all we have in Christ, robs believers from knowing that the new creation alone is the rule of life for those in him (Gal 6:15–16). The cross, through which we have been justified (Rom 3:24–26; 5:9), is the basis of the new creation (Gal 6:14–16). Thus, in one sense, in 6:14–16 Paul uses "the cross" and "new creation" interchangeably, for Christ died for our sins in order to make us a new creation, for to be a new creation I have already participated in his death and am thus delivered out of this present, evil age (Gal 1:4) into the world/age to come; for in Hebrews chapter 2, the subject is *salvation* (2:2), and the author defines salvation as "the world to come" (2:5). Thus, to be *justified* in Christ and to be a *new creation* are distinct realities, but they are inseparable. When Paul says that Christ lives in him (Gal 2:20), he means that he is a new creation who has died to the law and this entire age under the law. With Christ, the Christ-believer died (was justified) and rose to new life (is a new creation), and therefore "the cross" in which he glories is his shorthand for the justified/new creation complex (6:14–16). And in that sense the cross is the power of God (1 Cor 1:18), which energizes and empowers the person in Christ to live for him (Gal 2:20; see Phil 2:12, 13). Neither law-keeping nor lawbreaking mean anything before God, for the very flesh that outwardly does the law cannot trust God but only hates God. And the existence of indwelling sin alone would disqualify any works from being able to justify before God (Rom 8:3; 7–8). So, we cannot live to God unless we have died to the law, the ministry of condemnation, 2 Cor 3:9. Therefore the law, as the ministry of condemnation and death, does not recognize such a separate "use" or "function" that can be without its *condemnation unto death*.[45] Now if we have died to the lordship of the law (Rom 7:1-6), then the law is not our lord and ruler; and neither is it our rule. Martin Luther, following Paul the apostle in Gal 6:15–16, taught that the new creation is the Christian's *only* rule. Luther said:

---

45. Thus, a primary blind spot of those who teach that the law is the Christian's rule of life is that they do not understand that the Ten Commandments, "written and engraved on stones" (2 Cor 3:7), cannot be separated from its condemnation (3:9) unto (its penalty, which is) death (3:7). After God delivered Israel out of Egypt, Israel was given the Ten Commandments (see Exod 19:1; 20:1–17). With each commandment came the obligation to keep it on penalty of death. For example, transgressing the sixth commandment brought certain death: "He who strikes a man so that he dies shall surely be put to death" (Exod 21:12 NASB). Concerning the seventh commandment against adultery (Exod 20:14;) we read, "The adulterer and the adulteress shall surely be put to death" (Lev 20:10b NASB). So, one cannot scripturally separate the *commandment* of the law from the law's penalty and still call it "the law."

This is the only true rule by which we should walk, namely, the new creation.[46]

But let only this rule, about which Paul is speaking here, be blessed. By it we live in faith in Christ and are made a new creation, that is, truly righteous and holy through the Holy Spirit, not through sham or pretense.[47]

Faith in Christ itself *is* obedience to God, says the apostle in Rom 1:5. In "The Freedom of a Christian," Luther says:

It is clear, then, that a Christian has all that he needs in faith and needs no works to justify him; and if he has no need of works, he has no need of the law; and if he has no need of the law, surely he is free from the law. It is true that "the law is not laid down for the just" [I Tim 1:9]. This is that Christian liberty, our faith, which does not induce us to live in idleness or wickedness but makes law and works unnecessary for any man's righteousness and salvation.[48]

Luther's last word, "salvation," surely includes sanctification, definitive and progressive; for the gospel is the power of God unto salvation (Rom 1:17). The word of the cross *is* God's power to those who *are being saved* (1 Cor 1:18). Thus, Christ, the *last* Adam, the life-giving Spirit, is the *eschatological* end of the law for righteousness for all who believe (see Rom 10:4). However, even though Luther went further (in terms of closeness to Paul's gospel) than any other Reformer in his teaching on the law, as Pannenberg rightly says:

Nevertheless, in its doctrine of law and gospel *the Reformation did not unfold the finality of the eschatological turn* in its implications *for the theological understanding of law.*[49] As concerns the distinction of law and gospel, however, the finality of the turn that for Paul came with Christ's coming did not make its full impact because Luther, unlike Paul, viewed life in the flesh as a life still subject to law. Paul precisely did *not* say that Christian life "in the flesh" is still under the law. For him believers are already to let their earthly life be determined by the Spirit (Gal

---

46. *LW* 27:141.

47. *LW* 27:141.

48. *LW* 31:349–50.

49. Pannenberg, *Systematic Theology*, 3:86, emphasis mine.

5:18; Rom 8:4), so that they no longer live under the law but under grace (Rom 6:12–14).[50]

The essential truth about believers is that they are *no longer in the flesh*, but they are *in the Spirit* (Rom 7:5, 6; 8:9). Paul is saying that "the life I now live in the flesh" I live as one who is no longer in the flesh, but in the Spirit (8:9), for Christ lives in me (Gal 2:20). If (since) we have life in the Spirit, let us walk in the Spirit, (Gal 5:25). The old person in Adam (in the flesh) died (in his inner man) with Christ and now *Christ* lives in him, in the place of the old, independent-from-God "I." So that one is a new creation. *Christ*—and not "I under law"—*is* the life I now live in the flesh. For to live is Christ (alone), and to die is gain (Phil 1:21). So, my life in the flesh is not the issue before God—nor is it who I am! Being *in Christ* is the main eschatological change or turn. And, as the antidote to "antinomianism," most church leaders have neither understood nor taught the truth of Rom 6[51] nor 1 Cor 9:21—where Paul says that, because we are *in Christ*, we are, ipso facto, in the law of *Christ*, and thus not without the law of *God*. The indicatives in Romans chapter 6 do not contradict the radical and constant reality of indwelling sin in (the flesh of) those who are Christ's. Rather, Romans chapter 6 reveals the true identity of who we are *in Christ* and then gives that identity's imperatives. Pannenberg says:

> Luther could no longer primarily think of the relation between law and gospel as expressing the sequence of two epochs in salvation history. Ebeling found here the "striking difference" between Luther and Paul. Instead of a succession in a once-for-all irreversible turn, the Reformation schema had a distinctly simultaneous accompaniment, a permanent turn as it were, that raises the suspicion that it is no real turn at all. Of the switch *to* the new covenant the Reformation formula makes as it were the structure of existence *in* the new covenant.[52]

Regarding new testament imperatives, Pannenberg says:

> Reformation discussions of the concept of law did no more than medieval theology to distinguish between law and Christian paraclesis as exposition of our being in Christ.[53]

---

50. Pannenberg, *Systematic Theology*, 3:86.

51. See Schlink, *Theology of the Lutheran Confessions*, 300, 306; Lloyd-Jones, *Exposition of Chapter Six*, 19–78; 89–232; Nygren, *Commentary on Romans*, 241–59; 262–64.

52. Pannenberg, *Systematic Theology*, 3:80. It is as though the "new testament . . . of the Spirit" (2 Cor 3:6) never arrived.

53. Pannenberg, *Systematic Theology*, 3:90. By "paraclesis" Pannenberg means the admonitions, the imperatives that correspond to the new being (Rom 6:4; see 8:5) in

But the freedom of justification in Christ causes humans to bear spiritual fruit (Rom 7:5–6; Gal 5:6, 22), and only the life in Christ is that life which is not under law (Gal 5:18).

> If we view natural law as the normative expression of God's eternal will for us, we can no longer give full weight to what Paul says about *Christ* being the *end* of the law.[54]

And natural law is for the natural man. And that is not who we are in Christ.

> Now we have received, not the spirit of the world [of the natural man], but [we have received] the Spirit who is from God, that we might know the things that have been freely given to us by God. (1 Cor 2:12)

> But the *natural man* [soulish man, without the Spirit] does *not* receive the things of the Spirit of God, for they are foolishness to him; nor can he know them, because they are spiritually discerned [discerned by the Spirit]. (1 Cor 2:14)

Since natural law[55] is for the natural man (2:14), then it follows that spiritual law, "the law of the Spirit" (Rom 8:2), is for the spiritual man, the one indwelt by the Spirit. For Paul "spiritual" always means *of the Spirit of God* (e.g., 1 Cor 15:44). The Christian life is depending only on Christ—his Spirit—and not on ourselves. Thus, we discern God's will by renewing our minds (Rom 12:2). Therefore, nomism (law-ism) is not God's way for those in Christ, not because of anything wrong with the law, but because *the law is not Christ* nor of Christ, that is, not of faith in him (Gal 3:12).

> I beseech you therefore, brethren by the mercies of God [the grace which justifies], that you present your bodies to God, which [in light of grace] is your reasonable service of worship. And do not be conformed [in your thinking] to this age, but be transformed [in your thinking] by the renewing of your mind [according to the new creation you are *in Christ*, not according to the law], so that you may approve what is the will of God—the good, well-pleasing and perfect will of God. (Rom 12:1–2)

Christ. Those who hold to confessional Lutheranism are, in general, basically ignorant of what Luther taught on Gal 6:15–16. I believe this is because the Lutheran Confessions, far more than Paul's letters and/or Luther's 1535 Galatians, have historically dominated Lutheranism in their seminaries.

54. Pannenberg, *Systematic Theology*, 3:90.

55. See Rom 2:14, 15; and 1 Cor 2:14.

To the extent that Protestants have followed Rome in the fear (untrust) that clings to the law, they have not given the Spirit of Christ his rightful place in the Christian life—as the one who teaches, empowers, and guides the person in Christ. He or she may use apostolic imperatives, but, in one sense, he does not necessarily need them—see 1 Thess 4:9 and Rom 12:2. Christ reveals that the law demands that we serve God in spirit, from the heart (Rom 2:28–29). The OT scriptures, and even the gospels, must be interpreted in the light of the gospel of God—the light of the knowledge of the glory of God in the face of Jesus Christ.

The torah (the law) is *not* the new testament church's rule of life. The church is Spirit-indwelt and Spirit-led; and that means *Christ*-indwelt and *Christ*-led (see Rom 8:9–10, 12–14).

Now that the faith has come (Gal 3:23), everything outside of being led by the Spirit (through faith, Gal 5:5) is sin (Rom 14:23). Paul, in his letter to the Roman believers, says that the law of Moses was given, in covenant form, to the nation of Israel only; therefore, *Old Testament Israel* and *the law* are inseparable.[56] In contrast, the apostle says:

> Give no offense, either to the Jews [Israelites, Rom 9:3] or to the Greeks [gentiles] or to *the church of God*. (1 Cor 10:32 NKJV [see 12:1–2])

So those "in Christ" are neither Jews nor gentiles but are "the church of God." Thus, on the basis of all we have said so far, interpreting the apostle's words by the apostle's words, the risen Christ, through Paul, is saying:

> Now that the faith (of Christ) has come . . . whatever is not of faith is sin.[57]

> And that means, *whatever is not of the leading of the Spirit*—is of the flesh of sin.[58]

> But if you are being led by the Spirit, you are not under law. (Gal 5:18)

If the Spirit is in us, we are being led by him through faith in Christ for justification. Are we following? But human righteousness (Phil 3:9) is so deep in the flesh that, to the flesh, Paul's "no law but Christ" gospel can

---

56. "For as many as have sinned without law [gentiles] will also perish without the law. As many as have sinned in the law [Jews] will be judged by the law" (Rom 2:12). In the same context, he says: "Indeed you are called a Jew, and rest on the law" (Rom 2:17; see also Rom 5:13–14; 9:3–5.

57. Gal 3:23–25; compare Rom 14:23.

58. Gal 5:16–18; compare Rom 8:3 lit.

only seem like antinomianism: "If there's no law, they will sin all the more." But such people simply do not realize what "Christ in you" entails, namely, that I am *not* without the law of *God*, because I am *in Christ* ("Christ in me" means that God is in me, leading me every step of the way)—*in* the law of *Christ* (1 Cor 9:21), for Christ dwells in Paul and in all Christ-believers (Rom 8:9). The flesh is constantly opposing the Spirit with his desires and leading, distracting us from (the things of) Christ. But now that the new creation has arrived—now that the righteousness from God has been manifested through redemption—it is not "everyone shall be put to death for his own sin" (Deut 24:16c NASB) as *the law* says. But it is "if you *live according to the flesh* you will die" (spiritual unto bodily death) (Rom 8:13a)—*that* is a major difference between the old and new covenants. Therefore, now that Christ and his Spirit have come (Gal 3:22–25), to live according to the flesh means to live according to the law:

> For while we were in the flesh . . . But *now* we have been released from *the Law* [that is, from being "in the flesh"]. (Rom 7:5a,6a NASB)

The only freedom from the law of sin and of death is our union with Christ in his death to sin and the law and his resurrection to new life in the Spirit of God the Father. The old man is the sin-dominated, sin-enslaved man, but the new man is the God-dominated, Christ-enslaved man or woman who is therefore utterly free in Christ Jesus our Lord (Rom 6:3–22; 7:1–6; 8:1–10). In light of Rom 7:1–6, 10:4, and Gal 2:19–20, we agree with Gordon Fee's paraphrase of Paul's meaning in Gal 5:16 and 5:18:

> "It is all right to be done with Torah," he says, "because the Spirit can handle the flesh; indeed, to be led by the Spirit eliminates the need to be under law" . . . What is finally significant for the concern of this letter is that *Paul herewith places the flesh and the Law on the same side of things over against the Spirit* . . . This means that everything before Christ, which was fundamentally eliminated by his death and resurrection and the gift of the eschatological Spirit, belongs to the same "old age" sphere of existence. In that sense the Spirit stands over against both the flesh and the Law, in that *he replaces the latter and stands in opposition to the former.*[59]

Fee's statement is correct as far as it goes, but it is not adequate. For, after Fee said, "everything before Christ," he should have added ". . . and after Christ, that is, everything outside of Christ"—for, by the death of Christ,

---

59. Fee, *God's Empowering Presence*, 438, emphasis mine.

this age-world was judged, destroyed, and ended for those in Christ and that includes those who live in the flesh after Christ. Regarding Paul's admonitions, what Pannenberg calls "paraclesis," he says:

> Luther was materially right in contrast to his antinomian opponents to the extent that according to the NT witness and Paul's letters Christians are not just left on their own in matters of moral conduct. They receive apostolic paraclesis, which Paul bases on exposition of the new being in Christ . . . This paraclesis may be formulated positively as help but also as warning and threat in view of God's judgment. It is a mistake, however, to describe apostolic direction as law, for it is meant only as exposition of being in Christ. *For Christ has now replaced the law,* as Paul tells us in his saying that Christ is the end of the law.[60]

> Jesus Christ is the end of the law because in him the eschatological future of God's kingdom is already present.

> As believers, Christians do not in fact need any law but only the apostolic direction that leads them to use the freedom that they have in Christ that is inseparable from sharing in God's love for the world.[61]

> The Pauline formula that Christ is the end of the law (Rom 10:4) relates primarily to the Mosaic law as an expression of God's will for the chosen people. The formula states that this law is not the definitive form of God's righteous will. Here lies also the epochal significance in world history of the saying about the end of the law in Jesus Christ.[62]

Lincoln agrees:

> Since the law was a temporary provision, Christ brings its period of validity to an end, so that the believer in Christ is no longer under law as a rule of life.[63]

The reign of God is present *in the Holy Spirit*: "For the kingdom of God is . . . in the Holy Spirit" (Rom 14:17 NASB). This Spirit (of the crucified Christ who justifies) can be trusted. To be "not in the flesh, but in the Holy Spirit" means that Christ is in us (8:10), the Christ who is the end of the law for righteousness for believers (10:4). First, the law was given as a covenant to

---

60. Pannenberg, *Systematic Theology*, 3:88–89, emphasis mine.

61. Pannenberg, *Systematic Theology*, 95.

62. Pannenberg, *Systematic Theology*, 95.

63. Lincoln, "From Sabbath to Lord's Day," 370.

Israel only (Rom 9:4). Second, because the law is holy, righteous, and spiritual, humans are without excuse: The law is a power that brings all humans under the judgment and condemnation of God. But this is the bottom line:

> I, through law, died to the law, [for] I have been crucified [to death] with Christ, and I [in flesh] live no longer, but Christ lives in me [I, as new creation, have life in the Spirit, for *Christ alone* is my life]. And the life I now live in the flesh, I live by the faith of the Son of God [which faith-obedience procured my justification], who loved me and delivered himself up for me. (Gal 2:19–20)

All that he has accomplished in his death remains with Christ and thus "in him."[64] When the apostle says, "The law is not of faith," in context he means "the law for justification is not of faith in Christ" (Gal 3:11–12, 21; Rom 5:19–21); yes, but considering Paul's Spirit-taught words, he also means that, for the Christ-believer, who is indwelt by the Spirit (Rom 8:9), looking to the law for wisdom, righteousness, or sanctification is not of faith in Christ, who *is* our wisdom, righteousness, sanctification, and redemption (1 Cor 1:30; Gal 3:12), for Christ is in us (Rom 8:9–10).[65] Paul the apostle uses "the Spirit of Christ" and "Christ" interchangeably (Rom 8:9–10), so we know that the contrast between the flesh and the Spirit is a contrast between the flesh and Christ, which means that whatever is not of Christ is of the flesh. Whatever is not of the leading of the Spirit is disobedience to God. The fault lies not with the law but with the flesh of sin. There is now simply no need for the law, for in the new testament, the Spirit takes the place of the old covenant law. Because my true being is according to the Spirit of God (Rom 8:5), I can say, "I am not of this world; I am in and of *the Spirit* of *the age to come*."[66] Those believers who decry

---

64. Paul's revelation of Christ (Gal 1:12) also reveals the truth about the law. Now that "the faith of Christ has come," it has been revealed that "the law is not of faith" (Gal 3:12; 3:22–25). Moses could never have said "the law is not of faith" because the promised Messiah, with his faith, had not yet come nor died nor been raised from the dead. But now we have died with Christ to the law and have been joined to Christ who was raised by God from the dead (Gal 2:19, 20; Rom 7:4–6). Old covenant saints had faith because God gave it as a gift, and that only on the basis of Christ's death; but they did not have union with the crucified and risen Christ, as NT saints have.

65. Thus, the apostolic imperatives are not called "the law" nor are they the gospel. Rather, they flow out of the indicative of the gospel, that is, of who we are in Christ. Christ's commands are to those who are alive from the dead (Rom 6:11–13). And we are to believe the truth, to consider ourselves to be dead to sin and the law and alive to God in Christ Jesus—that the law already killed us with Christ, so we are beyond its jurisdiction, and we are alive in Christ. It is not the law but the grace of God that teaches us how to live in this present age (see Titus 2:11–14).

66. Gal 1:4; 6:15; 2 Cor 5:17; Rom 8:9, 11. Thus, we are *aliens* (1 Pet 2:11 NASB).

the belief of those holding to Luther's theology, New Covenant theology, etc., by saying, "They don't believe that the moral law[67] in Scripture applies to us" do not understand that Scripture never uses the phrase "the moral law," and that the Spirit of Christ in us replaces the law in all its "letter" forms (Rom 2:28–29; 7:1–6; 8:1–2; Gal 2:19–21; 6:15–16).

The Centrality of Justification
in Regards to Sanctification

After David committed adultery and sinned against Bathsheba, he said to God, "Against thee, thee only, have I sinned, and done this evil in thy sight" (Ps 51:4 RSV). All sin is essentially and uniquely against God.[68] Thus, if someone says, "Even though we are justified before God, we are obligated to the neighbor against whom we have sinned (to deal with the results of our sin)," in reality they are not sufficiently seeing the primary issue: Sanctification must be viewed in the light of the centrality and priority of justification (Rom 1:16–17; 1 Cor 15:1–4), precisely because against God only and uniquely we have sinned, and, in that sense, God is satisfied in propitiation unto justification, period. Only God is God; the neighbor is not God. So sanctification's works need to be understood in light of the gospel of God (Rom 1:1), which is as follows: With Christ we died to and are thereby released from the law (the obligation to do it,

---

Therefore, all fear of "antinomianism"—using grace as a license to sin, (1) does not understand that Paul views sin in light of Christ and faith in him and therefore as unbelief in Christ, rather than in light of the law (i.e., as law-transgressing); and (2) is ignorance of or unbelief in the truth of Christ in you, being led by the Spirit of Christ, which includes but is not limited to how his Spirit leads a believer to put to death the flesh-deeds (Rom 8) and to live in holiness.

67. People *like* the Ten Commandments because they feel they can have something with which *they* can control their lives. The flesh fears sinning, which is the fear of condemnation from God for sin. Only those in whom God in Christ reveals the bondage of being under law will know and be thankful for their freedom in Christ. The true gospel includes being led by the Spirit, whereby the believer is not under law (Gal 5:18). To the extent that this apostolic gospel is not preached, preachers and teachers will indeed be judged and suffer loss (1 Cor 3:11–15).

68. "Sin is a concept that is inseparably connected with the relationship to God. There is no sin which is not sin against God. It is meaningless to talk about sin if it has no relation to God. From this point of view the words of the 51st Psalm are unconditionally valid: 'Against thee, thee only, have I sinned' (Ps 51:4). From the viewpoint of Christian faith it would be meaningless to divide sins into two classes: sins against God and sins against the neighbor. There is no sin against the neighbor which is not sin against God. The sin against the neighbor becomes sin because it is sin against God" (Aulén, *Faith of the Christian Church*, 261).

Rom 7:1–6; Gal 2:19–21; 5:1–5, 18) and are now debtors to *the Spirit*, to be led by the Spirit (Rom 7:6;*8:9–14), whereby we are not under obligation to law (Gal 5:5:18) for salvation, which includes sanctification. Only as we are settled in (justification by) grace are we free to be led by the Holy Spirit in terms of doing God's will (Rom 12:1, 2). Christ in me (the new creation) does not need the law.

FIFTEEN

In One Word: Love . . .

The whole law has been fulfilled in *one word*:
You shall love your neighbor as yourself.

(Gal 5:14)

The Church of God (1 Cor 10:32) and
Its Lord's Commands (14:37)

Give no offense, either to the Jews or to the Greeks or to *the church of God.* (1 Cor 10:32)

WE FIND HERE THAT the church of God is a third entity—it is neither the Jews nor the gentiles. But then how does the church differ from them? The Jews and Greeks/gentiles are the ones being according to the flesh; but those in Christ are the ones being according to the Spirit (Rom 8:5). Paul was controlled by the love of Christ for us (2 Cor 5:14), and we are to imitate him (1 Cor 4:16). So, through the obedience of faith in Christ for justification (Rom 1:5, 16–17) the church is to heed the apostolic imperatives, which Paul calls "the commandments of the Lord" (1 Cor 14:37) and "the commandments of God" (7:19); thus, they are not Moses's commandments (see Rom 7:1–6). The commandments of the Lord Jesus are not the gospel; but on the other hand, they are consistent with the gospel and the living out of it; they are addressed only to those in Christ (1 Cor 1:2; 6:11). In 1 Corinthians, Paul uses a parallelism in which we find that there is both union and distinction between the Father and the Son.

> Yet for us there is only *one God*, the Father, of from whom are
> all things . . . and *one Lord* Jesus Christ, through whom are all
> things. (1 Cor 8:6)

Although there is a distinction between God (the Father) and the Lord (the
Son), nevertheless, there is only one God. Therefore, in the following texts
we can see that what Paul calls "the commandments of God" are the same
as "the commandments of the Lord."

> What matters is keeping the commandments of *God*. (1 Cor
> 7:19 NKJV)

> The things which I [Paul] write to you are the commandments
> of *the Lord*. (1 Cor 14:37c NKJV, emphasis mine)

Paul uses the two phrases interchangeably, for Christ the Lord is God. The
commandments of God are no longer the commandments of Moses (to OT
Israel, Deut 5:1–21); they are Christ's commandments, for in the new testament of the Spirit (2 Cor 3:6) we are the circumcision (Phil 3:3), the Jews,
for we have circumcised hearts (Rom 2:28, 29). Next, what Christ's apostle
commands, Christ commands. Paul wrote:

> And to the married I command, yet not I, but the Lord: A wife is
> not to depart from her husband. (1 Cor 7:10 NKJV)

As Christ's apostle, Paul says, "I command." This is just one of what Paul
calls "the commandments of the Lord" (1 Cor 14:37). This apostolic authority is the norm in Paul's letters, except for one instance, when what Paul
commands is not the Lord's command, but is only Paul's counsel; and then
he makes that clear (see 1 Cor 7:12–13). For Christ is the one who speaks
in Paul (2 Cor 13:3; Gal 1:12). So, Paul sums up his instructions to the Corinthians by saying, "If anyone thinks himself to be a prophet or spiritual, let
him acknowledge that the things which I write to you are the commandments of the Lord" (1 Cor 14:37 NKJV). Similarly, Paul, while telling the
Thessalonians to abstain from fornication, wrote, "For you know what commandments we [Paul the apostle, not Moses] gave you through the Lord
Jesus" (1 Thess 4:2 NKJV); then Paul says, "Therefore, he who rejects this
does not reject man, but God" (1 Thess 4:8 NKJV).

And these *commandments of the Lord* (1 Cor 14:37; 1 Thess 4:2, 8) are
what John's Gospel (from the perspective of the risen Christ) has Jesus calling "my commandments" (John 14:15, 21; 15:10), which are done not out of
the flesh as source (as law) but out of God's power, which is the gospel (Rom
1:16–17). For we were first *loved by Christ*, as the Johannine Jesus says:
"Love one another, *as I have loved you*" (in my death for you, John 13:34;

see 17:4; 19:30), *just as* the command to love is based on Christ's death in the Pauline corpus (see Eph 5:2; Col 3:13, 14; Rom 15:7). This is because John's Gospel is written from the perspective of the risen Christ, which, like Paul's, includes the already "now" of the Spirit having come, which is why the beloved disciple clarifies this for his readers in John 7:38–39, so that believing in Christ (John 7:38) is based upon the truth that God already "loved . . . and gave his only begotten Son" (3:16).

From Paul's words, we deduce the following truth: Just as Moses was God's servant through whom he gave the law to Israel according to the flesh (1 Cor 10:18; see Rom 9:4) under the old covenant, similarly, in the new, Paul is Christ's bond-slave in whom God revealed the gospel of God for the church of God. In Romans, in defense of the gospel, and to show that all humans are "without excuse," Paul speaks to the (natural) Jew, saying:

> But if you are named a "Jew" and rest on *the law*, and boast in God and *know God's will . . . being instructed out of the law . . .*
> (Rom 2:17–18 NKJV)

Paul says that the old covenant Jew "knows God's will" by being taught out of the law.[1] "The law" here is the Ten Commandments—that they should not steal, they should not commit adultery or idolatry (Rom 2:21–22). Furnish rightly says of Paul:

> Nowhere, however, does he speak of *the Christian* as having God's will available in the law. For the Christian, the will of God is not *possessed* but—as Rom 12:2 implies—ever newly sought and found.[2]

So, to the ones who are a *new creation* in Christ, Paul says:

> I beseech you therefore, brethren, by the mercies of God [God's grace having now come to you in Christ], that you present your bodies a living [alive from the dead with Christ] sacrifice to God, which [in light of God's grace] is your reasonable service. (Rom 12:1 NKJV)
> And do not be conformed to this age, but be transformed by the *renewing* of your mind [according to the *new* creation], so that you may prove and know what is good, acceptable and perfect— *the will of God.* (Rom 12:2)

Michael Gorman wrote:

1. Rom 2:17–18. Credit here goes to Westerholm, *Israel's Law*, 209, where I discovered this distinction.
2. Furnish, *Theology and Ethics*, 188–89. See Rom 12:1–2.

It is no accident that Paul's summary of believers' existence in Galatians 5:6 ("*Faith* working through *love*" [NRSV]) is a deliberate echo of Gal. 2:20b: "I live by the *faith* of the Son of God, who *loved* me by giving himself for me." It is the powerful presence of this paradigmatic person in Paul's life that enables him to live the life of faith before God and . . . of love for others. Gal 2:15–21, then, defines the life of faith, both as initial experience and ongoing reality. Paradoxically, this life is a death, a crucifixion, so that the Crucified One may live in the crucified one; the crucified but living Christ lives in and through the crucified but living believer. Also paradoxically, this life of faith, of trust, is first of all a life of *dis*trust, distrust of the self of the law . . . as the basis for justification. This death to the law . . . is an essential aspect of crucifixion with Christ. Most importantly, crucifixion with Christ is not a *supplement* to faith, it is the *essence* of faith.[3]

Referring to his call as apostle to the nations, Paul wrote:

> For though I am free from all, I have made myself a servant to all, that I might win more of them. To the Jews I became as a Jew, in order to win Jews. To those under law, I became as one under the law (though not myself being under the law), that I might win those under the law. (1 Cor 9:19–20 ESV)

> To those who are without law, [I became] as without law—*not being* without the law of *God*, but *in* the law of *Christ*—in order that I might win those who are without law. (1 Cor 9:21)

Here Paul refers first to Jews, and then proselytes to Judaism (those under law), and then to gentiles (those without the law). All these are outside of Christ. Because we are "in Christ" we are therefore *in* the law of *Christ* (1 Cor 9:21)—and thus we do not need the law of Moses, which was given to the nation Israel (Rom 2:12–14; 5:13–14; 9:4), many of whom were unregenerate and none of whom were in "the new testament . . . of the Spirit." The Greek translated is as follows: ἔννομος (in the law) Χριστοῦ (of Christ) (1 Cor 9:21). Therefore, believers are *not without the law of God* (1 Cor 9:21) for they are in union with Christ, and Christ is God. Christ cannot be ontologically severed from "the love of God which is in Christ Jesus," which controlled Paul (2 Cor 5:14), whom we are to imitate (1 Cor 4:16). So, Paul's gospel has both a negative (death) aspect and a positive (resurrection) aspect for those in Christ Jesus, who:

3. Gorman, *Cruciformity*, 139; all emphases are his.

- died to the law with Christ and are therefore dead to and released from the law; we are not under or in *the law* of Moses, including the work of *the law* in the hearts of the nations, hearts of those *in the flesh of sin,* Rom 8:3 (Rom 2:14, 15; 3:19 lit.; 7:1–6).

- are in *the law of Christ:* "*not being* without the law of *God,* but [being] *in the law of Christ*" (ἔννομος Χριστοῦ) (1 Cor 9:21; see Gal 2:19–20; Rom 7:1–6; 8:1, 2).

We are not without God's law precisely because we are *in Christ's law,* for *Christ* is *God.* Therefore, now that Christ has died and been raised, and we died and rose *with Christ,* the law of God is no longer the law of Moses but the law of Christ, for those *in Christ.* Thus, 1 Cor 9:21 is the clearest text against all arguments that would call Paul, and those who teach his gospel, "antinomian" (against law), for *in Christ* we are *not* without the law of God.

> Now as to the love of the brethren, you have no need for anyone to write to you, for you yourselves are *taught by God* to love one another. (1 Thess 4:9 NASB)

Most Christian traditions have not been taught the apostolic teaching of "Christ in you" that we have been presenting, which corresponds to the reality of not being under law but under God's grace, the grace of justification in Christ. Because God is working in us by his Spirit, *he is teaching and leading us to love one another.* The law of Christ *is* love for the neighbor, especially for our neighbors in Christ (Gal 5:13–15).

> For in Christ Jesus neither circumcision nor uncircumcision counts for anything, but faith working through love [Christ's love for us, which controls us and empowers us to serve one another in Christ]. (Gal 5:6)

Commenting on Gal 5:6, Luther says:

> As I have said, therefore, Paul is describing the whole of the Christian life in this passage: inwardly it is faith toward God, and outwardly it is love or works towards one's neighbor.[4]

---

4. *LW* 27:30.

In One Word

But *now*, apart from law, since God's saving righteousness has come, and, on the basis of an accomplished redemption in Christ, God has sent forth the Spirit of his Son into our hearts (Gal 4:4–7), Paul can say:

> The whole law has been fulfilled (not in ten words, as the Ten Commandments are called "the Ten Words" in Exod 34:28[5] and Deut 4:13[6] and 10:4,[7] but [now]) . . . in *one* word: *love your neighbor as yourself.* (Gal 5:14 ATP)

Now that the Spirit of Christ has been given, the BAG lexicon, on 5:14, says:

> Gal. 5:14 is . . . to be translated *the whole law has found its full expression in a single word.*[8]

This word—love your neighbor as yourself—is "the law of Christ":

> Bear one another's burdens, and so fulfill *the law of Christ.* (Gal 6:2)

In light of Gal 5:14, it is clear that *the law of Christ* is *love* (*your neighbor as yourself*).

In Gal 5:14 Paul is distinguishing the old covenant with its "ten words" and the new covenant, with its "one word." On Galatians chapter 5, Furnish says:

> Since believers live by the Spirit's presence and power in their midst, they should allow their lives to be ordered by its guidance, which is the guidance of love.[9]

Because such love is the fruit of the Spirit (Gal 5:22), it is not the fruit of the flesh nor of its law (Rom 8:2; see 8:5). To the saints at Rome, Paul wrote:

---

5. "So he was there with the LORD forty days and forty nights; he did not eat bread or drink water. And he wrote on the tablets the words of the covenant, *the Ten Words*" (Exod 34:28 [margin note, lit. "Words"] NASB).

6. "So He declared to you His covenant which He commanded you to perform, that is, the Ten Words; and He wrote them on two tablets of stone" (Deut 4:13 [margin note, lit. "Words"] NASB).

7. "He wrote on the tablets, like the former writing, the Ten Words which the LORD had spoken to you on the mountain from the midst of the fire on the day of the assembly; and the LORD gave them to me" (Deut 10:4 [margin note, lit. "Words"] NASB).

8. BAG, 677.

9. Furnish, *Love Command*, 99. On John 13:34, see 138, including footnotes.

> He who loves his neighbor has fulfilled the law. For the com-
> mandments, "You shall not commit adultery," "You shall not
> murder," "You shall not steal," "You shall not give false testimo-
> ny," "You shall not covet," and whatever other commandments
> there are, are all summed up in *this saying*, namely, "*You shall
> love your neighbor as yourself*." Love works not evil to the neigh-
> bor; therefore, *love is the fulfillment of the law*. (Rom 13:8b–10)

The whole law is completely fulfilled in "one" word: "You shall love your
neighbor as yourself." And we all know how to love ourselves, for we know
how we want others to treat *us*; and that is how we should treat others (Matt
7:12). Therefore, we are to walk in Christ (Rom 8:9–10; Gal 5:16), which is
to walk in love (Eph 5:2). Thus, there is no reason to fear antinomianism
if we walk in the Spirit, which is to walk in love. For the one who is a new
creation, his or her law is "Love your neighbor as yourself." The neighbor,
in context, means "one another" in the body of Christ (Gal 5:13, 15), but it
also applies in a secondary way to all others (6:10). But someone may ask,
"Why does Paul not command us to love God and then the neighbor, as
Jesus did (before his redeeming death)?" The answer is that "now" (Rom
3:21) that Christ died and rose again, God's saving righteousness, which
is "apart from law" (3:21) includes "apart from" (Jesus' previous summary
of) the law, because it is "now" (3:21) clearly *revealed* that our love for God
and neighbor (what the law demanded) could not save us (Rom 10:5–10).
Not only that, but because God's agape/love toward us is central in the gospel of God (Rom 5:8; 1 John 5:10), the life we are to live (in Christ) is one
of *faith in Christ* toward *God* and *love* toward *the neighbor* (Gal 5:1–14;
see 1 John 4). Since Christ died and rose again, God's love toward us is
central, not our love to God; and faith toward God includes love toward
him. Love for God is a fruit of faith; and God's love for us in Christ's death
provided faith for the elect (Gal 3:13–14; Rom 8:32–34; Phil 1:29). Anders
Nygren teaches that God's love is spontaneous in that it is not motivated
by anything outside of God. Therefore:

> Faith includes in itself the whole devotion of love, while em-
> phasizing that it has the character of a response, that it is recip-
> rocated love. Faith is love towards God, but a love of which the
> keynote is receptivity, not spontaneity.[10]

Only on the basis of redemption, which is the basis of God giving his Spirit
to indwell us, does Paul then say that the fruit of the Spirit is love (Gal

---

10. Nygren, *Agape and Eros*, 127.

5:22) and that the whole law is fulfilled in one word: Love your neighbor as yourself (5:14). A. T. Lincoln says:

> The Spirit produces love and love turns out to be the fulfilling of the law (cf. Gal 5:14).
>
> For Paul God's dealings in history, including the expression of His will, have moved on and he is no longer under the law of Moses but under the will of God in its fuller and later expression in "the law of Christ." When the four commandments from the Decalogue are quoted in Rom. 13:9 they have clearly been placed within the *new* framework of Rom. 13:8, 10, which stress that *love* is the fulfilling of the law.[11]

The love of Christ for us controls us and overflows from us toward others when we are filled with *the word of Christ* (Rom 10:17; Eph 5:18, 19; see Col 3:16) and walk in (obey) the Spirit. On God's agape (his love in Christ), Nygren first lists the following Scriptures: 1 Cor 13:5; Rom 15:1–3; Phil 2:21; 2:4, and then says that they show that:

> . . . the Christian has nothing of his own to give; the love which he shows to his neighbor is the love which God has infused into him.[12]
>
> Just as Paul made it his rule "not to know anything save Jesus Christ and him crucified," so he knew *no other love* than that which was inseparably bound up with the Cross of Christ.[13] It is not that he uses Agape as the name of two different things— *God's* love for us and *our* love for our neighbor. When Paul speaks of Agape, he always means the Divine love, never a merely human love. The Christian's love for his neighbor is a manifestation of God's Agape, which in this case uses the Christian, the "spiritual" man, as its instrument.[14]

Finally, Banks says:

> For Paul the gospel bound men and women to one another as well as to God. Acceptance by Christ necessitated acceptance of those whom he already accepted and welcomed (Rom 15:7); reconciliation with God entailed reconciliation with others . . .

---

11. Lincoln, "From Sabbath to Lord's Day," 370.

12. Nygren, *Agape and Eros*, 129.

13. Nygren, *Agape and Eros*, 117, emphasis mine.

14. Nygren, *Agape and Eros*, 129–30. See also Nygren, *Commentary on Romans*, 323–26 and 431–35 on agape in Christ's body.

union in the Spirit involved union with one another, for the Spirit was primarily a shared, not individual experience. The gospel is not a purely personal matter. It has a social dimension. It is a communal affair. To embrace the gospel, then, is to enter into community. One cannot have one without the other.[15]

Lord, help us hear, believe, and apply this truth, through the power of the gospel. Amen.

15. Banks, *Paul's Idea*, 33.

——— SIXTEEN ———

The Apostles' Confession

"Jesus Christ is Lord" was and is the confession of the apostles.

> Therefore, let all the house of Israel know assuredly that God has made this *Jesus*, whom you have crucified, both *Lord and Christ*. (Acts 2:36 NKJV)

> The word which God sent to the children of Israel, preaching peace [with God] through *Jesus Christ—he is Lord*. (Acts 10:36 NKJV)

> And that every tongue should confess that *Jesus Christ is Lord* to the glory of God the Father. (Phil 2:11 NKJV)

> That if you confess with your mouth "*Jesus is Lord*" and believe in your heart that God raised Jesus from the dead, you will be saved. (Rom 10:9)

And, when we compare 2 Cor 4:5, where Paul says, "We preach . . . Christ Jesus as Lord" with 1 Cor 15:1–4, where Paul says that he preached that "Christ died for our sins . . . was buried, and rose again," calling this "the gospel," we realize that "Jesus Christ is Lord" is shorthand for the gospel, because Jesus Christ is victorious Lord over all our enemies, including sin and death. So, all the essentials of "the faith which was once for all delivered to the saints" (Jude 3) are found in this simple confession of the apostles. This confession is completely in accordance with "the simplicity that is in Christ" (2 Cor 11:3); so those who confess Jesus as Lord are those who believe in him and are saved (Rom 10:8, 9; see 1 Cor 12:3). Paul says: No one can say "Jesus is Lord" except by the Holy Spirit (1 Cor 12:3). Since love believes all things, we are to trust that whoever confesses "Jesus is Lord" has the Spirit of Christ and therefore belongs to him (Rom 8:9). Therefore, to not fully accept a person in whom Christ dwells is to reject Christ, who died and rose for that person and to whom that person is joined (1 Cor 6:17). Paul said to the Galatians, "I have confidence in you in the Lord" (5:10); therefore, believers are to have confidence in the one who says, "Jesus is Lord," that the Spirit is in them. To the Romans, Paul wrote:

> Now the God of patience and comfort grant you to be like-minded one toward another *according to Christ Jesus* that you may with one mind [Christ's] and one mouth glorify God, even the Father of our Lord Jesus Christ. Therefore, *receive one another as Christ received us*, to the glory of God. (Rom 15:5–7 NKJV)

Note that in the above text, Paul said "that you may with one mind [the mind of Christ] and one mouth glorify God." By "one mouth" Paul means that they agree, just as he says to the Corinthian saints:

> Now I plead with you, brethren, through the name of our Lord Jesus Christ, that you *all speak the same thing*; and that there be no divisions among you, but that you be perfectly joined together in the same mind and in the same judgment. (1 Cor 1:10 NKJV)

All believers in Christ are to speak the same thing, that is, agree on the apostolic gospel with its doctrine, which they learned (Rom 6:17; 16:17). They can agree, insofar as they have the same mind (Christ's, see Rom 15:5–7), the Christ of the apostolic gospel of God (Roman 1:1), which says that we are justified by Christ's blood (5:9) through faith in Christ (5:1) and that we died with Christ to the sin and the law (Rom 6 and 7) and that Christ died for the elect and intercedes for them (Rom 8:33–34).[1] Paul says to "be like-minded toward one another" (Rom 15:5 NKJV). How are they to do this? "Receive one another, just *as Christ* has received us" (15:7 NKJV). For "*God* has received him" (Rom 14:3 NKJV), through faith in Christ alone (Rom 5:1). Therefore, we are to receive those who differ with us on nonessential matters, as he says in Romans chapter 14. Christ's mind is that we who are in Christ are one in our status before God, for in him there is neither Jew nor gentile, male nor female, slave nor free (black nor white, rich nor poor, conservative nor liberal, meat-eaters nor vegetarians, etc.). We are, in our human spirits, all one in the one Holy Spirit, because the one Spirit of the

---

1. God foreknew (fore-loved) his people (Rom 8:29, 30) and God in Christ died for them (Rom 8:33, 34; Acts 20:28; Eph 5:25–27; John 10:11–16) and indwells them (Rom 8:9).

one living God lives in each believer; therefore, we *are* one (Gal 3:28; 1 Cor 12:12–13). So, we are to keep the oneness of the Spirit by having the attitude of acceptance of one another in Christ (Rom 15:5–7; Eph 4:4-6), while at the same time strive to know the apostolic doctrine of the gospel (Rom 1:1; 6:17; 16:17). Such unity will exist as, having Christ's mind of acceptance of one another, we learn and obey the gospel of God found in Paul's letters, especially and systematically in Romans. The apostolic confession derives from and is a shortened form of the apostolic gospel. So it is not a merely human confession, as are all other creeds and confessions that have come after it! This is the confession of the apostles. Therefore, this confession has *the authority of God in Christ* behind it, that of the gospel given to the apostles who, for all time, laid the foundation, which is Christ (1 Cor 3:10, 11) for the church of God. Thus, the confession is in complete accord with the truth of justification and salvation in Christ alone, by grace alone, through faith in Christ alone. "By grace alone" means that Christ's death procured justification (the imputation of righteousness and the non-imputation of sin and sins)[2] freely for us, apart from anything in us (Rom 3:24; 5:9). And "through faith alone" is simply the corollary to "by Christ alone" and "grace alone," and that faith is a gift freely given by God (Eph 2:8, 9; Phil 1:29). Human confessions inevitably tend to usurp the apostolic confession and thereby cause division in Christ's body; thus they need to be subservient to the apostles' confession. In the gospel of God (Rom 1:1), Paul wrote:

> Now I urge you, brethren, note those who cause *divisions* and offenses, contrary to *the doctrine which you learned*; and avoid them. (Rom 16:17 NKJV)

Therefore, only "the doctrine which you learned" is that which belongs to and is in line with the gospel of God (Rom 1:1—16:27) and does not cause divisions. God's revealed will is that there *not be divisions* among members of an assembly of saints. So, according to Rom 16:17 and 1 Cor 1:10, there can truly be experiential unity in Christ's body to the extent we are of one mind in the gospel of God. And such unity should be the norm.[3] On one hand, the confession "Jesus is Lord" is sufficient for receiving one another *in Christ* (Rom 14:3; 15:5–7). At this point, we can imagine some leaders responding, "But a person can *say* 'Jesus is Lord' and yet be like Arius, who

2. See Rom 4:6, 8.

3. To the extent is it *not* the norm reveals how the church, immediately after the apostles died, departed from the (apostolic) gospel of God in its fullness and how it has never recovered, missing "the simplicity that is in Christ" (2 Cor 11:3). Thus, much of the "unity" in many American churches is more or less a superficial unity, where the unspoken reality is "We just won't talk about doctrine."

denied that Jesus was God—therefore, we need further (human) creeds, like the Nicene Creed and/or other confessions." To this we respond: On one hand, we agree that the Nicene Creed is very clear on Christ's deity. But on the other, Christ's deity *is* declared in the apostolic confession, and love believes all things (1 Cor 13:4–7), including those who confess Jesus as Lord, for those who confess Jesus as Lord do so by the one Holy Spirit of Christ, so in love we can trust that they belong to the one Christ. If we have the Spirit of Christ, we *are* in unity with all who are indwelt by the *one Spirit*, because Christ[4] is one. On the other hand, as we have shown, we need to strive to know (and believe) the apostolic doctrine (Rom 16:17; 1 Cor 1:10) of the gospel. We are free to use human confessions, but only under the authority of the Apostles' Confession (which includes its corresponding doctrine—that of the (apostolic) gospel of God (Romans 1:1).

> So then let no one boast in men [trust in men, with their confessions of faith[5]]. For all things belong to you, whether Paul or Apollos or Cephas or the world or life or death or things present or things to come; all things [including all creeds and confessions[6]] belong to you, and you belong to Christ; and Christ belongs to *God*. (1 Cor 3:21–23 NASB)

Summary

- The apostolic confession "Jesus Christ is Lord" is a shortened version of the gospel.

- The apostolic gospel has corresponding apostolic teaching, which includes its imperatives.

4. Both "Jesus" and "Lord" need to be understood in the light of the gospel of God. In none of the three ecumenical creeds do we find that Christ died for our sins. The Nicene Creed excellently teaches and defends the deity of Christ, but that truth already existed in the Apostles' Confession ("Jesus Christ is Lord"). And the Nicene Creed teaches baptismal regeneration (contra Paul, see my ch. 18) and disobeys Christ in Paul, who says "not to go beyond what is written" (1 Cor 4:6 ESV) when it adds "and the Son" to John 15:26; see Weinandy, *The Father's Spirit of Sonship*, 6–13; 25–104. The so-called Apostles Creed says that Jesus descended into hell (which is really Gehenna), but in truth he descended into the grave (Acts 2:27, 31). Humans think they know better than God, but the Apostles' Confession alone has the authority of God, that is, Christ, behind it.

5. See Phil 3:3 and Rom 4:2, 3, where boasting in is equated with trusting in.

6. Whether Paul or Apollos (or, deducing from Paul): the mature Luther on Galatians, the Canons of Dort, etc., *all things are yours* in Christ (1 Cor 3:22). But they are not to replace the apostolic gospel or its teaching.

- From Paul we have seen that any teaching that differs from the apostles' teaching will cause divisions in the body of Christ and does not glorify God. Those who in smugness reject the gospel's apostolic doctrine will indeed cause divisions, even if they think they are correct in their doctrine. Only the gospel of God glorifies God. We are to accept one another in Christ alone, but such unity will be superficial to the extent that it is not based upon the apostolic gospel with its doctrine. Therefore, in the light of Paul's words, we are to accept one another in Christ, for there needs to be grace toward one another while believers are learning apostolic teaching, while simultaneously striving by grace to keep the unity we already have in Christ through *thinking and speaking the same things*, the things freely given us of God, according to the apostolic gospel with its doctrine, knowing the truth as it is in Jesus. Therefore, all efforts to have unity apart from the truth of the gospel (Gal 2:14) are not of Christ's Spirit.

The Apostles' Confession (Gospel) with Its Doctrine

In the first century, God the Son took on himself a human body and soul— he was fully human without ceasing to be fully God. This is a great mystery (1 Tim 3:16). "Jesus" was the name given to him at his birth, meaning "Yahweh [the LORD] saves." An angel of the Lord said, "You shall call his name Jesus, for he will save his people from their sins" (Matt 1:21 ESV; see v. 20). "Christ" means *Messiah, Anointed One*, for he was anointed with God's Spirit without measure. "YHWH" ("LORD" in most translations) is the covenant name for God in the old covenant scriptures. That Jesus Christ is Lord (Yahweh) refers to the Son of God being very God. The apostles quote the prophet Joel (2:32) who uses the name "LORD" for Jesus—Peter in Acts 2:21 and Paul in Rom 10:13.[7] The Son of God was always the Lord of glory, even when he died on the cross (1 Cor 2:8). On the other hand, based upon what Jesus accomplished in his death, God the Father appointed his Son to the status of Lord over all our enemies that were against us (to destroy us): the wrath of God, the sin, the law, the death, and the authority of Satan. By raising his Son from the dead God gave Jesus the authority to judge the living and the dead on the day of the Lord.[8] God's wrath, sin, the law, death, and Satan with his principalities

---

7. Packer, *God's Words*, 50.

8. "But God raised him on the third day and made him to appear . . . he is the one who has been *appointed* by God to be judge of the living and the dead" (Acts 10:40, 42 ESV; also Acts 17:31); see also my ch. 4.

and powers lorded it over us, that is, had dominion and control over us, before and apart from Christ's redemptive death and his exaltation as LORD and before we came to faith in Christ. Thus, "Jesus Christ is Lord" means that "he must reign [as Lord] until he has put all his enemies under his feet" (1 Cor 15:25 ESV). To have Jesus as one's Lord is to have him as one's savior from sin and death. Paul says, "If you confess with your mouth 'Lord Jesus' and believe in your heart that God raised Jesus from the dead, you shall be saved" (Rom 10:9 AT; see 1:4). That Christ has been raised from the dead by God the Father is the result of our justification in Christ's blood and the proof that we have been justified (which is the imputation of righteousness and the non-imputation of sin, Rom 4:6–8) by Christ's death for us (Rom 4:25 lit.; 8:10; 1 Cor 15:17). Through Christ's death, resurrection, and exaltation for us, the Spirit of the risen Christ indwells us, and he is God's pledge that those in Christ will not perish but be raised bodily with Christ to eternal life and immortality in the age to come. We have this life already now in our spirits but not yet in our bodies.

The apostolic writings, especially 1 Cor 15 and Rom chapters 5 through 8, and John 5:24–29, will in no way allow a literal, thousand-year reign of Christ on this earth,[9] in which there are unbelievers (who are mortal) after Christ comes as exalted Lord and judge, when God's elect "put on immortality" to judge angels and God's enemies are finally destroyed.

The Apocalypse (which is apocalyptic literature and uses figurative language), written by a prophet (Rev 22:7, 10, 18, 19), should not be interpreted apart from the NT scriptures, especially Paul the apostle's writings. The prophet's "first resurrection" (Rev 20:4–6; see 2:10–11) refers to believers who were martyred and are now in heaven, implying that *not until they die* are they resurrected in this "first resurrection," whereas the NT scriptures outside of Revelation teach a *present* resurrection (in the spirit) of believers (Rom 6:4, 23; Col 3:1; Eph 2:5; John 11:25, 26) by regeneration, in this present life. But in Revelation, the "first resurrection" occurs at martyrdom (death). Thus, John's "first resurrection" is distinct from anything else in the NT, as is his millennium. The truth of the spiritual resurrection

9. The apostolic gospel does not allow premillennialism or postmillennialism; see Engelsma, *Millennium*; and Hoekema, *Bible and the Future*, chs. 4–7, 9, 16–20. Jesus reigns as Lord now (1 Cor 15:25). The worst thing about premillennialism is that, by its very nature, it denies the truth that Jesus has been (by God) *appointed Son of God in power*—as *Lord* over all the lords and powers that were aimed at our destruction (the wrath, the sin, the law, and the death [Rom 1:4; chs. 5–8]), thereby freeing us from their *destructive lordship* through Jesus *now* being our Lord*—by placing Christ's reign as (essentially) in a *future* "millennium."

* See Nygren, *Commentary on Romans*, 32, 71–349, 383.

(regeneration) taught in the rest of the NT is prior to (and yet would continue into) John's "first resurrection" in heaven.

Both Jesus and his apostles clearly taught two ages: this age and the age to come (Luke 18:30; 20:30–36; Eph 1:21; Rom 12:2 and 8:17–25; Gal 1:4 and 6:15 and 2 Cor 5:17; 1 Cor 1:20; 2:6 and 15:22–28 and 15:42–57). So, a person lives in this present age with a mortal body, and then in the age to come (at its inception), the elect will be raised as justified saints in immortal bodies and the non-elect will be raised in mortal bodies unto judgment (John 5:29), to be judged with wrath to endure wrath's affliction and anguish (Rom 2:5–10) unto destruction (Matt 10:28; Rom 9:22). *A literal millennium cannot fit into either of these two ages.* The NT scriptures, especially Acts 24:15, 1 Cor 15, Rom 2:5–10, 8:11–39, and John 5:24–29, will not allow a literal thousand-year reign of Christ on this earth, in which there are unbelievers (who are mortal) after Christ comes, that is, after God's elect are made immortal and in which the (supposed) judgment of believers occurs one thousand years before that of the lost. No. At the judgment seat of Christ (God), all humans will be judged according to their works; God's elect will be rewarded for the good (done of the Spirit of God) and will suffer loss for the bad (that done out of the flesh, not on the foundation of Christ) which they have done, which includes all teaching that is not in line with the apostolic gospel of God (Rom 1:1; 2:16; 1 Cor 3:9–15; 2 Cor 5:10). Since his exaltation, Christ has reigned as Lord of God's elect, having delivered them from the lordship of the wrath of God, the sin, the law, and the death (Rom 5, 6, 7, 8) and the authority of Satan (Acts 26:18; Col 1:13); and he will deliver them also in body, at the resurrection from the dead (1 Cor 15:25–28). Since Pentecost, the kingdom (reign) of God is "in the Holy Spirit" (Rom 14:17) of Christ (Rom 8:9–10; Col 1:13).

Christ is the foundation of those in him (1 Cor 3:11; see 1:30). The apostles are *servants*, and not masters, of the Lord (1 Cor 4:1; 2 Cor 4:5). Therefore Jesus Christ is the Lord of the apostles, some[10] of whose words

10. Of a certainty, we have Paul the apostle in his undisputed letters. Regarding the Fourth Gospel, by comparing Mark 14:12–26 with John 13:21–30, it is clear that "the disciple whom Jesus loved" was one of the twelve apostles, even John. Though both here and in the letters of John, he wished to remain anonymous. Johns' gospel is a revelation of the Word and only begotten Son of God—God who took on flesh and is eternal life for all who believe in him. In light of all that Paul says regarding his apostolic authority, it is wise to interpret John's gospel and letters, first, in light of themselves, and ultimately in light of Paul's gospel in his undisputed letters. Regarding the author of 1 Peter, see Boring and Craddock, *People's New Testament*, 724; Elliot, *1 Peter*, 118–38; Achtemeier, *1 Peter*, 1–43; Goppelt, *Commentary on 1 Peter*, 7–52. On 2 Peter's author, see *IB*, 12, 163–65. On the author of Revelation, see my ch. 20, including the footnotes. In light of the gospel, next to Paul's letters, 1 John (despite 1:9) and 1 Peter are the most relevant and helpful letters for those who are indwelt by

found their way into the NT scriptures. Since Jesus is the apostles' Lord, he therefore is Lord of the entire Scriptures.[11] So then, how much more is he Lord of the "confessions" and creeds of mere humans? Therefore, in terms of apostolic authority, all subsequent Christian confessions are under the confession of the apostles: "Jesus Christ is Lord" and its corresponding doctrine. Therefore, we conclude that all merely human creeds should be interpreted in the light of the apostles' confession, with its corresponding apostolic doctrine.[12] It is no wonder that, to the extent that this has not been done, there has been disunity in the church.

---

the Spirit of the risen Christ.

11. One example of applying the apostolic confession—"Jesus Christ is Lord"—is that our *unity is* in *him* alone and not in our views of baptism; as we believe that, we experience unity.

12. Therefore, to the extent that a church/denomination binds its pastors to a confession other than the apostles' confession, to that extent God's authority (behind it) is usurped and rejected. It would be acceptable for the church to say, "Insofar as our confessions are in line with Holy Scripture, especially the apostolic gospel (confession), we hold these confessions to be a true understanding of the Scriptures."

SEVENTEEN

Christ Indwells Redeemed Sons

THE CENTRAL REALITY OF the old covenant was *the law of Moses*, which could not and did not give the Spirit of Christ, due to the weakness of the flesh owned by sin (Rom 8:1–4, 9).

The central reality of the new covenant (testament) is justification through redemption by Christ's blood, through which those called by Jesus Christ are given *the Spirit of Christ* (Rom 1:6; 3:24–25; 1 Cor 11:25; 2 Cor 3:6; Gal 3:13–4; 4:4–7).

> The gospel of God . . . concerning his Son, having come from the seed of David according to the flesh, appointed *the Son of God in Power* according to the Spirit of holiness by the resurrection of the dead: *Jesus Christ our Lord.* (Rom 1:1a, 3–4)

As we have shown, "the Son of God in Power" is "Jesus Christ our Lord" (Rom 1:4). This truth—that God the Father appointed Jesus as Son of God in power (as Lord) through his resurrection from the dead, and the significance of this—has not been sufficiently taught to the church of God.

> This Jesus *God raised up again*, to which we are all witnesses. Therefore, having been *exalted* to the right hand of God, and having received from the Father the promise of the Holy Spirit, He [Jesus] has poured forth this [the Holy Spirit] which you both see and hear. (Acts 2:32–33 NASB)

> Therefore . . . know for certain that *God* has *made* Him both *Lord* and *Christ*—this Jesus whom you crucified. (Acts 2:36 NASB)

Because Jesus became obedient (to God the Father) to his death on the cross, therefore God also has highly exalted him, and given him a name which is above every name . . . that every tongue should confess that Jesus Christ is Lord to the glory of God the Father (Phil 2:8–11 summary). God the Father has now made Jesus what he is: the exalted and victorious Lord over our enemies: condemnation, sin, the law, and death, as taught in Romans, chapters 5 through 8. Thus, the "new testament . . . of the Spirit" (2 Cor 3:6), which Jesus poured out at Pentecost, did not go into effect until Jesus died.

> For where a *will* [or "testament," διαθήκην] is involved, the death of the one who made it must be established. For a *will* [as in *last will and testament: διαθήκην*] takes effect only at death, since it is not in force as long as the one who made it is alive. (Heb 9:17–18 RSV; see 10:1–14; Gal 3:13–22)

Therefore, Jesus, before he died, was under the old covenant (Gal 4:4); it was still in effect.[1] But, upon the death of Jesus, the new testament in his blood (1 Cor 11:25) takes effect for the chosen and is called "the new testament . . . of the Spirit."[2] Those in Christ are the "Israel" (true Israel, Rom 9:6) of whom the prophet (quoted in Heb 8:10) speaks. And in the new covenant, *all* covenant members *know the Lord* (8:11). Therefore, the children of Christ-believers are set apart (1 Cor 7:14), but they are not children of God until they come to faith in Christ (Gal 3:26). Paul wrote:

> Christ has redeemed us out of the curse of the law, having become a curse on our behalf, for it has been written, "Cursed is everyone who has been hung on a tree," in order that the blessing of Abraham [imputed righteousness] might come to the nations through Christ Jesus, in order that we might receive *the promise of the Spirit* through the faith. Brothers and sisters, to give a human example, though it is only a man's will (διαθήκην, "will/testament"), yet when it has been ratified, no one sets it aside, or makes additions to it. Now [with God] the

---

1. Thus, he could only teach the (old covenant) law for life, as we find in Luke 10:25–28; 18:18; Mark 10:17–19; and Matt 19:16, 17. Jesus' answer to the rich man is still, "Go and *do*" in Luke 10:37 NASB, and not "he who believes in me has eternal life" as John's Jesus repeatedly says (John 1:12; 3:16, 18; 5:24; 6:29, 40; 7:39; 8:34; 9:35; 11:25, 26; 20:31)—because John's gospel incorporates post-resurrection-of-Jesus *truth* into his account. It follows, then, that in John's gospel, Christ baptizes (present tense) with the Holy Spirit (John 1:33), because John knows that now, at the time of writing his gospel and until the Lord comes, he *does* give the Spirit; whereas in the Synoptic Gospels (Matt 3:11; Mark 1:8; Luke 3:16; [before Pentecost, Acts 1:4, 5]), it says that Christ *will* (at the then-*future* Pentecost and beyond) baptize with the Spirit.

2. 2 Cor 3:6; see Gal 3:13–14; Heb 8:7–12.

promises were spoken to Abraham and his seed. God does not say, "and to the seeds," as to many, but as to one, "And to your Seed," which is Christ. And I say this: a will (διαθήκην, "testament"), having been previously ratified by God, the law, having come into being four hundred and thirty years after the will/testament, does not annul [the will], so as to abolish the promise. For if the inheritance [the promise of *the Holy Spirit*] is of the law, it is no more of promise; but God has given it to Abraham through promise. (Gal 3:13–18)

God gave the covenant/testament to Abraham in the form of a *promise*, to be fulfilled in Christ. In Heb 9:16–17, the "testament" (διαθήκην), as in "last will and testament," went into effect when Christ died. And the death to which the author of Hebrews is referring is the death of Christ, just as in Gal 3:13–17. Also, "the inheritance" in Gal 3:18 is based upon a will (3:17; see 3:15), a last will and testament. So "the inheritance" came by the death of Christ, which resulted in those for whom Christ died receiving the Spirit through the faith (Gal 3:13–14). So "the inheritance" itself is *the Spirit* of Christ, for the Spirit is eternal life (Rom 8:10). The promise was confirmed by God with an oath (Heb 6:13–18); it *had* to go into effect "when the fullness of the time had come" (Gal 4:4). And it did. According to Heb 6:13, 17, the promise, by God's oath, was made to Abraham. And who are the heirs? Paul answers: "And if you are Christ's, then you are Abraham's offspring, heirs according to promise" (Gal 3:29 RSV). This is because Abraham's seed is ultimately *Christ* (Gal 3:16) and we who are in (union with) him, Gal 3:27, 29. Paul calls the testament of which we have been speaking "the new testament (διαθήκη) in Christ's blood" (1 Cor 11:25). Therefore, the Greek word διαθήκη in the NT scriptures usually means *testament*, as in *last will and testament*. With Hebrews chapter 9 in mind, commenting on Gal 3:15, Luther says:

> For when a man makes his last will, bequeathing his lands and goods to his heirs, and thereupon dies, this last will is . . . ratified by the death of the testator, so that nothing may now be added to it, or taken from it according to all law and equity. Now, if a man's will be kept with so great fidelity, that nothing is added to it or taken from it after his death, how much more ought the last will of God to be faithfully kept, which he promised and gave to Abraham and to his seed after him? For when Christ died, then it was confirmed in him, and after his death the writing of his last testament was opened; that is to say, "the promised

blessing of Abraham was preached among all nations dispersed throughout the whole world."[3]

In other words, "this completed and ratified covenant . . . about Christ" (the Seed, v. 16) "is just the arrangement . . . as to justification by faith to be extended to the Gentiles through the Messiah, which was . . . in the Divine declaration to Abraham."[4] But now, because this justification has come (Gal 3:22–25) through redemption, the Spirit has been placed into our hearts, so we cry "Abba, Father" (Gal 4:4–7). Abraham had the gospel preached to him in the form of a promise (Gal 3:8; Rom 1:1–2). But that promise has now been confirmed (Rom 15:8) and has *come* by the faith of Jesus Christ (Rom 1:1–4; Gal 3:22–25). So there is a difference between God's Spirit being with OT saints (including even with Jesus' disciples before the Christ event and Pentecost)—and those who have the risen Christ living in them by the Spirit based upon redemption. Of the Holy Spirit, Jesus said to his disciples, "But you know him, for he dwells with you and *will be in* you" (John 13:35; 14:17d). By "will be in you," John's Jesus is saying that from Pentecost henceforward the Spirit of the risen Christ would be in them. At the exultation of Jesus, "God made this Jesus, whom you crucified, both LORD and Christ" (Acts 2:36; see Phil 2:5–9). Thus, Peter says that *at Pentecost* he came to *believe* in the *Lord* Jesus Christ. Referring to the gift of the Holy Spirit being given to the gentiles (in Acts 10:44–47), Peter recounts the event and says:

> Then I remembered the word of the Lord, how He said, "John indeed baptized with water, but you shall be baptized with *the Holy Spirit.*" If therefore God gave them the same gift as He gave to us *when we believed on the LORD Jesus Christ*, who was I that I could withstand God? (Acts 11:16–17 NKJV)

Peter could not *believe* on the *Lord* Jesus Christ *until* Jesus was exalted to the status of lordship, when he was "appointed [ὁρίζω] Son of God in Power: Jesus Christ our Lord" (Rom 1:4 b). Thus, Paul says that we (in the new testament of the Spirit) no longer know Christ according to the flesh but according to the Lord, *the Spirit* (2 Cor 3:17)—according to an accomplished *reconciliation* (2 Cor 5:16–21). And that means not (knowing Christ) according to our flesh nor according to Christ's flesh, for neither Christ nor us

---

3. Luther, *Galatians*, 289–90. Commenting on Gal 3:16–18, Luther says, "Here Paul uses a new term and calls the promises of God a testament. A testament is nothing else than a promise, except that it has not yet been revealed but is still only signified. Now a testament is not a law, it is a gift. For heirs do not look for laws . . .; they look for an inheritance from a testament" (*LW* 26:298).

4. Brown, *Galatians*, 59.

(in union with him) are now "in the flesh" (Rom 7:6; 8:9). John the Baptizer lived before the faith of Christ had come; therefore, the Lukan Jesus says:

> For I say to you, among those born of women there is not a greater prophet than John the Baptist; but he who is least in *the kingdom of God* is greater than he. (Luke 7:28 NKJV)

Those *in* the kingdom of God are greater than John the Baptist because only those have the Spirit of the kingdom of God in them. Paul says, "The kingdom of God *is . . . in the Holy Spirit*" (Rom 14:17); and to be "in the Holy Spirit" is to have Christ crucified, risen, and exalted now dwelling in you (Rom 8:9–10). John was not in the kingdom because the kingdom did not come until the King ascended to his throne at God's right hand. This happened when Jesus ascended into heaven (Acts 2:32) and was exalted by God his Father—made both Lord and Christ, as Peter proclaimed on the day of Pentecost:

> This Jesus God raised up, and of that we are all witnesses. Being therefore exalted at the right hand of God, and having received from the Father the promise of the Holy Spirit, He [Jesus] has poured out this that you yourselves are seeing and hearing. For David did not ascend into the heavens, but he himself says: "The Lord said to my Lord, Sit at my right hand, until I make your enemies your footstool." Let all the house of Israel therefore know for certain that *God has made Him both Lord and Christ*, this *Jesus* whom you *crucified*. (Acts 2:32–36 ESV)

Although Jesus was Lord (1 Cor 2:8) before his incarnation, nevertheless, through his death, resurrection and exaltation, Jesus has now been "appointed Son of God in Power" (Rom 1:4); therefore Satan's kingdom no longer has *authority* (ἐξουσία, Acts 26:18; Col 1:13) over those who are in Christ. To be baptized/drenched in and by the Spirit is to be *given* the Spirit of God and of Christ, through which one belongs to Christ (Rom 8:9), and placed into Christ and thus in the body of Christ. Believers are those who have received the Spirit (1 Cor 2:12–16; 6:20–21; Rom 8:1–11; Gal 3 and 4). And Paul says that not all have the gift of speaking in tongues (1 Cor 12:30). Since Jews require signs, God gave Jewish Christians the sign of tongues[5] in order that they might know that the gentiles received the Holy Spirit. "By [the agency of] one *Spirit*, we were all *baptized* into one body—and all were given one *Spirit* to *drink*" (1 Cor

---

5. God gave the *Jews* (who require a sign, 1 Cor 1:22) the sign of tongues (1 Cor 14:22) to convince Christian Jews that gentiles did indeed receive the Holy Spirit (see also Acts 10:34–43; 44–47).

12:13).[6] In Mark's gospel (1:2–4) we find John the Baptist proclaiming a baptism of repentance for the remission of sins:

> And he [John the Baptist] preached, saying, "After me comes he who is mightier than I, the strap of whose sandals I am not worthy to stoop down and untie. I have baptized you with *water*, but he will baptize you with *the Holy Spirit*." (Mark 1:7–8 ESV)

This contrast, between John's baptism in water and Christ's baptism in the Holy Spirit, is set forth in all the Gospels (Mark: see above; Matt 3:11; Luke 3:16; and John 1:31–33). Just before his ascension, Jesus reminds his disciples of "the promise of the Father," regarding the baptism which John the Baptizer prophesied would come:

> And while staying with them, he ordered them [the apostles] not to depart from Jerusalem, but to wait for the promise of the Father, "which," he said, "you heard from me; for John baptized with *water*, but you shall be baptized with *the Holy Spirit* not many days from now." (Acts 1:4b–5 ESV)

Then this Spirit-baptism came—on Pentecost (Acts 2:1–4). And the basis of Christ receiving from the Father the promise of the Spirit is Christ's death and exaltation, whereby God appointed Jesus to be both Lord and Christ (Acts 2:32–36; Phil 2:8–11):

> Therefore [Jesus,] having been *exalted* to the right hand of God, and having received from [God] the Father the promise of *the Holy Spirit*, He has poured forth this [Spirit] which you both see and hear. (Acts 2:33 NASB)

Peter and the eleven *believed* in the now exalted Lord Jesus Christ. But when? At Pentecost (Acts 11:16, 17). Not until then did God give the gift of the Spirit of the risen Christ to them. Peter and the other disciples had the Spirit with them but not yet *in them* before Pentecost (John 14:17). Neither Peter nor anyone else could believe in the Lord Jesus Christ until he was first exalted as Lord to the right hand of God (Acts 2:32–36; see 11:15–17). The baptism with the Holy Spirit (Acts 11:16, 17) is the act of God whereby he *gives* people the Holy Spirit (Acts 15:7b, c, 8–9).

From Pentecost until this day, all those who are baptized by the Holy Spirit—who have received the Holy Spirit—are recipients of "the *firstfruits* of the Spirit" (Rom 8:23, that is, of the risen Christ, 8:11), which began at Pentecost, when "the new testament . . . of the Spirit" (2 Cor 3:6) went

---

6. Both "baptized" and "drink" are metaphors. "Baptized" (drenched) results in *us in Christ*. "Drink" results in Christ/the *Spirit in us*. See also ch. 18.

into effect. These are the "firstfruits" of the age to come, for the Spirit is the down-payment of salvation, the first installment of the Spirit toward the day when the *full* installment of God's kingdom-reign comes, when the spiritual body (1 Cor 15) will be put on, a body fully ruled by the Spirit, whereas now, although the Spirit is life in our (human) spirit, the body (outer man) is (spiritually) dead because of sin (Rom 8:10). When Paul is talking about the whole created order, which "groans and labors with birth pangs . . . until now" (Rom 8:22), he then says:

> And not only they, but we also who have the *first fruits of the Spirit*, even we ourselves groan within ourselves, eagerly waiting for the adoption, the redemption of our body. (Rom 8:23 NKJV)

Just as the risen Christ is the *firstfruits* of those who sleep in Christ, who will one day be raised from the dead by God's Spirit (1 Cor 15:20), even so "the *firstfruits of the Spirit*" (Rom 8:23) of the risen Christ (8:11) means the down-payment of the Holy Spirit himself, given based on Christ's historical resurrection and exaltation. Old covenant saints, including John the Baptist, did not have the "firstfruits of the Spirit' (8:23). Paul says to the Galatians:

> I mean that the heir, as long as he is a child [not yet an adult son], is no different from a slave . . . but he is under guardians and managers until the date set by his father. In the same way we also, when we were children [not yet adult sons of God], were enslaved to the elementary principles of the world. (Gal 4:1–3 ESV)

But now justification through *redemption* has brought the Spirit (4:4–7; see Rom 3:24).

Redemption in Christ enabled us to be adopted, adult sons, for through redemption we were justified before God (Rom 3:24). Paul continues:

> God sent forth this Son . . . to *redeem* those who were under law, so that we might receive adoption as *sons*. And *because* you are *sons*, God has sent *the Spirit of his Son* into our hearts, crying, Abba! Father! So you are no longer a slave, but a son, and if a son, then an heir through God. (Gal 4:4–7 ESV)

Because redemption has occurred by Christ's death, the redeemed are adopted by God. Because they are adopted, God has sent the Spirit of his Son into their hearts. So, by comparing Rom 3:24 with Gal 4:4–7, we learn that we are justified through the redemption in Christ (Rom 3:24) and, because we are justified, we are adopted as sons and, because of adoption, we received the Spirit of adoption, the Spirit who is eternal life (Rom 8:10; 6:23). The Holy Spirit is "the Spirit of God [the Father] who raised Jesus from the dead" (8:11). The Spirit was poured out upon the elect because Jesus redeemed them by his obedience unto death, and therefore God exalted him to the place of lordship over wrath, sin, the law, and death, that he might give the Spirit to his own (John 15:26; Acts 2:32–33; Gal 3:13–14; 4:4–7). Thus, *no one* could have been indwelt by the Spirit of the risen and exalted Christ (received "the *first*fruits of the Spirit," Rom 8:23) until God raised Jesus from the dead. So, John the Baptizer did not receive the promise of the Father (Acts 1:4), whereas all who are in the kingdom of God—who have the promised Spirit—are greater in privilege than John the Baptist. Hebrews says:

> But as it is, *Christ* has obtained a ministry that *is much more excellent* than the old [covenant] as the [new] covenant he mediates is better [than the old covenant], since it is enacted on better promises [which "better promises" in the new testament of the Spirit, 2 Cor 3:6, have *now* gone into effect]. For if the first covenant had been faultless, there would have been no occasion to look for a second. (Heb 8:6–7 ESV)

By "better promises" the author means first and foremost "the promise of the Father"[7] (i.e., of the Spirit, Gal 3:14) which was fulfilled at Pentecost. He then goes on to set forth the blessings of the new covenant (Heb 8:8–12), in which Christ makes the first covenant obsolete (8:13) and provides the fulfillment of the promise of Jer 31:33, where the Lord says, "I will put my laws into their minds and write them on their hearts, and I will be their God, and they shall be my people" (Heb 8:10b, c). This is what Paul refers to when he says that the Corinthians are "an epistle of Christ, ministered by us, written . . . by the Spirit of the living God . . . on tablets . . . of the heart" (2 Cor 3:3). According to Heb 10:1–18, this new covenant blessing of the Spirit is accomplished by Christ's taking away of sins through his one sacrifice. And after the author of Hebrews refers to the faith of some saints in the old covenant era, he writes:

> And all these, having obtained a good testimony through faith, *did not receive the promise*, God having provided something better for us [new covenant saints], that they [old covenant saints] should not be made perfect apart from us. (Heb 11:39–40 NKJV)

The phrase "that they should not be made perfect apart from us" means that the OT saints will not be glorified apart from us, from which we deduce that at *the resurrection from the dead* they will have received the Spirit of adoption

---

7. See also Andrews, *Spirit Has Come*, 73, 74 (and his ch. 4); and Long, *New Covenant Theology*, 73–81.

and the final adoption (Rom 8:23c), including every spiritual blessing of the new covenant (Eph 1:3; see 2 Cor 3:3–18). We will all together come bodily under the power and control of the Holy Spirit of Christ and of God the Father. So, the new testament in Christ's blood and of his Spirit is the fulfillment of the Abrahamic covenant (Gal 3:16, 29; Rom 15:8–12) and of the Mosaic covenant (Heb 8–10). John the Baptizer was not yet an adopted son of God, because the Spirit of the risen Christ was only given to adopted sons of God based on the accomplished redemption.[8]

In summary, now that redemption has been accomplished, and Jesus has been exalted to the place of authority at God's right hand, the Spirit of Christ *indwells* God's elect, for we are one spirit with him. And this *knowing Christ according to the Spirit* is incomprehensibly greater than knowing him (according to the flesh) as his disciples did before Pentecost. For God in Christ lives in us, in such a way that we have been called into the intimate fellowship with God the Father that belongs to the Son, in which also the Spirit guides us into all truth and takes the things of Christ and makes them known to us (John 16:13–16; 1 Cor 1:9; 2:11–16), and in which the Messiah continually leads his people, saying, in a sense, "This is the way: walk in it."

> Jesus Christ first accomplished and entered into immortal life for man by His resurrection from the dead. Christ being raised from the dead, *dies no more, "death has no more dominion over him"* (Rom 6:9). The life into which God raised Jesus Christ was a new kind of life for man, a life never lived before, a life never attainable by anyone else, the highest and best form of life, life that is spiritual, heavenly, incorruptible, immortal (1 Cor 15:45–48). Adam did not have this life; he could, and did, die. Jesus Himself did not have this life before His resurrection; he was "die-able" and he died. In Jesus Christ, and for Jesus Christ's sake, elect men and women share the immortal life of their head and savior in the grace of God.[9]

---

8. This reveals something of the magnitude of the worth of the death of the Son to the Father. But if Christ had not been raised, there would be no justification, adoption, or the Spirit of adoption given to anyone. The sins of God's elect were finally *propitiated* on Christ's cross (Rom 3:25) through which God removed his just wrath from them. There was not "one [body] in Christ" (Gal 3:28) until humans were baptized by the Holy Spirit (1 Cor 12:13; see Acts 1:5; 11:15–17) into Christ's body. The Spirit of Christ has come, who is eternal life, not only to seal us to the day of redemption but to lead and empower us to know and do God's will apart from law; *this* characterizes "the new testament . . . of the Spirit" (2 Cor 3:6; 3:3; Rom 3:21–24; 8:1–23; Gal 4:1–7).

9. Engelsma, "Intermediate State," 134, emphasis mine; Rom 6:9 changed from AV to modern English.

The outcome and fruit of the accomplished redemption is that *we* in the new covenant have the Spirit of the risen Christ (Rom 1:4; 8:11; Gal 3:13–14; 4:4–7) indwelling us. Old covenant saints were not baptized by the Spirit, even though they were regenerated.[10]

10. See also Long, *New Covenant Theology*, 73–81.

—— EIGHTEEN ——

Faith in Christ Alone

IN THE GOSPEL OF *God*, justification by *Christ* alone (his death alone) requires its corollary: justification through *faith* (in Christ) alone.

> Now I declare to you, brethren, the gospel[1] which I preached
> to you, which also you received[2] [believed], in which you also
> stand,[3] by which also you are saved,[4] if you hold firmly the

1. "For I delivered to you as of first importance that [word] which I also received: that Christ died for our sins according to the Scriptures, that he was buried, that he was raised on the third day according to the Scriptures, and that he appeared to Cephas, then to the twelve" (1 Cor 15:3–5). This is the gospel—and it is preached.

2. But following the preaching of the gospel (in Paul's letters and in the preaching in Acts) is the command to believe in the gospel (e.g., Rom 16:25–26; Acts 16:31, etc.) in order to be saved.

3. "Therefore, having been justified by faith, we have peace with God through our Lord Jesus Christ, through whom also we have had the access into this grace [of having been justified] in which we *stand*" (Rom 5:1–2a). Thus, "the gospel . . . in which you *stand*" means "this grace in which we stand" (Rom 5:1). Our standing, our status, before God, is one of having been justified in Christ, i.e., no longer being in Adam (5:12–21).

4. These words continue with the condition of faith, which says, "If you hold firmly [through faith] the word [the gospel] which I preached to you, unless you believed [the word] *in vain*." And to the Galatians Paul writes, "But now . . . why do you turn back again to the weak and miserable rudimentary principles [the law], to which you desire to be in bondage all over again? I fear for you, lest I have labored among you *in vain*" (Gal 4:9, 11). What he means is this: "You are severed from Christ, whoever of you are justified by law, you fell from the grace [from faith]. For we, by the Spirit, out of faith, eagerly expect the [certain] hope of righteousness" (Gal 5:4–5). We were saved (in hope) though faith, and yet we need to remain in faith to be saved; see also "believing" (present tense) in Rom 4:5 and 1 Cor 1:21; and Gal 2:21–3:3, 11, 12 (5:1–5); Col 1:22,

word [the gospel] which I preached to you, unless you believed [the word] in vain. (1 Cor 15:1–2)

Is salvation through faith in Christ alone, or is it through faith in Christ *plus* baptism? In what follows we will demonstrate from Paul's gospel, in his undisputed letters, the truth of the matter. In 1 Corinthians chapter 7, Paul says:

> For the unbelieving husband is sanctified by the wife, and the unbelieving wife is sanctified by the husband; otherwise your children would be unclean, but now they are holy. (1 Cor 7:14 NKJV)

Both the unbelieving spouse and the children are set apart; they are not as the heathen, because either the one spouse (or parent) or the other spouse (or parent) is in Christ, and the other spouse or child are in the believer's household. The apostle distinguishes between the way he uses "sanctified" (set apart) in 7:14, from "saved" in 7:16. Paul leaves no doubt as to whether a child of a believer or spouse of a believer was *saved* through their set-apart ("sanctified") relationship to the believer, for he says to the believer, "For how do you know, O wife, whether you will save your husband? Or how do you know, O husband, whether you will save your wife?" (1 Cor 7:16 NASB). The saint's spouse was not yet saved, and this also applies to any children of the marriage: They are not saved unless and until they believe in Christ. So, this text reveals that each child (regardless of its age) of a Christ-believer who was baptized in household baptism[5] is not thereby regenerated by the act of baptism itself, or Paul would have noted that here. Paul wrote:

> Now I make known to you, brethren, *the gospel* which I preached to you, which *also you received*, in which also you stand. (1 Cor 15:1 NASB)

As noted above, the apostolic norm for preaching is that the gospel, when preached, is followed by words such as this: "Believe in the Lord Jesus Christ and you shall be saved" (Acts 16:31a; see 13:38; Rom 1:17; 10:8–9). In my experience, gospel preaching ending with words like "Believe on the Lord Jesus Christ, and you will be saved" is rarely heard in Lutheran

---

23; Heb 11:38, 39; John 15:4–10. Faith is not a work (Rom 4:5), so there is no boasting (3:27–28). But salvation is wholly God's doing, and, according to Rom 5 and 8:28–39; Phil 1:6; Eph 4:30; 2 Cor 1:22; John 10:26–29; 1 Pet 1:23; 1 John 3:9; 5:18; those who are elect and regenerated will be saved.

5. The apostles baptized the believer's entire household; on this, see Irons, "*Oikos* Formula." Also, in Acts, of the three times in which household baptism is mentioned, only one says that the entire household believed.

and Reformed churches. For example, in a lectionary text such as 1 Cor 1:18–21, the thing preached on and heard would be on the word of the cross being the power of God to salvation (1:18) but not (continuing with) "God was well-pleased . . . to save those who *believe*" (1:21 NASB). But Paul's need to tell people to believe does not deny that they, of themselves, *cannot believe* (which is the fear of confessional Lutherans and Reformed). Could this lack of saying, "You need to receive Christ, to believe on him to be saved" be related to the way most of them (1) have their thinking pre-shaped by their confessions and traditions, and (2) have not considered enough texts such as in 1 Cor 1:17–21—that salvation is by faith in Christ alone, which means apart from baptism (even though the apostles or their coworkers baptized in God's name)? And could this be because Lutherans are taught that their infants are already children of God by baptism?[6] And does this lack exist in most Reformed and Presbyterian churches which hold that, through simply being born of believers, infants are adopted children of God, which adoption baptism seals? For the Reformed tradition has believed that, through simply being born of believers, infants are adopted children of God.[7] Calvin believed this, and his thinking made its

---

6. Luther's view on baptism goes back to Augustine, influenced by him. On the plurality of influences on Luther regarding what became his view of baptism, see Preus, *Theology to Live By*, 190. At times Luther said that infants have faith to justify infant baptism; see Ferguson, *Baptism in the Early Church*, 810–11. To Luther's words regarding baptism with water, "faith must have something on which to cling" (LC), we believe that Paul's response would be "God forbid that I should glory [trust] except in *the cross of our Lord Jesus Christ*" (Gal 6:14a; see Phil 3:3 and Rom 4:2–3, where *to boast* in means *to trust in*; also pertinent are 2 Cor 13:5 and 1 Cor 1:17, 21).

7. See Beisner, *Auburn Avenue*, 93, 191, where John Calvin himself is quoted as having taught this. The Reformed read baptism *into* Rom 4:11 (teaching that baptism is the NT circumcision) but it is not there. The Scriptures never call baptism "a sign of the covenant." What follows is what Paul the apostle says about signs.

"For Jews ask for *signs*, Greeks seek after *wisdom*, but we preach *Christ crucified*; a *stumbling block to* Jews, and foolishness to Greeks, but to those who are *called*, both Jews and Greeks, *Christ* is the power of God [unto salvation] and the wisdom of God" (1 Cor 1:22, 23).

What many miss here is that Paul is saying that *signs* are *antithetical* to *the gospel*. This aligns with the words of Jesus in Matt 12:38–40, that a sinful generation seeks a sign. John the Baptist's baptism (not Christian baptism, see Acts 19) was a sign to the Jews (John 1:33 and 1 Cor 1:22). The flesh seeks signs, but God will not give the flesh what it desires. Instead, God gives *Christ crucified*, who saves those who *believe* (through faith alone, 1 Cor 1:21) for we walk by faith and not by sight (2 Cor 5:7). So, to the extent that anyone calls baptism a "sign," they are living in the old covenant. Paul says signs are for unbelievers and not for believers: "Therefore, tongues are for a sign, *not* to those who believe, but to unbelievers; but prophesying is not for unbelievers but for those who believe" (1 Cor 14:22). But the Reformed insist that baptism is "a sign of the covenant" without scriptural proof.

way into the Heidelberg Catechism, in Q. & A. 74, which says, "*Infants* as well as adults are in God's covenant and *are his people. They* are promised the forgiveness of sin through Christ's blood and the Holy Spirit who produces faith."[8] But this can be understood as saying that believing adults and their children (irrespective of their children's faith or unbelief) are given an *unconditional promise* by God that they will be saved. No. The Scriptures say that *the promise*—of the forgiveness of sins and the gift of the Holy Spirit—is for those who repent (Acts 2:38[9]), which includes faith.

> For the promise[10] [of the forgiveness of sins and the gift of the Spirit] is to you [Jews] and to your children, and to all [adults and children] who are afar off [among nations], as many as the Lord our God may *call*. (Acts 2:39)

"As many as the Lord our God may call"—as many as God calls (chooses, 1 Cor 1:24–30).

This last phrase, "as many as the Lord our God will call" (2:39), is omitted in the (Reformed) Heidelberg Catechism. It is only referenced to in the footnotes ("Acts 2:38–39"). But only those called by God will receive the Holy Spirit unto life. Thus, God never gave an unconditional promise to Abraham, or Isaac, or any believer that his or her children would be accounted righteous (saved) by God. Paul, in Rom 9:7–24, bears this out. So, when it comes to this text: "Now I make known to you, brethren, *the gospel* which I preached to you, which *also you received*, in which also you stand, by which also you are saved" (1 Cor 15:1–2 NASB), Reformation churches have preached the gospel but have been weak on telling their hearers that they need to *receive* (by faith, believe[11]) the gospel (1 Cor 15:1b). On the

---

8. See *ECRC*, 44, emphasis mine. For an updated version, see https://www.crcna.org/welcome/beliefs/confessions/heidelberg-catechism.

9. Acts 2:38 (including its baptism) must be interpreted in light of the knowledge of God's glory in Christ (2 Cor 4:6), that is, Paul's (not Luke's) gospel (Gal 1:11–12), as this chapter demonstrates.

10. "For the promise to Abraham and his seed [Gal 3:29], that he would be heir of the [new] world . . . was through . . . . faith [not faith plus circumcision or baptism]. Because of this, it [the promise] is of faith, that it may be according to grace . . . to those [Jews] who [not only are circumcised, natural Jews, but] also are of the faith of Abraham, who is the father of us all [Jews and Gentiles who believe, Rom 4:9–16] (Rom 4:13, 16).

11. Paul, the apostle to the nations, consistently preached that salvation from sin and death is through faith (believing) in Christ: "The gospel . . . is the power of God for salvation to everyone *believing*" (Rom 1:16); "even a righteousness from God through the faith of Jesus Christ to all and upon all those *believing*" (Rom 3:22) "a man is justified by *faith*, apart from works of the law" (3:28). "Abraham *believed* God, and it was accounted to him for *righteousness*" (4:3b). "But to the one not working, but *believing*

other hand, evangelical churches have not neglected to say of the gospel, that "you need to receive it" as the apostles did. But often thereafter the *gospel* (that Christ died to remove our sins, to justify us—and he did) is *assumed*. And the gospel assumed is the gospel denied.

In Paul's gospel of God, *faith* (in Christ) *alone* (1 Cor 1:21) aligns with "the simplicity that is in Christ" (2 Cor 11:3). So, the Reformation's slogan "faith alone" was indeed in line with the apostolic gospel. In line with that, the truth about Mark 16:16—that it was not in the original Gospel of Mark—supports what Paul says in 1 Cor 1: 17 and 21. The Reformers, Luther[12] and Calvin,[13] use Mark 16:16, which says, "He that believes and is baptized will be saved." This text—over against the apostolic word in 1 Cor 1:17–21—greatly influenced Luther and Calvin in their views on baptism. But now we can know from textual evidence that what is authentic in Mark's Gospel is Mark 1:1 through 16:8—not Mark 16:16. The Roman Catholic Church uses Mark 16:16 to say that their church, with their baptism, is necessary for salvation.[14] The original ending of Mark, if there was one, was lost. Mark 16:16 was not in the original Gospel of Mark at all, but was added later.[15] The truth on this issue rightly allows and enables

---

. . . his faith is counted for *righteousness*" (4:5). "Having been *justified* by *faith*, we have peace with God (5:1); "the Gentiles . . . attained to righteousness, even the *righteousness which is of faith*" (9:30–32). "For Christ is . . . for *righteousness* to everyone who *believes*" (10:4). "That if you . . . *believe* in your heart that *God raised Jesus from the dead*, you will be saved. For with the heart, one *believes* unto righteousness" (10:8–10). "Not having my righteousness, the one of law, but [having] the one of the faith of Christ—the righteousness of God bestowed on *faith*" (Phil 3: 8d, 9); "even we *believed into Christ Jesus, that we might be justified*" (Gal 2:16). "Did you receive the Spirit by the works of the law, or by the hearing of *faith*? . . . He therefore supplying the Spirit to you, and working works of power among you, does he do it by the works of the law, or by the hearing of *faith*? Even as Abraham *'believed* God, and it was reckoned to him for righteousness.' Know therefore, that those who are of *faith*, these are sons of Abraham" (Gal 3:2, 5, 6, 7) ". . . in order that we might receive the promise of the Spirit through *faith*." (Gal 3:14) "In order that the promise, by the faith of Jesus Christ, might be given to those *believing*. So that the law has become our supervisory-guardian up to Christ, in order that out of *faith* we might be justified. For you are all sons of God through *faith* in Christ Jesus." (Gal 3:22, 24, 26) "It pleased God through the foolishness of the proclamation to save those who believe" (1 Cor 1:21).

12. LC, 4.5, 6, 31; and SC, 4.7, 8.

13. *ICR*, 4, ch. 15, n1.

14. See CCC, sect. 846.

15. See Bible Research, "Ending of Mark"; Boring, *Mark*, 448–53; Byrne, *Costly Freedom*, 261–62; Comfort, *New Testament Text*, 157–63; Gould, *Mark*, 299–309; Gundry, *Mark*, 1016–21; Streeter, *Four Gospels*, 333–60; Stein, *Mark*, 727–38; Spivey and Moody Smith Jr., *Anatomy of the New Testament*, 91–92; NA26, 44 (defining what double brackets mean), and 147–49.

the risen Jesus Christ in Paul (2 Cor 13:3; Gal 1:11–12 and 1 Cor 1:17–21) to speak clearly to us today.[16] Note the following contrast between Mark 16:16 and the apostolic gospel.

He who believes *and is baptized* will be *saved*; but he who does not believe will be condemned. (Mark 16:16 NKJV)	For Christ sent me, *not to baptize*, but to *preach the gospel* . . . For since, in God's wisdom, the world through [its] wisdom did not know God, God was well-pleased through the proclamation [the gospel] to *save those who believe* (1 Cor 1:17, 21).

For the apostle Paul, it is not "he that believes and is baptized," because God "saves those who believe" in Christ. Therefore, since "faith alone" is God's corollary to "Christ alone" (justification/salvation by *Christ's death alone*), this adds even more proof to the textual evidence (see above footnote) that Mark 16:16 was added to Mark's Gospel. But Paul's apostleship is from God and Jesus Christ his Son (Gal 1:1). And thus, Paul's "my gospel" (Rom 2:16) "is not according to man" (Gal 1:11), and that undoubtedly includes the man who added 16:16 to Mark's Gospel, an addition that contradicts Paul the apostle, both in his letters and in his preaching in Acts.

Excursus 7: Paul's Antithetical "Not . . . But(s)"

Paul's frequent antitheses are often marked with the words: "not . . . but. . ." For example, Paul did *not* receive the gospel from man . . . *but* (instead) Paul received it and was taught it through a revelation of Jesus Christ (Gal 1:11–12). What follows are some of these gospel antitheses from Romans (AV/AT):

- ". . . for not the hearers of the law are justified, but the doers of the law" (2:13)

- "For he is *not* a Jew who is one outwardly . . . *but* he is a Jew who is one inwardly . . . and his praise is *not* from men, *but* from God" (2:28–29).

- "*Not* by a law of works, *but* through a law of faith" (3:27).

- "But to the one who does *not* work, *but* [instead] believes on the God justifying the ungodly" (4:5).

- "How then was righteousness reckoned to him? *Not* in circumcision, *but* in uncircumcision" (4:10).

- "For the promise to Abraham . . .was *not* through the law, *but* through the righteousness of faith" (4:13).

- "[He] did *not* decide against the promise of God by unbelief, *but* was strong in faith" (4:20).

16. Regarding Acts 2:38, Peter's gospel was to the Jews (Gal 2:2–9). The Book of Acts was not written by an apostle; only Paul is the world-apostle (Rom 11:11–13).

- "Likewise reckon yourselves to be dead [*not* alive] to sin, *but* alive to God through Jesus Christ our Lord" (6:11).

- "For sin shall *not* have dominion over you, for you are *not* under law, *but* [you are] under grace" (6:14)

- ". . . because we are *not* under law, *but* under grace?" (6:15) "so that we serve *not* in oldness of the letter [law] *but* in newness of the Spirit" (7:6) "who walk, *not* according to the flesh, *but* according to the Spirit" (8:4).

- "*But* you are *not* in the flesh, *but* in the Spirit" (8:9).

- "For you did *not* receive the spirit of bondage . . . *but* you received the Spirit" (8:15).

- "*But* hope that is seen is *not* hope . . . *But* [rather] if we hope for what we see *not*, then do we with patience wait for it" (8:24b–25).

- "We do *not* know what we should pray for . . . *but* the Spirit makes intercession" (8:27).

- "For they are *not* all children [of God]" (9:8) "*but* 'through Isaac your seed will be named'" (9:7).

- "It is *not* the children of the flesh who are children of God, *but* the children of promise" (9:8), "that . . . election might stand, *not* of works, *but* of him that calls" (9:11).

- "So, then it is *not* of him what wills, or of him that runs [works], *but* of God" (9:16).

- "The Gentiles, who followed *not* after righteousness, attained righteousness; *but* Israel has *not* attained to righteousness . . . because they sought it *not* by faith, *but* . . . by works" (9:30–31); ". . . a zeal for God *but not* according to knowledge" (10:2).

- "I was found by them who sought me *not*" (see 3:11; 4:5) ". . . *but* to Israel he says . . ." (10:20–21).

- "*But* if it is by grace, it is *not* any longer based on works" (11:6).

- "Israel has *not* obtained that which he seeks for, *but* the election has obtained it" (11:7).

- "Be *not* conformed to this world, *but* be transformed" (12:2).

- "*Not* in rioting and drunkenness . . . *not* in strife and envying, *but* [instead] put on the Lord Jesus Christ" (13:13, 14).

- "For the kingdom of God is *not* eating and drinking, *but* righteousness, peace, and joy in the Holy Spirit" (14:17).

Therefore, when Paul says:

> For Christ sent me *not* to baptize, *but* [rather], to preach the gospel, *not* with wisdom of [human] words, [*but* with (divine)

words taught by the Spirit[17]], lest *the cross of Christ [the gospel]* be made of no effect (1 Cor 1:17)

. . . he is saying that, apart from (faith in Christ through) *the gospel, baptism* is just as ineffectual to save sinners as the wisdom of (mere) *human words* are to save sinners. In 1:17, both the wisdom which is expressed in merely human words and baptism are contrasted with *the preached gospel*, which is *God's word* and is thus effective to save sinners. There is no getting around the fact that this is what Paul says in 1:17; yet this truth has been missed in the Lutheran, Reformed, and Anglican churches with their "word and sacrament," primarily because of Augustine's heavy catholic–sacramental[18]

17. "which things also we speak, *not* in *words* taught from human wisdom, *but* in those [*words*] *taught by the Holy Spirit*, communicating spiritual things by [means of] *spiritual words* [that is, Spirit-taught words, such as Christ, justified, grace, faith, etc.]" (1 Cor 2:13).

18. *The Lord's Supper* differs from baptism in this regard—see below on the Supper. And regarding the original text of Matt 28:19, the words "baptizing them in the name of the Father, and of the Son and of the Holy Spirit" were *absent* in the Greek text that Eusebius used in the many places where he quotes Matt 28:19. Matthew's original text reads as follows:

All authority in heaven and on earth was given to me; go therefore, and disciple all the nations *in my name*, teaching them to keep all things which I have commanded you.

See Hastings, *Encyclopedia of Religion*, 380; Eusebius, *Proof*, and/or "Everlasting Gospel." This is in line with Jesus using "in my name" elsewhere in Matthew: see Matt 1:21, 25; 7:22; 18:5, 20; 24:5 (compare Luke 24:47). All honest scholarship has shown that the "baptizing" and trinitarian words were *added* no earlier than the second century. And the great commission in Luke 24 has nothing of baptism in it. In Christ dwells all the fullness of the Godhead bodily (Col 2:10 AV). The apostles believed in the God revealed in Christ—one triune God, in which each person in the Godhead fully shares the *one* divine nature: Matt 3:16, 17; 1 Cor 12:4–6; 2 Cor 13:14; Rom 1:1–4; 8:11; 8:15–17; 15:16; Acts 2:32, 33; John 14:16, 17, 26; 15:26 (Gen 1:26; 18:1–5). These Scriptures are sufficient to show the truth of the one triune God in three persons, each fully sharing one divine nature. Thus, Matt 28:19 is not needed to do so. Because in not one, but five places, in the NT scriptures we find baptism in (or into) "the name of our Lord Jesus Christ," a statement in the WCF can and should be rightly applied to the *one* and only use of the triune God's name in relation to baptism, that in Matt 28:19. It says, "The infallible rule of interpretation of Scripture is Scripture itself: and therefore, when there is a question about the true and full sense of any Scripture (which is not manifold, but one), it must be searched and known by other places that speak more clearly" (*WCF* 1.9). The "more clearly" here are the following texts: 1 Cor 1:13; Acts 2:38; 8:16; 10:48; 19:5, where we find that the apostles, in obedience to Christ as Lord (Acts 1:1, 2), baptized people "into the name of Jesus Christ" for "there is no other *name* under heaven given among humans whereby we must be saved" (Acts 4:12 AT). "Most scholars think that Matthew's church had developed and adopted a 'Father, Son, Holy Spirit' for their own baptismal liturgy, and that Matthew read back this feature of their worship into Jesus' words to the disciples" (Long, *Matthew*, 327); see also Keck, *Proclamation*

influence on Luther and Calvin. In 1 Cor 2:13, Paul contrasts the wisdom of merely human words with words taught by *the Spirit*, who reveals that Christ is the wisdom of God in 1:24. In the light of 1 Corinthians chapter 2, the contrast in 1:17 is that of humans, with their words, versus *God*, with *God's words*, which Paul uses in his preaching. Thus, God's weakness in Christ crucified is stronger (in terms of being able to *save*) than human strength in whatever form (1:25). Again, merely human words of wisdom would make God's word of the cross (1 Cor 1:17–18) of no effect to save. God inspired Paul to put human words of wisdom and baptism with water on the same level when he says that neither of them saves, contrasting both with the gospel—and that believed, which alone saves from sin and death (1:18, 21). Paul, as an apostle, was sent not to baptize but to preach the gospel, which saves those who believe (1 Cor 1:17, 21). He is not only saying that "others can baptize, I was sent to preach." He is saying that only the gospel, and that believed, saves. Later in this letter the apostle says, "For though you have ten thousand instructors in Christ, yet you have not many fathers: for in Christ Jesus, I have begotten you through the gospel" (4:15b NKJV)—not through baptism. So, the fact that not only Hitler but millions of others who were baptized as infants (whether in Orthodox, Roman Catholic, Anglican, or other churches) never came to believe in Christ and confess Christ as Lord (Rom 10:8–9) fully coincides with the apostle's words in 1 Cor 1:17–21. Note again the contrasts in Paul's important words in the following text:

For Christ sent me not to baptize, not with wisdom of [human] words be made of no effect.	but to preach the gospel, [but with divine words taught of the Spirit, 2:13] lest the cross of Christ
foolishness to the ones perishing,	For the word of the cross is but to us who are being saved it is the power of God. (1 Cor 1:17–18 NKJV)
the world, through [its] wisdom did not know God,	For since, in the wisdom of God, it pleased God through the foolishness of the message preached to save those who believe. (1 Cor 1:21 NKJV)

Commentaries, 55. Martin Luther knew that baptism "in the name of Jesus Christ" was apostolic practice and fully acceptable; see *LW* 36:63. But most Protestants have not followed him (or Paul) in this freedom but remained with Rome, contra the above (five) texts. In light of the "eyewitnesses" of Luke 1:2, we should consider Luke's version of the great commission (Luke 24:46–53) as legitimate. My sons, at ages three and one, were baptized in the name of Jesus Christ and both are still trusting in him.

Notice that the phrases "the gospel," "the cross of Christ," "the word of the cross" and "the message preached" are all the same reality—the gospel. Again, we find that, in the left column, "baptism," in light of the gospel, is placed in the same category as that of "the wisdom of [mere] human words," of "foolishness," and "the world's wisdom," through which they did not know God, precisely because *none* of these is *the gospel*, which Paul (in 2:13) says are God's Spirit-taught words, which alone are able to *save* the ones believing (1:21). Therefore, we submit that "not to *baptize*" (βαπτίζειν) in 1 Cor 1:17 cannot be "the baptism" (τοῦ βαπτίσματοσ) of Rom 6:4, which unites with Christ, according to Rom 6:5. Charles Hodge says it well:

> The gospel is thus efficacious . . . to everyone that believes, not to everyone who is circumcised, or baptized, or who obeys the law, but to everyone who believes, that is, who receives and confides in Jesus Christ as he is offered in the gospel.[19]

Justification by *Christ* alone—that is, Christ's death alone—requires its corollary: justification through *faith* (in Christ) *alone, for* only *faith is not a work* (Rom 4:5).

For even though, in Luther's view, baptism is not considered as a human work (but a divine work)—for Paul, the only thing that is not a human work is believing (4:5). If justification is not through faith alone, then it is some act of man that contributes to one's justification. This is the apostle Paul's consistent "theology of the cross." And Dunn says:

> Finally, we may note that in Acts Christians are called "those who have believed in the Lord," and "those who call upon the name of the Lord," but never "the baptized." The essential characteristic of the Christian and that which matters on the human side is in the last analysis faith and not water-baptism.[20]

19. Hodge, *Romans*, 28. John the Baptizer was regenerated even in his mother's womb, and some infants trusted God (Ps 22:9–10); see Matt 18:4 NRSV, which refers to "infants" as "these little ones who *believe*" (18:6 NRSV). Thus, some infants do trust God, *if* God has regenerated them. But these things prove neither the Lutheran nor the Reformed view of baptism, with their multi-worded theologies of baptism, neither of which correspond with "the simplicity that is in Christ" (2 Cor 11:3; see 1 Cor 1:17–21). Yes, God works in families, but the bottom line is that the elect will be saved (see Rom 9:7–16). The claim that baptism (in water) gives the Holy Spirit is proved wrong by Acts 10, where they received the Spirit and after that were baptized; but this error comes from interpreting "baptized" in Rom 6 and Gal 3 literally, whereas it is a metaphor, as is "put on" in Gal 3:27 and "grown together" in Rom 6:5.

20. Dunn, *Baptism in the Holy Spirit*, 96. Dunn's book was written years before he fell into the "New Perspective on Paul" movement.

Contrary to calling believers "the baptized," Paul calls them οἱ ἐκ πίστεως, "the ones of *faith*" (Gal 3:9).

Paul would not say, as did Luther, that "faith needs something on which to cling,"[21] for Paul says, "God forbid that I should boast [trust] except in the cross of our Lord Jesus Christ" (Gal 6:14), for what one boasts in is that which he trusts in—see Phil 3:3; Rom 4:2–3. Paul's way of assuring the saints at Corinth that they are not reprobate is this: Christ is in them (2 Cor 13:5).

Excursus 8: "The Baptism" of Romans 6:4

In 1 Cor 1:13(–16), Paul clearly infers that the Corinthian saints were baptized into (εις) the name of Christ, which refers to their Christian baptism in water. This same language is also used regarding Christian baptism in water in Acts 8:16; 10:48; and 19:5. Because "the name" of Jesus Christ means Christ himself, it appears that this baptism is identical to "the baptism" of Rom 6:[3], 4, where Paul says to the Roman believers, "As many of us as were *baptized into Christ Jesus* were baptized into His death" (6:3 NKJV). So, we do understand the strength of this argument (we held it for years)—that the baptism in Rom 6:3–4 is Christian water baptism. Thus, Anglicans, along with Lutherans (and Catholics), use this argument to support their view of baptism. Paul says that we were buried with Christ (and thus died with Christ, 6:5) "through baptism." Therefore, "the baptism" in 6:4, whatever kind it is, does *unite us to Christ*, as is evident from Paul's words in Rom 6:5.

The proclaimed gospel, as Lutherans say, is a totally outside-of-us act. In response, we say, "Yes, but then, the gospel does not need *another* outside-of-us act like baptism, in order to *not* originate within *us*. It originates in God, and the outside-of-us word of faith, which is preached, is near us, in our mouth and in our hearts (Rom 10:8); but only those who are called by God believe in Christ (1 Cor 1:21–29)." We know that baptism in water is not called a "work" in Scripture, but that does not make it God's act unto salvation. And people were baptized with the Holy Spirit (received the Spirit unto life) *before* they were baptized in water (Acts 10:44–48; see 11:14–18). Also, the idea of a saving complex of repentance/faith/baptism, as taught by some scholars, cannot align with Paul's words in 1 Cor 1:17–21, for baptism is not intrinsically attached to the repentance that belongs to faith.

Because this (Catholic/Lutheran/Anglican) saving view of baptism is ultimately inconsistent with justification through faith in Christ alone, which Paul teaches in his letters, we will offer a different interpretation of Rom 6:3–5, which accords with the truth of justification through faith in Christ

21. BC-T 8.28–29, 440.

alone, especially because of what Paul teaches in 1 Cor 1:17–21, as explicated above, but also because of the Greek definite article, which is not translated in most Bible translations. Now "the baptism" (lit.) in Rom 6:3–4 *saves*, by uniting us with Christ (6:5). So, while we acknowledge that our view—that there is no water in the baptism of Rom 6—has not been the dominant view of the church, neither was the truth that Christ was fully *God* the dominant view of the church (including the bishops) in the time of Athanasius, which is why he battled the heresy of Arius and was often rejected by the church while doing so. Similarly, the truth of justification through faith in Christ alone was, for the most part, lost in the church after Paul died (inferred in Paul's prophecy in Acts 20:29–30) until the Reformation. In both Rom 6:3 and Gal 3:27, the words "were baptized" are in the Greek passive voice, which means that "the baptism" (Rom 6:4) in these texts was *done to* us by God; that is, we *passively received* it. Thus, "the baptism" in these texts is not work which humans do, not even an act of obedience to God, as evangelicals usually call it (as if their being baptized as believers somehow counts before God). But what we just said about the human passivity in "the baptism" (which includes the fact that it is God's uniting–us–with–Christ act) of Rom 6:4–5 eliminates views where baptism is *only* a *sign* of our death, burial, and resurrection with Christ. This leaves us with the Catholic (similarly, Lutheran and Anglican) view, which teach that the baptism in Rom 6 is Christian baptism in water that does unite us with Christ. We acknowledge that many scholars hold this view.[22] But *we also* believe that this baptism does *unite us* with Christ, but that God does it by his Spirit, independently of water; for only such a view is consistent with (salvation through) faith in Christ alone. Thus, either the (above-mentioned) Catholic, etc., view is correct, or the view which we set forth here is apostolic (correct). This view is also held by John Brown,[23] Dr. D. Martyn Lloyd-Jones,[24] others,[25] and myself. Paul wrote:

22. See, for example, Elliot, *1 Peter*, 672–76.

23. On the words "*baptized into Christ*" in Gal 3:27, the Presbyterian says, "We cannot understand the apostle's words as applying to all who, either in infancy or mature age, have undergone the rite of Christian baptism, for they are not true of them all. They plainly refer to those who have received the doctrine of Christ, who 'by one Spirit have been baptized into one body, and have been made to drink into one Spirit' (1 Cor 12:13); who are saved by the washing of regeneration, which is not baptism, 'and'—even 'the renewing of the Holy Ghost' (Tit 3:5). The baptism here spoken of is the "one baptism" which belongs to those who have one God and one Lord—one Spirit, one faith, one hope. It is that of which external baptism is the emblem" (Brown, *Exposition of Galatians*, 74).

24. See Lloyd-Jones, *Exposition of Chapter Six*, ch. 3; and/or the quotes from him in my ch. 9.

25. Some of these others include Puritan John Owen, who wrote, "For by the Spirit

> For *by one Spirit* we were all baptized into one body. (1 Cor
> 12:13a)

The context of 1 Cor 12:13 is important in determining how the Greek
word εν should be translated in 12:13. We shall argue that the Greek word
εν—according to how it is used in its context, should be translated as "by"
in 1 Cor 12:13. Paul uses the Greek εν twice in 1 Cor 12:9 where the Spirit of
God is the agent *by* whom the Spirit's gifts come and in 12:8, where he says
that "through the Spirit," the Spirit is the agent through whom the spiritual
gifts come. Both 12:8 and 9 show that *the Spirit* is the agent *by whom* they
come. In what follows, note that "Spirit," "Lord," and "God" are used interchangeably in 12:4–6, for there is *one* God—for there is *union*, and not only
distinction, between the three persons in the *one God*.

> 3 No one can say, "Jesus is Lord," but *by* [εν] the Holy Spirit.
> 4 Now there are various kinds of gifts, but the same *Spirit*. 5
> There are various kinds of service, and the same *Lord*. 6 There
> are various kinds of workings, but the same *God*, who works
> all things in all. 7 But to each one is given the manifestation of
> *the Spirit* for the profit of all. 8 For to one is given through *the
> Spirit* the word of wisdom, and to another the word of knowl-
> edge, through the same *Spirit*; 9 to another faith, *by* [εν] *the
> same Spirit*; and to another, gifts of healings, *by* [εν] *the same
> Spirit*. . . 11 But *the* one and the same *Spirit works* all of these
> [gifts], distributing to each one separately as he [the Spirit of
> God] desires. . . 13 For *by* [εν] *one Spirit* [of Christ] we were all
> *baptized* into one body, whether Jews or Greeks, whether bond-
> slave or free; and one Spirit we were all *given* to *drink*. 14 For
> the [human] body is not one member, but many [members] . . .
> 18 But now *God* has *set* the members, each one of them, in the
> [one] body, just as he desired. (12:3b–14, 18)

Notice that the Spirit (v. 3, v. 12) and God (v. 18) are used interchangeably,
and that εν is rightly translated as "by" in 12:3, 9, 13. Thus, he means "by
[the agency of] one Spirit we were baptized into one body."

---

are we baptized into the death of Christ" (*Works*, 6:86;) and Unger, in *Baptizing Work*,
7, 15–18, 33–34, 39, 41–47, 50–54, 62; 78–99. However, unlike Unger, neither Lloyd-
Jones nor myself are dispensationalists, nor is Gaffin Jr., who interprets the baptism
of 1 Cor 12:13 as being that of *the Spirit*, by which/whom we receive the Holy Spirit,
thereby giving this baptism its rightful importance; see Gaffin Jr., *Perspectives on Pentecost*, 21–24; 29–31. "By the *Spirit*" (1 Cor 12:13) means not by water, yet "by *God's*
doing" (1:29–30, "*His*" in NASB).

Next, the extent to which the apostle used metaphors[26] has not been sufficiently understood or taught. For example, in 1 Cor 12:13, both "baptized" and "drink" are metaphors that Paul used for *spiritual* realities: "baptized" (12:13) refers to being *placed* (12:18 NASB) *into Christ* and his body. And "to drink of one Spirit" means *to receive* the Spirit of Christ into us; for Christ is now in us (Rom 8:9-10). And in John's Gospel, "drink" is likewise used as a metaphor for *receiving* God's life, the Spirit—see John 4:14 and 7:37-39. So, by "we were all given one Spirit to drink" (v. 13d), he means we were given the Holy Spirit (John 4:14; 7:37-39). The Lord Jesus is the last Adam, the life-giving Spirit (1 Cor 15:45). Christ is the author of this baptism (see Acts 2:32-33; and Mark 1:7, 8; Acts 1:5; 11:15-17) which issues in newness of life (Rom 6:4; see 2 Cor 3:6). Paul says, "Now the Lord is the Spirit" (2 Cor 3:17). Therefore, *the Spirit* is the agent by which the Lord Christ delivers all the benefits of the new testament in his blood (1 Cor 11:25); thus, it is called the "new testament . . . of the Spirit" (2 Cor 3:6). Commenting on 1 Cor 12:13, Charles Hodge writes:

> The church is one, *for* by one Spirit we were all baptized into one body. The word is not in the present tense, but in the aorist. "We *were*, by the baptism of the Spirit, constituted one body." This is commonly, and even by the modern commentators, understood of the sacrament of baptism; and the apostle is made to say that by the Holy Ghost received in baptism we were made one body. But the Bible clearly distinguishes between baptism with water and baptism with the Holy Ghost.[27]

Below, when Hodge refers to "this present passage," he means 1 Cor 12:13; but first he refers to Matt 3:11; John 1:33; and Acts 1:5, of which he says:

> These passages not only distinguish between the baptism of water and the baptism of the Spirit, but they disconnect them. The baptism to which Acts 1:5 refers took place on the day of Pentecost, and *had nothing to do with the baptism of water*. . . . And in the present passage there does not seem to be even an allusion to water baptism, any more than in Acts 1:5. Paul does not say that we are made one body by baptism, but by the baptism of the Holy Ghost . . . Any communication of the Holy Spirit is called a baptism, because the Spirit is said to be poured out, and those upon whom he is poured out . . . are said to be baptized . . . It is not therefore by baptism as an external rite,

---

26. See Dunn, "'Baptized' as Metaphor," especially 294-98; 300-310.

27. Hodge, *First Epistle to the Corinthians*, 253.

but by the communication of *the Holy Spirit* that we are made members of the body of Christ.[28]

It is by the agency of God the Spirit (by this baptism) that Paul can say "that no man should boast before *God*. For *by His doing* you are *in Christ Jesus*, who became to us wisdom from God, and righteousness and sanctification and redemption, that, just as it is written, 'Let him who boasts, boast in the Lord'" (1 Cor 1:29–31 NASB). Paul, who believes in one triune God, using the human body as a metaphor for Christ's spiritual body, is saying:

> For as the (human) body is one, and has many (bodily) members, but all the (physical) members of that one (human) body, being many, are one body, *so also* is *Christ* (one body—one *spiritual* body, yet having many members).

> For by one Spirit/Lord/God [see 1 Cor 12:4, 5, 6] we were all *baptized* [*placed*, 12:18 NASB] into one body [of Christ], where there is neither Jew nor Greek, neither slave nor free; and all have been made to *drink* of one Spirit. (1 Cor 12:12–13)

The triune God is one God. Therefore, Paul can and does say that *God* placed the members in the body in 12:18 (see 1:29–30).

Next, Jesus used both "baptized" and "drink" as metaphors:

> And Jesus said to them . . . "Are you able to *drink* the cup that I *drink*, or to be *baptized* with *the baptism* with which I am *baptized*?" And they said to him, "We are able." And Jesus said to them, "The cup that I *drink* you will *drink*, and with *the baptism* with which I am *baptized*, you will be *baptized*; but to sit at my right hand or at my left is not mine to grant, but it is for those for whom it has been prepared." (Mark 10:38–40 RSV)

Jesus is talking about his death, and Jesus uses both "baptized" and "drink" as metaphors for his suffering and death and then as metaphors of such sufferings for those two disciples. Jesus here uses "baptized" as a metaphor; so how much more of a precedent do we need? Paul imitates Christ (1 Cor 11:1). Just as Jesus used "baptized" as a metaphor for his death (Mark 10:38), Paul also used the metaphor "baptized" (into Christ's death) in Rom 6:3 and 4, so that we become *united with Christ* in his *death* (6:5). So the only way that we can savingly partake of "the baptism" (Rom 6:3) with which Christ was baptized is by the Spirit of *God* uniting us to Christ in the likeness of his death. John the Baptizer prophesied of the time when Christ would baptize with/in/by the Holy Spirit:

28. Hodge, *First Epistle to the Corinthians*, 253–54, emphasis mine.

And he [John the Baptist] preached, saying, "After me comes he who is mightier than I, the strap of whose sandals I am not worthy to stoop down and untie, I have baptized you with water, but *he will baptize you with the Holy Spirit.*" (Mark 1:7–8 ESV)

Before his exaltation, Jesus reminded his apostles of "the promise of the Father," regarding the baptism the Baptizer prophesied would come:

And while staying with them, he ordered them not to depart from Jerusalem, but to wait for *the promise of the Father,* "which, he said, you heard from me; for John baptized with water, but you shall be *baptized with the Holy Spirit* not many days from now." (Acts 1:4b, 5 ESV)

This baptism with the Spirit came on Pentecost (2:1–4).

Therefore [Jesus] . . . having received from [God] the Father the promise of *the Holy Spirit*, He has *poured forth* this [Spirit] which you both see and hear. (Acts 2:33 NASB)

Then, in Acts 10, we find this same baptism in the Spirit comes to the gentiles: "The gift of the Holy Spirit had been poured out upon the Gentiles also" (Acts 10:45 NASB). Peter says that "the Gentiles *received the Holy Spirit* just as we did" (Acts 10:47 NASB). Just as when the Jews received the Spirit at Pentecost, so now the gentiles received the Spirit. Then, in Acts chapter 11, Peter recounts to Jewish Christians (11:2) all that happened:

And as I began to speak, the Holy Spirit fell upon them, just as he did upon us at the beginning. And I remembered the word of the Lord, how He used to say "John baptized with water, but you *shall be baptized in the Holy Spirit.*" If then God gave to them [the Gentiles] the same gift as he gave to us when we believed in the Lord Jesus Christ, who was I, that I could withstand God? (Acts 11:15–17)

The saints at Rome were already (through word of mouth and teaching) familiar with terms and experiences that believers in the book of Acts heard of and experienced, namely, this baptism with the Holy Spirit (Acts 1:5; 11:15–18; see 15:7–9). And so Paul wrote:

Therefore, we were buried with Christ through *the baptism* [του βαπτίσματοσ] into the death [of Christ, and his burial] in order that, as Christ was raised from the dead through the glory of the Father, so also, we, in newness of life, might walk. For if we have become *united* [*grown together as one plant*] *with him* in the likeness of his death [through the baptism], so also, we shall certainly be united with him in the likeness of his resurrection. (Rom 6:4–5)

The Greek words τοῦ βαπτίσματοσ should be translated as "the baptism." The translators have erred in omitting the definite article τοῦ ("the"). If they were consistent in doing this, then, for example, Rom 5:5b would have been translated as "poured out in our hearts through Holy Spirit given to us." But of course, it is correctly translated "through the [τοῦ] Holy Spirit given to us," for the definite article is there in the Greek. Likewise, 6:4 should be translated "we were buried with him through *the baptism*." Nor is Rom 6 the only place the translators have omitted the article.[29] In Col 2:12, referring to the spiritual baptism of Rom 6:4, the Greek has the definite article there also, the meaning being "the baptism." Because it has been omitted in bible translations in Rom 6 and Col 2, the church has, for the most part, considered it to be baptism in water. At least one translation, translated by scholars who know that this baptism accomplishes our union with Christ, includes a translation of the Greek definite article.

> Or do you not know that all of us who were baptized into Christ Jesus were baptized into his death? We were therefore buried with him by this baptism into his death, so that just as he was raised from the dead through the glory of the Father, we too would also walk in a new life. (Rom 6:3–4 EHV)

In 1 Cor 12:13, both "baptized" and "drink" are metaphors for spiritual realities here. "Baptized" refers to being immersed in the Spirit (into Christ, for "Christ" is used interchangeably with "the Spirit" in Rom 8:9–10), so that we are now *in the Spirit* (*in Christ*, Rom 8:9–10). And to "drink of one Spirit" refers to the *receiving* (*in us*) of *the Spirit of God* (Rom 8:9–10). Using Paul's words from Rom 8, we correlate them with words from 1 Cor 12:

> But you are not in the flesh, but in the Spirit [by having been baptized by the Spirit of God, 12:13, 18] if indeed the Spirit of God dwells *in* you [if you were *given one Spirit* to "drink," so that he is now in you]. (Rom 8:9; 1 Cor 12:13)

In Rom 6 Paul avoids mentioning the Spirit (he is waiting until later), yet, by comparing Scripture with Scripture, we know that the Spirit was nevertheless in his thinking. He says, "We walk in the newness of *life*" (6:4), and that means we walk "in newness of *the Spirit*" (in 7:6) who *is* life (Rom 8:10). In 6:4 he says we were raised from the dead by *the glory* of the

---

29. See, for example, the literal translation from Greek of Rom 5:12—6:23 in my ch. 9, in which Paul uses the definite article ("the") before both "sin" and "death."

Father, and that means "by *the Spirit* of the Father" in Rom 8:11. Therefore we can, by Paul's authority, substitute the words from 7:6 and 8:11 for "walk" and "glory" in Rom 6 with "the Spirit"—and add "Spirit" from 1 Cor 12:13; then Rom 6:4 would read and mean as follows: "Therefore we were buried with him through *the* Spirit's *baptism* into his (Christ's) death, in order that, just as Christ was raised from the dead through the Spirit of the Father, even so, we should walk in newness of the Spirit." The closest parallel in Scripture to Rom 6:3–5 is Col 2:11–12. In Col 2, we find that, just as there is a spiritual (without human hands) circumcision, there is also a spiritual (by the Spirit, without-hands) baptism:

> In whom [Christ] also you were circumcised with a [spiritual] *circumcision* made *without [human] hands*, in the putting off the flesh [Rom 2:29, the body of sin, Rom 6:6], by the circumcision of Christ [the *circumcision* of the heart (through Christ's death, Rom 8:3–4), by which (redemption) *the flesh* (of sin) was (by the Spirit of Christ) cut off (from the heart), so that the Spirit of Christ now dwells in the inner man (Eph 3:16). This circumcision occurred "through the baptism," Col 2:12] co-buried with Christ through *the baptism* [τῷ βαπτίσμτι, also without (human) hands], in whom also you were co-raised through the faith of the working of God [regeneration] the [One] raising him [Christ, and you with him] from the dead. (Col 2:11–12)

Just as "the circumcision made without hands" is without human hands, so also is "the baptism" (τω βαπτίσμτι) without human hands. This is του βαπτίσματοσ, "the baptism" of Rom 6:4. The "by one Spirit" baptism of 1 Cor 12:13 results in this: that in Christ's body "there is no longer Jew nor Greek [Gentile], and there is no longer slave or free," for we are all one in Christ. But this is precisely what Paul says in Gal 3:27–28;,where he also says that "in Christ there is neither Jew nor Greek, neither slave nor free, male nor female," which refers to those who have been "baptized into Christ" (3:27), which baptism put us into Christ, in whom we are a new creation. Thus, in 1 Cor 12:13 and Gal 3:27, the apostle is referring to the very same baptism. And, when Paul says:

> For you are all sons of God through *faith* in Christ Jesus. For as many of you as were *baptized* into Christ have *put on Christ* (Gal 3:26, 27),

he means:

> You are all sons of God through faith in Christ, because you have been *baptized* by God (the Spirit) *into* Christ, (or you

would never have believed) whom you have *put on* like a garment (see 1 Cor 12:18, 13).[30]

To *Put On* Christ

In Gal 3:27, the Greek word ενδυω (to "put on") is a metaphor for a spiritual putting on of Christ. And, as in the phrase "have put on Christ" (3:27), "put on" is a metaphor for the unseen, spiritual reality of being clothed with Christ, the believer's righteousness; even so, the phrase "have been *baptized* into Christ" (3:27) refers to the believer's having been *baptized* into Christ and thus *baptized* (*placed* [1 Cor 12:18 NASB]) into his body.[31] Remembering that the Galatians were tempted to go back to the law, for them primarily circumcision (Gal 5:1–4), and, commenting on Gal 3:27, Dunn shows that the words "put on" (Christ) and "baptized into" (Christ) are metaphors:

> The sense is disrupted if we take one as a physical metaphor and one as a physical description of a physical act. (ii) The context revolves round the contrast between the old covenant, where the relationship with God is through the law and which is entered by an outward, physical rite, and the new covenant, where relationship with God is through the Spirit of Christ and which is entered by the act of believing; the contrast, in fact, between sonship κατὰ σάρκα and sonship κατὰ πνεῦμα (4:28f.) [sonship—according to the flesh and according to the Spirit].[32]

Dunn continues:

> Paul makes his contrast between circumcision and faith, *not* between circumcision and baptism. If baptism was an "effective symbol" which achieved what circumcision could not achieve, Paul could have met his opponents by pointing out that in baptism all that they had hoped to achieve had already been

---

30. Because you have been baptized by God, therefore "into Christ Jesus we believed" (εἰς Χριστὸν Ἰησοῦν ἐπιστεύσαμεν), "in order that we might be justified by Christ's faith" (Gal 2:16c, d).

31. When Paul wrote, "For as many of you as were baptized into Christ have *put on* Christ" (Gal 3:27), in all of Paul's letters, the Greek word for "put on" (ἐνδύω) is *always* used metaphorically, that is, for spiritual, unseen reality (see Rom 13:12, 14; 1 Cor 15:53–54; 2 Cor 5:3; Gal 3:27; 1 Thess 5:8 [Eph 4:24; 6:11, 14; and Col 3:10, 12]); so why should "baptized" in the same verse (Gal 3:27) not be a metaphor? As in 1 Cor 12:13 (where both "drink" and "baptized" are metaphors), so also in Gal 3:27—both "put on" and "baptized" are metaphors.

32. Dunn, *Baptism in the Holy Spirit*, 111. Words in brackets mine.

achieved. But Paul's contrast is circumcision and *faith*. He could not attack one material rite as he does here if at the same time, he believed that another was necessary for the reception of the Spirit. The Christian does not say to the Jew "Your rites are ineffective, but ours are effective." He points rather to the cross and the resurrection, *to faith* and the Spirit.[33]

If we have "believed into Christ" (Gal 2:16c), then it follows that the Spirit was actively involved in this *baptism into Christ* (Gal 3:27); and the Spirit was indeed involved in the faith given us, as Scripture teaches in 1 Cor 12:3, 13; 2 Cor 4:13; Gal 3:3; 5:5; and 2 Thess 2:13. Paul, like the writer of Acts in 11:16–17 (see 15:7–9), refers to this baptism as *the receiving of the Spirit*, as in 1 Cor 12:13b. Thus, if you are in Christ, then you were baptized with "the baptism" of Rom 6:5, Col 2:12, Gal 3:27, and 1 Cor 12:13. Therefore, *"the baptism"* (τοῦ βαπτίσματοσ) of Rom 6:4 unites us with Christ (6:5); this is the baptism of Acts 1:5; 11:11–17; 1 Cor 12:13 and see v. 18 (by God); and Col 2:11–12—otherwise, Paul could not say what he did in 1 Cor 1:17–21, which aligns with all of Paul's "faith" (alone) texts: Rom 4:5; 5:1; 9:30; Gal 2:16; 3:9, etc.

Furthermore, many commentators have read Christian water baptism *into* texts that do not use the words "baptized" or "baptism" at all, such as 1 Cor 6:11 and Titus 3:5, which refer to "washed" and "washing" respectively. But "wash" in both cases is a metaphor for the reality of spiritual cleansing, as it is in Psalm 51:2. So, in Titus 3:5, it means, "he saved us, by the *washing* of regeneration"—in other words, "So God . . . acknowledged them, by *giving* them the Holy Spirit, just as He did to us, and made no distinction between us and them, *purifying* their hearts by faith" (Acts 15:8–9 NKJV); and (Titus continues), "the *renewing* of the Holy Spirit" (in regeneration, Titus 3:5). Another, closely related, view by Gordon Fee, commenting on Titus 3:5, is as follows:

> Thus, the Spirit not only renews, but in Pauline theology effects the washing away of sins and the making new of the believer's life.[34]

---

33. Dunn, *Baptism in the Holy Spirit*, emphasis mine. Yes. In support of Dunn's words, "*to faith* and the Spirit," we set forth as proof of *faith* (in Christ) *alone*, the following texts: Rom 1:16–17; 3:21–28; 4:1–8; 5:1–2; 9:30–33; 10:4–9; Phil 3:9; Gal 2:16–17; 3:1–9, 14–26; 5:1–5; 1 Cor 1:21 (15:1–4).

34. Fee, *God's Empowering Presence*, 782.

Similarly, Matera writes, "God saves people *through* a regenerative washing which is the renewal that comes through the Spirit, whom the Savior God poured out *through* the Savior Jesus Christ."[35]

The Spirit is the seal of redemption and salvation (2 Cor 1:21–22; Eph 1:13; 4:30). Paul never says that baptism is the seal, for the Spirit is the seal. The Reformed purport to get the idea that baptism is a seal in Rom 4:11, but there Paul only refers to *circumcision* (not baptism) as a sign and seal.[36] Surely, then, "the baptism" of Rom 6:4 and Col 2:12 is the "one baptism" of Eph 4:5—the one Spirit's baptism into the one body of Christ. Notice the order of these seven "one" words (of unity, below), from left to right, appearing in the same order as it is written in Ephesians chapter 4. There is:

one Lord

one hope   one faith

one Spirit   one baptism

one body   one God

and Father who is over all, and through all, and in you all (from Eph 4:4–6). Note that "one Spirit" is, in God's wisdom, appropriately across from "one baptism," for it is the *one Lord's* (one) baptism by *one Spirit* into *one body* (Mark 1:8; 1 Cor 12:13) to which the writer refers. These seven divine unities of "the church which is Christ's body" (Col 1:18, 24; Eph 1:22–23) are *all unseen* to the human eye, in accordance with 2 Cor 5:7,[37] the one baptism being no exception. Yet for all who remain in human tradition that presumes this must be a baptism with water,[38] one of these seven uni-

---

35. Matera, *New Testament Christology*, 172.

36. The Scriptures never refer to baptism as a sign or seal. John's baptism (before Pentecost) was in order that the Messiah might be made manifest to Israel (John 1:31), not to the new covenant church. Both the unbelieving Jews (1 Cor 1:22) and unbelievers (14:22) require signs; thus, *neither* Christian baptism with water nor the Lord's Supper are signs to Christ-believers; see Lane's utter refutation of the Presbyterian/Reformed view of baptism in "Infant Baptism View," 121–29. The Jew trusted in circumcision, and when Paul says that circumcision for Abraham was a sign and seal of the righteousness of faith (Rom 4:11), he says nothing about baptism. But if Paul believed baptism was a seal, then Rom 4:11 would have been the perfect place to teach it, by adding something like this: "even as baptism is now a sign and seal of the righteousness of faith." But he does not. Thus, the Reformed use of the word "seal" in connection with baptism is deceptive, for in Scripture all those sealed (by the Spirit) are saved. This argument of the Reformed (and others) from Rom 4 is an argument from silence; it interprets Rom 4:11 and Col 2:11–12 in the light of the OT scriptures, instead of vice-versa, as the apostles do.

37. Compare 4:16–18.

38. Baptism in (visible-to-sight) water would nullify the other (six) *unseen divine*

ties is *seen*, for water is seen with eyes of flesh. From Christ's exaltation, until the end of the age, Christ is Lord (1 Cor 8:6; 15:25). And *"God is over all . . . and in you all"* (Eph 4:6; see 1 Thess 1:1) because through the one Spirit's baptism (1 Cor 12:13) we were all given one Spirit to drink (12:13b), that is, to indwell us (Rom 8:9). In other words:

> The new identity of the believer must also be understood in connection with what Paul termed "the body of Christ." The work of *the Holy Spirit* joins every new believer to the body of Christ upon conversion (1 Cor 12:13).[39]

Therefore, from all of the preceding scriptural points, we deduce the following points which prove our position:

1. All four gospels and Acts 1:5 predicted a baptism εν (in, and/or by) the Holy Spirit, and the "baptized" of 1 Cor 12:13 and Acts 11:15–17 is that baptism.

2. The "baptized" of 1 Cor 12:13 and of Gal 3:27 both result in there being *"neither Jew nor Greek, neither male nor female"* in Christ. Therefore, both 1 Cor 12 and Gal 3 are referring to the same "by one Spirit" baptism.

3. Since Gal 3:27 and Rom 6:3 both say that "we were baptized into Christ" we deduce that the baptism of 1 Cor 12:13 *is* the baptism of Gal 3:27 and Rom 6:3–4. This means that Christ, through the agency of the Spirit of God (1 Cor 12:18[40]), is the baptizer in "the baptism" (τοῦ βαπτίσματοσ) of Rom 6:4 and in "the baptism" (τῷ βαπτίσματι) of Col 2:12.

When Paul says we were *buried with him* (Rom 6:4), he uses a synecdoche, where the part ("buried") stands for the whole—Christ's death, burial, and resurrection. The apostle is saying that we, in spirit, died with Christ, were buried with him, and raised with him to new life, "through the [Spirit's] baptism" (6:4). Being "grown together with Christ" (6:5) is also a metaphor for the spiritual reality of our union with Christ in his death. Paul loves metaphors:

---

unities; thus, it has caused only disunity in the body of Christ; see, e.g., Bridge and Phypers, *Water That Divides*, which deals with two Protestant views on baptism. Even the Eastern Orthodox differ from Roman Catholics in their practice of baptism.

39. Arnold, *Powers of Darkness*, 113, emphasis mine.

40. Compare Acts 2:33.

- Just as the "if we have become *grown/planted/united with* Christ in the likeness of his death" in Rom 6:5 is not a literal planting/grafting but a metaphor for a spiritual grafting/union with Christ, so also "the baptism" of 6:4 is not a literal baptism in water but a spiritual baptism.

- Christ's baptism by and with the Holy Spirit (Acts 1:5; 11:15–17) in which people receive the Spirit of Christ (Acts 11:15–17; 15:7–9) is the baptism of 1 Cor 12:13, where he says "for by one Spirit we were all baptized into one body" so that we are in Christ; "and all were *given one Spirit* to drink [so that Christ, by his Spirit, is in us]" (Rom 8:9–10).

- According to 1 Cor 1:17–21, either baptism in water or mere words of human wisdom would make God's "word of the cross" of no effect, if either of them replaces *the gospel* (and that believed), for salvation (1:21). So, 1 Cor 1:17–21 verifies our interpretation of 1 Cor 12:13, Rom 6:3–5, Gal 3:26–27, and Col 2:11–12.[41]

Luther and Calvin were raised in Roman Catholic theology; and, regarding baptism, they came only a few steps out of that mindset, and their teachings have been passed on to all the generations of theologians and church leaders who followed them. Thus, referring to the assumption that such scholars and leaders have made, Dunn remarks:

> The *assumption* is that the presupposition of *centuries of* Christian *sacramental* theology must have *already been operative* in the case of *Paul* and his first audiences.[42]

Such scholars impute the theology of the church fathers back to Paul himself! These "centuries of sacramental theology" are primarily due to Augustine's powerful influence on the church, including the Reformers. But the witness of Paul's letters, not only all his statements of salvation through faith

---

41. In 1 Cor 1:21, Paul did *not* say, "God was well-pleased through the foolishness of the proclamation to save the ones who believe *and are baptized.*" Yet this what those churches within the Catholic tradition have forced Paul to say, when they read a *non*-metaphorical baptism with water into Rom 6—because they omit the definite article "the" in "the baptism," and they ignore the fact that Paul in 1 Cor 12:13 uses both "baptism and drink" as metaphors. Also, the Spirit (Life, Rom 8:10) was received before Peter's converts were baptized in water (Acts 10:43–48); therefore the two baptisms are distinct. Also, Paul's churches were never taught to baptize those who believe; but the Lord's Supper was delivered to Paul, to be done in the churches. Nor does Paul tell saints to preach Christ, for preaching is done by those sent to preach (Rom 10:14–17).

42. Dunn, *Theology of Paul*, 445, emphasis mine. Clement (35–95 AD) taught that keeping the commandments in love issues in the forgiveness of sins; see Nygren, *Agape and Eros*, 247–49; 1 Clem 50:4. Sacramental theology (in which sacraments saved) also developed early; see Brunner, *Christian Doctrine*, 3:67–69; Schaff, *History*, 2:253–54.

in Christ alone but also in 1 Cor 12:13 and 18, as well as Acts chapters 1, 10, 11, and 15 is, in Dunn's words, as follows:

> The benefits of Jesus' death and resurrection were made over to humanity not by water baptism, but by the Pentecostal baptism in Spirit.[43]

And this is not "the baptism of the Holy Spirit" of which modern day Pentecostals speak. It is the one that first occurred on the day of Pentecost, based upon the exaltation of Jesus to God's right hand, in which humans receive the gift of the Holy Spirit, whereby they are placed into Christ and his body, and whereby Christ now indwells them by his Spirit. That baptism baptized us into Christ Jesus, in whom the flesh of Sin was condemned to death (destruction) in order that the Spirit of *Christ* might now instead indwell us in our inner man (Rom 8:3–10; Eph 3:16).

Thus, regarding Paul's use of "baptism" in 1 Cor 1:17–21, E. R. Rogers wrote:

> It occupied a subordinate position in his evangelistic practice. Otherwise, how could he say that he was thankful that he had baptized so few of the Corinthians and insist that Christ did not send him to baptized but to preach the gospel. Viewed in context this means that Paul did not regard the rite of baptism as an essential element in a saving response to the gospel.

> Returning to Ephesians 4:5 I want to suggest that the reference to "one baptism" is best understood in terms of baptism in the Spirit. The unity which the "Ephesians" were urged to preserve is described as being produced by the Spirit. Read against this background the first two pillars of unity, "one body and one Spirit" inevitably recall 1 Corinthians 12:13, which . . . refers to baptism in the Spirit." . . . The "one Lord" is the object of the "one faith" which is the regular precondition for the receiving of the Spirit. Such a reception may be seen as the "one baptism." This interpretation finds a measure of early support in 1 Clement 46:6 which, clearly reflecting the Ephesian passage, asked, ". . . or do we not have one God and *one Spirit* of grace who has been *poured out* upon us?" At the very least it can be said that Clement had *the Pentecostal baptism in the Spirit* suggested to his mind by the Pauline appeal to unity.[44]

---

43. Dunn, *Pneumatology*, 55.
44. Rogers, "Yet Once More," 48, 49, emphasis mine.

Yes, Clement did have the Spirit's baptism in mind when thinking of the Ephesian passage on unity, because "poured out" is NT terminology for Christ's baptism by the agency of the Spirit—Luke says so in Acts 10:45 (see 2:33). And, yes, as the gospels and Acts say, Christ baptizes in the Holy Spirit; and to be "in the Holy Spirit" is to be "in Christ" (Rom 8:9, 10) by the agency of the Spirit.

This is the bottom line: The baptism that *saves* from sin and death is Christ's baptism by the agency of the Holy Spirit, by which sinners receive the gift of the Holy Spirit, being placed into Christ and thus into his body (see 1 Cor 12:18). In this baptism we were made to "drink" of the Spirit (12:13) which means we *receive the Holy Spirit* into our inner man (Eph 3:16), the Spirit who is life (eternal, Rom 8:10; 6:23). This is the "one baptism" referred to in Eph 4:5.[45] Christian baptism in water is not Christ's baptism by the agency of the Spirit (see Acts 10:44 and 47). And so, in terms of preaching and teaching, it should be clearly taught that only the Spirit's baptism saves. After thirteen pages of scriptural study on baptism, Anglican D. W. B. Robinson, near his conclusion, wrote:

> To this we must add the evidence of Paul, that although he had baptized a handful of people at Corinth, he did not consider baptism to be part of his essential apostolic mission to the Gentiles. I can see no reason why we should not accept this as indicating that Paul regarded water baptism as ultimately an adiaphoron, a matter of indifference.[46]

A primary issue here is the Reformation tradition's ignorance of *Christ's* baptism with and by the Holy Spirit as being essential and primary and as distinct from baptism with/in water—not only John's baptism, but even Christian baptism (Acts 10:43–48; 19:1–5), which Paul was *not* sent as apostle to do (1 Cor 1:17). So, the bottom line is that "the baptism" of Rom 6:4–5 *is* efficacious, for it *unites us to Christ* (v. 5). We were united with him "through the baptism" (6:5 lit.). This truth does not deny that baptism in or with water of the believer's entire household in Jesus' name was the apostolic norm, the initiation of such ones. And, in Ephesians chapter 5, regarding "the washing of water with the word," (1) the writer does not call it "the baptism" into Christ, and (2) it most likely means the spiritual washing/

45. The "one baptism" of Eph 4:5 does *not* of necessity prove that no baptism in water should ever be practiced, for Ephesians is not one of Paul the apostle's genuine, undisputed letters. At the same time, we conclude that Eph 4:5 shows that one who learned from Paul understood him in 1 Cor 12:13 and elsewhere.

46. Robinson, "Towards a Definition of Baptism," 14. It took years from my first reading of this to be convinced.

cleansing that the gospel gives (see Act 15:9) and not the water of baptism, as it is called "the washing of *regeneration*" in Titus 3:5. One text that many have used to support baptismal regeneration is as follows: "Unless a man be born of water and of the Spirit, he cannot enter into the kingdom of God" (John 3:3b). Regarding the new birth, Nicodemus asked Jesus if a man can enter his mother's womb, but:

> Christ, in his answer, repeats what he had said of the necessity of regeneration, and in addition clears the way of it for Nicodemus's information, showing that this birth was not natural, but spiritual, wrought by the Spirit, whose working is likened to water cleansing filth. To understand this water [as that] of baptism will not agree with this place, for this water does certainly regenerate, but everyone that is baptized is not certainly regenerate, as witness Simon Magus, Acts 8:13, 23, and others. Further: this water is pressed as absolutely necessary to salvation, whereas men may go to heaven without baptism if it be not held in contempt; as of old, the elect seed of Abraham who died in the wilderness without circumcision, were saved; so the thief on the cross was saved without baptism; therefore, as [in] Matt 3:11, "*the Holy Spirit and fire*," signify *one* thing, of *the Spirit* like the *fire* in purging dross, [even] so the "*water and Spirit*" signifies *the Spirit* working like *water*. Hence it is that, *ver. 6, he repeats only "the Spirit," as including* all that here signified by the "*water and Spirit*;" and this expressing of *the Spirit's* working, under the name of *water*, is no unusual expression in the *Old Testament*, [see] *Isa 44:3; Ezek 36:25.*[47]

Water is a metaphor for God's *Spirit* in Isa 44:3; and in Ezek 36:25–27 water is a metaphor for *the Spirit's* creating a cleansed and new heart when the new covenant comes into being; similarly in John 3, the author was undoubtedly thinking of those OT texts.

The unity that already exists in the body of Christ (Gal 3:28) is to be kept (Eph 4:3) through the truth of *the one baptism* (4:5), which resulted in "Christ in you, the hope of glory" (Col 1:27; see "hope" in Eph 4:4). So, division over baptism is unnecessary, if we accept the fact that only Paul was given the gospel of and to the uncircumcision (gentiles/nations, see Gal 2:2–9). We scripturally deduce from this that letters written by or in the name of Peter (and James and John) are *not* the gospel to and for the world ("gentiles" and "world" are interchangeable in Rom 11:12–13; see Gal 2:2–9), for they were not written by the apostle of the world/nations (Rom

47. Hutcheson, *John*, 42, emphasis and modern English mine. On baptism in 1 Peter 3:21, see Dunn, *Baptism in the Holy Spirit*, 217–219.

11:12–13). Therefore, we are to accept doctrine for the church that is Christ's body from Paul and interpret other NT letters in the light of Paul's gospel (Rom 2:16; Gal 1:1–2:9), knowing that the saints referred to in Peter's and John's epistles were in that body also, though the writers of those letters wrote to Christ-believers of Jewish descent. There is both *union* (Gal 1:23) and distinction (2:2–9) between Peter's and Paul's gospel; it is a both/and situation; the "and" falls on the union: one gospel.[48] Israel's being *baptized into Moses* meant that they were *identified with Moses*, God's appointed leader of Israel. Likewise, we have been baptized into Christ, who is God's appointed Lord and leader of the church, which is his body, who are identified with Christ (Col 1:18; 2:12). Both Moses' and Christ's baptisms are metaphorical. Neither baptism is a literal drenching in water. Both are dry baptisms. Thus, it is unwise to base a doctrine of baptism upon 1 Cor 10:1–2.[49]

The Lord's Supper

The Lord's Supper is a remembrance of Christ's death for us. It is an audible and visible form of proclaiming the gospel (1 Cor 11:26). It should not be confused with the gospel, for Paul says that the preached gospel, and that believed, saves sinners (Rom 10:4–9; 1 Cor 1:21). Therefore, a person is saved from sin and death through faith in Christ, before and apart from partaking in the Lord's Supper, for those who are to partake of the Supper are already saints (1 Cor 1:2; see 11:17–34). The Lord's Supper is a proclamation of the Lord's death until he comes (1 Cor 11:26) and a looking forward to his coming as exalted Lord (1 Cor 11:26; Luke 22:15–20). In the following texts, Paul says that in the Lord's Supper, the consecrated bread and wine, with Christ's words of institution, is the body and blood of Christ: a communion with Christ in his once-for-all sacrifice for our sins. The New Testament church in fellowship "broke bread" (Luke 24:35; Acts 2:42) every Lord's Day, for Acts 20:7 says that the Supper was why

48. See 1 Cor 15:3–11. The bottom line is that the Reformed (who baptize infants of believers), Reformed Baptists, and Baptists make *too* much of water baptism and, conversely, not enough of the baptism by the Spirit, which is God sovereignly baptizing people into Christ and his body (1 Cor 12:13, 18), whereby they *receive* the gift of *the Spirit of Christ* (Acts 11:15–18; see 15:7–9) who is *life* (Rom 8:10). This occurs when they, by God's power, believe in Christ.

49. "Now I would not have you ignorant, brethren, that our fathers were all under the cloud, and all *passed through the sea*; and were all baptized into Moses in the cloud and in the sea" (1 Cor 10:1–2 WEB/AT). "When OT Israel passed through the sea, were they immersed in water? Or did they remain dry? By faith, they *passed through* the Red Sea as on *dry land*. When the Egyptians tried to do so, they were swallowed up" (Heb 11:29 WEB). Israel's enemies were drowned in water; but Israel remained dry.

they came together on the first day of the week. Also, the uses of the word "blood" in the Torah (in Exod 12 and 24 and Leviticus) were mere shadows (Heb 10:1) of Christ and not Christ himself (see Heb 9:16—10:18). "For Christ our Passover has been sacrificed for us" (1 Cor 5:7b). Therefore the new testament in Christ's blood (11:25) is not a shadow but the substance of what *was* a shadow in the entire old covenant era.[50] And Paul says, "The *bread* which we break, is it not the *communion* of *the body of Christ*? And the *cup* of blessing which we bless, is it not the *communion* [the *partaking*] of *the blood of Christ*? For we, being many, are one bread and one body; *for* we all partake of that one bread" (1 Cor 10:16–17 NKJV). Paul does not say, "The cup of blessing which we bless, is it not *a sign of* the communion of the blood of Christ?" Nor does he say, "The bread which we break, is it not *a sign of* the communion of the body of Christ?" Neither is the (substance of) the bread and wine transformed into the body and blood of Christ, as in Rome's "transubstantiation," for the bread is still called "bread" in 10:16, because it is.[51] Paul wrote:

> For I received from the Lord what I also delivered to you, that the Lord Jesus on the same night in which He was betrayed took *bread*, and . . . He broke it and said, "This is *My body* which is broken for you. Do this in remembrance of Me." In the same manner He also took *the cup* after supper, saying, "*This cup* is the new covenant in *My blood*. This do, as often as you drink it, in remembrance of Me." (1 Cor 11:24–25 NKJV)

> Whoever, therefore, eats *the bread* and drinks *the cup* [of wine] in an unworthy manner will be guilty of profaning *the body and blood of the Lord*. (1 Cor 11:27)

In 11:27 Paul uses "the bread and cup" and "the body and blood of the Lord" interchangeably. The Supper is the Lord's new testament[52] in his blood that was shed for many for the remission of sins (Matt 26:28). What makes the Supper *the Lord's* Supper is that the Lord's words of institution in 1 Cor 11:23–26 are spoken at the Supper, along with (eating and drinking) the

---

50. See Andreae and Beza, *Lutheranism*, 60, which helped me understand this.

51. Referring to Luther (his theology), Vajta wrote, "Reason is bound to misinterpret the real presence. A deeper understanding of Christology made transubstantiation pointless to him. For in Christ he found both *human and divine* nature to be present, *without change* and *without mixture*. Human nature therefore needs no transubstantiation for the divine to dwell in it [*WA* 6, 511]. Faith can see both natures in one. Reason alone remains baffled." "Though both [bread and wine, body and blood] remain at the same time, it can truly be said: 'This bread is my body, this wine is my blood . . . ' " (Vajta, *Luther*, 94, emphasis mine).

52. On *the new testament* in Christ's blood, see Forde, *Preached God*, 149–51.

bread and wine. Self-examination (11:28) for the Supper means *discerning* the Lord's body (11:29; compare v. 27)—recognizing the distinction between this bread and all other bread, that the bread and wine consecrated by the words of institution is a communion in Christ's body and blood, and that we examine ourselves as to whether we are having a proper consideration for the other members of Christ's body (see 1 Cor 11:27–34, where the apostle reminds them of what he said in 11:17–22). The word "sacrament" is never applied to either baptism or the Lord's Supper in the Scriptures.

> The New Testament does not possess the concept of "a sacrament," nor is it primarily interested in sacred rites in themselves. That interest, and the development of the idea of "sacraments," only came *later* . . . The Greek term *mysterion* ("mystery"), which is commonly translated into Latin as *sacramentum*, does indeed appear several times in the New Testament. There, however, its meaning is not that of "sacred rite," but of "mystery" or "secret," and it most usually refers to the hidden things of God which are disclosed in Jesus Christ: it speaks of revelation, not ritual. There is a warning here that needs to be heeded.[53]

But that warning has not been heeded. For Paul refers to "words taught by the Spirit," which are the words that he used in preaching and are found in his letters. Referring to "the things freely given to us by God" (1 Cor 2:12), such as justification (Rom 3:24), he says:

> Which things we also speak, not in *words* taught from human wisdom [that of the flesh], but in those [words] taught of the Holy Spirit, communicating spiritual things [the things freely given us by God] by spiritual words [words *taught* (διδακτοῖς) of the Spirit]. (1 Cor 2:12–13)

Paul was *taught* these things by Jesus Christ (Gal 1:11–12). But the church has not been faithful to remain satisfied with these Spirit-taught words. Instead, it has imported words such as "sacrament," from the Latin "sacramentum" for "mystery" and applied it to baptism, the Lord's Supper, and, in some traditions, other things also. For when NT writers used the word μυστήριον ("mystery"), they used it to mean things like Christ's death as it was ordained before the ages (1 Cor 2:7–8 [see 1:23–24] and Rom 16:25), or that a partial blindness has happened to natural Israel, so that gentiles may be saved, until all the elect gentiles come in (Rom 11:25). On the Lord's Supper, Brunner wrote, "If it were a sacrament, that is, the bestowal of salvation, then it would necessarily be clearly taught as the decisive thing, and

---

53. Heron, *Table and Tradition*, 55, emphasis mine.

would be made the central theme of the preaching."[54] The Lord's Supper, as a gift from God to the church of God, is the normal practice of the church, handed down through Paul the apostle, and in a secondary sense, the Synoptic Gospels. John R. Stephenson, referring to 1 Cor 10:16, wrote:

> But any intelligent and attentive layperson can establish the apostle's intent to teach that communion/participation in the body and blood of Christ occurs through the oral acts of eating and drinking bread and wine. The blest bread and cup themselves are the κοινωνια of the Lord's body and blood (1 Cor 10:16). This point is reinforced as Paul compares partaking of Holy Communion with joining in Jewish and pagan sacrificial worship. At the time First Corinthians was written, practicing Jews became "sharers in the altar" . . . as they ate of the sacrifices . . . (1 Cor 10:18). Practicing pagans likewise partake of the table and cup of demons as they eat and drink what has been offered to idols (1 Cor 10:19–21). The whole passage stoutly resists Reformed interpretation; according to Paul, the mystical body is constituted as we partake of one bread (1 Cor 10:17), which happens only through its eating. Lutheran talk of the oral eating and drinking of Christ's body and blood proceeds from faithful listening to the words of institution which are paraphrased in 1 Cor 10:16–17. Paul corroborates 1 Cor 10:16 by following the words of institution with caution that unworthy eating of the bread and drinking from the cup of the Lord involves its perpetrators in guilt against His body and blood (1 Cor 11:27). He admonishes the church in Corinth to discern the Lord's body in the sacramental eating and drinking.[55]

Commenting on the context of this text, namely, 1 Cor 10:14–22, Alasdair Heron says:

---

54. Brunner, *Christian Doctrine of the Church*, 3:64. The Lord's Supper is not as central to the faith as is *the gospel* itself, otherwise Paul would have included it in "the gospel of God" (Rom 1:1)—his letter to the Romans. Thus, there is a distinction and a union between the gospel and the Lord's Supper.

55. Stephenson, *Lord's Supper*, 47. See also SD VII, 2–90 (74–123); and, on Christ, VIII, 17–87 (594–608); and Althaus, *Theology of Martin Luther*, 384–96. On 1 Cor 11:28, see Lockwood, *1 Corinthians*, 235–36, and *LW* 40:186. The Lord's Supper is for justified saints; so Lutherans should note that Paul never says that those who partake unworthily are unbelievers, though an unbeliever would be such. We agree with Luther, that we go to Paul and the Synoptic Gospels for teaching on the Lord's Supper. John's "eating and drinking" means to believe in Christ (6:40, 47, [44, 64]); and (through faith) to partake of the body and blood of Christ in the Lord's Supper (6:53-58); but on John and the Supper, see also Heron, *Table and Tradition*, 42–56.

The key ideas here are "sharing" or "participation" . . . These are all extremely strong terms: they describe such a sharing in someone or something that one is bound to and united with him or it. What Paul is saying is that in the Eucharist we really participate in the body and blood of Christ, and so in him and in his death for us; but if we also wish to take part in idolatrous worship, this sets up an impossible conflict. While the pagan gods as such do not exist, the demons do, and pagan worship is in fact offered to and bound up with real demonic powers, so that through it, people are bound to the demons in the same way as in the Eucharist they are united with Christ.[56]

That, we believe, is the main thing to know regarding the Lord's Supper. Heron also says of the Lord's Supper:

It is *not an addition* to the sacrifice of Christ, *nor is it a repetition* of it; for *the sacrifice has been completed once and for all upon the cross.* The Eucharist is, rather, a sacramental sharing in that sacrifice. . . . the sacrifice itself is present—the same that was offered to God on Calvary—for Christ himself is present, both as victim and as priest.[57]

Hasting's *Dictionary of the Bible* agrees:

The Eucharist, therefore, is a sacrifice, not as the commemoration of the death of Christ, but as the means of participation in the Paschal lamb slain for us (1 Cor 5:7) in the offering of the body of Christ once for all on the cross (Heb 10:10; cf. John 19:36; 1 Cor 10:17).[58]

And, commenting on 1 Cor 10:16, *The Book of Concord* says:

From these words we learn clearly that not only the cup which Christ blessed in the Last Supper and not only the bread which Christ himself broke and distributed, but also that which we break and bless is participation in the body and blood of Christ, so that all who eat this bread and drink this cup truly receive and partake of the true body and blood of Christ.[59]

56. Heron, *Table and Tradition*, 36; also SD 7.56–58.

57. Heron, *Table and Tradition*, 103, 104, emphasis mine.

58. *DB*, 275.

59. SD 7.54, 579. The opponents of Luther charged him with cannibalism, calling it a "Capernaitic" way of understanding the Supper, taking literally what was said by Jesus at Capernaum (John 6:17–59), i.e., "unless you eat the flesh of the Son of man and drink his blood, you have not life in you" (6:53), which literalism Lutherans rightly rejected, for they only sought to do justice to Paul's words in 1 Cor 10:16–17; 1 Cor

Those who partake of it were already saved in hope (Rom 8:24) through faith (5:1). Yet the bread and wine, consecrated by the words of institution, is a communion in Christ's body and blood; so we do not deny that partaking of his body and blood are not *excluded* from the process of "being saved" (1 Cor 1:18). This true participation is to be accepted by faith in Christ, in this case his words of institution, apart from our reason. Scripturally, we find that the presider at the Supper was most likely the host of the dinner in which the house-church met. Thus, the notion that only "the ordained" can preside at the Lord's Supper has no support in Scripture;[60] such is the tradition of men (see Mark 7:8).

In conclusion, the teaching of Paul the apostle interpreted and as presented in this chapter on baptism and the Lord's Supper is in accordance with the gospel, which proclaims salvation from sin and death on account of Christ alone, through faith (in him) alone.

Summary: The First Importance of Christ's Death for Justification

1. When Paul says, "For I delivered to you as of first importance what I also received: that Christ died for our sins in accordance with the Scriptures, that he was buried, that he was raised on the third day in accordance with the Scriptures, and that he appeared to Cephas, then to the twelve" (1 Cor 15:3–5 ESV), he is saying that Christ's death for our sins, which justifies the ungodly, is of first importance, and that we are saved if we hold fast to the gospel through faith in Christ.[61] The gospel, that Christ died for our sins and was raised to life, includes the law in that he died for *our sins—our transgressions of the law.*[62] The gospel proclaims that deliverance from sin, wrath, and death unto eternal life is received through faith in Christ alone, to the glory of God alone.

11:24–25; and 11:27; all of which use "*bread and cup* [*wine*]" interchangeably with "*the body and blood*" of Christ. Therefore, in the Lord's Supper we have communion with Christ's body and blood, not in a local manner (which Lutherans acknowledge), but in a mystery which transcends human comprehension and rationalism. Therefore, since it is not a local presence, we believe that wisdom dictates that Lutherans, on Christ's presence in the Lord's Supper, should refrain from using the words "in, with, and under" (the bread and wine), for these words add to Paul's "words taught by the Spirit" (1 Cor 2:13), and this is one of many instances in which human creeds "go beyond what is written" (from 1 Cor 4:6 ESV).

60. See Dunn, *Pneumatology*, 2:299–307; esp. 304–5.

61. 1 Cor 15:1–2; see Gal 5:1–5 (Col 1:21–23).

62. 1 Cor 15:1–4; Rom 3:9–26; 4:25; Gal 2:17–19; Col 2:13.

2. The source of "my righteousness" is the flesh, whose heart and mind cannot trust God for salvation (Phil 3:3, 9). Thus, by God's act I died (passed away) with Christ[63] and was made a new creation who *does* (again) trust God. Sinners are justified by an imputed righteousness through the redemption that is by Christ's death for God's elect, which results in their regeneration and ultimate glorification (Rom 1:6, 7; 3:23–26; 4:6—5:2; 8:10, 30–34).

3. The gospel of God reveals that there are only two worldviews, which are in reality two religions—for humans worship either God or the creature in God's place: one distinguishes between the Creator and the creation; the other does not.[64] Apart from the obedience of faith in Christ, humans are bound to worship the creation rather than the Creator. Although *grace* was in God's plan from before the creation of the world (2 Tim 1:9; Rom 8:29–30; Eph 1:3–14), grace by redemption occurred after sin entered the world,[65] through God's only begotten Son's death and resurrection.[66]

4. The (old covenant) holy scriptures, wherein the gospel was promised (Rom 1:1–2), along with the NT scriptures, are the trustworthy and authoritative writings for the faith of the church. And the Scriptures include the law, which works wrath against sinners, shutting them up to Christ alone for salvation. They also include the Lord's indicatives and imperatives for his New Testament church that is his body and the truth about the final judgment.[67] There is a distinction between the law and the promise, the promise of *the Spirit* having now come

63. Gal 2:20; Rom 6:6–7; 2 Cor 5:17.

64. See Jones, *Other Worldview*, chs. 2–3, 10–13; and, destroying the lie of human evolution, see Varvel, *Genesis Impact*. Secular psychology has too often greatly influenced the church through its leaders. But secular psychology can only lead toward self-justification or a license to do the deeds of the flesh, both of which are not in line with the gospel. Psychology has its place in this world, (which in one sense believers are still in), but in the kingdom of God, Christ is sufficient.

65. Rom 3:24; 5:12–21.

66. Rom 3:24–26; 4:25—6:23; Gal 4:4–7.

67. For example, Rom 1:18–32; 4:15; 2:5–10; 12:1—14:13. Such apostolic teaching (as is written, 1 Cor 4:6) should not be ignored, things such as church discipline (1 Cor 5) or headship in marriage (1 Cor 11; Eph 5:22–33); for the apostolic gospel teaches both complementarianism in this age (1 Cor 11) and egalitarianism in Christ (Gal 3:28), and the judgment seat of Christ—that humans will appear before God's judgment seat (Rom 14; 1 Cor 3; 2 Cor 5), when God will judge humankind's secrets (heart-motives) according to Paul's gospel (Rom 2:16); and church-leaders will incur a stricter judgment (Jas 3:1; 1 Cor 3:11–15), and believers will be judged according to their stewardship with those gifts which God gave them (Luke 12:48; 1 Cor 3).

by Christ's death, granting the Spirit and faith (Gal 3:13–14; Phil 1:27–29) to the called (Rom 1:6–7). Similarly, there is union and distinction between the law and the gospel.[68]

5. For us in the new testament, who believe in the God who has raised Jesus from the dead (Rom 4:24), the OT (and NT) Scriptures are to be interpreted in the light of the knowledge of the glory of God in Christ (2 Cor 4:6)—in the light of the apostolic gospel of God,[69] which Paul calls "my gospel" (Rom 2:16), found (primarily [with apostolic authority], but not solely) in the undisputed letters of Paul.[70] The church is repeatedly told by Paul to imitate him as he imitates Christ.[71] Imitating Paul includes his teaching that, since we are already in the (future)kingdom/reign of God in the Holy Spirit (Rom 14:17), there is neither male nor female (Gal. 3:28). and thus, women can be co-workers with Paul and other men in the work of the ministry (see note 70), proclaiming his gospel with its indicatives and its imperatives, and for all believers, the working out of this salvation in our everyday lives (Phil 2:12–13).

68. The union is that the righteous requirement of the law (through faith in the gospel) is fulfilled *in* those who are according to the Spirit and walk thereby (Rom 8:5, 4). The gospel fulfills the law, "You shall have no other gods besides me," for Christ is our (indwelling) God (8:10), through faith. The distinction is that Christ is not the law; Christ is the end of the law for righteousness (10:4), for the law says, "Do," and it cannot be done (Rom 8:3); the gospel says, "Believe in God who raised Christ from the dead, and be justified unto life" (Rom 10:4–10).

69. Rom 1:1–4 and 11:13 Gal 1:1—2:9; 1 Cor 2:12–13 and 1:22—2:16; 1 Cor 3:10; 4:9–17; 9:1–6; 12:28; 14:37; 15:1–11; 2 Cor 3:1–6 and 4:1–6, 12:12; 1 Thess 4:2–8. The Scriptures preserve the gospel of God.

70. They are: Romans, 1 and 2 Corinthians, Galatians, Philippians, 1 Thessalonians, and Philemon. Next to these, Colossians is the closest, but there is enough evidence (differences from Paul), as with the other disputed letters, to hold that it was probably written in Paul's name by a disciple of Paul. For such a practice (pseudonymity) was acceptable in those times if it meant carrying on an important person's teaching; on this see Schnelle, *Theology of the New Testament*, 534–38. On the Pastorals and Ephesians, see Meade, *Pseudonymity and Canon*, 118–61; Boring and Craddock, *Peoples New Testament*, 594–95; 655–66. This reality enables us to understand Paul's consistency with texts like Gal 3:28, that *in Christ Jesus there is neither male nor female*; that is, believers are *all* in the same (eschatological) reign of God in the Holy Spirit (Rom 14:7). Thus, there are women apostles (Rom 16:7), women ministers (16:1–2 [Greek], see 1 Cor 3:5; 2 Cor 3:6); women who are coworkers with Paul in the gospel (Phil 4:1–2). Correspondingly, 1 Cor 14:34–35 is without doubt an interpolation, added by a scribe who was influenced by 1 Tim 2:11–12; see Conzelmann, *First Corinthians*, 246; Hays, *First Corinthians*, 244–46; Fee, *First Corinthians*, 699–708; Koester, *History and Literature*, 2:11, 54.

71. 1 Cor 4:16; 11:1; Phil 3:17; 4:9; 1 Thess 1:6; compare Phil 2:12–13; Rom 6:1—8:15; 12:1–2. Thinking in Hebrew, paradoxical thought, none of these things denies the inspiration and importance of all the Scriptures in the NT canon.

—— NINETEEN ——

Justification Revisited

There is an already-now aspect to our salvation in Christ Jesus, but there is also a not-yet aspect to it. The already-now aspect of salvation relates to the inner man; and the not-yet aspect relates to the outer man.

- We are already saved (Rom 8:24), yet we will be saved (5:9–10).
- We are already redeemed (3:24), yet we wait for the redemption of our body (8:23).
- We are already adopted (8:15), yet we wait for the adoption (8:23, 25).
- We are already justified (5:1, 9), yet we wait for the (certain) hope of righteousness, when we will be acquitted[1] before all creation (Gal 5:5; Rom 8:23–25).

We Now Have Obtained Mercy

THE NEW TESTAMENT SCRIPTURES teach that there are two ages: this age and the age to come.[2] Because the already/now aspect of salvation in Christ was not clearly taught by the church fathers,[3] it is not surprising that the church's liturgy developed into things like the *Kyrie Eleison*,

1. "If believers appear at the final judgment as already resurrected bodily, then they will appear there as already openly justified" (Gaffin Jr., "Justification and Eschatology," 21).

2. Eph 1:21; Matt 12:32; Mark 10:30; Luke 20:33–36; Rom 8:18.

3. See Torrance, *Doctrine of Grace*, the conclusion.

298

which is Greek for "Lord, have mercy." In all the extant writings in the history of the early church, the first time the *Kyrie Eleison* (hereafter, the *Kyrie*) is mentioned is in the latter part of the fourth century.[4] So, the *Kyrie* developed centuries after the apostles fell asleep in Christ. In one sense, the *Kyrie* is imploring God to have mercy over our whole lives through Christ; and because, insofar as we remain in the flesh, we are still sinners (Rom 3:7); in that sense we acknowledge that there is a constant need for the mercy of God. However, now that redemption has come in Christ, we *have obtained* mercy in Christ, for God continually justifies believers in Christ (Rom 4:5; 8:33–34, both say "justifying").[5]

Writing to gentile believers, Paul said:

> For as you were once disobedient to God, yet *now have obtained mercy* though their [Israel's] disobedience, even so these also have now been disobedient, that through the mercy shown you they also may obtain mercy. (Rom 11:30–31)

Here, the apostle is referring back to the foundation that he laid in chapter 3, that God *has* had mercy, and it is called "grace," in and by Christ's death for sinners—"being justified freely by his grace, through the redemption in Christ Jesus, whom God set forth as a propitiation through [Christ's] faith, by his blood" (Rom 3:23–25a). Thus, it is significant that, where in the old covenant the psalmist says, "Blessed are those whose transgressions are forgiven," when Paul uses this text in Rom 4:7, in the *new* testament in Christ's blood,[6] he uses the past tense (ἀφέθησαν), "were forgiven."

4. Fortescue, "Kyrie Eleison."

5. As we have shown, the old covenant saint's cry, "God, be merciful to me" is echoed in our Lord's parable, in which he has the publican crying out, "God, be *merciful* [literally, *propitious*] to me the sinner" (Luke 18:13). In the Gospels, the phrase "Lord, have mercy" (Mark 10:46–52; Matt 9:27–31; 15:21–28; 17:14–18) is not specifically for forgiveness. It has to do with people asking the Lord to have mercy regarding their situations, e.g., for the blind to receive sight, for the demon-possessed to have the demon exorcized, etc. But now that Christ has died, this old covenant prayer has been answered once and for all in Christ's death. "In this the love of God was manifested toward us, that God has sent His only begotten Son into the world . . . to be the propitiation for our sins" (1 John 4:9a, b, 10c NKJV; see Rom 3:24–26).

6. 1 Cor 11:25; see Rom 3:25.

God in Christ Has Redeemed His People:
God Justified Them

> Blessed are they of whom the lawless deeds were forgiven, and
> of whom the sins were covered over; blessed is the man of whom
> the Lord by no means may reckon sin. (Rom 4:7–8)

Similarly, we read: "*having forgiven us* all our transgressions" (Col 2:13c
NASB; compare Col 1:14; 3:13; Eph 1:7; 4:28). This is why, in Rom 4, when
Paul teaches on justification through faith in Christ (4:24–25), he does *not*
use Ps 51, which says, "Have mercy upon me, O God." Why? Because God
has had mercy on us in Christ, who is *the propitiation* (or mercy seat[7]) for
our sins (Rom 3:25; 11:30–31). And Ps 51:1 (AV) also says, "Blot out my
transgressions," but God now in Christ has already blotted them out (Col
2:14). Ps 51 continues, "Wash me thoroughly from mine iniquity" (v. 2), but
God has already washed us: "You were washed" (1 Cor 6:11a). The psalmist
says, "Blot out my transgressions . . . *for* I acknowledge my transgressions"
(51:1, 3). "But now" (Rom 3:21) God's justifying righteousness has been
manifested (through Christ's faith, his obedience unto death, 3:22), in that
we are justified through redemption[8] in *Christ*, God's propitiatory sacrifice
and mercy seat (3:24–25), that God might be the justifier of not him who
works (3:28; 4:5) but "the one [who's] of the faith of Jesus" (3:26). So, it is
not because of what we do—even confessing our sins—that God blots out
our transgressions, for when we were still dead in our transgressions, that
is when he made us *alive*, having forgiven us all our transgressions (Col
2:13 ATP; see Eph 2:4–6). While we were still sinners (unbelievers) Christ
died for us, which justified us (Rom 5:8–9). And being *alive* means being
a new creation in Christ[9] (2 Cor 5:17). This grace through redemption has
justified the gentiles through faith alone (Rom 3:27—4:11); they *have* obtained mercy (11:30); so it is *not* that they have not yet obtained it and so
must constantly plead for it, with or without a *Kyrie* liturgy. Thus, we find
no such pleas for mercy as in the *Kyrie* in the NT letters.

---

7. See Nygren, *Commentary on Romans*, 156–60.

8. Redemption is the basis of the giving of the Spirit (Gal 4:4–7), the seal unto the
day of redemption (2 Cor 1:22; Eph 1:13; 4:30). OT saints were not sealed in this manner, for David said, "Take not your Holy Spirit from me" (Ps 51:11b). There is union
and distinction between OT and NT saints.

9. In the old covenant, the psalmist said "a prayer to the God of *my* life" (Ps 42:8);
but now, since I have died with Christ, and I (as in flesh) live no longer, but Christ lives
in me (Gal 2:20; Rom 6:6), instead of "the God of *my* [soulish] life" (1 Cor 2:12, 14), it
is "*Christ* our Life" (Col 3:4 AT).

Paul was called by Christ, not in Jerusalem but on the road to Damascus (Acts 9:3–6), and then, having received his revelation of Jesus Christ, he *did not* go up to Jerusalem to those who were apostles before him (Gal 1:11–17). Three years later Paul went to Jerusalem to get to know Peter, and he stayed fifteen days (Gal 1:18). Then, after a period of fourteen years, Paul went to Jerusalem because of a revelation from God in Christ, and he set forth and submitted to the so-called pillars (James, Peter, and John) *the gospel that he preached among the gentiles*, Gal 2:1–7. It was there, at Jerusalem, that James, Peter, and John *first came to discover* and *know the gospel of grace to the nations* that was given by Christ to Paul as the nations' apostle (Gal 2:9). Paul said that to Peter there was entrusted "the gospel of the circumcision" to the Jews, who could retain their Jewish ways while having faith in the Messiah, and that God entrusted to Paul the law-free "gospel of the uncircumcision" to the gentiles (Gal 2:7–8 AV and lit. Greek trans.). Although the apostleship of Peter was distinct from Paul's, ultimately all the apostles preached the gospel of Christ—see Gal 1:23; 1 Cor 15:1–11—so there is both distinction and union between the gospel to the gentiles and the gospel to the Jews. Sometime after Paul's trip to Jerusalem, Peter came to Antioch, where Paul opposed him to his face (2:11).

> For prior to the coming of certain men from James [from Jerusalem], he [Peter] used to eat with the Gentiles, but when they came, he began to withdraw and hold himself aloof, fearing the party of the circumcision. (Gal 2:12 NASB)

This was a powerful law-keeping influence coming from "the party of the circumcision," who came from the Jerusalem church. The use of the *Kyrie* began in the East, and the most liturgically Jewish church today, in terms of using the *Kyrie* the most often, is the Eastern Orthodox Church. Thus, it is significant that the Eastern Orthodox Church boasts of its origins as the church that had its beginning in Jerusalem.[10] So, the *Kyrie* comes from Jewish Christianity and not from the gospel of God—the grace of Christ which Paul preached among the gentiles. Later, the West (Rome) put the *Kyrie* into its liturgy. But the letters of the NT scriptures never teach the *Kyrie*, for it is not in line with the apostolic gospel. We continually need mercy from God, but God continually justifies the ungodly who trust in him (Rom 4:5 lit.; 8:33); not those who beg for mercy as *if God has done nothing* in his Son's death (Gal 2:21). What God desires is repentance

10. See Carlton, *Faith*, 21.

when needed (1 Cor 11:31; 2 Cor 12:20–21); thus, the NT scriptures know nothing of a corporate confession of sins.[11]

Paul says, "Where there is no law, neither is there transgression" (Rom 4:15), and "Christ is the end of the law for righteousness to everyone who believes" (10:4).

> For if those things (of the law) I destroyed (by faith in Christ, through my death with him to the law) I build again, I establish myself as *a transgressor* (of the law). But (in Christ I am *not* a transgressor, for) I . . . died to the law, in order that I might live to God. (Gal 2:17–19; see 2:20–21)

Paul is saying:

> The law is nullified to me (Gal 6:14) by faith in Christ; for if not, the promise (of salvation) is nullified and destroyed by the law. (see Rom 4:14–15)

Therefore, in Christ, with whom we died to the law, there are no transgressions, in that they are not "put to our account" (Rom 4:6–8); thus there are no transgressors in Christ; and neither is there (a need for) the *confession* of transgression for the forgiveness of those transgressions, as *there was under the law* of Moses, as when David said:

> I said, "I will *confess* my transgressions unto the LORD," and You *forgave* the iniquity of my sin. (Ps 32:5b)

For David knew *the law*, which said:

---

11. Nor can such a confession be deduced from the NT scriptures. If, in corporate worship, for the sake of reminding believers of the truth of sin and *grace*, with its *assurance* of forgiveness in Christ to comfort and renew the minds of God's people, it is deemed good to have such a confession of faith, it should align with the gospel of God. One example of such would be as follows:

Leader, with the whole assembly:

Our God and Father, as long as we live in this world, we continually need your justification, for *in the flesh* we are in bondage to sin, to desiring things other than God in God's place. But we thank you, Father, that you have delivered us from the reign of Sin, and that you *will* deliver us from the body of this death, through Christ our Lord—for we died with Christ, and by your doing we are not in the flesh, but *in the Spirit of Christ*, in whom we *have* the forgiveness of sins—we *are justified* from Adam's sin, indwelling sin, and all our sins, for the purpose of eternal life with You and your Son, in the Holy Spirit. Amen.

Leader: There is therefore now no condemnation for those who are in Christ Jesus. For the "law" of the Spirit, the rule of *life in Christ Jesus*, has set us free from the law, the one of Sin and of Death.

Leader, with the rest of the assembly: Amen!

(Those who would use this Confession of Faith are free to do so.)

It shall be, when he is guilty in any of these matters, that he shall *confess that he has sinned in that thing.* (Lev 5:5)[12]

Blot out my transgressions . . . *for* I acknowledge my transgressions. (Ps 51:1, 3)

For Us in Christ, to Ask God to Forgive Us
Is to Ask God to Redeem Us

Redemption was accomplished when Christ died for us. Redemption means that we have been set free from the debt of sin by God himself when he purchased his people back from the ownership of and slavery to sin. Referring to Christ, the writer says:

> In him *we have redemption* through his blood, *the forgiveness of our trespasses*, according to the riches of his [God's] grace. (Eph 1:7 ESV)

In Christ we *have* redemption, the forgiveness of sins. *Redemption* and *the forgiveness of sins* go together, for justification (forgiveness) is based upon redemption. So, a person cannot be "in Christ" without the forgiveness of sins! Redemption is the basis of and for justification, including the forgiveness of sins. We do not get redeemed again and again, for we were justified through the once-for-all, historical redemption that is in Christ (Rom 3:24; 6:10), which we received through faith in Christ alone (5:1) and not by confessing sins or doing anything else. If we needed to be forgiven each time we sinned, then we would have to be redeemed each time we sinned (Eph 1:7). We were justified when we believed in Christ, at a point of time in the past (Rom 5:1; 1 Cor 6:11), with the full effects remaining to the present. To the saints at Corinth, Paul said:

> God is faithful, through whom you were called [unto salvation] into the fellowship of his Son, Jesus Christ our Lord. (1 Cor 1:9)

The saints were called by God into "the fellowship of his Son," which is Christ's unbroken fellowship with God the Father. Through Christ's death, resurrection, and exaltation, those in him share that same fellowship with God the Father! And God never stops fellowshiping with his Son, for "no unrighteousness is in Him" (John 7:18 NKJV). In 1 Corinthians chapter 11,

---

12. Forgiveness under the law of Moses was inextricably tied to the Levitical priesthood; Lev 4:20, 26, 31; 5:6, 10, 13; 16:21; 26:40, 42; Num 5:6–8.

Paul seeks to correct those at Corinth who were taking the Lord's Supper in an unworthy manner.[13] He says:

> For he who eats and drinks in an unworthy manner [sins, and therefore] eats and drinks *judgment* to himself, not discerning the body of the Lord. For this reason, many are weak and sickly among you . . . [judgment follows the sin not repented of], and many sleep. (1 Cor 11:29–30 NKJV)

But then Paul says:

> For if we would *judge ourselves* [that we sinned, and repented of it] we would *not be judged* [by the Lord]. But [if we do not judge ourselves] when we are *judged, we are chastened by the Lord*, that we *may not be condemned with the world.* (1 Cor 11:31–32 NKJV)

In other words, if we judged ourselves (repented), we would not be judged by God. But if we did not discern the Lord's body, then, not judging ourselves (not repenting of this sin), when we are judged, we are chastened by the Lord (disciplined by him), not condemned by him. So, if we sin, there needs to be a change of mind, a judging of ourselves—that we have sinned—in which we turn from sin, back to the Lord. However, according to Rom 8:29–34; 1 Cor 6:10–11; and 1 John 2:19, we believe that those who remain unrepentant really are the children of disobedience and not children of God. God's faithfulness to his own means that, if we do not judge ourselves, the Lord will judge us, and that such discipline ensures that we will not be condemned along with the world. But it is significant that, in referring to this *judging* of one's self, which is *repentance*,[14] Paul does not use the language of "confession of sins." This does not mean a believer will never say to our Father, "Forgive me" in the relational sense.

God's *love does not*, even for one moment, consider our wrongs (1 Cor 13:5 AP); so, we (by the power of his justifying love for us) are not to account the wrongs of others against them. When a believer is walking in this love of Christ, if I sin against him, he does not hold it against me (13:5). But that does not mean that I never say, "Forgive me" when I sin against such a one. Likewise, when I sin against God, we sin against his love and grieve his Spirit, I may say, "Forgive me" (or similar words) for I have a personal relationship with God that I want to remain healthy. And since the "no condemnation" of the gospel is a pronouncement of justification ahead of the actual time of acquittal (on the last day, *the day of judgment,*

---

13. See 1 Cor 11:27 and 11:17–22, 33, 34. Even though he does not use "repent" in these texts (as he does in 2 Cor 12:(20), 21), it is clear that that is what he means.

14. As we have shown above (in 1 Cor 11:31).

Rom 2:5–10, for "we by the Spirit *wait* for the hope of righteousness/justification, Gal 5:5), since we still live in the flesh, the "God, I repent" (or even "Forgive me") is an expression of the present reality of sinful flesh. But knowing I am justified in Christ (Rom 5:1; 4:5; 8:33) and thus without legal compulsion, I am free, if and as God leads, to use words that express my repentance (the real issue), for repentance is a change of mind/heart, and God looks on the heart (Rom 2:28, 29; Acts 1:24; 15:8). Knowing that Scripture presents both sides—God's sovereign grace and human responsibility—the most that we can say is as follows: Those who *practice* the deeds of the flesh—who persist in such things without repentance—will not inherit the kingdom of God (Gal 5:21). Those who habitually practice those things cannot be those whom God foreknew (Rom 8:29), for the elect are sealed to the day of redemption (2 Cor 1:22; Eph 4:30). Just as the natural man (flesh) cannot receive Christ by faith (1 Cor 2:14), similarly, the elect saint, because of the flesh of sin and Satan, cannot persevere in faith—unless *God* in his faithfulness keeps him in faith to the end; and he does (see Phil 1:6; Rom 8:32–39). And any confession of sins to one another in the household of faith is to be according to the Spirit's leading, not out of legal compulsion, the source of which is the fear of condemnation.

True Faith, Which Includes Repentance, Is the Issue

In light of these things, according to Paul's gospel:

Any confession of sin done *in faith* is done, not to obtain forgiveness of that sin from God, but only as an expression of *repentance*, which is the fruit of *faith in Christ*, in whom *we have* the *forgiveness of sins* (Rom 4:5–8; Eph 1:7).

Christ-believers are not to live in fear that they have forgotten to confess some sin. God disciplines his children when they turn from him (Heb 12). A confession of sin does not change God's mind from being his enemies to being his friends, for God, by Christ's death, did that (Rom 3:24–26; 5:8–10). God's determination to reconcile us was accomplished by Christ's death, and God made sure we participated in this through the baptism into Christ's death and his resurrection life. So, if we sin, we are by the power of God (the gospel) to repent and believe in Christ—in the grace in which we stand, the grace of justification wherein we have peace with God (5:1). So, to repent is to return to Christ—to the obedience of faith—in whom we were justified (1 Cor 6:11). The clarity of Paul's gospel of free justification apart from the works of the law through Christ to all who believe in him been dulled by a verse in the "catholic letters," so that one *could* think that a person could be (justified) in Christ one day and back in Adam (in flesh, condemned) the next—back and forth, on and on. The letter to which I am referring is 1 John. Let us look at it in its context:

> That which was from the beginning, which we have seen and heard [Christ], which we have seen with our eyes . . . concerning the Word of life—the life was manifested, and we have seen and bear witness, and declare to you that *eternal life* [Christ, 1 John 5:10] . . . that which we have seen and heard we declare to you, that *you also* may have fellowship with *us*; and truly *our* fellowship is with the Father and with His Son Jesus Christ. (1 John 1:1–3 NKJV)

The writer clearly says that the people to whom he speaks in 1:3 did not yet have fellowship "with us," and thus they did not yet have fellowship with the Father or his Son Jesus Christ. This is also clear from the verses that follow (vv. 4–9). These people *said* they had fellowship with God, but they did not: "If we *say* that we have fellowship with him [the Father], and walk in darkness, we lie and do not the truth" (1:6 AV). Three things characterize those who "say" they have fellowship with God but do not. First, they *walk in darkness*.[15]

Second, they *lie*.[16] Third, they *do not the truth*.[17] So, in 1 John 1:1–2, the writer is evangelistically proclaiming the Messiah to his readers, some of whom were most likely influenced by Gnosticism, who thought that they were without sin. To make sure they were real Christians, he tells them that they need to stop denying that they are sinners, that is, no longer think or

---

15. "If we say we have fellowship with him, and [yet] *walk in darkness* . . ." (1:6). Anyone who *walks in darkness* is *not* walking in *light*; for "God is light, and in Him is no darkness at all" (1:5c). To be *in God*, where there is *no darkness*, is to be in "eternal life, which is *in his Son*" (5:11). So, being in the darkness is the same as walking in darkness. "But he who hates his brother is *in darkness* and *walks in darkness*, and does not know where he is going, because the darkness has blinded his eyes" (1 John 2:11). "He who *says* he is in the light and hates his brother, is *in darkness* even until now" (1 John 2:9 NKJV). "Whoever hates his brother [is in darkness] is a murderer, and you know that *no murderer has eternal life* abiding in him" (1 John 3:15 NKJV). In contrast, he later says, "We know that the Son of God has come and has given us an understanding, that *we may know* Him who is true; and we are in him who is true, in his Son Jesus Christ. This is *the true God*, and *eternal life*" (1 John 5:20 NKJV).

16. "*We lie*" (1:6 AV), "and no *lie* is of the truth" (2:21c AV); i.e., no lie is of Jesus Christ, who is the truth (John 14:6).

17. "*We . . . do not the truth*" (1:6 AV) .They are unbelievers, for "he who *does the truth* comes to the light, that his deeds may be clearly seen, that they have been done in God" (John 3:21 NKJV).

say, "We have no sin," and believe in the Christ who is being proclaimed in 1:1–3. In 1 John 1:8, John says, "If we say that we have no sin, we deceive ourselves, and the truth is not in us" (1:8). Now, the natural antithesis to this phrase "if we say that *we have no sin*" would have been "if we say that *we have sin.*" But instead, he says, "If we *confess our sins.*" If we understand the writer's background as a Jew, who was familiar with the law, with its "confess your sins,"[18] then we can understand that it was natural for John to say "confess your sins." But Paul, to whom God gave the gospel to the nations, never uses the phrase "confess your sins." He does not use those words because his gospel is law-free and that means free from "the Jews' religion" (Gal 1:12–16); and the phrase "confess your sins" (for forgiveness), is found in the (old covenant) law. Thus, 1 John 1:9 *can* be understood to mean that one is obligated to confess his sins to be forgiven—but such an idea is, according to Paul, to be justified by the works of *the law* (Gal 5:1–5), for the law includes the confession of sins, as we have shown. Again, only if and when they yield to the flesh does Paul tell Christ-believers to judge themselves (1 Cor 11:31; see 1 Cor 5), to repent (2 Cor 12:20–21). But the light of Paul's gospel (Rom 2:16) has been darkened and obscured by some things in the catholic epistles, (especially 1 John 1:9). Beker wrote:

> The theological tendencies behind the formation of the canon had enormous consequences for the interpretation of Paul's letters. Paul was not only harmonized with the other canonical witnesses, but became as well a witness for doctrinal uniformity. This construction of a catholic Paul yielded disastrous consequences for the understanding of the authentic, "historical" Paul in the church.[19]

And so it has been, down to this very day. But Christ is my life; thus, I am no longer in Adam but in Christ alone. According to Paul's gospel and his imperatives, the only thing required for continued life with God is faith in Christ, whose Spirit obliges mortification (Rom 1:5; 8:12–13) and repentance as needed (1 Cor 11:31; see 1 Cor 5; 2 Cor 12:20–21).

> God's unchangeable *love* for his people issued in his pre-creation, pre-fall *choice* of Christ's own people, resulting in God's justification of his people in time, unto eternal life.[20]

18. Lev 5:5; 16:21; 26:40; Num 5:7; Ps 32:5; contra Rom 3:21.

19. Beker, *Triumph of God*, 8. He continues, "The catholic Paul is a synthesized Paul, constructed from Acts, the Pauline letters, and the Deutero-Pauline letters (Colossians, Ephesians, and the Pastoral Epistles)" (*Triumph of God*, 8).

20. See Rom 8:28–34 ATP; compare Eph 1:4, 5; 5:25; and Christ died for those under the first covenant (Heb 9:15), that they should not be made perfect (glorified)

Just as God's foreknowledge of his people (wherein he intimately knew them before the world began) is unconditional—it is *not* conditioned upon a foreseen faith of ours, for faith is a gift unconditionally granted[21] to the elect, so that they come to faith—even so justification is not conditioned on anything in us, for we are justified freely by God's grace, through the redemption which is in Christ Jesus received by faith alone, which is a gift from God, and we receive this grace that justifies through faith alone. Therefore, any liturgy that says, "*If* we confess our sins, God will forgive us our sins" is not in line with the apostolic gospel,[22] the grace in which we stand (Rom 5:1–2). A conditional justification/forgiveness is ignorance of the purity and sufficiency of faith in Christ alone, which (alone) is the grace of God in Christ.

> If human existence under law is bondage to a divinely sanctioned structure of obligation which must be met in order to be rightly related to God . . . then one can understand why Paul's theological analysis of law shows no interest whatever in distinguishing one law from another: for example, the ritual from the moral, the permanently valid from the transient . . . for the problem is not certain laws but law.[23]

Amen. This "obligation which must be met" to be right with God includes the obligation to confess one's sins. And yes, that is "law." And Keck also says:

> A resolute affirmation of the *adequacy* of *trust/faith* to relate one *rightly to God* will always appear "negative" with respect to every other mode that, however subtly, supplements sheer *reliance on what God has done in Christ* with prerequisites. Theologically, the demand for "circumcision" can take many forms, even today. It appears whenever one thinks along these lines: "Faith in Christ is fine as far as it goes, but your relation to God is not really right and your salvation is not adequate *unless . . .* " It does not matter how the sentence is completed.[24]

And that includes when the sentence is completed with "*unless* you confess your sins."

---

apart from us (Heb 9:15; 11:40b).

21. Phil 1:29.

22. Even if this writer was the apostle John, this can be compared to Peter's lapse at Antioch (Gal 2:11–21; see 2:6).

23. Keck, *Proclamation Commentaries*, 84.

24. Keck, *Proclamation Commentaries*, 84–5, emphasis mine.

"The new testament . . . of the Spirit" of Christ has superseded the old covenant law of Moses (2 Cor 3:6–18) and that includes confession in its relation to the forgiveness of sins. Luther understood that Jesus' ministry did not begin until his baptism, when the Spirit was poured out upon him. But Luther wrongly equated Christ's baptism (by John the Baptizer) with the beginning of grace and of the new covenant (testament).[25] Luther rejected Rome's view of Penance, but he revised it to be what Lutherans call "Confession and Absolution," which they claim to get from Matt 16:19, 18:15–18, and John 20:23. But those texts are dealing with the *discipline* of members of Christ's church and not with a confession of sin (with a corresponding assurance of forgiveness). This blind spot of Luther on primary aspects of the new covenant/testament was so influential that it caused him, and those who have followed him, to preach (like Rome) primarily from the four Gospels, over against the Epistles, where God's grace based upon Christ's accomplished redemption is most clearly revealed.[26]

25. See Luther, *Complete Sermons*, 1:128.

26. Of course, we are *not* saying that preachers should never use any of the four Gospels in their preaching.

——— TWENTY ———

Death and Eternal Life

> For the wages that the Sin pays is Death, but the free gift of God
> is eternal life, through Jesus Christ our Lord. (Rom 6:23)

The Resurrection of the Dead Is Eternal Life

PAUL SAYS, "IF CHRIST has not been raised, your faith is futile and you are
still in your sins. Then also those who have fallen asleep in Christ have
perished [ἀπώλοντο]" (1 Cor 15:17–18 ESV). And Paul concludes his argument with the following words: "If the dead are not raised, then 'Let us eat
and drink, for tomorrow we *die*'" (15:32b ESV). It is clear from these texts
that Paul means that to *perish* (v. 18) is to *die* (v. 32), just as we still use
these words today. So Paul is saying, "If the dead are not raised, death is the
ultimate end." Corresponding to this, Jesus in the Synoptic Gospels uses
the phrase "the resurrection out of the dead" *only* for the children of God,
because, for Jesus and for (Christ in) Paul, "resurrection from the dead"
means *life* and *immortality*—the opposite of *death*. "For the wages of the Sin
is *Death*, but God's gift is *Eternal Life* in Christ our Lord" (6:23).

A Resurrection . . . of Both Just	and Unjust (Acts 24:15)
"The children of this world marry, and are given in marriage. But those who shall be accounted worthy to obtain that world-age, and *the resurrection from the dead, neither marry . . . neither can they die anymore*; for [in this way] they are equal to the angels; and are *children of God*, being *children of the resurrection*" (Luke 20:34–36 AV/AT).	Therefore, conversely, we deduce that "the children of this world" are *not* accounted worthy to obtain that age (of resurrection and immortality), for they can (and will) *die*; they are *not* equal to the angels, they are *not* children of God; they are *not* children of the resurrection (deduced from Luke 20:35–36 AV/AT).
So also, *is the resurrection of the dead*: It is sown: In corruption (1 Cor 15:42) In dishonor (15:43) In weakness (15:43) In flesh and blood (15:50) In mortality (15:53, 54) a natural body (15:44) . . . The image of the earthy (15:47–49) It is raised: In incorruption (1 Cor 15:42) In glory (15:43) In power (15:43) In immortality (15:53–54) A *spiritual* (of the Spirit) *body* (15:44) Bearing the image of the heavenly one, i.e., the last Adam (15:45–49)	Since they are *not* "children of the resurrection" (Luke 20:36) unto *immortality* (1 Cor 15:53–54; 2 Tim 1:10), we scripturally deduce that *the unjust* will be raised in flesh and blood (15:50); a natural body (15:44); in mortality (15:53, 54); bearing the image of the first man, *not* the image of the last Adam; the image of the earthy (15:47–49), for flesh and blood cannot inherit the kingdom of God, neither does corruption (mortal body) inherit incorruption (immortal body, 1 Cor 15:50). They will "come forth unto the resurrection of *judgment*" (John 5:29), when they will receive God's wrath (Rom 2:5, 8) and experience tribulation and anguish (Rom 2:9) unto *destruction* (Rom 9:22; Matt 7:13; 10:28). So, the wages of sin (truly) is *death* (Rom 6:23).
"Christ, having been raised from the dead, *dies no more*" (Rom 6:9 NKJV). He is the firstfruits of *our* resurrection.	Thus, for those "in Adam" raised for judgment, it cannot be said that they "die no more."
—Delivered from death[1]	—Not delivered from death[2]

Scripture gives *no* hint of a third kind of body for the resurrection to judgment of the unjust.

---

1. 1 Cor 15:26 (50–57). Unless otherwise noted, the AV was used in this chart.

2. Rom 6:21–23; see Phil 3:19; 1 Cor 15:16–22; Matt 10:28. Regarding this entire chart, some credit goes to Peter Grice, from whom I received the basic idea, in his "Neglected Doctrines of Resurrection."

Thus, the phrase "the resurrection from the dead" applies only for those who will be saved from death, never to die again. While Luke has Paul referring to "a resurrection of both the just and unjust" (Acts 24:15), Paul, in his letters, never applies the word "resurrection" to the lost. Why? Because for Jesus (in Luke 20) and Paul (in 1 Cor 15), the *resurrection out of the dead* is a resurrection *to life and immortality*—nothing less than that (2 Tim 1:10)! Thus, for the historical Jesus and Paul, any "resurrection" from the dead of the lost (such as that of Acts 24:15 and John 5:29), is not worthy to be called "resurrection," precisely because the end of those who practice lawlessness is *death* (Rom 6:19 lit., 21, 23); their end is *destruction* (Phil 3:19; Matt 7:13, 21–23; 10:28). Thus, "resurrection" for such falls short of being an appropriate term, for it is not a resurrection out of the dead to life and immortality but to judgment (John 5:29) and ultimately to death (Rom 1:32; 5:21; 6:23), that is, to destruction (Rom 9:22). At the same time, however, from what Paul says in Rom 2:5–10, we deduce that Paul (without using "resurrection") is there describing the very same judgment to which Acts 24:15 and John 5:29 refer. For *the day of . . . the righteous judgment of God* (Rom 2:5) includes both those who through patient endurance seek immortality (who will be given eternal life), and those who do not obey the truth, who will on that day receive wrath.[3]

John's words in 5:29 are not necessarily the words of the historical Jesus, any more than are those in John 3:16 or John 19:30, but are the theological *truth* of the risen Christ woven into the work by the evangelist. For example, the author of John has Jesus saying, "It is accomplished" (or "finished") to convey the truth that his death was "the work" that he came to do, as we find throughout his Gospel. But Jesus' work was not accomplished until he actually *died* (and thus could no longer speak) according to the apostolic gospel. This is not me being a literalist; it is gospel truth. So, in John 19:30, 5:29, and elsewhere in his Gospel, the writer puts the truth of the risen Christ into the words of Jesus while he is still in the flesh. But we should not ignore differences such as the contrast between Luke 20:35–36 ("the resurrection" of the children of God only) and John 5:29 (the resurrection of just and unjust), nor the radical difference between what Jesus says in Luke 10:25–28; 18:18; Mark 10:17–19; and Matt 19:16–17—where the historical Jesus, before his death accomplished redemption, says that to attain to eternal life one must keep the Ten Commandments—with the Christ of John's Gospel, which says that eternal life comes by *believing* in Jesus Christ (John 1:12; 3:16, 18; 5:24; 6:29, 40; 7:39; 8:34; 9:35; 11:25, 26; 16:9; and 20:31)—the latter being in line with *the risen Christ* in the

3. According to Paul's gospel, Rom 2:5–10, 16.

apostolic gospel (Rom 10:5–10). When one understands that the only basis for preaching "the word of faith [in Christ]" unto salvation (Rom 10:6–10) is Christ's death and resurrection, then all else falls into place, including the fact that Jesus could not have preached that gospel *before* his death and resurrection (Rom 3:24–26; 4:24, 25 lit.; 10:5–9; 2 Cor 5:16–21).

God's Wrath Revealed (Romans 1:18)

God's wrath is indeed a revelation from God, not only in its dynamic action but in the revelatory enlightenment which comes through Paul's words about God's wrath. For in this present age, God's wrath is against those who suppress the truth in unrighteousness (Rom 1:18), the effect being that they are "receiving in themselves the due penalty for their error" (Rom 1:27c ESV). But Paul says that this "receiving in themselves" a reprobate mind with its corresponding wicked passions *is* the just recompense and penalty for their error—it *is* "the wrath of God" dynamically revealed *now* in this present age (1:18–27). But logically, there is a correspondence between the nature and degree of the present (revelation of the) wrath of God (1:18–32) and the future revelation of God's wrath in the day of wrath (2:5–10). Although God's wrath in the ultimate sense will be expressed in "the day of wrath and revelation of the righteous judgment of God" (Rom 2:5[–10]), the way the *wrath of God* is expressed in this present age (God gives them over to a reprobate mind, to do the things that are not proper), does not begin to correspond to the future wrath of God on the day of wrath if the wrath is defined as "eternal conscious torment"! Instead, it is a wrath (2:8) that results in "tribulation and anguish" for its recipients (v. 9), a wrath far worse than the present form of God's wrath, which is God giving them over to a reprobate mind, receiving "in themselves the due recompense of their error" (1:27), which results in "such things" (1:32) as resulted from rejecting God through unbelief: "*God gave them up* to a reprobate mind, to *do those things not being right . . . unrighteousness, fornication, covetousness, evil; full of envy, murder*" (from Rom 1:28–29). We emphasize that "the wrath to come" will finally be experienced in terms of "affliction" and "distress" ("anguish," Rom 2:9), utterly surpassing[4] the negative experience

---

4. "Is *anything* too hard for the Lord?" (Gen 18:14a AV). Thus, God surely can cause the unjust to endure wrath's "affliction and anguish" for a long period of time before that person finally dies (Rom 6:21–23; 9:22). Many Christians, often pastors, who are leading people to Christ in Africa, Indonesia, etc., are *murdered* by men of anti-Christian religions; those men will experience hell, and when their intense affliction in conscience and body has satisfied retributive *justice*, they will finally die (Rom 2:5–10; 6:23), which is also in accordance with divine justice (Rom 1:28–32).

of what that same individual has endured of God's wrath *in this* age, as we have shown. Therefore, in "the day of wrath" (2:5) there will be a spectrum of a near-infinite degree of broadness—*of* suffering "*affliction*" (v. 9), that is, the recompense according to God's justice, depending on what *each* has done in the body, considering the vast differences of humans, each with his or her own individual life. And the (temporal) "wrath" on that "day" is in contrast to "*eternal* life" (2:5–10). Returning to Rom 6:23, the contrast is between eternal life and death—not eternal life in suffering—not eternal *existence* (*being*) in suffering versus eternal life. For there are only two kinds of being: Paul contrasts the ones *being* (ὄντες) according to *the flesh*, with *the ones* (*being*) according to *the Spirit* (in Rom 8:5). This corresponds to Galatians, where he writes, "Because the one sowing to his flesh will of the flesh reap *corruption*, but the one sowing to the Spirit, of the Spirit will reap *life eternal*" (Gal 6:8). Relating to this text and others, Fudge says:

> The most natural opposite of life is *death* or *non-life*. It is not life in misery. The fact that "eternal life" involves so much more than mere existence only increases Paul's contrast of "life" and "corruption." . . . By what means can "loss of life" be converted to "life of loss"? If the "life" is of a more precious and enduring quality than any we now fully experience, that makes the loss of it all the more tragic, but it is more terrible precisely because it is loss.[5]

Death (Θάνατος)

There are four apostolic texts which reveal that, in contrast to those to whom God will render eternal life, the end of those who "do not obey the truth" is described by these words: "*death*," "*corruption*," and "*perish*." These three words all stand in antithesis to *eternal life*.

> Do not be deceived; God is not mocked [outwitted]; for whatever a man sows, that he will also reap, because the one sowing to his flesh will of the flesh reap *corruption*, but the one sowing to the Spirit, of the Spirit will reap *life eternal*. (Gal 6:7–8)

> But what fruit were you getting at that time from the things of which you are now ashamed? For the end of those things is *death*. But now that you have been set free from sin, and have become slaves of God, the fruit you get leads to sanctification, and its end, *eternal life*. (Rom 6:21–22 ESV)

5. Fudge, *Fire That Consumes*, 203.

For the wages of the Sin is *death*,[6] but the gift of God is *eternal life*, through Christ Jesus our Lord. (Rom 6:23)

For God so loved the world, that he gave his only begotten Son, that those believing in him may not *perish*, but have *life eternal*. (John 3:16)

All these texts coincide with what Paul says in Rom 2:7–8, where he contrasts "wrath," which is unto *destruction* (Rom 9:22), with *eternal life*. But he does not call *the day of wrath and of the righteous judgment of God* (when *the lost* will be judged) "the resurrection of the dead," or even a "resurrection." Even apart from John's Apocalypse, we scripturally deduce that "the death" (Rom 5:12, 14, 17, 21, lit.) has two aspects: the first death and the second; but these two are ultimately *one* death. John's resurrection to *judgment* of those who have done evil (John 5:29; compare who did "not obey the truth," Rom 2:5–10), when they will be judged and recompensed according to their works, does *not* occur in this present life. If it did, there would only be one death. But since that judgment does not occur in this life, there is a "resurrection to judgment" (5:29), after which they die[7] and from which there is *no resurrection unto life*. This truth is clearly deduced from 1 Cor 15:16–22 (where Paul teaches that "in Adam all *die*") and then in 1 Cor 15:42–57, where he teaches that there is *immortality* in Christ alone (see earlier, in 15:22). Thus, in Paul's letters, sin leads to death; death is seen holistically and with ultimate finality, i.e., to not ever be broken by a kind of resurrection that would *undo* or *reverse* death. What makes *death* to be *death* is that it *deprives* one of *eternal life with God in Christ*. Thus, the so-called "resurrection" of the lost in Acts 24[8] and John 5 is only for a short

---

6. When Christ died on our behalf for sin (Rom 5:8), the wages of which are death, he did not suffer eternal conscious torment. Hear the unanswerable argument for this in Date's podcast, "Precious Blood of Christ." Regarding the lost, that God can and will destroy both body and soul (which Date rightly calls "embodied life") in Gehenna (Matt 10:28), Date says, "Accordingly, conditionalists believe the consequences of sin, borne by Jesus for those who accept his gift, is the death he died in their stead: the privation of embodied life. Defenders of eternal torment, however, seem unable to explain how Jesus' death can be considered substitutionary if those in whose stead he died would have lived forever in hell" ("Righteous for the Unrighteous," 92).

7. These two deaths (yet one) are analogous to the two comings of Christ. Whereas the Jews expected only *one* coming; it is *one* and *the same Christ* who came, first in humiliation to redeem a people, and will come the second time as exalted Lord, unto salvation for his people (Heb 9:28); there is both union and distinction between them.

8. Those who would use Dan 12:2 to support eternal conscious torment (ECT) are wrong. The text is not referring to a universal resurrection of the just and unjust; see Gowan, *Daniel*, 152–53; Newsom and Breed, *Daniel*, 363; and Collins, *Daniel* 392, 394–97; thus, the text is a merely a shadow of what is clear in the NT. Regarding

duration, a mere moment in relation to *God's* time, in which "a thousand years [is] as one *day*" (2 Pet 3:8; see Rom 2:5), that each unredeemed sinner will receive his or her *just* punishment according to what was individually done in the body, only to return to death.[9]

"contempt" see Peoples, "Introduction to Evangelical Conditionalism," 16n19.

9. Θάνατος ("death") is translated (in English) in italics in the following texts: "Then the serpent said to the woman, 'You shall not die by *death*'" (Gen 3:4 SAAS). Regarding Hagar and her son: "Then she went and sat down across from him . . . for she said to herself, 'Let me not see the *death* of the boy'" (Gen 21:16a, b SAAS). "So Abimelech charged all his people, saying, 'He who touches this man or his wife shall surely be put to *death*'" (Gen 26:11 SAAS).

"Those who practice such things are worthy of *death*" (Rom 1:32). "As through one man the Sin entered the world, and through the Sin, the death [entered]—and so the *death* entered into all men . . ." (5:12), "the *death* reigned from Adam until Moses" (Rom 5:14a, referring to a spiritual-unto-bodily *death* of the whole man—of those who lived from Adam until Moses; for Paul is referring to Genesis, where it says of Adam): "and all the days that lived were nine hundred and thirty years: and he died" (Gen 5:5 AV). And then, beginning with Seth and then others, it says, "and he died" (Gen 5:8 AV); "and he died" (5:11 AV); "and he died" (5:14 AV); "and he died" (5:17 AV); "and he died" (5:20 AV); "and he died" (5:27 AV); "and he died" (5:31 AV). Paul the Hebrew knew of no other "*death*" than this. So he continues: "For if by the trespass of the one, *death reigned* through the one" (Rom 5:17) ". . . in order that, as the sin reigned in the *death*, even so might the grace reign . . . unto *eternal life*, through Jesus" (5:21). "As many of us who were baptized into Christ Jesus, into the *death* of him we were baptized? Therefore we were buried . . . into the *death* . . . we have become united with him in the likeness of his *death*" (6:3–5). "*Death* no longer lords it over him" (6:9). "For the end of those things is *death*" (6:21). "Bearing fruit unto *death*" (7:5; see 6:23). "For the wages that the Sin pays is *death*" (6:23). "Who will deliver me out of the body of this *death*?" (7:25). "For the law of the Spirit . . . has set you free from the law of sin and of *death*" (8:1–2). "For I am persuaded that neither *death*, nor life . . . will be able to separate us from God's love" (8:39).

What follows are other texts that translate Θάνατος as *death*, using WEB translation: "Behold . . . the Son of Man will be delivered . . . they will condemn him to *death*" (Matt 20:18). "They all condemned him to be worthy of *death*" (Mark 14:64). "It had been revealed . . . that he should not see *death* before he had seen the Lord's Christ" (Luke 2:26).

"And I, if I am lifted up from the earth . . . signifying by what kind of *death* he should die" (John 12:32, 33). "The Jews said to him, 'It is not lawful for us to put anyone to *death*,' that the word of Jesus might be fulfilled, which he spoke, signifying by what kind of *death* he should die" (18:31–32), ". . . what kind of *death* he would glorify God" (21:19).

"And killed; whom God raised up, having freed him from the agony of *death*" (Acts 2:23b, 24). "I persecuted this Way to the *death*, binding . . . men and women" (22:4). "I found him to be accused . . . but not to be charged with anything worthy of *death*" (23:29). "But . . . he had committed nothing worthy of *death*" (25:25). "This man does nothing worthy of *death*" (26:31) ". . . because there was no cause of *death* in me" (28:18).

"For all things are yours, whether Paul . . . or the world, or life, or *death*" (1 Cor 3: 22). "You proclaim the Lord's *death*" (11:26) "For since *death* came by man, the resurrection

Destroy, perish (ἀπόλλυμι)

is also an important word in this discussion, because θάνατος ("death") and ἀπόλλμι ("destroy") are often used synonymously, as we see when Paul, referring to Jesus, said, "Though they found no ground for putting him to *death* [θανατος], they asked Pilate that he be *destroyed* [απολλμι]" (Acts 13:28 [margin note, lit. "destroyed"] NASB). Similarly, since "kill" means put to death, it follows that Matthew's Jesus also equates death with destruction:

> And do not fear the ones *killing* the body, but not being able to *kill* the soul; but rather, fear him [God] who is able to *destroy* [απόλλμι] both body *and soul* in Gehenna. (Matt 10:28)

Although I am not alone in the belief that the author of Matthew (written decades after Jesus died) in the above text was most likely influenced by Platonic philosophy,[10] we nevertheless let it stand; it proves that for God the "soul" is not indestructible. He can and will destroy the unjust in Gehenna. This word is usually translated as *destroy*, which is defined as "to put out of existence, kill."[11] In the scriptures below (see footnote), the English translation of ἀπόλλυμι (*apollumi*) appears in italics (using the WEB, unless otherwise noted).[12]

---

of the dead also came by man" (15:21). "The last enemy that will be abolished is *death*" (15:26). "But when this perishable will have become imperishable, and this mortal will have put on immortality, then what is written will happen: '*Death* is swallowed up in victory.' '*Death*, where is your sting? Hades, where is your victory?'" (15:55). "The sting of *death* is sin, and the power of sin is the law" (15:56).

"Christ will be magnified in my body, whether by life, or by *death*" (Phil 1:20). "He humbled himself, becoming obedient to *death*, yes, the *death* of the cross" (2:8). "For indeed he was sick, nearly to *death*" (2:27). "For the work of Christ he came near to *death*, risking his life" (2:30). "And the fellowship of his sufferings, becoming conformed to his *death*" (3:10).

"Yet now he has reconciled in the body of his flesh through *death*" (Col 1:22). "Christ Jesus, who abolished *death*, and brought life and immortality to light through the Good News" (2 Tim 1:10). "Jesus, because of the suffering of *death* crowned with glory . . . that by the grace of God he should taste of *death* for everyone" (Heb 2:9). "That through *death* he might bring to nothing him who had the power of *death*, that is, the devil, and might deliver all of them who through fear of *death* were all their lifetime subject to bondage" (Heb 2:14, 15). "To him who was able to save him from *death*" (Heb 5:7; also Heb 7:23; 9:15–17; 11:5).

10. "Matthew expresses his warning in the Hellenistic language that distinguishes 'body' and 'soul.'" Boring and Craddock, *People's New Testament*, 49.

11. *Merriam-Webster*, "Destroy," 2a.

12. "From the blood of Abel to the blood of Zachariah, who **perished** [died] between the altar and the sanctuary" (Luke 11:51). "Unless you repent, you will all *perish* [be destroyed] in the same way" (13:3). "Or those eighteen, on whom the tower in Siloam fell, and *killed* them; do you think that they were worse offenders . . . ? I tell you, no, but,

unless you repent, you will all *perish* in the same way" (13:4–5). "I *perish* with hunger" (15:17). "Until the day that Noah entered into the ship, and the flood came, and *destroyed* them all" (17:27). "But in the day that Lot went out from Sodom, it rained fire and sulfur from the sky, and *destroyed* them all" (17:28–29). "He was teaching daily . . . but . . . the people sought to *destroy* him" (19:47). "What therefore will the lord of the vineyard do to them? He will come and *destroy* these farmers" (20:16).

"For God so loved the world, that he gave his only begotten Son, that whoever believes in him should not **perish** [die], but have eternal life" (John 3:16). "Do not work for the food which *perishes*, but for the food which remains to *eternal life*, which the Son of Man will give to you" (6:27). "The thief only comes to steal, kill, and *destroy*" (10:10). ". . . should die for the people, and that the whole nation not **perish**" (11:50). "Caiaphas . . . advised the Jews that it was expedient that one man should *perish* for the people" (18:14). ". . . as have sinned without law will also *perish* without the law" (2:12).

"For the word of the cross is foolishness to those who are *dying* [*perishing*, AV], but to us who are saved it is the power of God" (1 Cor 1:18). "For it is written, 'I will *destroy* the wisdom of the wise, I will bring the discernment of the discerning to nothing'" (1:19). "And through your knowledge, he who is weak *perishes*, the brother for whose sake Christ died" (10:9). "Let us not test Christ, as some of them tested, and *perished* [were *destroyed*, AV] by the serpents. Do not grumble, as some of them also grumbled, and *perished*" (10:10 WEB/AT). "For if the *dead* are not raised, neither has Christ been raised. Then they also who are fallen asleep [died] in Christ have *perished*" (15:17–18).

"For we are the aroma of Christ to God among those who are being saved and among those who are *perishing*, to one a fragrance from death to death, to the other a fragrance from life to life" (2 Cor 2:15–16 NKJV). "The gospel is veiled in those who are *dying*" (4:3). "We are pressed on every side . . . struck down, yet not *destroyed*" (4:9).

"Only one is the lawgiver, who is able to *save* and to *destroy*" (Jas 4:12). ". . . by which means the world that then was, being overflowed with water, *perished*" (2 Pet 3:6). ". . . not wishing that any should *perish*, but that all should come to repentance" (2 Pet 3:9). "The Lord, having saved a people out of the land of Egypt, afterward *destroyed* those who did not believe" (Jude 5). "For they went in the way of Cain and *perished* in Korah's rebellion" (Jude 11).

We continue with ἀπόλλυμι (translated in italics) from the SAAS translation of the LXX except where noted (note how *destroyed* means put to death, and vice versa): "Would You also *destroy* the place and not spare it for the fifty righteous in it?" (Gen 18:24) "'Would You *destroy* all the city for lack of five?' He replied, 'If I find there forty-five, I will not *destroy* it.' 'But suppose there should be forty found there?' . . . 'I will not *destroy* it for the sake of forty'" (18:28, 29). "So He said, 'I will not *destroy* it for the sake of twenty.' . . . suppose ten should be found there?' So He said, 'I would not *destroy* it for the sake of the ten'" (18:31–32). "Then take them out of this place! For we will *destroy* this place, because their outcry has become great before the Lord, and the Lord sent us to *destroy* it" (19:12c–13). "O Lord, will You *destroy* an ignorant and just nation?" (20:4). "The people of the land will stone him with stones. I will set my face against that man and will *destroy* him from among his people" (Lev 20:2d, 3a). "I will . . . *destroy* them from among their people" (20:5c). "I will . . . *destroy* him from among his people" (20:6c). "Any soul who does any work on that same day, that soul shall be *destroyed* from among his people" (23:30) ". . . and I will utterly *destroy* the bad wild animals from the land" (26:6c).

"You shall *perish* among the Gentiles" (26:38). "I will strike them with death and *destroy* them" (Num 14:12a). "So they and all with them went down alive into Hades, and the earth covered them; and they *perished* from the midst of the congregation" (16:33).

Incorruption (ἀφθαρσία), Which Is the Opposite of Corruption (φθορά)

Flesh and blood cannot inherit the kingdom of God, nor does *corruption* inherit incorruption (1 Cor 15:50). Paul uses "flesh" to refer to the whole man, the person, in the following text: "that no flesh should glory in His presence" (1 Cor 1:29). The whole man, body and spirit, is flesh and will ultimately perish without Christ. Therefore, we must be born according to the Spirit (Gal 4:29), who is life (Rom 8:10 lit.). Paul says:

> For the trumpet will sound, and the dead will be raised *incorruptible*, and we will be *changed*. For this *corruptible* must put on *incorruption*, and this *mortal* must put on *immortality*. But when this corruptible will have put on incorruption, and this mortal will have put on immortality, then what is written will happen: "Death [corruption and mortality] is swallowed up in victory [incorruption and immortality]." (1 Cor 15:52–54 WEB)

"And the children of Israel spoke unto Moses, saying, 'Behold, we die, we *perish*, we all *perish*'" (17:12 AT). "Their seed shall *perish*" (21:30). "He shall rise up out of Jacob, And *destroy* the survivors of the city" (24:19). "Amalek was the first of the nations, but their seed shall *perish*" (24:20). "But they themselves with one accord shall *perish*" (24:24). ". . . and *destroyed* the Amorites dwelling in it" (32:39). "Then you shall *destroy* all the inhabitants of the land . . . and as for all their molten idols, you shall *destroy* these; and you shall remove all their pillars" (33:52). "You shall also *destroy* all the inhabitants of the land and dwell in it" (33:53). "But if you do not *destroy* the inhabitants of the land from before your face . . ." (33:55).

"But the sons of Esau rooted them out and *destroyed* them" (Deut 2:12). "But the Lord *destroyed* them before their face" (2:21). ". . . you will be utterly *destroyed* from the land you are crossing over the Jordan to inherit" (4:26). "But the Lord your God will deliver them into your hands and *destroy* them with a great destruction until they are *destroyed*" (7:23). "So He will deliver their kings into your hands, and will *destroy* their name from that place; no one shall be able to stand against your presence until you *destroy* them" (7:24). "Thus it shall be, if you forget the Lord your God, and follow after different Gods, and serve and worship them . . . you shall surely *perish*" (8:19). "As the remaining nations the Lord *destroys* before your face, so you shall *perish*" (8:20). "He will *destroy* them . . . and you will *destroy* them as the Lord God said to you" (9:3). ". . . how He made the water of the Red Sea overflow them . . . the Lord *destroyed* them to this day" (11:4). "Lest the Lord's anger be aroused against you and . . . you *perish* quickly" (11:17). "The Lord will send on you poverty . . . until he *destroys* you and lays you waste quickly" (28:20). "The Lord will strike you with perplexity . . . murder, blight . . . shall pursue you until you *perish*" (28:22). "May the Lord give dust as the rain of your land . . . until it wears you out and *destroys* you" (28:24). "Curses shall . . . overtake you until you are *destroyed* and wasted, because you did not obey the voice of the Lord your God" (28:45).

> Because the creation itself also shall be delivered from the
> bondage of *corruption* [Φθορασ] into the glorious freedom of
> the children of God. (Rom 8:21 NKJV)

If you will not be *delivered* from corruption, into the glorious freedom of
the children of God (Rom 8:20–25), your end will be corruption (8:21; Gal
6:7–8); you will die (Rom 8:12). You will be raised for judgment in a corruptible body (Rom 2:5–10; John 5:29) and then return to corruption.

> So also, is the resurrection of the dead. It [the dead person/
> body] is sown in corruption [φθορά].[13] It is raised in *incorrup-
> tion* [ἀφθαρσία]. It is sown in dishonor, it is raised in *glory*: it
> is sown in weakness, it is *raised in power*: It is sown a natural
> [psychical, of the soul] body, it is raised a spiritual [Spirit-ruled]
> body. There is a natural body, and there is a spiritual body. And
> so, it is written, "The first man Adam [by creation] was made a
> living soul" [and thus able to die *or* to live]. The last Adam [by
> resurrection from the dead] was made a life-giving Spirit [un-
> able to die]. (1 Cor 15:42–45 AV/AT)

The natural body is of the earth; it was a natural body even before Adam's
fall into sin.

> However, that which was spiritual was not first, but that which
> is natural; and *afterward* that which is spiritual [of the Spirit].
> The first man is of the earth, earthy: the second man is the Lord
> from heaven. As is the earthy [Adam], such are those also who
> are earthy: and as is the heavenly [the last Adam], such are they
> also that are heavenly. And as we have borne the image of the
> earthy [Adam], we shall also bear the image of the heavenly [the
> last Adam]. Now this I say, brethren, that *flesh and blood* cannot
> inherit the kingdom of God, neither does *corruption* [flesh and
> blood] inherit *incorruption*. Behold, I show you a mystery. We
> shall not all sleep [in death], but we [in Christ, 15:22] shall all
> be changed [into incorruption, with incorruptible bodies]: in a
> moment, in the winking of an eye, at the last trumpet; for the

---

13. In Gal 6:8, "corruption" is the English translation of φθορά, and is translated as
such in the following texts: "It [the body] is sown in *corruption*; it is raised in incorruption" (1 Cor 15:42); "flesh and blood cannot inherit the kingdom of God, nor does
corruption inherit incorruption [that is, immortality]" (15:54). As we have shown, Paul
uses "corruption" in contrast to "eternal life" in Gal 6:8. And that is what Paul is saying
in Romans, but in different words: "If you live according to the flesh, you are about to
die [that is *corruption, with its end*], but if by the Spirit you put to death the deeds of the
body you will live [*in life eternal*]" (Rom 8:13). It is that simple (2 Cor 11:3). And the
"eternal life" of Gal 6:8 is the same as the "eternal life" of Rom 6:23. Also, "corruption"
is contrasted with its opposite, "incorruption," in 1 Cor 15:42, 50, 54.

trumpet shall sound, and the dead shall be raised *incorruptible*, and we will be changed [from corruption to incorruption]. For this *corruptible* must put on *incorruption*, and this *mortal* must put on *immortality*. So, when this *corruptible* shall have put on *incorruption*, and this *mortal* [person] shall have put on *immortality*, then shall be brought to pass the saying that is written "*Death* is swallowed up in victory. O *Death*, where is thy sting? O *Hades*, where is thy victory?"[14] The sting of *death* is Sin; and the power of Sin is the law. But thanks be to God who gives us the victory [over the lordship of the sin, the law, and the death] though our Lord Jesus Christ. (1 Cor 15:43–57 AV/AT)

This is the essence and climax of "what God has prepared for those who love him" (1 Cor 2:9). Therefore, this "mystery" (15:51) is an aspect of the mystery of the gospel (1 Cor 2:7)—that only those who love God by knowing him will put on immortality. Much of the church has ignored Paul's words in 1 Cor 15:24–28, where he says that, after all of Christ's enemies are destroyed (done away with), then, at "the end" (v. 24), death will be *destroyed* for God's elect, by means of Christ's resurrection becoming theirs when they put on *immortality*. Yet, premillennialists believe that there will still be mortal (dying unto death) sinners walking around on this earth, together with immortal saints. And this is due to the influence of John's Revelation and ignorance of Paul's words in 1 Cor 15:24–28, where, once there is the immortality of God's elect, there will be no more death anywhere; for, in Christ all (in him) will be made alive (1 Cor 15:22), that is, abide forever (1 John 2:17), "in order that God may be all things in all [who are *not* destroyed: the redeemed (and innumerable elect angels)]" (1 Cor 15:28).

> Eye has not seen, nor ear heard, nor have entered into the heart of man, the *things which God has prepared* for those who love him. But God has revealed *them* to *us* through his Spirit. (1 Cor 2:9 NKJV; see 1 Cor 15:19–57)

These are "the things unseen and eternal" (2 Cor 4:17–18), which we by faith "look at" and earnestly wait for (2 Cor 5:7; Gal 5:5). Unbelievers have nothing to do with these things, for they, born only according to flesh, are not eternal. Thanks be to God for the gift of life and immortality in Christ alone (2 Tim 1:10)! The author of Hebrews refers to "another priest [Christ], who is made, not according to the law of a fleshly commandment, but according to the power of an *indestructible* life" (Heb 7:15c, 16). Thus,

---

14. Note the synonymous parallelism between "death" and "Hades" (the grave). For, *throughout Scripture*, death and Hades (the grave) always go together—meaning the *end* of man in Adam, so Paul does not say "death and eternal conscious torment."

"the gift of God is *eternal [indestructible] life*" (Rom 6:23; but for the lost, their soul/life will be destroyed (Matt 10:28), for they do not receive an indestructible life, as that referred to in Heb 7:16. They never receive immortality (Rom 2:7; 1 Cor 15:50–56). Where does it say in the Scriptures that they receive *another kind* of *immortality*? Nowhere.

Therefore, when the apostle says, "For the one who sows to his flesh will from the flesh reap *corruption* [death]; but the one who sows to the Spirit shall from the Spirit reap *life eternal* "(Gal 6:8) he is saying:

> For if you live according to the flesh [not mortifying its deeds], you are about to die [now, and in the age to come (you will not be immortal)]; but if, by the Spirit *you* put to death the deeds of the body, you will live [now, and in the age to come (you will have put on immortality)]. (Rom 8:12–13; see 1 Cor 15:52–54)

> Professing themselves to be wise, they became foolish, and changed the glory of the *incorruptible* God into the likeness of an image of *corruptible* man, and of birds, and four-footed animals, and creeping things. (Rom 1:22–23)

> For our light affliction, which is only for a moment, works for us more and more exceedingly an eternal weight of glory; while we look not at the things which are seen, but at the things which are not seen. For the things which are seen are *temporal*, but *the things which are not seen are eternal*. (2 Cor 4:17–18)

> For the ones being according to the flesh [seen and temporal beings] mind the things of the flesh [the things which are seen and temporal], but the ones being according to the Spirit mind the things of the Spirit [the things which are unseen and eternal[15]] (Rom 8:5).

This text (Rom 8:5), in light of the one that preceded it (2 Cor 4:17–18), proves that Paul knows nothing of flesh inheriting immortality, that is, the kingdom of God (1 Cor 15:50); just as when he contrasts *corruptible* man with the *incorruptible* God in Rom 1:23.[16] Regarding the final destiny of the lost in the Old Testament scriptures, Fudge says, "The OT uses about fifty different Hebrew words to describe this fate, and about seventy figures of speech. Without exception they portray destruction."[17]

---

15. 2 Cor 4:18.

16. Only God is immortal (1 Tim 6:16).

17. Fudge, "Final End of the Wicked," 31. He says, "The Psalms repeatedly say that the wicked will go down to death, their memory will perish, and they will be as though they had never been. The righteous on the other hand will be rescued by God from

Destruction (ἀπώλεια)[18]

Destruction is the next pertinent word for this study. It is translated in italics below, in Romans, Philippians, Hebrews, 2 Peter, Matthew, and Acts, to give a clear understanding of its meaning.

What if God . . . endured with much long-suffering the vessels of wrath fitted for *destruction*. (Rom 9:22)

For many walk, of whom I told you often . . . as the enemies of the cross of Christ, whose **end** is *destruction*. (Phil 3:18–19a WEB)	But what fruit were you getting at that time from the things of which you are now ashamed? For the **end** of those things is *death*. (Rom 6:21 ESV)

The above comparison shows that Paul uses "destruction" and "death" interchangeably. And then Hebrews says, "But we are not of those who shrink back and are *destroyed*, but of those who have faith and preserve [do not destroy, but save] their souls" (Heb 10:39 ESV). And similarly. Others:

But by the same word the heavens and earth that now exist are stored up for fire, being kept until the day of judgment and *destruction* of the ungodly. (2 Pet 3:7; note the parallelism between "day of judgment" and "destruction." The judgment (Gehenna) is ultimately their destruction—as in Rom 2:5, 8, 9; 9:22).

Enter by the narrow gate, for wide is the gate and broad is the way that leads to *destruction*, and there are many who go in by it. (Jesus, Matt 7:13 NKJV)

Regarding the phrase "eternal ἀπώλεια ['destruction']" in 2 Thess 1:9, we interpret it as meaning a destruction that never ends—is never undone. For if "those who know not God" were undestroyed, they would return to life. On 2 Thess 1:6–9, Boring and Craddock say, "The Paul of the undisputed letters does not dwell on the fate of unbelievers. Second Thessalonians is more explicit about the future judgment of persecutors than the future reward of believers."[19] And, the writer of 2 Thessalonians was not content to use the word "destruction" alone, as Paul always does. He adds

death and then will enjoy him forever (Pss 9; 21:4–10; 36:9–12; 49:8–20; 52:5–9; 59; 73; 92)" (Fudge, "Final End of the Wicked," 31).

18. "the *destruction* that one experiences, *annihilation*" BAG, 103. Nygren, in *Commentary on Romans*, aptly and often uses "destroying" and "destruction" throughout his commentary in the way that Paul does; for ἀπώλεια is one of Paul's "words taught of the Spirit" (1 Cor 2:13).

19. Boring and Craddock, *People's New Testament*, 649, emphasis mine.

the adjective "eternal" to emphasize how righteous (1:6), and how extreme the judgment is, in order to amplify God's repaying *affliction* on those who afflict believers. Furnish gives one of the reasons that demonstrate that Paul did not write 2 Thessalonians:

> It is . . . very difficult to see how Paul's description of the manner of the Lord's coming (1 Thess. 5:1–3) leaves any room for the extended scenario that is presented in 2 Thess 2:3b–12. And why is there no trace of this scenario in any subsequent Pauline letter, even in 1 Corinthians where the apostle is having to deal with some form of realized eschatology?[20]

Similarly, and most importantly, Schnelle says, "The *fundamental differences* between the eschatological teachings in 1 Thess 4:13–18 and 5:1–11 on the one hand, and 2 Thess 2:1–12 and 1:5–10 on the other, are clearly obvious."[21] There is no way that the same author wrote both letters.

Eternal Punishment

The Westminster Confession of Faith says:

> The infallible rule of interpretation of Scripture is Scripture itself: and therefore, when there is a question about the true and full sense of any Scripture (which is *not* manifold, but *one*); it must be searched and known by *other places that speak more clearly.*[22]

This is true, and the phrase "eternal punishment" in Matt 25:46 is found only in this *one* text. Therefore, we should interpret Matt 25:46 in the light of all the other scriptural texts on the end of the unjust.[23] Then we discover that it cannot refer to an eternal *punishing* in the sense of an *eternal life in suffering.*[24] The Greek word αἰώνιον, translated "eternal" in Matt 25:46,[25] means *eternal*, but the punishment is eternal in that its punishment, its

20. Furnish, *1 Thessalonians 2 Thessalonians*, 136.

21. Schnelle, *Theology of the New Testament*, 575, emphasis mine; see 574–78 for further evidence that Paul did not write 2 Thess; and see 534–38 on the reality of pseudepigraphy in the NT scriptures.

22. WCF 1, 9, emphasis mine.

23. Not only that, but the word κολασιν ("punishment" in 25:46) is used to mean *death* in 2 Macc 4:28 and 3 Macc 7:10, 14.

24. Or eternal wrath; for Paul contrasts "wrath" with *eternal* life, Rom 2:7–8, as we have shown.

25. On Matt 25:41–46, see Beare, *Matthew*, 495–97.

destruction (2 Thess 1:9), abides forever, not to be undone. The same Greek word is used in Hebrews, where Jesus obtained for us "*eternal* [αἰωνίαν] redemption" (Heb 9:12). This is not an eternal, perpetual redeeming, but a redemption that was once accomplished in Christ's death, with its corresponding eternal life. The same is true when Hebrews refers to "*eternal* [αἰωνίου] salvation" (5:9). Similarly, the "eternal [αἰωνίου] inheritance" (Heb 9:15) means the inheritance that will never end; it is not an eternal *inheriting*. And the blood of the *eternal* (αἰωνίου) covenant (13:20) is Christ's blood that established the basis for the covenant which the eternal, triune God purposed in times eternal (Rom 16:25) that has eternal effects, so it is called an "eternal covenant" in Hebrews. Lane writes:

> In God's innermost being, his attributes are perfectly united. There is no love of God that is not holy and no holiness of God that is not loving.[26]

In the very same way, *there is no love of God that is not just and no justice of God that is not loving.* There is no justice of God that is not affected by God's love; and this is in line with what is called "the simplicity of God."[27] So, the justice of God that is to be demonstrated on the day of judgment toward the lost is not disconnected from his love. Yes, God hates the reprobate (Rom 9:13), but he is still the same God who loved and died for his people and who sends the rain on the just and on the unjust. He is not a devil nor is he the Allah of Islam.[28]

The Book of Revelation

Regarding John's "Revelation," Luke Timothy Johnson similarly wrote, "Few writings in all of literature have been so obsessively read with such generally disastrous results as the Book of Revelation. Its history of interpretation is largely a story of tragic misinterpretation, resulting from a

26. Lane, "Wrath of God," 162.

27. See Taylor, "Simple Explanation."

28. God's (kind of) love is totally beyond the flesh's comprehension, and his judgment (including that of the lost) is not unaffected by his love. The *evil* heart of unbelief (Heb 3:12), "the mind of the flesh," *hates* God (Rom 8:6–8). *Sin* has *so darkened* our hearts that we cannot think rightly of God; and we underestimate how deep (this) sin's effects go, for the flesh easily believes in a "God" who sentences his enemies to never-ending, conscious suffering in body and soul in hell (contra all the clear texts in Paul's letters, Acts, 2 Peter, Genesis, the Psalms, Matt 3:12; 7:13; 10:28, etc.), whether it be the flesh-mind of Christians or of approximately two billion Muslims, with the "hell" of their Qur'an—see, for example, Qur'an 43:74 and 78:30.

fundamental misapprehension of the work's literary form and purpose."[29] And Boring and Craddock say, "Revelation does not claim to be written by an apostle, but speaks of the twelve apostles as others who belonged to the founding generation of the church (21:14; see Eph 2:20). The author speaks of his composition as 'prophecy' (1:3), belongs to a group of prophets (22:9) and describes his ministry as 'prophesying' (10:11)."[30] A Bible dictionary describes the *recurrent prophetic method*, which John's Revelation uses, as follows:

> This method assumes that the book was composed primarily to meet a present need within its day, and was designed to be understood by the men of that generation which know and used apocalyptic language. Its allusions are largely to the current affairs of the day.[31]

Koester agrees: "The Revelation of John is directly focused upon *the events and problems of its own time* . . . The acceptance . . . of the book, however, in the history of the Christian churches was always based upon its understanding as a writing about *the future*."[32] In line with this important reality, on the narrative in the book of Revelation, Beker wrote:

> How can a sequential and chronological narrative . . . do justice to the expectation of the one ultimate disclosure event—the triumph of God that alone should occupy Christian hope? . . . is it not true that the present time is the only penultimate time before the end time of God's theophany? However, Revelation's narrative sketches a sequence of events to come, reinforced by continuous references to "what is to take place hereafter" (1:19; 4:1–2; 7:1, 9; 9:12; 15:5; 18:1; 19:1; 20:3). . . . For such a narrative suggests that we presently do not actually live in the end time—but rather in a plurality of penultimate times, which give birth to a series of further events to come *before* God's kingdom can be actualized. Since Revelation deflates *our* time as the end time and points to other times to come as preliminary to the end time, it runs counter to a genuine Christian apocalyptic theology, such as we find in Paul's end time hope (cf. 1 Thess 4:15; 5:1–11; Rom 8:18–19; 1 Cor 15:51).[33]

29. Johnson, *Writings of the New Testament*, 512.

30. Boring and Craddock, *People's New Testament*, 760–61.

31. *Standard Bible Dictionary*, 740. That "need" was to die as a martyr rather than deny Christ as Lord (and worship the emperor).

32. Koester, *History and Literature*, 261, emphasis mine.

33. Beker, *New Testament*, 131–32.

Referring to the millennium of Rev 20:4–6, Boring comments:

> The only persons we see in this scene are the faithful martyrs who are raised from the dead to participate with Christ in the eschatological rule during the thousand-year reign, who are further described as blessed, reigning as priests (20:6). These are specifically identified as those who had not worshiped the beast or its image and had not received its mark, those who had not participated in the *emperor* cult. The scene is thus intensely focused to portray only one picture: the eschatological reign of the martyr church.[34]

This proves that John was addressing a situation in his own time (that of emperors). His main motive for writing Revelation was that the Christians to whom he wrote would be willing to be martyred for their faith rather than deny Christ. Regarding a thousand-year reign of Christ, Boring says, "John . . . is influenced here as elsewhere by the story line of Ezekiel . . . The 'first resurrection' and millennial period (20:4–6) corresponds to Ezek 37, the defeat of Gog and Magog (20:7–10) to Ezek 38–39, and the coming of the Holy City (21:1–22:25) to Ezek 40–48 . . . It was the *Jewish* tradition that provided the elements for John's picture."[35] McDonald writes:

> Krister Stendahl . . . asserts that the many variations and differences in the NT are real and that "they cannot be overcome by harmonization." Or we would even say, when they are overcome by harmonization, the very points intended by the writers are dulled and distorted.[36]

These differences between Paul's apostolic gospel, his revelation of Jesus Christ (Gal 1:11–12; see 1:1) and John the prophet's revelation, sent through "the angel" (Rev 1:1; see Gal 1:8), are clear, and so throughout history, Paul's revelation of Jesus Christ has been dulled by John's. John's "thousand years" has been (wrongly, in the light of Jesus' words, Paul, and other NT scriptures) interpreted as meaning a literal thousand-year reign on earth of Christ (bodily, in which mortals and immortals will coexist, contra 1 Cor 15:22–28) *before* he returns to judge the living and the dead. Luther said:

> About this book of the Revelation of John, I leave everyone free to hold his own opinions. . . . I miss more than one thing in this book, and it makes me consider it *to be neither apostolic*

34. Boring, *Revelation*, 203–4, emphasis mine.

35. Boring, *Revelation*, 207, emphasis mine; contrast this with Paul on the *Jewish religion* (Gal 1:13–14 RGT, in the context of 1:1–16).

36. McDonald, *Formation*, 149, citing Stendahl, *Meanings*, 63.

nor prophetic. First and foremost, *the apostles do not deal with visions, but prophecy in clear and plain words, as do Peter and Paul, and Christ in the gospel. For it befits the apostolic office to speak clearly of Christ and his deeds, without images and visions.* Moreover, there is no prophet in the Old Testament, to say nothing of the New, who deals so *exclusively with visions and images* . . . For me this is reason enough not to think highly of it: *Christ is neither taught nor known in it.* But to teach *Christ,* this is the one thing which an *apostle* is bound above all else to do.[37]

And in a footnote from this section of *Luther's Works,* it says, "In terms of order, Hebrews, James, Jude and Revelation come last in Luther's New Testament because of his *negative* view of their apostolicity."[38] The answer as to how to interpret this NT mix of scriptures, with its multiple authors, lies in that of *apostolic authority.* Paul gives full weight to the reality and uniqueness of his *apostolic authority* in Rom 1:1–4; 11:13; 1 Cor 2:12–13;[39] 3:10; 4:9–17; 9:1–6; 14:37; 15:1–11; Gal 1:1—2:9; 2 Cor 3, 4, 5, 11, 12:12; 13:3; 1 Thess 4:2–8. According to Gal 1:1, it is the God who raised Jesus from the dead who also called Paul to be an apostle. "Since Paul has been called by the risen Lord, the power of God, who raises from the dead, stands behind his apostleship."[40] Thus, of Christ's resurrection by God, Ebeling can say, "This eschatological event has instead entered into the legitimation of the apostle himself and determined the nature of his apostleship."[41] Thus, it follows that Paul can say, "And God has appointed these in the church: *first apostles, second,* prophets, third, teachers" (1 Cor 12:28).

We scripturally deduce from these words an important truth about *apostolic authority:* that NT prophets and others with their writings are

37. *LW* 35:398–99, emphasis mine. These are powerful words, and we basically agree.

38. *LW* 35:394, emphasis mine. Luther "denied its functional canonical status because, in his view, it was not theologically adequate. The Swiss reformer Ulrich Zwingli likewise refused to base Christian teaching on Revelation, pronouncing it 'no biblical book.' John Calvin passed over it in silence in his biblical exposition, writing commentaries on twenty-*six* New Testament books" (Boring, *Revelation,* 3). Boring also says, "As late as the fourth century, when Eusebius (d. 340) classified the Christian literature purported to be Scripture into 'accepted,' 'rejected,' and 'disputed,' Revelation was still classified as 'disputed.' Cyril of Jerusalem (315–86) was even more negative, omitting it from the list of canonical books and forbidding its use publicly or privately" (*Revelation,* 3). See also pp. 4–5 for Boring's difference between the Christ of "Revelation" and Christ's teaching in the Gospels.

39. Compare 1:22—2:16, Gal 1:12.

40. Ebeling, *Truth of the Gospel,* 16–17.

41. Ebeling, *Truth of the Gospel,* 17.

second to and under the Christ-given authority of the apostles.[42] There-fore, Revelation, James, Hebrews, etc., which scriptural research has found to be not apostolic in origin, should be interpreted in the light of those writings that are apostolic. Paul, the apostle to the world (Rom 11:12–13), says that Peter, James, and John *added nothing* to him (Gal 2:6), by which he means his gospel (1:1–12; 2:2, 6–9; Rom 2:16). In one sense, the other writers in the NT scriptures do add things that are complementary to him; nevertheless, in the ultimate sense of the word, they "added nothing to" Paul, that is, to *Paul's gospel* (Gal 1:11, 12; 2:2–9; Rom 2:6), which includes his doctrine. Therefore, concerning *the end of the unjust*: either the clear words of Paul the apostle are interpreted in the light of the figurative words of John's prophecy,[43] or the words of one who was *not an apostle* are inter-preted in the light of the clear words of Paul the apostle to the world (Rom 11:12–13)—"death," "corruption," "perishing," "destruction," ("immortal" and "eternal life"). We are utterly convinced that it is to be the latter, for the Spirit of the Lord Jesus Christ bears witness with "the revelation of Je-sus Christ," which Paul calls "my gospel" in Gal 1:11–12; 2:2; Rom 2:6; and 16:25. In the following comments, notice the important differences between Paul the apostle (Gal 1:1, 11–12) and John, who identifies himself a prophet in that he calls his writing "prophecy" in Rev 22:7, 10, 18, 19.

42. Paul says that saints are to discern (διακρινέτωσαν) what prophets say (1 Cor 14:29); this includes John's prophecy in Rev 22:7, 10, 18, 19. See "discern" in 1 Cor 11:29 and Matt 16:3. Its root means to *judge*.

43. The John of Revelation was a prophet (Rev 22:7, 10, 18, 19); he nowhere claims to be an apostle; Revelation's John was not; see Charles, *Revelation*, 1:xxix–l; Hays, *NIB* 12:350–72; Boring, *Revelation*, 200–212, 234; Boring and Craddock, *Peoples New Testa-ment*, 760–64; Johnson, *Writings of the New Testament*, 512, 520–21; Koester, *History and Literature*, 253–62; Kummel, *Introduction to the New Testament*, 497–99.

Paul the apostle ("first, apostles"*)	John the prophet ("secondarily, prophets"*)
The entire theology of Paul, and especially 1 Cor 15, allows for no literal millennium. For Christ reigns now, as Lord of those who belong to him, until he has put all his enemies (reprobate humans and satanic powers) under his feet, that is, until he destroys them—brings them to nothing. That is "the end" (15:24–28), for God will be all in *all* (who remain forever) because all in Christ will put on *immortality* (15:22, 53; 1 John 2:17).

* 1 Cor 12:28 infers that apostles have precedence over prophets. Also, Paul says that (we) saints are to *judge/discern what prophets say* (1 Cor 14:29). I do. | The "thousand years" (Rev 20) is a figurative term, meaning a period of completeness. In light the of the NT scriptures, it must refer to Christ's present reign, from his exaltation until just before he comes in glory. But John the prophet's (Revelation's) weakness is that Rev 20 has been often, throughout history, misinterpreted as meaning either premillennialism or postmillennialism, neither of which are in line with the apostolic gospel, and have therefore caused division in Christ's body (1 Cor 1:10; Rom 16:17).

* From 1 Cor 12:28 AV |
| Paul the apostle | John the prophet |
| If *God* is *for* us, *who* can be *against* us? *Christ*, who *died*? (from Rom 8:31, 34).

"All things are lawful for me," but not all things are profitable. "*All things are lawful for me*," but not all things build up. Let no one seek his own, but each one his neighbor's good. Whatever *is sold in a meat market, **eat***, asking no question for the sake of conscience, for "*the earth is the Lord's, and its fullness*." But if one of those who do not believe invites you to a meal, and you are inclined to go, eat whatever is set before you, asking no questions for the sake of conscience. But if anyone says to you, "This was offered to idols," do not eat it for the sake of *the one who told you*, and for the sake of conscience. Conscience, I say, not your own, but the other's conscience. For why is *my freedom* [in Christ] judged by another's conscience? If *I* **partake** [eat] with thankfulness, why am I denounced for something I give thanks for? Whether therefore you eat, or drink, or whatever you do, do all to the glory of God. (1 Cor 10:23–31 WEB/AT) | ("Christ" speaking):

But I have this *against* you, that you permit the woman Jezebel, who calls herself a prophetess who teaches and deceives my slaves to commit fornication and *to eat idol sacrifices* (Rev 2:20) . . . the end of which is *death* (Rev 2:23). |

John the prophet conveys Jesus' words to the church in Thyatira, in which his Jesus *threatens* those in that church who did not repent (2:21) of committing fornication and *eating food sacrificed to idols* (2:20)[44] *to "kill* her children with *death"* (2:23). So, unlike the apostle, the prophet's Jesus puts *committing fornication* and the *eating of meat sacrificed to idols* on the *same, forbidden* level—both being worthy of *death,* and that means the opposite of eternal *life* (see Rom 8:12–13; Gal 6:7–8). For Paul the apostle, believers are free to each such meat, but on the other hand, those who *practice fornication* will *not* inherit the kingdom of God (1 Cor 6:9–11), not have eternal life (Rom 8:12–13; Gal 5:19–21).

There is no way that these two views—which deal with the ultimate issues of death and eternal life—can be reconciled.[45] And those who would attempt to do so for the purpose of enabling the flesh to possess an error-free Bible (for the flesh desires such, as a kind of security blanket; it feels good to flesh) need to be reminded that the Bible did not die and rise again for them, but Christ, the Lord of glory, did. The saint does not need an inerrant Bible, because his God is the one true God who has revealed himself in the gospel, that is, in the Son of God, *the Lord Jesus Christ*; and he needs no other gods. And though the Scriptures are in the main sense trustworthy, our trust is ultimately in God and not in a book, lest we be idolaters, for what you trust in is your god. Our faith was and is first in the (preached) Christ, and then Christ is known to us through Scripture. There is a basic difference between believing (trusting) in Christ and believing in the Bible. They are not the same thing, for Christ is not the Bible. In Paul's day and after, many believed in Christ and lived and died *without* possessing a Bible. The Scriptures firstly preserve the preached gospel of the apostles. "Therefore the apostles are the legitimate and, in their proclamation of Christ,

---

44. Similar to Revelation's view of not eating meat sacrificed to idols (but without the warning to "kill her children with death") is that which is imputed to Paul by Luke in Acts 15:22–30, where Luke has Paul agreeing with a decree "which had been decided upon by the apostles and elders who were *in Jerusalem*" (Acts 16:4 NASB) on the teaching that the gentiles should "*abstain* from things sacrificed to idols and from blood" (Acts 15:29a NASB). Luke has Paul quote this decree (21:25). But according to Paul in his letters, gentile believers are *not forbidden* to eat meat that has been sacrificed to idols; they are only told to use their freedom in love for one another (1 Cor 10:23–32)! Luke portrays the Jerusalem church, with their apostles, as the apex of authority. (That is, as if the church of Jerusalem was the ultimate authority, similar to what "the Church of Rome" has been to Roman Catholicism. On *Jerusalem*, see Paul's words in Gal 4:25–26 in the light of Gal 1:1, 11.) For, in Acts 15, the apostles in the Jerusalem church have the authority of "the apostles," and Luke proceeds to *distinguish* "the apostles" from Paul, as if Paul (and Barnabas) were merely their servants—see Acts 15:4, 22–29.

45. "From the moment of its composition, Revelation has been a controversial writing" (Boring, *Revelation,* 2).

the infallible teachers of Christendom . . . The proclamation of the apostles was originally also a spoken word. This corresponds to the nature of the gospel."[46] "The fact that the New Testament is in writing is not essential to its basic character."[47] "The church's decision is never under any circumstances an authority standing above *the word* of God but only beneath it."[48] And since, in my chapter 1 (footnotes) and in this chapter we have shown the reality of Paul's apostolic authority (e.g., Gal 1:1–12; 2:20), and, throughout the book of Acts and Paul's letters, *"the word of God"* is called *"the gospel"* or *"Christ,"* it is true that *the church's* "authority" to put John's Revelation into the canon of Scripture is one that was *lesser in authority than God*, in his *gospel of God* (Rom 1:1; see Gal 1:1–12). Thus, whenever the church decides to exalt John's non-apostolic Revelation above *the apostolic gospel* by giving it equal or *greater authority* than God's gospel (including 1 Cor 15) in its status or its *interpretation of Scripture—*the church is thereby, in reality (though unintentionally), to some extent *rejecting the gospel of God*, which has been preserved in those same canonical Scriptures. Insofar as the living *God* uses the Scriptures, they do not point to themselves but to Christ, in whom alone we are to trust; so there is a distinction between the living Word/Logos/Christ and the written Scriptures. This is not being "liberal"—it is being a believer in Christ, one who trusts in *Christ crucified*, who is the Way. This is seeing Scripture in light of Christ.[49]

> The insistence that scripture interprets itself is simply the hermeneutical correlate of justification by faith alone.[50]

This is true because *Christ*, through *the gospel*, interprets Scripture—and does so "according to the Spirit" by (us) comparing Scripture with Scripture (1 Cor 2:11–16; see 1 John 2:27; 2 Cor 5:16).

> Luther's ultimate authority and standard was not the book of the Bible and the canon as such but that Scripture which interpreted itself and also criticized itself from its own center: from Christ and from the radically understood gospel. For Luther the authority of Scripture is strictly gospel-centered.[51]

46. Althaus, *Theology of Martin Luther*, 72.

47. Althaus, *Theology of Martin Luther*, 73.

48. Althaus, *Theology of Martin Luther*, 75; from WA 30², 420.

49. Around six or seven years after coming to faith in Christ in 1971, I began to see this reality. And since then it has become clearer and clearer to me, more now than ever, by the grace and Spirit of God.

50. Forde, *More Radical Gospel*, 66; see also Käsemann, *Perspectives on Paul*, 152.

51. Althaus, *Theology of Martin Luther*, 336. If Paul would have lived to see the books in the church's canon, he would have had the same view.

For the prophet John's Jesus, if they continue to eat meat sacrificed to idols and do not repent of it, they will die—and that means forever. In light of these things, who are we going to hear and follow—the apostle or the prophet? The Spirit of Christ witnesses with Paul, the apostle to the world (Rom 11:12–13), whom we are to imitate (1 Cor 4:16; 11:1; Phil 3:17; 4:9; 1 Thess 1:6). And therefore, the same reality (as to "who?") applies to the truth regarding the end of the unjustified sinner. For, Jesus says not to fear those who can kill (destroy) the body but rather fear him who is able to *destroy* both body and soul in Gehenna (Matt 10:28). This aligns with the apostle's words everywhere, especially in 1 Cor 15:24, that *all* of God's enemies will be *destroyed* (καταργέω, "brought to nothing"), the same Greek word that is used when he says that, for those in Christ, death will be *destroyed* (15:26)—it will *no longer exist.*

> During the second and third centuries after Christ, a number of pagan philosophers became Christians and devoted their talents to reasoning with non-Christian thinkers. Chief among them was a man from Carthage, a fiery-tempered philosopher named Tertullian. He was a convert from the followers of Socrates and Plato, who believed that every human being had a mortal body and an immortal soul. . . . Tertullian was practically obsessed with thoughts of the soul. *For proof that the soul is immortal, the church father appealed to Plato.* In a work titled "Resurrection of the Flesh," Tertullian wrote: "I may use, therefore, the opinion of Plato, when he declares, 'Every soul is immortal.'" Because the soul is immortal already, Tertullian reasoned, it does not need saving. Christ came only to save the body. But most important to our inquiry is Tertullian's reasoning about the immortality of the soul and hell. When Jesus warns that God can destroy the soul (Matt. 10:28), we should not think of destruction, said Tertullian, for immortal souls cannot be destroyed. Jesus really means that the soul will suffer conscious punishment in hell. . . . The assumption was wrong but the logic was straight and simple. If souls are truly "immortal," they cannot *die, perish,* or be *destroyed*—the three words used most often in the Bible to describe the final end of the wicked. And if they will never die but live forever, there are but two possibilities: either the souls of the wicked live forever in torment or they are eventually purified and graduate to heaven. The church fathers were never consistent about the destructibility of the soul, always acknowledging that God is able to destroy whatever he creates, but reasoning about hell as if that were not the case.[52]

52. Fudge, *Hell*, 152–53, emphasis mine.

Thus, the unscriptural belief in the immortality of the soul is *the* presupposition for those who hold to ECT. For if the soul cannot die (cannot be destroyed), then it must live somewhere forever. Similarly, the unscriptural word "eternity" implies the same thing. But "eternal" is the scriptural adjective that, when applied, means that which never ends, which lasts forever. So, when it is used with the word "destruction," it means that which is *never un*destroyed.

ψυχή (Psukee: *Soul or Life*)

BAG defines "soul," the Greek ψυχή, as "*soul, life*; it is often impossible to draw hard and fast lines between the meanings of this many-sided word. 1. lit.—α (breath of) *life, life-principle, soul* of animals . . . (Gen 9:4). As a rule of human beings (Gen 35:18)."[53]

> The Biblical concept of soul appears in the Hebrew *nephesh*, which in various contexts may be rendered "soul," "life," or "self." It can usefully be compared with bāśār, "flesh." The soul is not an entity with a separate nature from the flesh and possessing or capable of a life of its own. Rather it is the life animating the flesh.[54]

This is seen in the Messiah's death for his people, where *nephesh* is translated as "soul."

> Because he poured out His *soul* unto death. (Isa 53:12c).

So, when the life (the soul) is poured out, there is no longer life; there is death. Cooper would agree with this when he says:

> Genesis 2:7 states that God made Adam as a soul or living being (*nephesh chayah*), forming him from the dust of the ground and giving him the breath of life (*neshamah*). A human does not *have* a soul but *is* a soul, a single being consisting of formed earth and breath/spirit (*neshamah*, a synonym of *ruach*).[55]

Therefore, "the *breath/spirit* of life" (Gen 2:7) "is an empowering non-material force . . . the power of life and reproduction is shared with other

53. BAG, 901.

54. *DB*, 932. This is the Hebrew (OT) view of the soul, with which Paul agrees. Thus the person, not some soul, must put on immortality (1 Cor 15:50–56).

55. Cooper, "Current Body-Soul Debate," 36. Since "*man is a soul*" (scripturally), it is absurd to speak of "the immortality of the soul." Here Cooper explains the unity of humans but not the duality of holistic dualism, which he purports in *Body, Soul*.

living things, but our personal, cognitive, moral, and spiritual abilities uniquely image God. God combines earthly stuff in bodily form and spiritual power to make living human individuals."[56] Thus, for man to become a living *soul* is for him to have become a living *life*, for "soul" means "life." Regarding 2:7, Schwarz agrees: "The distinction is made not between body and soul but between a lifeless and a living human being."[57] What follows are some examples from the Scriptures, wherein ψυχή is translated into English in italics, usually as "life" but sometimes as "soul."

> Do not worry about your *life*. (Matt 6:25)

> Is it lawful on the Sabbath . . . to save *life* or to kill? (Mark 3:4)

> For whoever desires to save his *life* will lose it; but whoever loses his *life* [*soul*] for My sake and the gospel's will save it [shall *have life*, the kind that is eternal]. (Mark 8:35, 36)

> Or what will a man give in exchange for his *soul* [his *life*]? (Mark 8:37)

> For even the Son of Man came not to be served, but to serve, and to give His *life* [*soul*] a ransom for many. (Mark 10:45)

Jesus gave his ψυχή (life) unto death, not some semi-death. It is clear from the above verses that the ψυχή is the life of a person and that it can be killed (Mark 3:4) as Jesus was for the many (10:45). Therefore, the idea of a "soul" or "life" that cannot be killed is a contradiction in terms. ψυχή can be used for person(s) (see Acts 7:14; 27:37)—the entire person, not just a part of them—but usually ψυχή means one's *life*: "Neither count I my *life* dear unto myself" (Acts 20:24; see Mark 8:35). Therefore, ψυχικόν ("soulish," as in *soulish* or *natural* body in 1 Cor 15:44), the root of which is ψυχή ("soul"), means:

> *pertaining to the soul or life*, in our literature, always denoting the life of the natural world and whatever belongs to it, in contrast to the supernatural world, which is characterized by πνεῦμα.[58]

As we saw earlier, Paul, the Hebrew of Hebrews (Phil 3:5, not a follower of Plato), in accordance with the entire Hebrew scriptures, says if Christ is not risen, "Then also those who have fallen asleep in Christ have *perished*" (15:18

---

56. Cooper, "Current Body-Soul Debate," 36.

57. Schwarz, *Eschatology*, 274.

58. BAG, 902. That is, πνεῦμα, when used for *Spirit* (*of God*) is contrasted with ψυχή, which is of *this* creation.

ESV). And later, "If the dead are not raised, then 'Let us eat and drink, for tomorrow we *die*'" (15:32b ESV). As in the meaning of these words today, "perished" and "die" are used synonymously. Therefore, death is *death*—unless somehow there is a resurrection out of the dead unto immortality. Paul is speaking to believers, for death applies to all sinners, for the body is dead (mortal: dying unto death) because of sin (Rom 8:10; compare 5:12; 6:12). Paul believed that "death" means that all humans "perished" if they were not in the future raised to resurrection life (1 Cor 15:18). Since believers are joined to Christ, their life is Christ (Col 3:4) for his Spirit dwells in their inner man; they never die (John 11:26; Phil 1:21–24; 1 Thess 5:10). But unbelievers go their place[59] and must wait for the day of judgment as well as believers. John W. Cooper says, "The soul is not an absolute substance, as Plato taught."[60] Elsewhere, he says:

> Although some traditional Christian thinkers have argued that the soul was created essentially immortal and indestructible, there is nothing in Scripture which implies that a part of humans is naturally impervious to death and disintegration . . . In the Old Testament, the dead are thought of as ghosts who depart to *Sheol* . . . a dark and lifeless place below the earth, quite unlike Paradise.[61] They are most often called *Rephaim* . . . but *nephesh* (soul) refers to those in Sheol in Gen 35:18; Ps 16:10; 30:3; 49:15; and 139:8.[62]

And Hughes says:

> True though it is that for the Christian the sting of death has been removed (I Cor 15:55–57), yet death in itself is not something in which he takes pleasure. It still means a state of nakedness and a period of waiting until he is clothed with his resurrection body. Like the souls of the martyrs in the Apocalypse, there is a sense in which he cries "How Long?" (Rev 6:9–10). Death, although no longer feared, is still repulsive to the Christian; it is still a disruptive event; it is still the reminder that he has not yet come to that *ultima thule* where there will be no more death.[63]

And the OT scholar Delitzsch says:

59. Acts 1:25.

60. Cooper, *Body, Soul,* 216.

61. Cooper, "Current Body-Soul Debate," 37.

62. Cooper, "Current Body-Soul Debate," 48.

63. Hughes, *Second Corinthians,* 171. "Ultima thule" means the highest degree attainable.

The souls of the Old Testament dead, and indeed of those who died in faith in God the Redeemer, not less than of the godless, went to Hades. The souls of the former were, it is true, in the midst of Hades in God's hand, but still in a state of subjection to wrath and in need of redemption.[64]

The expressions of the Old Testament Scripture . . . all agree in this, that the state of Hades is a state of *death still unabolished* . . . certainly dreamlike, and only darkly conscious in the shadows of the previous bodies; and that the special horror of . . . Hades consists of being cut off from God's love in the land of the living.[65]

In order to redeem humanity from death, the Redeemer must, as the Sinless One, suffer the wrathful destiny of death. He must die and be buried without seeing corruption, and go down into Hades without being holden of Hades (Acts 2:27). The descent into Hades . . . is the extreme lowest point contrasted with the ascension above all the heavens (Eph 4:9); for heaven and Hades (Matt. 11:23), or heaven and the underworld (Phil 2:10; Rev 5:3), or heaven and the abyss (Rom 10:6) are opposite poles.[66]

Then ascending out of Hades, arising out of the grave, and rising toward heaven, The Lord led captivity captive . . . For He has triumphed over the angelic powers (Col 2:15); and when He had subjected to Himself the spirits that rule in the kingdom of death and of darkness, He led the men who in Hades honored Him as a Redeemer with Himself toward heaven, for the Paradise is from that time forth above the earth (2 Cor 12:1–4). And the souls of the blessed dead are, according to the constant testimony of New Testament Scripture, henceforth in heaven—in the Jerusalem which is above.[67]

We know of no other explanation than this to explain the difference between the intermediate state in the OT scriptures and in the NT. More than a millennium before Franz Delitzsch wrote those words, John of Damascus said of Jesus:

64. Delitzsch, *System of Biblical Psychology*, 498.

65. Delitzsch, *System of Biblical Psychology*, 499. And, according to all that Paul (the Hebrew) teaches in his letters, we have no reason to believe that he believed anything different about death and Hades—see 1 Cor 15:50–55.

66. Delitzsch, *System of Biblical Psychology*, 482. He means "held" in Hades (Acts 2:27).

67. Delitzsch, *System of Biblical Psychology*, 484.

Just as He brought . . . release to the prisoners and sight to the blind, and became to those who believed the author of everlasting salvation . . . so he might become the same to those in Hades . . . And thus after He freed those who had been bound for ages, straightway He rose again from the dead.[68]

Likewise, Philip E. Hughes wrote:

If our Lord descended into hades, it was to liberate the souls of the just who had been awaiting His triumph and thence to lead them to the heavenly *paradise* won for them through His conquest on the Cross. It was there that the penitent thief was *with him* on the day of His death. It was thither that Paul was transported in this rapture which he experienced. It is there that, after death, the souls of believers are *with Christ* even now (Phil 1:23), rejoicing in His presence.[69]

There, it may be presumed, he witnessed the state of the disembodied spirits of the redeemed who had been overtaken by death—a blissful and desirable state (5:8), but still and imperfect state until the day when their nakedness is covered by the assumption of the glorified and incorruptible resurrection body . . . Then at last redeemed humanity will shine forth in the full splendor of eternal Christlikeness.[70]

We may take it as certain that the Apostle, when he was caught up "even to the third heaven" was taken into the heavenly presence of the exalted and glorified Savior—a transcendental and unparalleled experience by no means to be explained in ordinary terms of locality and space . . . .[71]

Hughes is referring to Paul's ability to leave the body in 2 Cor 12, where Paul says, "I know a man in Christ who . . . whether in the body or out of the body I do not know—such a one was caught up to the third heaven" (2 Cor 12:2) ". . . how he was caught up into Paradise and heard inexpressible words (12:4a NKJV). Earlier, he applies that ability to Paul's words in chapter 5, where he says, "We are confident, yes, well pleased rather

68. *NPNF*, 9, 72–73.
69. Hughes, *Second Corinthians*, 436, emphasis mine. Paul says that to be *with Christ* is "*very much better*" (Phil 1:23).
70. Hughes, *Second Corinthians*, 437–38.
71. Hughes, *Second Corinthians*, 434.

to be absent from the body and to be present with the Lord" (2 Cor 5:8 NKJV).[72] And Hebrews says:

> But you have drawn close to Mount Zion, and to a city of the living God, to a *heavenly* Jerusalem, and myriads of angels, to an assembly and *church* of first-born ones, having been enrolled in *heaven*, and to God the judge of all men, and to *spirits* of just men having been made *perfect*. (Heb 12:22–23)

This could not have been written before Christ's death and resurrection; for then, the "spirits" referred to were not spirits "having been made perfect" by being joined to *Christ*.

And of the phrase "spirits . . . having been made perfect," Healy says:

> The phrase refers to all the deceased faithful of both the old and new covenant eras, those who have died looking forward in faith (11:13) and those who have fallen asleep in Christ (1 Cor 15:18) . . . Now the saints of the old covenant and the new, having been perfected by Christ's grace, are rejoicing together before the throne of God. The term "spirits" here, is synonymous with "souls" (as in Wis 3:1), referring to souls that have been separated from the body. They are still looking forward to the final consummation of God's plan, the resurrection of the dead.[73]

Referring to Rev 14:13, Delitzsch says of these spirits, "They wait in peace, as already perfected, for the conclusive perfection even of their bodies, by their being made alive again and glorified."[74] We agree with Cooper when he says:

> Souls are radically contingent and dependent on God's continuing providence for their very being. Total extinction at death is a very real possibility. It is just that God does not will to destroy people in death completely. He chooses instead to maintain them in disembodied existence.[75]

To his last sentence, we would add: "until when, on the day of wrath, the disobedient will receive the wrath of God (Rom 2:5–10) and are thereby

72. See Hughes, *Second Corinthians*, 431–38.

73. Healy, *Hebrews*, 277. So even though, in the OT scriptures, all went to Sheol, there was the hope that "the righteous" would be finally delivered from Sheol: "But God will redeem my soul from the power of the *grave*, for He shall receive me" (Ps 49:15); Johnston, *Shades of Sheol*, 84, alludes to this text.

74. Delitzsch, *System of Biblical Psychology*, 498.

75. Cooper, *Body, Soul*, 216–17. I agree with Cooper; see his *Body, Soul*, chs. 3, 5–8; and Delitzsch, *System of Biblical Psychology*, 477–520.

finally destroyed, body and soul, in Gehenna (Matt 10:28)."[76] Therefore, we conclude that the disembodied existence of the human spirit after one dies *is* the person's continuity that exists between one's bodily death and future resurrection unto judgment by God; but that does *not* mean that such spirit or soul is indestructible.

The Hebrew לִשְׁאֹל (Sheol) translated into Greek is ᾅδης (Hades). Gilmour says:

> As in the LXX, Hades represents the Hebrew word Sheol. In early Hebrew thought Sheol was a gloomy subterranean pit to which the spirits of men went after death and in which they suffered some shadowy . . . existence . . . Gradually the belief arose that there would be some separation of the righteous from the wicked even before the resurrection. In 1 Enoch 22 the author speaks of special places reserved in Sheol for the evil and the good "until the great day of judgment." The Lukan parable moves within a similar framework of thought.[77]

As a second witness, Goppelt says:

> According to OT and Jewish tradition, לִשְׁאֹל, the ᾅδης, is an underworld realm of the dead, where the dead are not differentiated. Subsequent layers of the tradition refer to a preliminary separation already in Sheol between the just and sinners on the basis of a schema of recompense (e.g., *1 En 22*, Luke 16:24–26). . . . In the rabbinic literature, Sheol is replaced by Gehinnom/Gehenna as the intermediate and final place of punishment.[78]

Thus, the very tradition which had been *believed* by Jews *for centuries*, Jesus used in his *parable* of the rich man and Lazarus, on which Craddock comments:

> The first part of the parable (vv. 19–26) is a much-traveled story, forms of it being found in several cultures . . . At least seven versions are to be found in the rabbis. In one version the characters are a rich merchant and a poor teacher; in another, a rich and haughty woman and a servile husband. The story in Luke is, of course, Jewish in orientation (Father Abraham), appropriate to an audience of Pharisees and to the point Luke is making. Theologically it is most congenial to Luke, not only

76. See Rom 6:23 and 9:22; Phil 3:19; also, hear Date, "Traditional Objections Answered."

77. Gilmour, "Luke," *IB* 8:290.

78. Goppelt, *1 Peter*, 260–61.

in its perspectives on rich and poor but also in the reversal of the fortunes of the rich man and Lazarus. An eschatological reversal is central in Luke's understanding of the final reign of God. *The parable reflects popular beliefs about the hereafter and the state of the dead.*[79]

The weight of the OT and NT Scriptures,[80] especially Paul in 1 Cor 15:17–32, conflicts with this parable as being used for theological dogmatism. Smith's Dictionary of the Bible says:

> It has been the prevalent, almost universal, notion that Hades is an intermediate state between death and resurrection, divided into two parts, one the above of the blessed and the other of the lost. This was the belief of the Jews *after the exile*, who gave to the places the names of Paradise and Gehenna. . . . In holding this view, main reliance is placed upon the parable of Dives and Lazarus, but it is impossible to ground proof of an important theological doctrine on a passage which confessedly abounds in Jewish metaphors. "*Theologia parabolica non est demontrativa*" (parabolic theology is not demonstrative [as clearly true, in comparison with other views]) is a rule too valuable to be forgotten.[81]

The influence of a two-fold division in Hades influenced some translators of the Bible. "The Hebrew word *sheol* appears 66 times in the Old Testament and is translated in the King James Version 32 times as 'hell,' 31 times as 'the grave' and 3 times as 'the Pit.' How the King James translators rendered *sheol* was determined purely by whether the passage referred to the wicked or the righteous . . . Scholars agree that there is simply no justification for this lack of uniformity in translating *sheol*."[82]

Someone may ask, "If Christ died for us, why do we still die?" In Christ, we do not die; as John's Jesus says, "The one living [by the Spirit's life] and [thereby] believing in me will never die" (John 11:26; compare Phil

---

79. Craddock, *Luke*, 195, emphasis mine. See also Schnelle, *Theology of the New Testament*, 521n406.

80. On the apparent exception of 1 Pet 3:19, see Goppelt, *Commentary on 1 Peter*, 261–63; and Acts 2:29–32.

81. *SDB*, 1038, emphasis mine. I repeat this because this parable is considered as dogma, due to two thousand years of tradition that ignores the rest of Scripture. But whether the unjust, after dying, are in the condition described in OT Hades texts, which aligns with 1 Cor 15:17–32 (compare v. 55) and Acts 2:27, or suffer, as in Luke 16's Hades, the predominant scriptural witness is that the suffering of the lost will be on "the day of wrath and revelation of the righteous judgment of God" (Rom 2:5–10).

82. Waren, *Sheol Know!*, 19.

1:21–24). We die bodily because the body is dead because of sin, but the Spirit (of God) is life (Rom 8:10); therefore we live ("with Christ") in spirit, awaiting the resurrection, the redemption of our body (Phil 1:23; Rom 8:24). The Spirit (of God) is life, not an immortal soul. "When participating in Christ, the believer shares in an ontological and real manner in what is death to death, i.e., life."[83] How then can he die? Note how the following passage from 1 Thessalonians seems to infer "soul-sleep."

> But we do not want you to be uninformed, brethren, about those who are asleep, that you may not grieve, as do the rest who have *no hope*.[84] For if we believe that Jesus *died* [our death] and *rose again* [*to life*], even so God will bring *with Him* [those asleep were *always with God* in Christ] those who have fallen asleep [died] in Jesus. For this we say to you by the word of the Lord, that we who are [bodily] alive [not "asleep"] and remain until the coming of the Lord, shall not precede those who have *fallen asleep* [died; but it is *not* forever,[85] so Paul calls it "sleep" from which we will *awake*]. For the Lord Himself will descend from heaven with a shout, with the voice of the archangel, and with the trumpet of God; and the *dead in Christ*[86] shall rise first. Then we who are *alive and remain*[87] shall be caught up together with them in the clouds to meet the Lord in the air, and thus we shall always be with the Lord.[88] (1 Thess 4:13–17 NASB)

Until Christ rose from the dead, death was not yet abrogated. For, the grace "which was given us in Christ Jesus before times eternal was not yet manifested, but now [is] manifested, through the appearance of our Savior Christ Jesus, on one hand *abrogating the death*, and on the other, bringing to light *life and incorruption* through the gospel" (2 Tim 1:9c, 10–11). *Life and incorruption (immortality)* had *not* been revealed before Christ, because *death and Hades* had *not* been abrogated until *Christ rose*

83. Mannermaa, *Christ Present in Faith*, 37.

84. That is, *no hope* of resurrection from the dead, of life and immortality.

85. Thus implying that death (in Adam) *is* forever, and that only those who sleep in Jesus have the hope of resurrection unto life eternal.

86. "The dead in Christ"—he does not say "the bodies of the dead in Christ." This is why many hold to "soul-sleep." But we agree with Delitzsch on hades, contra soul-sleep.

87. "We shall *not all* sleep [die], but we shall all be changed . . . at the last trumpet, for the trumpet will sound, and the dead will be *raised imperishable*, and we shall be *changed*" (1 Cor 15:51, 52 NASB)

88. To "be with the Lord" here refers to the parousia; similarly: "we . . . prefer to be absent from the body and to *be* at home *with the Lord*" (2 Cor 5:8 NASB); that is, "in this house we groan, longing to be clothed with our dwelling from heaven . . . in order that what is *mortal* may be swallowed up by *life*" (2 Cor 5:2, 4c; see 1 Cor 15:51–55).

from the dead—see 1 Cor 15:20–23. And thus, to the degree that a person does not understand what *death* really is—that the soul is not immortal/indestructible—to that extent one will not appreciate the awesomeness of Christ's resurrection from the dead—his victory over "the last enemy," which is death, with its utter finality of being cut off from the God who is life, *never* to be revived—and therefore deprived of life eternal with the eternal God. OT scholar Delitzsch says, "The souls of the righteous are only still awaiting the overcoming of death in their bodies (Rom 8:11), and the overcoming of death generally."[89] And yet, in light of Phil 1:21–24, Rom 8:10, and John 11:26, Delitzsch can say:

> Nothing is more certain than that the Old Testament knows as yet nothing of blessed men who are in heaven. It was not until *the ascension of Christ* that heaven became open for men, and became the place of assembly for a human *ecclesia triumphans*.[90]

Schwarz sums up the view of Benoit in "Resurrection: At the End of Time or Immediately after Death,"[91] as follows:

> He affirms that we are already here united in the Holy Spirit with the body of the risen Lord in a union that will not be interrupted by death. Thus there is no continuance through an immortal soul, but through the already initiated union with Christ.[92]

Yes. Commenting on what Paul calls the *man of the Spirit* (in 1 Cor 2:14 ATP), Boussett says:

> For Paul the ἄνθρωπος πνευματικός [man of the Spirit] is in truth a being of another and higher category than the natural man. Over against him the sarkics are simply (plain) men (1 Cor 3:3; cf. 15:32), "only" souls (ψυχικοί).[93]

"Sarkics" are his term for those who are according to the *flesh* (σάρξ, *sarx*), for they are soulish (ψυχικός), "natural" men. Humans of *the Spirit* are beyond ψυχικός ("natural" or "soulish"), being according to the Spirit of God[94] (Rom 8:5). Paul's contrast between ψυχικός ("soulish" man) and πνευματικός ("man of *the Spirit*") has not been given its rightful emphasis in theology.

89. Delitzsch, *System of Biblical Psychology*, 497.

90. Delitzsch, *System of Biblical Psychology*, 496n1, emphasis mine.

91. Benoit's chapter is from the book *Immortality and Resurrection*.

92. Schwarz, *Eschatology*, 291. Cullmann, "Immortality of the Soul," 40–43, preceded Benoit in teaching these things.

93. Bousset, *Kyrios Christos*, 174, words in brackets mine.

94. See (especially the Greek in) 1 Cor 2:12, 14–16 and 3:1, 3; compare Rom 8:5.

The chart below contrasts the soulish, earthy body and the spiritual from 1
Corinthians chapter 15.

The First Adam	The Last Adam
44) ψυχικόν=natural, soulish (body)	πνευματικόν=spiritual (of the Spirit) (body)
45) ψυχὴν ζῶσαν (became) a living soul	πνεῦμα ζωοποιοῦν (became) a life-giving Spirit
47) Out of earth, earthy	Out of heaven
48) Such as the earthy man, such also are the earthy ones (in him)	Such as the heavenly man, so also are the heavenly ones (in him)
49) As we bore the image of the earthy man	we shall bear the image of the heavenly man

John W. Cooper, referring to Paul, says:

> He always employs the grammar of persons: the "I," the self,
> the core person is what continues in unbroken fellowship with
> Christ during this life, from death to the second coming, and
> forever. If Paul is a dualist, he is strictly speaking a self-body,
> person-body, or ego-body *dualist, not a soul-body* dualist.[95]

Yes. Paul the saint, the person in Christ, is *no longer a soulish* or natural man
but a person of *the Spirit of God*, for "the one being joined to the Lord is
one spirit [with him]" (1 Cor 6:17). "Now the Lord *is* the Spirit, and where
the Spirit of the Lord is, there is freedom" (2 Cor 3:17), including freedom
from the flesh (Rom 8:9). For man "in the flesh" is soulish, having only the
mind of the flesh (Rom 8:6). The natural (soulish) man (1 Cor 2:14) has only
the life of Adam, who was made a living *soul* (ψυχὴν) (15:45). Peters would
agree; for, referring to Paul's words in 1 Cor 15, he says, "Hence, the soul
dies. As if to rub it in, Paul says it is not the ψὺχη that we find in the resurrection; it is the σῶμα"[96]—the body, not the soul. A Greek root of ψυχικος
("soulish"/"natural"), which refers to "body" in 15:44, is φυικός, which Paul
uses as follows: "Their women exchanged the *natural* [φυσικὴν] use for what
is against nature" (Rom 1:26). This refers to what is *natural* in this age. But
of the coming age, Jesus says, "Those who are accounted worthy to attain
that age, and the resurrection from the dead, neither marry nor are given in

---

95. Cooper, *Body, Soul*, 171, emphasis mine. This could be because, for Paul, the
inner man/spirit is the person's true self.

96. Peters, *God*, 313.

marriage; nor can they die anymore, for they are equal to the angels and are sons of God, being sons of the resurrection" (Luke 20:35–36 NKJV). The *natural* (*soulish*) man or woman has marital sex according to his or her *nature*. But the one who has *divine* life (*God's* life, *Spirit-life*) will not marry[97] and will be immortal, since we are now joined to the Lord, the Spirit, and we are to be strengthened by God's Spirit in the inner man (Eph 3:16). Since God (who is immortal, whose life is eternal) by his Spirit lives in *us*, our inner man, then how can *we* die in the same way that the natural (soulish) man dies (without Christ)? We do not. That is why Paul says only of Christ-believers that they "sleep" in Jesus (only to awake in the resurrection out of the dead); for they are those who are "dead in Christ" (1 Thess 4:14, 16). Schnelle says, "Paul is certain that the finitude of the world cannot abolish the reality of the Christian's life, for the Spirit of God/Christ continues beyond death as the believer's true selfhood."[98] To saints, Paul wrote:

	But we have received,
not the spirit of the world	but the Spirit which is from God.[99]
(i.e., not the mind of the world, of the natural/soulish [ψυχικος] man)	But we have the mind of Christ[100] (of the Spirit)[101]
Thus, the mind of the soulish man will *perish* with him.	Thus, the mind of the *Spirit*ual man will remain unto *eternal life*.

Death denotes a demarcation between this life and the hereafter, a demarcation so radical that it could hardly sustain the idea of continuance, unless we talk about a "shadowy existence" in analogy to existence in Sheol. But the Old Testament writers never talked about continuity, for they realized that Sheol allowed for no life in the real sense. The notions of a new creation and a resurrection, so central to the New Testament,

97. On the other hand, "To conclude from passages such as 'in the resurrection they neither marry nor are given in marriage . . .' (Matt 22:30) that the state of the resurrection is an asexual state, is a gross misconception" (Schwarz, *Eschatology*, 289–90); see also Hoekema, *Created in God's Image*, 98 (a Lutheran and a Reformed theologian are in agreement here).

98. Schnelle, *Theology of the New Testament*, 342; because the Spirit (the Lord) is joined to our spirit (1 Cor 6:17; 2 Cor 3:17).

99. 1 Cor 2:12 (AV).

100. 1 Cor 2:16. For the one being joined to the Lord is one spirit (with him, 1 Cor 6:17). Thus the "soul" is saved not by living but by dying with Christ and having his resurrection life. We are "saved in his [resurrection] life" (Rom 5:10).

101. Rom 8:6.

point to something so different from our life here that they contradict the idea of a continuity through and beyond death and a reuniting of body and soul.[102]

Here Schwarz is saying what Cooper said (above) about how "Paul is not a soul-body dualist."[103] But there must be some continuity between the person in this age and the person the age to come. But it will not be a reuniting of body and *soul* (this earthy *life*) because, as we have shown, the soul (ψυχὴν)—the natural, soul-life of Adam, even before the fall, is *not* the "life in Christ Jesus" (Rom 8:2). The *naked* or *unclothed* state to which Paul refers in 2 Cor 5:3–4 is a bodiless state, which completely accords with what he says in 2 Cor 12:2–4. Thus, we deduce that Paul meant that *he, as spirit, would be without a body*, which accords with what he says in 1 Cor 6:20 NKJV.[104] This seems to be as close as we can get to the answer. In conclusion, Hughes says:

> There is a progressive intensity in the believer's experience of closeness to his Lord: first of all in the pilgrimage of this life, then more so in the period of waiting between death and resurrection, and finally most of all when the Lord appears in glory and the human soul is clothed with its resurrection body, thus attaining the full perfection of humanity for which man was all along destined by the Creator.[105]

> There is altogether no room for doubting that, first, at the last judgment God will mete out condign punishment in accordance with the absolute holiness of his being, and, second, the Scriptures allow no place whatsoever to the wicked for complacency as they approach that dreadful day when they will stand before the tribunal of their righteous Creator. This Day of the Lord is depicted as one of indescribable terror for the ungodly, who will then be confronted with the truth of God's being which they had unrighteously suppressed and experience the divine wrath ... They will then learn firsthand that "it is a fearful thing to fall into the hands of the living God" (Heb 10:31). The horror of everlasting destruction will be compounded, moreover, by the unbearable agony of *exclusion*. To be inexorably excluded from the presence of the Lord and from the glory of his kingdom, to see but to be shut out from the transcendental joy and bliss of

102. Schwarz, *Eschatology*, 278.

103. Cooper, *Body, Soul*, 171.

104. "Therefore glorify God in your body and in your spirit, which are God's [possession]" (1 Cor 6:20). The NKJV here follows the Majority Text and the Received Text. See also Rom 1:9 for a similar anthropology.

105. Hughes, *True Image*, 397.

the saints as in light eternal they glorify their resplendent Redeemer, to whose likeness they are now fully and forever conformed, to be plunged into the abyss of irreversible destruction, will cause the unregenerate of mankind the bitterest anguish of weeping and wailing and gnashing of teeth. Thus God's creation will be purged of all falsity and defilement, and the ancient promise will be fulfilled that "the former things shall not be remembered or come to mind" as the multitude of the redeemed are glad and rejoice forever in the perfection of the new heaven and the new earth (Isa 65:17; Rev 21:1–4).[106]

Thus the curse of futility which man through the perverting of his nature brought upon himself and upon the creation over which he had been placed will be removed by virtue of the redeeming work of him who became accursed for us (Gal 3:13), as at last "the creation itself will be set free from its bondage to decay" and will participate in "the glorious liberty of the children of God" (Rom 8:19–21). And man at last will attain the full actualization of the marvelous potential implicit in his beginning as the creature uniquely privileged by being constituted in the image of God, so that his latter will far exceed his former glory as by divine grace he reaches the ever-intended goal of Christiformity and his will becomes one with the Son's will, which is one with the Father's. In this harmony of all things, which is God's kingdom of peace and holiness, the great multitude of the redeemed "will reign for ever and ever" (Rev 22:5). . . . the atmosphere of the new heaven and earth will be totally pervaded by the love of God, who will be all in all.[107]

Only God has immortality (1 Tim 6:16), and God will confer it on God's elect at the resurrection of the dead (1 Cor 15:53–54). And even though, in the ECT view, Satan and his innumerable angels along with all reprobate sinners would be fully under God's control, having no chance of escaping their hell (which is really Gehenna), or to bother the redeemed in any way, nevertheless, we believe that all of God's enemies will be judged in Gehenna and done away with (1 Cor 2:6; 15:24, 25; Phil 3:19; Matt 10:28; 7:13), in order that God may be all things in *all*, that is, be everything to *everyone* (1 Cor 15:28 ATP). In contrast, an acceptance of ECT coincides with the flesh's having no problem with unrighteousness, wickedness, and pure evil (in beings who are possessed by such) existing somewhere in God's creation *forever*. And this would be the case, even though those who hold to

106. Hughes, *True Image*, 406–7.

107. Hughes, *True Image*, 413–14.

ECT would argue that God's "justice" requires it. But this implies that there will some place *outside* the new heavens and new earth, contrary to 1 Cor 15:24–25, 28. One looks in vain throughout Paul's letters (and throughout the preaching in the Acts of the Apostles) for the idea of death and Hades (those in them) being cast into a lake of fire, where the lost are tormented day and night forever and ever. If such was the case, human decency, not to mention God's Spirit and love itself, would demand for Paul to teach it. Instead, he *defines* "death" in 1 Cor 15:18 (compare 15:32), 15:42–57, and in Rom 5:12–14 (compare Gen 5). We believe that immortality in Christ alone, by God's sovereign grace alone, allows no such existence of sin, evil, and thoroughly wicked beings existing for all "eternity" (an unscriptural word). God will be glorified in his justice on the day of wrath and praised for his grace in giving eternal life to his elect (Rom 2:5–10; 8:29–39; Eph 1:5–14). Scriptural immortality in Christ alone is an inexpressibly wonderful, uplifting, edifying, glorious, joy-filled, God-glorifying, certain hope of *eternal life*, experientially knowing God's agape/love in the age to come, where God's elect will participate in the loving fellowship of God the Father with his Son in the Holy Spirit, when the creation will be delivered from the bondage of corruption into the freedom of the glory of the children of God, where *only* righteousness dwells (2 Pet 3:13; Rom 8:18–23). Thus, we believe that Paul the apostle taught what an Orthodox theologian said about the relationship between evil and God:

> Evil is not coeternal with God.[108]

Belief in the immortality of the soul crept into the church through Tertullian and through those who were steeped in Platonic philosophy and, "as it were from the time of Origen (the first half of the third century), that we are to regard the idea of natural, as opposed to that of Christian, immortality as beginning to gain a firm foothold in the Christian Church"[109]—and increased in popularity with Augustine, who:

> fixed the lines along which the thought of the civilized world ran from the sixth century onwards; but it was not till the year 1513 that any denial of the natural immortality of the soul was officially condemned. In that year there was issued a Bull of Pope Leo X, which includes the following words:—"*Damnamus et reprobamus omnes asserentes animam intellectivam mortalem*

108. Ware, *Orthodox Way*, 59.
109. Bennet, *Resurrection of the Dead*, 21.

esse—"We condemn and reprobate all those who assert that the intellectual soul is mortal."[110]

Peoples notes that, among the early church fathers, "Writers like Ignatius of Antioch, the author of the *Epistle of Barnabas*, Irenaeus of Lyons, Arnobius of Cicca, and even Athanasius the Great" were conditionalists.[111] But for many of the leaders of the church for the first six centuries, their presupposition was Plato's belief in the immortality (indestructibility) of the soul. Augustine's words are as follows:

> And Plato's doctrine, which in philosophy is the purest and most clear, the clouds of error having been removed, showing forth especially in Plotinus.[112]

But in the Scriptures, philosophy is equated with "empty deception" (Col 2:8 NASB)—something overlooked by Augustine. Both before Augustine and since, many, if not most, theologians have reasoned from a supposed immortality (indestructibility) of the soul to eternal conscious suffering.[113]

Regarding Adam's one sin: God's judgment concerning it was condemnation (the verdict was "guilty"), and the sentence thereof was death. And 2 Tim 1:10 states that the abolishing of death, and thus the opposite of spiritual-unto-bodily death, is "life and immortality," (lit., incorruptibility). Until we *remove* from our thinking the lie of natural immortality in humans, *we will not be able to behold* the wonder of *the gospel: immortality in Christ alone*—living with the one triune God (and his people) forever, in the joy of the Holy Spirit! And the world is passing away and the lust of it; but the one doing the will of God remains forever (1 John 2:17). "This implies that he who follows the ways of the world will not abide forever."[114]

> The wages that the Sin pays is *death*, but the free gift of God is *eternal life* in Christ Jesus our Lord. (Rom 6:23)

110. Bennet, *Resurrection of the Dead*, 25. Rome's denial of the mortality of the soul (which is really of *man*) for many centuries before that, and officially in the centuries since, has been convenient for them in their use of the threat of eternal conscious torment over people. Sometimes conservative Christians will accuse conditionalists of going by their emotions on their rejection of the traditionalist view of hell for conditional immortality and the real Gehenna that destroys (Matt 10:28). Nothing could be further from the truth. It is a matter of the interpretation of Scripture—in this case, what do the *apostolic* writings, including 1 John 2:17, clearly teach?

111. Peoples, "Introduction" in *Rethinking Hell*, 14; see also *Rethinking Hell*, ch. 19; Roller, *Doctrine of Immortality*; Peoples, "Church Fathers."

112. Augustine, *Against the Academics*, 148.

113. See Fudge, *Fire That Consumes*, 32.

114. Plummer, *Epistles of St. John*, 54.

That is the gospel of God (Rom 1:1). Hence, any diversion from that, whether it be teaching a natural immortality in humans (contra Rom 1:23 and 1 Cor 15) or a mingling of the law[115] with Christ's grace for those (gentiles) in Christ, Paul calls "another gospel" (Gal 1:6–7).[116] For, Paul's gospel is indeed freedom from the law to be guided by the Spirit of Christ, thus we "walk" and live as already freed from our righteousness, to be led by God's Spirit in Christ, through faith (Phil 3:9; Gal 5:1–18). For any other "Christ" than the Christ of the gospel of God involves "another Jesus":

> A different spirit . . . [and thus] a different gospel (2 Cor 11:4).
> Amen.

115. Paul wrote: "You were running well! Who hindered you that you should not obey the truth [of the gospel of grace, Gal 1:6]? This persuasion is not from him who calls you. A little yeast [of the law] leavens the whole lump [of dough] . . . But I, brothers, if I still preach circumcision [the law, 5:1–4], why am I still persecuted? Then the offense of the cross [the gospel] has ceased" (Gal 5:7–11). Any mixing of law with grace nullifies the grace alone through faith alone gospel of God.

116. This sentence reveals that the Christ whom Paul preached has been mostly rejected in the church throughout history. For Christ crucified (in whom alone we are to glory) remains an offense to the flesh, with all its wisdom and its righteousness (Gal 5:11; 6:13–14; Phil 3:9; 1 Cor 1:18–25).

—— APPENDIX A ——

The Glory of the Old and New Covenants

The law was given to old covenant Israel. Christ's indwelling Spirit is given to new covenant Israel. These things are included in Paul's admonition to "distinguish between the things which differ" (Phil 1:9–10). There are two kinds of glory: that of Moses and that of Christ.[1] The glory of *Moses* was an outer, seen, and *temporal glory*. It was glorious, but it was to be done away with. But the glory of *Christ* is an inward, unseen (in this age), and *eternal glory*.[2] In 2 Cor 3, Paul asks the Corinthians if they need a letter of recommendation (3:1); but then he says that the Corinthian saints themselves "are our letter, known and read by all men; being manifested that you are a letter of Christ . . . written not with ink, but with the Spirit of the living God, not on tablets of stone [the law], but on tablets of human hearts" [severed from the flesh by the Spirit of God, who now indwells the heart] (2 Cor 3:2–3 NASB). Paul refers to God:

> Who also made us [apostles,[3] particularly Paul[4]] adequate as servants of a new covenant, not of the letter, but of the Spirit; for the letter [the law] kills, but the Spirit [of Christ] gives life. But if the ministry of death, in letters engraved on stone, came with *glory*, so that the sons of Israel could not look intently

1. See the word "glory" in 2 Cor 3:7–11, 18; 2 Cor 4:4, 6, 15, 17; where Paul repeatedly contrasts the (temporal) glory of Moses with the (eternal) glory of Christ.

2. 2 Cor 3:3; 4:6, 16–18.

3. See 1 Cor 4:9.

4. 2 Cor 3:15, 16; 4:1–3 and Rom 2:16.

at the face of Moses because of the *glory* of his face, fading [temporal] as it was, how shall the ministry of the Spirit [of life eternal] fail to be even more with *glory*? For if the ministry of condemnation has *glory*, much more does the ministry of righteousness [justification] abound in *glory*. For indeed what had [past tense] *glory* [the old covenant, the law] in this case has *no glory* [at all] on account of the [eternal] *glory* [of Christ, in "the new testament" (3:6 lit.)] that surpasses it [the law]. For if that which fades away was with *glory*, then what which remains [forever][5] is in *glory*. (2 Cor 3:6–11 NASB)

The new testament of the Spirit is written with *the Spirit* of the living God *in the heart*.[6] The ministry of justification exceeds that of condemnation in terms of *glory*, for Christ justifies and gives life (3:6, 9); therefore, the law now has *no* glory when compared to Christ.[7] Paul was not "as Moses, who used to put a veil over his face that the sons of Israel might not look . . . at the end of what [glory] was fading away" (2 Cor 3:13 NASB); it was a fading (temporal) glory (3:7).

But Israel's thoughts were hardened. For until the present day, the same veil [veiling, hiding the end of the old covenant (law)], remains on and at the reading of the old covenant, it not being unveiled [revealed (in the OT, without the gospel of God)], that in Christ it [the old covenant law] is being done away. For until today, whenever Moses [the law] is read, a veil lies on Israel's heart, but whenever it [the heart] turns to the Lord, the veil is taken away. Now the Lord is *the Spirit*,[8] and where *the Spirit* of the Lord is, there is freedom. But we all [in Christ], with [our] face having been unveiled, beholding as in a mirror the *glory* of the Lord, are being transformed [in our inner man, 4:16; by the renewing of the mind, Rom 12:2] into the same image [of Christ] from *glory* to *glory*, even as from the Lord, the Spirit. (2 Cor 3:14–18)

Of the gospel of the glory of Christ (4:4b), Paul says, "For God . . . is the One who has shone in our hearts to give the light of the knowledge of *the glory of God* in the face of Christ" (2 Cor 4:6 NASB), which is "a far more exceeding and *eternal* weight of *glory*" (4:17), ". . . *while we look not at the things which are seen* [not only the outer man, but also the law, written

5. In John's words, "remains forever" (1 John 2:17).
6. 2 Cor 3:6 and 3:3; also Heb 8:7–12; 9:15–17; 10:1–2, 8–10, 15–18.
7. 2 Cor 3:10.
8. The Spirit gives life (2 Cor 3:6).

with ink and on stone, and ultimately anything written or seen], life, as if it were God], *but at the things which* are *not seen* [Christ, with his 'things freely given us of God,' for the Scriptures witness to Christ and point away from themselves to God in Christ]; *for the things which are seen are temporal, but the things which are not seen are eternal* (2 Cor 4:18 NASB).[9] Jewish tradition says the law is eternal. But Christ says, "I am the *end* of the law for justification; I am eternal; I am God, not the law."[10] Immediately after God spoke the words of the law in Exod 20:1–17, it says:

> Now when all the people saw the thunder and the flashes of lightning . . . the people were *afraid* and trembled, and they stood far off and said to Moses, "You speak to us, and we will listen; but do not let God speak to us, lest we *die*." (Exod 20:18–19 ESV)

But the grace in the new covenant in Christ's blood is explained as follows:

> That through death He [Jesus] might destroy him who had the power of *death*, that is, the devil, and release those who *through fear of death* were all their lifetime subject to bondage [to death and its fear]. (Heb 2:14c–15 NKJV)

The church which is Christ's body is a third entity (1 Cor 10:32). Thus, the church has not come to the mountain that burned with fire, where Moses said, "I am exceedingly *afraid* and trembling." "But you have come [not to Sinai but] to Mount Zion and the city of the living God, the heavenly Jerusalem . . . to the . . . *church* of the firstborn [from the dead: Jesus] who are registered in heaven . . . to *Jesus* the Mediator of *the new covenant*" (Heb 12:18, 21–24). "Knowing that *the law* is not made for a righteous person, but for the lawless and insubordinate" (1 Tim 1:9). "For *the grace of God* that brings salvation has appeared to all men, *teaching* us that, denying ungodliness and worldly lusts, we should live soberly" (Titus 2:11–12a). The world's (the flesh's) image of God is that of *the god* of (this age, who deceives through) *the law*, through the law's glory (its right–ness, its righteousness), in contrast to Christ, who is the true image of God (2 Cor 4:4b, c). Referring to "our gospel," Paul says that it remains "hidden in the ones who are perishing, in whom the god of this age has blinded the thoughts of the unbelieving, so that the enlightenment of the gospel of the glory of *Christ*, who is the image of God, should not shine forth in them" (2 Cor 4:3–4). (Satan, through) the law, blinds and deceives this world to trust in *its* righteousness, which is of the law (2 Cor 4:4; Phil 3:3–9). We say "through the law" because

---

9. See also John 5:39–47. For we walk by faith and not by sight (2 Cor 5:7).

10. Rom 10:4; Rom 7:1 ("*lords* it over"); compare "released from the law . . . through Christ," (7:4–6); "I am" (John 18:3–6).

of the context of 2 Cor 4:4 (2 Cor 3:6 through 4:6; especially 2 Cor 3:7, 14). Thus, both Satan *deceives* (2 Cor 11:3) and Sin *deceives* (Rom 7:11) humans. In Christ, the image of God is *not* that of the law, "written and engraved in stones," as if we could be justified by law, or as if God is the one who, through the law, still condemns us who are in Christ. Instead, God is preached and beheld in "the light of the glorious gospel of *Christ*, who [utterly apart from the law] is *the image of God*" (2 Cor 4:4 AV; see Rom 3:21–22).

— APPENDIX B —

The Reality of Sin and of Grace

1. Man in the flesh would rather destroy[1] himself than to submit to the grace of God (no condemnation) in Christ Jesus. For, to be severed from life[2] (Christ) is death.

2. *The grace* of God is *Christ's death for justification* in God's sight (Gal 2:21; Rom 5:9, 15–19).

3. (Man in) the flesh can only trust in himself and not in Christ for righteousness. Apart from faith in Christ he destroys himself, for he is born and lives in Adam, in total bondage to the sin (as power, as lord, as unbelief in Christ), the end of which is death.[3]

4. Therefore, unless God intervenes through the gospel, accompanied by God's effectual call[4] that results in faith in Christ, man is destroyed—his end is death.[5]

5. The grace of God always involves the lordship of Jesus Christ; the grace cannot be severed from the lordship of Jesus Christ; but his lordship over us is based upon having been justified by the grace of

---

1. Through the gospel, I know this is true of my flesh; thus, it is true of all flesh.

2. Gal 3:21–22; Col 3:4; Gal 5:1–4; Rom 7:9–13.

3. Rom 5:12–21; 6:17–22; 8:5–8; 1 Cor 2:12–14. In Rom 5 and 6, the definite article is used: "*the* Sin" (that condemned).

4. Rom 1:1, 6, 7, 16; 8:30.

5. Rom 6:23; 9:22.

God.[6] Therefore, God's grace (gospel) is of first importance ("first of all," 1 Cor 15:1–4).

6. To submit to God's grace is to submit in faith to the gift of righteousness (justification) in Christ, which is to simultaneously submit to the same Christ as Lord.[7]

7. There is union and distinction between God's grace (having God's righteousness in Christ[8]) and his lordship: Christ is your Lord; therefore, you are free from the Sin—no longer its slaves—and so you are obligated to obey this Christ by his Spirit, his leading in mortification and all things.[9]

8. While we were still sinners, enslaved to the sin that condemned us, Christ died for us,[10] whereby the old man of us (in the flesh), who cannot submit in faith to God in Christ, God put to death with Christ (so the person as owned by sin has been done away with and thereby justified and freed from [the lordship of] the sin and the law,[11] in order that we might be indwelt instead by the Spirit of God and of Christ, raised a new creation[12] for the purpose of eternal life, Rom 5:21). In the inner man, saints are joined no longer to sin but to God (Christ) alone. We have been bought with a price: God's blood; we belong to God alone. God's Spirit, who is life, indwells and owns us.[13]

There is no other gospel than this one.[14]

6. Rom 3:24; 5:1, 9, 15, 17, 21; 6:14, 15.

7. Rom 1:5; 5:17; 6:20–23; 10:1–4; see 8:7, 8.

8. Grace: see Rom 3:24; 5:17–21; 6:3–11, 14 (*justified* from the sin, 6:7 lit.); having God's (imputed, Rom 4:1–9) righteousness (Phil 3:9).

9. Lordship: see Rom 6:2–22; 8:3–5; 9–14. The Spirit's desires are opposed by the flesh's desires continuously; thus, we are to walk by the strength and leading of the Spirit (Gal 5:16–18).

10. "The Sin" that *condemned all to death* is Adam's one sin (Rom 5:12–21 lit.); the "us" of Rom 5:8 is defined in Rom 1:6–7 and 8:33–34.

11. Rom 6:2–11; 7:1–6.

12. Eph 2:4–6; 2 Cor 5:17; the new creation (Christ in us) is our rule (Gal 6:15–16). The new creation can and does *trust* God (Rom 4:13; see Eph 4:24). The inner man is indwelt by *the Spirit of Christ* (Eph 3:16), whereas before it was indwelt by *the spirit of the world* (1 Cor 2:12), of *disobedience* (Eph 2:2), of *Satan* (1 John 4:4).

13. 1 Cor 6:19–20; Acts 20:28; Rom 8:10–13.

14. Gal 1:6–12; compare Romans. Just as *the gospel* assumed is the gospel denied, even so *faith* (in Christ) assumed is faith denied. Paul says, "*The gospel* which I preached to you, which *also* you *received* [by faith, Rom 5:1, 17], in which you also stand, by which also you are saved, if you hold firmly [by faith] *the word* which I preached to you, unless you *believed* in vain" (1 Cor 15:1–2).

——— APPENDIX C ———

The Sabbath in the Light
of Christ

Stephen Westerholm says:

> Anyone obligated to observe the law's demands must recognize that some food is clean, other food unclean (Lev 11; Deut 14:3–21). Paul does not: "I know and am persuaded in the Lord Jesus that nothing is unclean in itself" (Rom 14:14). The law demands that the seventh day be kept holy, and that other festival days be observed as well. For Paul, such observance is entirely optional: "One man esteems one day as better than another, while another man esteems all days alike. Let everyone be fully convinced in his own mind" (v. 5).[1]

Paul writes to the believers at Galatia:

> However at that time, when you did not know God, you were slaves to those which by nature are no gods. But now that you have come to know God, or rather to be known by God, how is it that you turn back again to the weak and worthless elemental things, to which you desire to be enslaved all over again? You observe days and months and seasons and years. I fear for you, that perhaps I have labored over you in vain. (Gal 4:8–11 NASB)

Earlier in this letter, Paul had said that his gospel is to and for the uncircumcision, the gentiles (Gal 2:2, 7). So, in Gal 4:8–11, Paul is saying, "Don't listen to those teachers of the law who would add works of the law to the

---

1. Westerholm, *Israel's Law*, 207.

gospel of Christ." He speaks of the law repeatedly in this way throughout Galatians. Therefore how could the "days" of 4:10 *not* include Sabbath days? The Paul who, in this letter, says, "The law is not of faith" (Gal 3:12; see Rom 2:17–23; 3:20) is not saying, "The law—except, of course, the fourth commandment—is not of faith." Longenecker rightly says:

> While not, as yet, submitting to circumcision, Gentile Christians of Galatia seem to have begun to observe the weekly Jewish Sabbaths, the annual Jewish festivals, and the Jewish high holy days—all, as they evidently were led to believe by the Judaizers, as a means of bringing their Christian faith to completion.[2]

> One person esteems one day above another; another esteems every day alike. Let each man be fully convinced in his own mind. He who observes the day, observes it to the Lord; and he does not observe the day, to the Lord he does not observe it. (Rom 14:5–6a)

In Rom 14:1–6 Paul writes about Christian freedom in the grace of Christ, and that specifically in terms of what one eats, and what day or days one observes (if any), and how we are not to judge one another regarding these things, because God in Christ does not do so. This includes the Sabbath day, first, because Christ is the end of the law for righteousness for everyone who believes in him (Rom 10:4). Second, in this way, Christ, though Paul, forever ends the basis of believers judging one another, including on the issue of observing days for Christ-believers, because God has received us in Christ alone.

It appears that the apostolic church gathered on the first day of the week. It was not the law; that is, it was not the Sabbath that was being followed or kept (see Acts 20:7; 1 Cor 16:1, 2). The Gospel of Mark, in 16:2, 9, records that Christ rose from the dead on the first day of the week. This is why Christ-believers eventually assembled and worshiped corporately on the first day of the week. Concerning the first day, A. T. Lincoln wrote:

> The oldest designation for the Lord's Day is "the first day of the week" (ἡ μία τοῦ σαββάτου/τῶν σαββάτων, Mark 16:2; John 20:1, 19; Acts 20:7; 1 Cor. 16:2). This designation presupposed the weekly division of time based on the Old Testament Sabbath and signifies "the day which is number one in the sequence of days determined by the Sabbath." Thus despite the radical discontinuity involved in the church's beginning to assemble on the first day to commemorate their fellowship with

2. Longenecker, *Galatians*, 182, 83.

the risen Lord, there is also a definite continuity with the Old Testament people of God in that this was done on a weekly and not a monthly or yearly basis. In this the early church acknowledged the sabbatical sequence of time.[3]

Apostolic teaching is that the law is not the Christian's rule, for Christ was their rule, and the Sabbath day was not kept, at least not by the predominantly gentile part of the church. And later, the church father Tertullian wrote:

> It follows, accordingly, that, in so far as the abolition of carnal circumcision and of the old law is demonstrated as having been consummated at its specific times, so also the observance of the Sabbath is demonstrated to have been temporary.[4]

After Lincoln shows from numerous texts in the Gospels and in Hebrews that Jesus repeatedly fulfilled the Old Testament scriptures,[5] he says:

> It has become clear from these passages that the coming of Jesus Christ fulfills the concept of rest tied up with the Old Testament Sabbath and that because of the situation of the church between the Resurrection and the Parousia of Christ, there is an "already" and a "not yet" to that fulfillment.[6]

> As should also have become clear from these passages, *the "already" is of such profound epoch-making significance* that in the process of fulfillment the old categories are *reinterpreted and transformed.* Thus, the true Sabbath, which has come with Christ, is not a literal, physical rest but is seen as consisting in the salvation that God has provided . . .

> Believers in Christ can now live in God's Sabbath that has already dawned. Jesus' working to accomplish this superseded the Old Testament Sabbath (John 5:17) and so does the doing of God's work that He now requires of his people—believing in the one God has sent (John 6:28–29). In fact, the Sabbath keeping now demanded is the cessation from reliance on one's own works (Heb 4:9–10).[7]

---

3. Lincoln, "Sabbath, Rest, and Eschatology," 200–201.

4. *ANF* 3:155.

5. See Lincoln, "Sabbath, Rest, and Eschatology," 201–14.

6. Lincoln, "Sabbath, Rest, and Eschatology," 214.

7. Lincoln, "Sabbath, Rest, and Eschatology," 215; emphasis mine. See also 368–75; 166–77; 200–215; 388–90.

On the errors of the medieval church in this area, the Augsburg Confession says:

> These errors crept into the church when the righteousness of faith was not taught with sufficient clarity. Some argue that the observance of the Lord's Day is not *indeed* of divine obligation but is *as it were* of divine obligation and they prescribe the extent to which one is allowed to work on holy days. What are discussions of this kind but snares of conscience?[8]

At the same time, it could be argued that, for humans, the principle of resting one day after six days of work is intended by the creator for humans as those who have been created in the creator's image; for after six days of work, God rested. So, if and as we are led by the Spirit, we are free to rest one day a week, as the Spirit leads and not as the law obliges. The Augsburg Confession puts it well:

> Those who hold that the observance of the Lord's Day in place of the Sabbath was instituted by the Church's authority as a necessary thing are mistaken. The Scriptures, not the church, abrogated the Sabbath, for after the revelation of the Gospel all ceremonies of the Mosaic law can be omitted. Nevertheless, because it was necessary to appoint a certain day so that the people may know when to assemble, it appears that the church designated the Lord's day for this purpose, and it seems that the church was the more pleased to do this for the additional reason that men would have an example of Christian liberty and would know that the keeping neither of the Sabbath nor of any other day is necessary.[9]

On the other hand, without nullifying our freedom in Christ, there are wise reasons for the setting aside of one day a week for rest and corporate worship.[10]

---

8. AC, Article 28, 91–92.

9. AC, Article 28, 91.

10. See, e.g., Hodge, *Princeton Sermons*, 302.

Bibliography

Achtemeier, Paul J. *1 Peter*. Minneapolis: Fortress, 1996.

———. *Inspiration and Authority: Nature and Function of Christian Scripture*. Grand Rapids: Baker Academic, 1999.

———. *Paul and the Jerusalem Church: An Elusive Unity*. Eugene, OR: Wipf & Stock, 1987.

Alleine, Richard. *The World Conquered by the Faithful Christian*. Morgan, PA: Soli Deo Gloria, 1995.

Althaus, Paul. *The Theology of Martin Luther*. Philadelphia: Fortress, 1966.

Andreae, Jakob, and Theodore Beza. *Lutheranism vs. Calvinism*. St. Louis: Concordia, 2017.

Andrews, E. H. *The Spirit Has Come*. Darlington, UK: Evangelical Press, 1982.

Arnold, Clinton E. *Powers of Darkness: Principalities and Powers in Paul's Letters*. Downers Grove: InterVarsity, 1992.

Augustine. *Against the Academics (Contra Academicos)*. Translated by John J. O'Meara. Ramsey: Paulist, 1951.

———. *On the Trinity*. Bk 4. Translated by Arthur West Haddan. Logos Virtual Library. https://www.logoslibrary.org/augustine/trinity/0413.html

Aulén, Gustaf. *Christus Victor: An Historical Study of the Three Main Types of the Idea of Atonement*. Eugene, OR: Wipf & Stock, 2003.

———. *The Faith of the Christian Church*. Philadelphia: Fortress, 1948.

Aune, David E. *Revelation 1–5*. WBC 52A. Dallas: Word, 1990.

Ballew, J. Richard. *Heavenly Worship*. Mount Hermon: Conciliar, 1983.

Banks, Robert. *Paul's Idea of Community: The Early House Churches in Their Historical Setting*. Grand Rapids: Eerdmans, 1980.

Barrett, Matthew. "Divine Simplicity." Gospel Coalition, 2023. https://www.thegospelcoalition.org/essay/divine-simplicity/.

Batten, Don, ed. *The Creation Answers Book*. Powder Springs, GA: Creation, 2014.

Bauckham, Richard. "Life, Death and the Afterlife in Second Temple Judaism." In *Life in the Face of Death: The Resurrection Message of the New Testament*, edited by Richard N. Longenecker, 80–95. Grand Rapids: Eerdmans, 1998.

Bauer, W., et al. *Greek-English Lexicon of the New Testament and Other Early Christian Literature*. Chicago: University of Chicago Press, 1957.

Baugh, Steven M. "The New Perspective, Mediation, and Justification." In *Covenant, Justification, and Pastoral Ministry*, edited by R. Scott Clark, 137–63. Phillipsburg, NJ: P&R, 2007.

Bavinck, Herman. *Reformed Dogmatics*. Vol. 2, *God and Creation*. Grand Rapids: Baker Academic, 2004.

Beare, Francis Wright. *The Gospel According to Matthew*. San Francisco: Harper & Row, 1981.

Beker, J. Christiaan. *The New Testament: A Thematic Introduction*. Minneapolis: Fortress, 1994.

———. *Suffering and Hope: The Biblical Vision and the Human Predicament*. Philadelphia: Fortress, 1987.

———. *The Triumph of God: The Essence of Paul's Thought*. Minneapolis: Fortress, 1990.

Beisner, E. Calvin. *The Auburn Avenue Theology: Pros and Cons*. Fort Lauderdale: Knox Seminary, 2004.

Bennet, F. S. M. *The Resurrection of the Dead*. London: Chapman & Hall, n.d.

Benoit, Pierre, and Roland Murphy. *Immortality and Resurrection*. Freiburg, Germany: Herder and Herder, 1970.

Berghoef, Gerard, and Lester DeKoster. *The Great Divide: Christianity or Evolution?* Edinburgh: Banner of Truth, 1989.

Bible Research. "The Ending of Mark: Mark 16:9–20." https://www.bible-researcher.com/endmark.html.

Boring, M. Eugene. *Mark: A Commentary*, Louisville: Westminster John Knox, 2006.

———. *Revelation*. Interpretation. Louisville: Westminster John Knox, 1989.

Boring, M. Eugene, and Fred B. Craddock. *The People's New Testament Commentary*. Louisville: Westminster John Knox, 2004.

Bornkamm, Günther, et al. *Tradition and Interpretation in Matthew*. Philadelphia: Westminster, 1963.

Bousset, Wilhelm. *Kyrios Christos*. Translated by John H. Steely. Nashville: Abingdon, 1970.

Braaten, Carl E., and Robert W. Jenson, eds. *Christian Dogmatics*. 2 vols. Philadelphia: Fortress, 1984.

Bridge, Donald, and David Phypers. *The Water That Divides: Two Views of Baptism Explored*. Fearn, UK: Christian Focus, 2008.

Brown, John. *An Exposition of Galatians*. Grand Rapids: Christian Classics, 1960.

Brown, Michael. "John Owen on Republication in the Mosaic Covenant: The Covenant of Works Revived." *CPJ* 4 (2008) 151–61.

Brownson, James V. *The Promise of Baptism*. Grand Rapids: Eerdmans, 2007.

Bruce, F. F., ed. *The International Bible Commentary*. 2nd ed. Grand Rapids: Zondervan, 1986.

Brunner, Emil. *The Christian Doctrine of the Church, Faith, and the Consummation*. Vol. 3, *Dogmatics*. Philadelphia: Westminster, 1962.

Buchanan, James. *The Doctrine of Justification*. Edinburgh: Banner of Truth, 1984.

Bultmann, Rudolf. *Theology of the New Testament*. Vol. 1. Translated by Kendrick Grobel. New York: Scribner, 1951.

———. *This World and Beyond*. New York: Scribner, 1960.

Byrne, Brendon. *A Costly Freedom: A Theological Reading of Mark's Gospel.* Collegeville, MN: Liturgical, 2008.

Calvin, John. *Institutes of the Christian Religion.* Vol. 1. Edited by John T. McNeill. Philadelphia: Westminster, 1960.

Carlton, Clark. *The Faith: Understanding Orthodox Christianity.* Salisbury: Regina Orthodox, 1997.

Catechism of the Catholic Church. Second ed. Vatican City: Libreria Editrice Vaticana, 2019. https://www.usccb.org/sites/default/files/flipbooks/catechism/226/.

Charles, R. H. *The Revelation.* Vol. 1. ICC. New York: Bloomberg, 1920.

Collins, John J. *Daniel.* Hermeneia. Minneapolis: Fortress, 1994.

Comfort, Philip W. *New Testament Text and Translation Commentary.* Carol Stream, IL: Tyndale, 2008.

Conzelmann, Hans. *A Commentary on the First Epistle to the Corinthians.* Hermeneia. Philadelphia: Fortress, 1988.

Cooper, John W. *Body, Soul, and Life Everlasting: Biblical Anthropology and the Monism-Dualism Debate.* Grand Rapids: Eerdmans, 1989.

———. "The Current Body-Soul Debate: A Case for Dualistic Holism." *SBJT* 13 (2009) 32–50.

Craddock, Fred B. *Luke.* Interpretation. Louisville: Westminster John Knox, 1990.

Crowder, Stephanie Buckhanon, and Dennis E. Smith. " A Jewish Christian Gospel: The Gospel of Matthew." In *Chalice Introduction to the New Testament*, edited by Dennis E. Smith et al., 152–74. St. Louis: Chalice, 2004.

Cullmann, Oscar. "Immortality of the Soul or Resurrection of the Dead." In *Immortality and Resurrection: Four Essays by Oscar Cullman, Harry A. Wolfson, Werner Jaeger, and Henry J. Cadbury*, edited by Krister Stendahl, 9–53. New York: Macmillan, 1965.

D. Martin Luthers Werke. Kritische Gesamtausgabe: Weimar, 1883–.

Date, Chris. "The Precious Blood of Christ: A Response to James White." *Rethinking Hell*, Dec 16, 2018, podcast. https://rethinkinghell.com/2018/12/16/episode-115-the-precious-blood-of-christ-a-response-to-james-white/.

———. "The Righteous for the Unrighteous: Conditional Immortality and the Substitutionary Death of Jesus." *MJTM* 18 (2016–17) 92.

———. "Traditional Objections Answered with Chris Date." *Rethinking Hell*, Oct 4, 2012, podcast. https://rethinkinghell.com/2012/10/04/episode-7-traditional-objections-answered-with-chris-date/.

Delitzsch, Franz. *A System of Biblical Psychology.* Edinburgh: T. & T. Clark, 1890.

Dunn, James D. G. *Baptism in the Holy Spirit.* Philadelphia: Westminster, 1970.

———. "'Baptized' as Metaphor." In *Baptism, the New Testament and the Church: Historical and Contemporary Studies in Honor of R. E. O. White*, edited by Stanley E. Porter and Anthony R. Cross, 294–310. Journal for the Study of the New Testament Supplement 171. Sheffield, UK: Sheffield Academic Press, 1999.

———. *Pneumatology.* Vol. 2 of *The Christ and the Spirit.* Grand Rapids: Eerdmans, 1998.

———. "The Messianic Secret in Mark." *Tyndale Bulletin* 21 (1970) 92–117. https://www.academia.edu/1463303/The_Messianic_Secret_in_Mark.

———. *The Theology of Paul.* Grand Rapids: Eerdmans, 2006.

Easton, Burton Scott. *The Interpreter's Bible in Twelve Volumes.* New York/Nashville: Abingdon, 1957.

Ebeling, Gerhard. *The Truth of the Gospel: An Exposition of Galatians.* Philadelphia: Fortress, 1985.

Ecumenical Creeds and Reformed Confessions. Grand Rapids: CRC Publications, 1988.

Elliot, John H. *1 Peter.* Anchor Yale Bible Commentary. New York: Doubleday, 2000.

Engelsma, David J. *The Millennium.* Vol. 1 of *The Church's Hope: The Reformed Doctrine of the End.* Jenison, MI: Reformed Free, 2021.

———. "The Intermediate State." *SB* 85.6 (Dec 15, 2008) 132–34.

Eusebius. "The Everlasting Gospel: Eusebius' Quotes Referring to Matthew 28:19." http://jesus-messiah.com/html/evr-last-gosp.htm.

———. *The Proof of the Gospel.* Eugene, OR: Wipf & Stock, 2001.

Fee, Gordon D. *The First Epistle to the Corinthians.* Grand Rapids: Eerdmans, 1987.

———. *God's Empowering Presence: The Holy Spirit in the Letters of Paul.* Peabody, MA: Hendrickson, 1994.

Ferguson, Everett. *Baptism in the Early Church.* Grand Rapids: Eerdmans, 2013.

Fergusson, James. *An Exposition of the Epistles of Paul to the Galatians, Ephesians, Philippians, Colossians, Thessalonians.* Evansville, IN: Sovereign Grace, 2001.

Fesko, J. V. *The Covenant of Redemption: Origins, Development, and Reception.* Göttingen: Vanden Hoek and Ruprecht, 2015.

Forde, Gerhard O. *The Captivation of the Will: Luther vs. Erasmus on Freedom and Bondage.* Grand Rapids: Eerdmans, 2005.

———. "Christian Life." In *Christian Dogmatics,* edited by Carl E. Braaten and Robert W. Jenson, 2:395–469. Philadelphia: Fortress, 1984.

———. *Justification by Faith: A Matter of Death and Life.* Philadelphia: Fortress, 1982.

———. *A More Radical Gospel.* Grand Rapids: Eerdmans, 2004.

———. *On Being a Theologian of the Cross.* Grand Rapids: Eerdmans, 1997.

———. *The Preached God.* Edited by Mark C. Mattes and Steven D. Paulson. Grand Rapids: Eerdmans, 2007.

———. "The Viability of Luther Today: A North American Perspective." *W&W* 7.1 (1987) 22–31.

———. *Where God Meets Man.* Minneapolis: Augsburg, 1972.

Fortescue, Adrian. "Kyrie Eleison." *The Catholic Encyclopedia.* Vol. 8. New York: Robert Appleton, 1910. https://www.newadvent.org/cathen/08714a.htm.

Fryer, N. S. L. "The Intermediate State in Paul." *HTS Teologiese Studies* 43.3 (1987) 448–84.

Fudge, Edward William. "The Final End of the Wicked." In *Rethinking Hell: Readings in Evangelical Conditionalism,* edited by Christopher M. Date et al., 29–43. Eugene, OR: Cascade, 2014.

———. *The Fire That Consumes.* Third ed. Eugene, OR: Cascade, 2011.

———. *Hell: A Final Word.* Abilene: Abilene Christian University Press, 2012.

Furnish, Victor Paul. *1 Thessalonians 2 Thessalonians.* Nashville: Abingdon, 2007.

———. *The Love Command in the New Testament.* Nashville: Abingdon, 1972.

———. *Theology and Ethics in Paul.* Louisville: Westminster John Knox, 2009.

Gaffin, Richard B., Jr. "Justification and Eschatology." In *Justified in Christ: God's Plan for Us in Justification,* edited by K. Scott Oliphant, 1–22. Fearn, UK: Mentor, 2007.

———. *Perspectives on Pentecost.* Phillipsburg, NJ: P&R, 1979.

———. *Resurrection and Redemption: A Study in Paul's Soteriology.* Phillipsburg, NJ: P&R, 1987.

Gathercole, Simon. "Does Faith Mean Faithfulness?" *MR* 13.4 (Jul/Aug 2004) 31–36.

Gilmour, S. Maclean. "Luke: Text, Exegesis, Exposition." In *The Interpreter's Bible*, edited by George Buttrick, 8:26–434. New York: Abingdon, 1952.

Goppelt, Leonhard. *A Commentary on 1 Peter*. Edited by Ferdinand Hahn. Grand Rapids: Eerdmans, 1993.

Gorman, Michael. *Cruciformity: Paul's Narrative Spirituality of the Cross*. Eerdmans, 2001.

Gould, Ezra P. *A Critical and Exegetical Commentary on the Gospel According to Mark*. New York: Scribner, 1896.

Gowan, Donald E. *Daniel*. Abingdon Old Testament Commentaries. Nashville: Abingdon, 2001.

Grice, Peter. "Neglected Doctrines of Resurrection and Bodily Transformation." Rethinking Hell, Dec 12, 2017. https://rethinkinghell.com/2017/12/12/the-neglected-doctrines-of-resurrection-and-bodily-transformation/.

Gundry, Robert H. *Mark: A Commentary on His Apology for the Cross*. Grand Rapids: Eerdmans, 1993.

Haldane, Robert. *The Epistle to the Romans*. London: Banner of Truth, 1966.

Hastings, James. ed. *Dictionary of the Bible*. Rev ed. by Frederick C. Grant and H. H. Rowley. New York: Scribner, 1963.

———. *Encyclopedia of Religion and Ethics*. Vol. 1. New York: Scribner. 1908.

Hays, Richard B. *First Corinthians*. Interpretation. Louisville: John Knox, 1997.

———. *The New Interpreter's Bible*. 11:183–348. Nashville: Abingdon, 2000.

———. "'The Righteous One' as Eschatological Deliverer: A Case Study in Paul's Apocalyptic Hermeneutics." In *Apocalyptic and the New Testament: Essays in Honor of J. Louis Martyn*, edited by Joel Marcus and Marion L. Soards, 191–216. Sheffield: Sheffield Academic Press, 1989.

Healy, Mary. *Hebrews*. Grand Rapids: Baker Academic, 2016.

Heron, Alasdair. *Table and Tradition: Toward an Ecumenical Understanding of the Eucharist*. Philadelphia: Westminster, 1983.

Hoekema, Anthony A. *The Bible and the Future*. Grand Rapids: Eerdmans, 1979.

———. *Created in God's Image*. Grand Rapids: Eerdmans, 1986.

———. *Saved by Grace*. Grand Rapids: Eerdmans, 1989.

Hoeksema, Herman. *Reformed Dogmatics*. Grand Rapids: Reformed Free, 1966.

Hoeksema, Homer C. *The Voice of Our Fathers: An Exposition of the Canons of Dordrecht*. Second ed. Jenison, MI: Reformed Free, 2013.

Hodge, A. A. "The Ordo Salutis: Or, Relation in the Order of Nature of Holy Character and Divine Favor." *PR* 54 (1878) 304–21.

Hodge, Charles. *Commentary on the Epistle to the Romans*. Philadelphia: Alfred Martien, 1864.

———. *An Exposition of the First Epistle to the Corinthians*. Grand Rapids: Eerdmans, 1973.

———. *Princeton Sermons: Outlines of Discourses Doctrinal and Practical*. London: Banner of Truth, 1958.

———. *Systematic Theology*. Vol. 2. Grand Rapids: Eerdmans, 1940.

Horton, Michael, ed. *Christ the Lord*. Grand Rapids: Baker, 1992.

———. *Pilgrim Theology*. Grand Rapids: Zondervan, 2011.

Hughes, Philip Edgcumbe. *Paul's Second Epistle to the Corinthians*. Grand Rapids: Eerdmans, 1962.

———. *The True Image: The Origin and Destiny of Man in Christ*. Grand Rapids: Eerdmans, 1989.

Hutcheson, George. *An Exposition of the Gospel According to John*. Evansville, IN: Sovereign Grace, 1959.

Irons, Lee. "The *Oikos* Formula." Upper Register. https://www.upper-register.com/papers/oikos_formula.pdf.

Johnson, Luke Timothy. "Romans 3:21–26 and the Faith of Jesus." *CBQ* 44.1 (1982) 77–90.

———. *The Writings of the New Testament: An Interpretation*. Philadelphia: Fortress, 1986.

Johnston, Philip S. *Shades of Sheol: Death and Afterlife in the Old Testament*. Downers Grove: InterVarsity, 2002.

Jones, Peter. *The Other Worldview: Exposing Christianity's Greatest Threat*. Bellingham, WA: Kirkdale, 2015.

Käsemann, Ernst. *Commentary on Romans*. Grand Rapids: Eerdmans, 1980.

———. *Perspectives on Paul*. Philadelphia: Fortress, 1971.

Keck, Leander E. *Romans*. Abingdon New Testament Commentaries. Nashville: Abingdon, 2005.

———. *Proclamation Commentaries: Paul and His Letters*. Philadelphia: Fortress, 1988.

Keil, C. F., and F. Delitzsch. *Commentary on the Old Testament in Ten Volumes*. Grand Rapids: Eerdmans, 1980.

Kingston Siggins, Jan D. *Martin Luther's Doctrine of Christ*. New Haven: Yale University Press, 1970.

Kittel, G., and G. Friedrich, eds. *Theological Dictionary of the New Testament*. Translated by G. W. Bromiley. 10 vols. Grand Rapids: Eerdmans, 1964–76.

Koester, Helmut. *History and Literature of Early Christianity*. Vol. 2 of *Introduction to the New Testament*. Second ed. Berlin: de Gruyter, 2000.

Krodel, Gerhard A. *Acts*. Augsburg Commentary on the New Testament. Minneapolis: Augsburg, 1986.

———. *Augsburg Commentary on the New Testament: Revelation*. Augsburg, 1989.

Kummel, Werner G. *Introduction to the New Testament*. Nashville: Abingdon, 1966.

Lane, Anthony N. S. "Infant Baptism View: Dual-Practice Baptism Response." In *Baptism: Three Views*, edited by David F. Wright. Downers Grove: IVP Academic, 2009.

———. "The Wrath of God as an Aspect of the Love of God." In *Nothing Greater, Nothing Better: Theological Essays on the Love of God*, edited by Kevin J. Vanhoozer, 138–67. Grand Rapids: Eerdmans, 2001.

Lee, Witness. *Life-Study of Galatians*. Anaheim: Living Stream Ministry, 1984.

Lincoln, A. T. "From Sabbath to Lord's Day: A Biblical and Theological Perspective." In *From Sabbath to Lord's Day: A Biblical, Historical, and Theological Investigation*, edited by D. A. Carson, 343–412. Grand Rapids: Zondervan, 1982.

———. "Sabbath, Rest, and Eschatology in the New Testament." In *From Sabbath to Lord's Day: A Biblical, Historical, and Theological Investigation*, edited by D. A. Carson, 197–220. Grand Rapids: Zondervan, 1982.

Linebaugh, Jono. *Liberate Online* blog, 2012. No longer online. Quotations used with permission of the author.

Lloyd-Jones, D. Martyn. *An Exposition of Chapter 8:17–39: The Final Perseverance of the Saints*. Romans. Grand Rapids: Zondervan, 1975.

———. *An Exposition of Chapter Five: Assurance*. Romans. Grand Rapids: Zondervan, 1971.

———. *An Exposition of Chapter Six: The New Man*. Romans. Grand Rapids: Zondervan. 1972.

Lockwood, Gregory J. *1 Corinthians*. Concordia Popular Commentary. St. Louis: Concordia, 2010.

Long, Gary D. *New Covenant Theology: Time for a More Accurate Way*. Self-published, 2013.

Long, Thomas G. *Matthew*. Philadelphia: Westminster John Knox, 1997.

Longenecker, Richard N. *Galatians*. WBC 41. Dallas: Word, 1990.

Luther, Martin. *Commentary on Saint Paul's Epistle to the Galatians by Martin Luther*. Philadelphia: John Highlands, 1891.

———. *Complete Sermons of Martin Luther*. Reprint ed. 10 vols. Grand Rapids: Baker, 2000.

———. *Martin Luther's Basic Theological Writings*. Edited by Timothy F. Lull. Minneapolis: Fortress, 1989.

———. *Letters of Spiritual Counsel*. Edited and translated by Theodore G. Tappert. LCC 18. Philadelphia: Westminster, 1955.

———. *Luther's Works*. 55 vols. American ed. St. Louis: Concordia (vols. 1–30), 1955–86, and Philadelphia: Fortress (vols. 31–55), 1955–86.

Mack, Wayne. *To God Be the Glory: A Study in the Biblical Doctrine of Particular Redemption*. Reformed Baptist Publications.

Madson, Meg H. *The Cross and the Crown: An Eight Lesson Study in Lutheran Basics*. Graham, NC: Sola, 2019.

Mannermaa, Tuomo. *Christ Present in Faith: Luther's View of Justification*. Edited by Kirsi Stjerna. Minneapolis: Fortress, 2005.

Martyn, J. Louis. *Galatians*. Anchor Yale Bible Commentaries. New Haven: Yale University Press, 2004.

———. *Theological Issues in the Letters of Paul*. Nashville: Abingdon, 1997.

Matera, Frank J. *New Testament Christology*. Louisville: Westminster John Knox, 1999.

McDonald, Lee Martin. *The Formation of the Christian Biblical Canon*. Nashville: Abingdon, 1988.

Meade, David G. *Pseudonymity and Canon: An Investigation into the Relationship between Authorship and Authority in Jewish and Early Christian Tradition*. Tubingen: Mohr, 1986.

Merriam-Webster. "Destroy." July 4, 2023. https://www.merriam-webster.com/diction ary/destroy.

Montefiore, C. G., and H. M. J. Loewe, eds. *A Rabbinic Anthology*. New York: Schocken, 1978.

Mortenson, Terry, ed. *Searching for Adam: Genesis and the Truth about Man's Origin*. Green Forest, AR: Masters, 2016.

Murray, John. *Collected Writings of John Murray*. Vol. 2. Edinburgh: Banner of Truth, 1977.

———. *The Epistle to the Romans*. Vol. 1. Grand Rapids: Eerdmans, 1959.

Nestle, Eberhard, et al., eds. Novum Testamentum Graece. Twenty-sixth ed. Stuttgart: German Bible Society, 1979.

Newsom, Carol A., and Brennan W. Breed. *Daniel: A Commentary.* Louisville: Westminster John Knox, 2014.

Nygren, Anders. *Agape and Eros.* 1 vol. Philadelphia, Westminster, 1953.

———. *Commentary on Romans.* Philadelphia: Fortress, 1944.

———. *Essence of Christianity: Two Essays.* Translated by Philip Watson. Grand Rapids: Eerdmans, 1973.

———. *The Significance of the Bible for the Church.* Philadelphia: Fortress, 1963.

Olyott, Stuart. *The Gospel as It Really Is: Romans Simply Explained.* Darlington, UK: Evangelical Press, 1979.

Ord, David Robert. *What Is the Mystery of the Gospel?* Glen Ellyn, IL: Union Life Ministries, ca. 1970.

Owen, John. *The Doctrine of Justification through the Imputation of the Righteousness of Christ: Explained, Confirmed, and Vindicated.* Grand Rapids: Reformation Heritage, 2006.

———. *The Works of John Owen.* Vol. 6. Edited by William Gould. London: Banner of Truth, 1967.

Packer, J. I. *God's Words: Studies of Key Biblical Themes.* Grand Rapids: Baker, 1981.

Palmer, Edwin H. *The Five Points of Calvinism, Enlarged Edition.* Grand Rapids: Baker, 1980.

Pannenberg, Wolfhart. *Systematic Theology.* Vol 3. Grand Rapids: Eerdmans, 1997.

Papias. "Fragment 2." *Fragments of Papias.* Translated by J. B. Lightfoot and J. R. Harmer, edited by Daniel R. Jennings. http://www.seanmultimedia.com/Pie_Fragments_of_Papias.html.

Payton, James R., Jr. *Light from the Christian East: An Introduction to the Orthodox Tradition.* Downers Grove: IVP Academic, 2007.

Peoples, Glen. "Church Fathers Who Were Conditionalists." YouTube video. *Rethinking Hell,* 2016. https://www.youtube.com/watch?v=je3AW6QeXzk&list=PLzzKdEy3zkxOy9oaukIL6Ed5JpDOHAjaE.

———. "Introduction to Evangelical Conditionalism." In *Rethinking Hell: Readings in Evangelical Conditionalism,* edited by Christopher M. Date et al., 10–24. Eugene, OR: Cascade, 2014.

Pester, John. "The Faith of the Son of God in Galatians 2:20 Being the Initiating Source and Constant Supply for the Believers' Organic Union with Christ." *A&C* 25 (Fall 2020) 11–22.

Peters, Ted. *God: The World's Future.* Minneapolis: Fortress, 1992.

Plummer, Alfred. *The Epistles of St. John.* Grand Rapids: Baker, 1980.

Preus, Herman A. *A Theology to Live By.* St. Louis: Concordia, 2006.

Robinson, D. W. B. "Faith of Jesus Christ: A New Testament Debate." *RTR* 29.3 (1970) 71–81.

———. "Towards a Definition of Baptism." *RTR* 34.1 (1975) 1–15.

Rogers, E. R. "Yet Once More: One Baptism?" *RTR* 50 (1991) 41–49.

Roller, John. *The Doctrine of Immortality in the Early Church.* Self published, 2012 Kindle ed.

Sanders, E. P. "Is Paul's Legacy Relevant Today?" YouTube video. Villanova University, 2010. https://www.youtube.com/watch?v=SZNijc_-4Lk.

Schaff, Philip, and Henry Wace, eds. *A Select Library of Nicene and Post-Nicene Fathers of the Christian Church.* Translated by S. D. F. Salmond. 14 vols. Edinburgh: T. & T. Clark, 1997.

Schlink, Edmund. *Theology of the Lutheran Confessions*. Philadelphia: Muhlenberg, 1961.

Schmithals, Walter. *An Introduction to the Theology of Rudolph Bultmann*. Minneapolis: Augsburg, 1968.

Schnelle, Udo. *The History and Theology of New Testament Writings*. Translated by M. Eugene Boring. Minneapolis: Fortress, 1998.

———. *Theology of the New Testament*. Grand Rapids: Baker Academic, 2009.

Schwarz, Hans. *Eschatology*. Grand Rapids: Eerdmans, 2000.

Shaw, Robert. *An Exposition of the Westminster Confession of Faith*. Fearn, UK: Christian Heritage, 1998.

Silversides, David. "Benefits Accompanying Justification." Sermon, May 28, 2000. https://www.sermonaudio.com/sermoninfo.asp?SID=1190454935.

Smith, D. Moody. *Proclamation Commentaries: John*. Second ed. Philadelphia: Fortress, 1986.

Smith, William. *Smith's Dictionary of the Bible*. Revised and edited by H. B. Hackett. Cambridge: Riverside, 1869.

Spivey, Robert A., and D. Moody Smith, Jr. *Anatomy of the New Testament*. New York: Macmillan,1974.

Sproul, R. C. *Defending Your Faith: An Introduction to Apologetics*. Wheaton: Crossway, 2003.

Stein, Robert H. *Mark*. Baker Exegetical Commentary on the New Testament. Grand Rapids: Baker Academic, 2008.

Stendahl, Krister. *Meanings: The Bible as Document and as Guide*. Philadelphia: Fortress, 1984.

———. *Paul among Jews and Gentiles*. Philadelphia: Fortress, 1976.

Stephenson, John R. *The Lord's Supper*. Vol 12 of *Confessional Lutheran Dogmatics*. St. Louis: Luther Academy, 2003.

Stott, John. *Romans: God's Good News for the World*. Downers Grove: InterVarsity, 1994.

Streeter, B. H. *The Four Gospels: A Study of Their Origins*. Eugene, OR: Wipf & Stock, 2008.

Strimple, Robert. "Was Adam Historical?" Westminster Seminary California Resource Center, Jul 26, 2010. https://www.wscal.edu/resource-center/was-adam-historical.

Sturz, Harry A. *The Byzantine Text-Type and New Testament Textual Criticism*. Nashville: Thomas Nelson, 1984.

Swanson, Reuban J. "The Gospel of Matthew as an Anti-Pauline Polemic." In *Reflections on Biblical Themes by an Octogenarian*, 69–90. Eugene, OR: Wipf & Stock, 2007.

———. *New Testament Greek Manuscripts: Variant Readings Arranged in Horizontal Lines against Codex Vaticanus: Romans*. Wheaton: Tyndale, 2001.

Tappert, Theodore G., ed. "The Apology of the Augsburg Confession." In *the Book of Concord: The Confessions of the Evangelical Lutheran Church*, 97–286. Philadelphia: Fortress, 1959.

———. "The Augsburg Confession." In *the Book of Concord: The Confessions of the Evangelical Lutheran Church*, 23–96. Philadelphia: Fortress, 1959.

———. *The Book of Concord: The Confessions of the Evangelical Lutheran Church*. Philadelphia: Fortress, 1959.

―――. "Formula of Concord and Solid Declaration." In *the Book of Concord: The Confessions of the Evangelical Lutheran Church*, 501–636. Philadelphia: Fortress, 1959.

―――. "Large Catechism." In *the Book of Concord: The Confessions of the Evangelical Lutheran Church*, 357–462. Philadelphia: Fortress, 1959.

Taylor, Justin. "A Simple Explanation of Divine Simplicity." Gospel Coalition, Jan 6, 2021. https://www.thegospelcoalition.org/blogs/justin-taylor/a-simple-explanation-of-divine-simplicity/.

Taylor, Walter F., Jr. *Paul: Apostle to the Nations*. Minneapolis: Fortress, 2012.

Thielicke, Helmut. *Theological Ethics*. Vol. 1. Grand Rapids: Eerdmans, 1979.

Tipton, Lane E. "Union with Christ and Justification." In *Justified in Christ: God's Plan for Us in Justification*, edited by K. Scott Oliphint, 23–49. Fearn, UK: Mentor, 2007.

Torrance, Thomas F. *The Doctrine of Grace in the Apostolic Fathers*. Edinburgh: Oliver and Boyd, 1948.

Unger, Merrill F. *The Baptizing Work of the Holy Spirit*. Findlay, OH: Dunham, 1962.

Vajta, Vilmos. *Luther on Worship: An Interpretation*. Philadelphia: Muhlenberg, 1958.

Varvel, Brett, dir. *Genesis Impact*. Folsom, CA: Genesis Apologetics, 2020. DVD.

Versteeg, J. P. *Adam in the New Testament: Mere Teaching Model or First Historical Man?* Phillipsburg: P&R, 2012.

von Loewenich, Walther. *Luther's Theology of the Cross*. Minneapolis: Augsburg, 1976.

Ware, Kallistos. *The Orthodox Way*. Crestwood: St. Vladimir's Seminary, 1979.

Waren, Dick. *Sheol Know! The "Intermediate State" between Death and Resurrection*. Youngstown: Soaring Eagle, 2015.

Webster's New World Dictionary of the American Language: College Edition. New York: World, 1959.

Weinandy, Thomas G. *The Father's Spirit of Sonship: Reconceiving the Trinity*. Eugene, OR: Wipf & Stock, 2011.

Wengert, Timothy J. *A Formula for Parish Practice*. Grand Rapids: Eerdmans, 2006.

―――. *Reading the Bible with Martin Luther*. Grand Rapids: Baker Academic, 2013.

Westerholm, Stephen. *Israel's Law and the Church's Faith*. Eugene, OR: Wipf & Stock, 1988.

―――. *Justification Reconsidered: Rethinking a Pauline Theme*. Grand Rapids: Eerdmans, 2003.

―――. *Perspectives Old and New on Paul: The "Lutheran" Paul and His Critics*. Grand Rapids: Eerdmans, 2004.

The Westminster Standards. Suwanee, GA: Great Commission, 1978.

White, A. J. Monty. *What about Origins?* Leominster, UK: Day One, 2010.

White, Blake. "Israel in Romans 11." *Barabbas* blog, Mar 24, 2016. http://ablakew.blogspot.com/2016/03/israel-in-romans-11.html.

Wigram, George V., and Ralph D. Winter. *The Word Study Concordance*. Pasadena: William Carey Library, 1978.

―――.*The Word Study New Testament*. Pasadena: William Carey Library, 1978.

Witsius, Herman. *The Economy of the Covenants between God and Man*. Kingsburg: P&R, 1990.

Zachman, Randall C. *The Assurance of Faith: Conscience in the Theology of Martin Luther and John Calvin*. Minneapolis: Fortress, 1993.

Made in the USA
Las Vegas, NV
14 October 2023

79112652R00216